Democratic Vistas

ALAN TRACHTENBERG, associate professor of English and American Studies at Pennsylvania State University, is the author of *Brooklyn Bridge, Fact & Symbol.*

The American Culture

NEIL HARRIS—General Editor

DEMOCRATIC VISTAS
1860-1880

Edited,
with Introduction and Notes by

Alan Trachtenberg

George Braziller   New York

Published simultaneously in Canada by Doubleday Canada Limited.
All rights reserved.
For information address the publisher:
George Braziller, Inc.
One Park Avenue
New York, N. Y. 10016

Standard Book Number:
        0-8076-548-4, cloth;
        0-8076-547-6, paper
Library of Congress Catalog Card Number: 75-103170
Designed by Jennie Bush
FIRST PRINTING
Printed in the United States of America

Acknowledgments

I am grateful to the American Council of Learned Societies for making it possible for me to spend a year at the Center for Advanced Study in the Behavioral Sciences, where this project was completed. The staff of the Center provided generous help in the preparation of the manuscript. I wish to thank Miriam Gallaher in particular, for her close scrutiny of the entire typescript, and for her shrewd and invaluable suggestions. The project also benefited from the support of the Central Research Fund, Pennsylvania State University. I am indebted to Steve Spector for his very able assistance. Alan Fern and Milton Kaplan of the Prints and Photographs Division, Library of Congress, generously helped in the selection of prints.

I would like to express my gratitude to several scholars who read and commented upon the Introduction: Ray Birdwhistell, Irving Howe, Merrill Peterson, David Potter, and Henry Nash Smith. They are not to blame for whatever errors or infelicities that remain. Neither is my wife Betty Trachtenberg, who intervened on several occasions to prevent some unusual mistakes. This volume is another item of my indebtedness.

Preface

"Do not tell me only of the magnitude of your industry and commerce," wrote Matthew Arnold during his visit to the United States in the 1890's; "of the beneficence of your institutions, your freedom, your equality: of the great and growing number of your churches and schools, libraries and newspapers; tell me also if your civilization—which is the grand name you give to all this development—tell me if your civilization is *interesting*."

The various volumes that comprise THE AMERICAN CULTURE series attempt to answer Matthew Arnold's demand. The term "culture," of course, is a critical modern concept. For many historians, as for many laymen, the word has held a limited meaning: the high arts of painting, sculpture, literature, music, architecture; their expression, patronage, and consumption. But in America, where physical mobility and ethnic diversity have been so crucial, this conception of culture is restricting. The "interesting" in our civilization is omitted if we confine ourselves to the formal arts.

The editors of THE AMERICAN CULTURE, therefore, have cast a wider net. They have searched for fresh materials to reconstruct the color and variety of our cultural heritage, spanning a period of more than three hundred years. Forgotten institutions, buried artifacts, and outgrown experiences are included in these books, along with some of the sights and sounds that reflected the changing character of American life.

The raw data alone, however fascinating, are not sufficient for the task of cultural reconstruction. Each editor has organized his material around definitions and assumptions which he explores in the volume introductions. These introductions are essays in their own right; they can be read along with the documents, or they can stand as independent explorations into social history. No one editor presents the same kind of approach; commitments and emphases vary from volume to volume. Together, however, these volumes represent a unified effort to restore to historical study the texture of life as it was lived, without sacrificing theoretical rigor or informed scholarship.

NEIL HARRIS

Contents

III CULTURE AND DEMOCRACY

Illustrations

A POPULAR ARTIST: ENGRAVINGS BY WINSLOW HOMER/320

Introduction

ALAN TRACHTENBERG

I

The intention of this volume is to offer a perspective on American culture in the two decades including and following the Civil War. By culture I mean the pattern of ideas, feelings and behavior which comprise a society's collective version of "reality." Some of the documents presented here may be useful as accounts of concrete historical events, but their primary value lies in what they represent as idea and feeling. The selections are drawn almost entirely from public sources, from newspapers, periodicals and published books; I have deliberately excluded private sources such as journals, diaries and unpublished correspondence. A more significant exclusion is material drawn from what might be called "subcultures"—the life of immigrant, ethnic or regional groups. Much of this very rich and valuable material is contained in oral expressions and in handicrafts. My exclusion is not meant to slight the value of such documents. I was guided by the intention of depicting forms and themes common to large numbers of people.

The principal focus of the book is, moreover, on a particular idea of culture, a creed, which came to occupy a commanding place in American society. This creed was a distinct product of the times, of the conflicts and tensions wrought by the Civil War, by industrialization, and by changing social patterns. Allan Nevins has described this period as "the emergence of modern America," and perhaps the dominant emergent pattern was an increasingly standardized national way of life. Mechanization created a continental market, and the official creed of culture soon began to find its way into all sections and regions. The source of dissemination was the eastern seaboard, especially Boston and New York. Compounded of "genteel" ideas of art, architecture, and home furnishings, and of sentimental notions of family, children, females, the poor, and Negroes, the official creed imposed its version of reality on virtually all aspects of

American life. The mass media, beginning to flourish in this period, became an almost irresistible agent of standardization. Ideality and a benevolent religion of the heart came to prevail in popular fiction and illustrations.

But the picture was not as single-minded as this account implies. Although popular culture began to develop an official idea of what constitutes an American—an idea essentially middle-class in its complacency and in the value it placed upon affluence—the culture as a whole contained currents of doubt and resistance. A study of the serious art between 1865 and 1900 reveals, for example, considerable uneasiness with the drift of American life. In works by writers like Mark Twain, William Dean Howells, Henry James, Henry Adams, and Emily Dickinson—in the frustration, disenchantment, isolation, and even self-imposed exile of their careers—we can detect serious misgivings about and, in some cases, outright rejection of what George Santayana called "the genteel tradition." But (with one exception) nowhere, not even in the pioneering work in pragmatism by Charles Sanders Peirce, Chauncy Wright and William James, can we find a fully developed negative critique of the leading idea of culture.

The one significant exception is Walt Whitman's *Democratic Vistas* (1871). Whitman had already passed the crest of his poetic creativity in the 1850's and early 1860's and, like Emerson and Melville, figured in the period more or less as an outsider, a voice from an earlier time. But his argument in *Democratic Vistas* stands as the sole perspective fundamentally and unequivocally at odds with the emergent creed, and for that reason I have chosen to place a selection from that essay at the conclusion of this volume. And as a foil, as an example of unresolved tensions in the troubled consciousness of the period, I shall refer frequently in this introduction to *The Gilded Age* (1873), in which, in collaboration with Charles Dudley Warner, Mark Twain attempted—admittedly with only partial success—to write a realistic novel of the times. The esthetic faults of the book are themselves characteristic of the culture.

II

A feeling that the nation had reached a turning point pervades the post-Civil War years. "The eight years in America from 1860 to 1868," wrote Mark Twain and Charles Dudley Warner in their novel which pinned its title as epithet on the age, "uprooted institutions that were centuries old, changed the politics of a people, transformed the social life of half the country, and wrought so profoundly upon the entire national character that the influence cannot be measured short of two or three generations."

To many Americans the Civil War seemed a watershed, and in response to—perhaps defense against—the rush of change, many seized upon an image of the past as uncomplicated and idyllic. In his study of Hawthorne, Henry James wrote in 1879 that the war had shattered the provincialism of the "earlier and simpler generation," and had "introduced into the national consciousness a certain sense of proportion and relation, of the world being a more complicated place than it had hitherto seemed, the future more treacherous, success more difficult."

To be sure, the prewar generation was considerably more complex than James allows, and the transformation Mark Twain speaks of was well under way before 1860—the transformation of a predominantly rural and agricultural society into an expanding urban and industrial power. Some recent historians have argued that the war may indeed have retarded this change. But there is no doubt that in the years between 1860 and 1880 modern industrial society established itself as an irreversible fact. And with it came a sense of dislocation. True, most Americans approved the change, some even rapturously. But it was no longer easy to believe, as many Americans had for generations, that their society was immune from the class conflicts and the struggles of the Old World.

The existence of vacant land to be settled—or, as became apparent with the Indian wars of the 1870's, often to be wrested from resisting aboriginal inhabitants had seemed since Jefferson's day to sanction the idea of a special providence, of an exemption from the travail of history. The Mexican War of 1848 and the growing agitation over slavery began to tarnish the image of a Peaceable Kingdom in the New World. With the Civil War, and its unprecedented scale of destruction (over a half million dead), history made its unequivocal presence felt in American society. The war was an initiation into social violence. And bloodshed continued, in organized terrorism against Negroes in the South, in their armed resistance, in pitched battles between workers and militia in the 1870's, and in a steady increase in urban crime. By the 1880's violence seemed to loom as a permanent threat to social order.

"We sail a dangerous sea of seething currents," wrote Whitman, "all so dark, untried—and whither shall we turn?" The achievements themselves of the period seemed contradictory.

On one hand, feats of industry provided tangible proof of strength. The lofty towers of Brooklyn Bridge, in construction through the 1870's (the bridge was completed in 1883), were understandably regarded as evidence of a coming period of technological magnificence. New processes in iron and steel and the extension of mass production to household goods and food gave the nation its first taste of an abundance spawned by machinery. In 1869 the transcontinental railroad was joined at Promontory Point, Utah, helping to secure a continental market for an expanding economy. With the spread of public higher education, books, magazines and lithographs became major commodities. But not all the evidence pleased the eye. With spreading mechanization came aggravated labor conditions, the rise of militant unions, and a period of violent strikes. Scandals of corruption in government became common news; a new class of financiers and industrialists seemed to operate like feudal barons, without regard for public interests. A major depression occurred in 1873, followed by the first nationwide strike of railroad workers in 1877. Henry George's *Progress and Poverty* (1879), an eloquent condemnation of the paradox of poverty alongside ostentatious wealth and mechanical progress, initiated a political protest movement for a Single Tax; the growing appeal of socialism, anarchism, and cooperativism among workers and farmers added to the ferment of the period. In addition, feminism reached a new level of militancy in its campaign against the most cherished ornament of genteel society, the "sacred" place of women.

The dominant note of the period however—a note struck by an interpid chorus of silver-throated orators—was optimistic. A typical view of the war, for example, described it as a victory of "order against faction, law against conspiracy." After the war, popular spokesmen like Henry Ward Beecher were able to draw on two new sources to bolster the traditional American outlook—Herbert Spencer's "Social Darwinism," which made *laissez faire* appear a social policy true to "nature," and Hegelian Idealism, which guaranteed that history and nature were guided by "moral ideas." Armed with new pseudoscientific and theological support, and fed by impressive technological progress and spreading middle-class affluence, optimism swelled into a rapturous outpouring as the nation approached the centennial celebration of 1876.

At the same time a sense of menace insinuated itself as an undercurrent. It was felt most keenly as a social menace by members of the established classes, especially in the East—a threat from labor agitators and anarchists below, and from the new tycoons above, the *nouveaux riches* who were seizing economic and political power. But anxiety in subtler form appeared even at the height of self-congratulation. Bayard Taylor's official Centennial Ode, for example, speaks of the "perils of prosperity," and of fallow pastures awaiting "purer seed." "But keep thy garments pure," he warns the "shepherds" who "stray"; "Pluck them back, with the old disdain,/ From touch of the hands that stain!" Pastoral imagery had by this time become ceremonial in patriotic poems, and indeed some advice about the corruption of the world was always a convention of such poetry. But against the contemporary setting in 1876 the pastoralism seems considerably strained, and the warnings more genuine.

In his Ode for the occasion James Russell Lowell also evokes the conventional image of "happy homesteads hid in orchard trees," but speaks more feelingly about "this inert prosperity,/ This bovine comfort in the sense alone." He refers to the "stolen fruit" of public officials, and although he has a visionary's hope for the future, confesses "the present still seems vulgar." Melville's mood in this period was of course much darker than any of these minatory mumblings—which in fact those who felt themselves oppressed in American society would have considered mild indeed—but the words of a character in *Clarel* (1876) epitomize what a significant number of people seemed to feel: "Negation, is there nothing more? . . . . *Some other world*: Well, there's the New—/ Ah, joyless and ironic too." No wonder Whitman described these years as a "sea of seething currents."

III

The meaning of the Civil War—why it was fought, what its major issues were—is still today an unsettled, even obscure, matter. But one unmistakable feature of the war, if not its direct purpose, was the destruction of the system of chattel slavery. The Emancipation Proclamation of 1863 was received by the Negro and his friends as a deliverance, but as many even then realized, it was little more than a paper document unless followed by massive government aid to implement complete liberation, from the effects of slavery as well as the fact. Such a program held out the prospect of full social and political equality for Negroes, a prospect unpalatable to most white Americans. Frederick Douglass wrote in 1864 that "the freedom of our race and the welfare of our country tremble together in the balance of events," but it would take another hundred years before the message struck home. By the 1870's the federal government, to the relief of most Northerners, had virtually abandoned the freed slaves to the local control of white society, and the promising experiment of Reconstruction was scuttled. By 1900, as C. Van Woodward has shown in *The Strange Career of Jim Crow*, segregation, supported by stereotypes of the Negro as inferior to the white man, had been enacted into law throughout the South, and it is probably accurate to say that many white Americans throughout the nation accepted this as an appropriate solution.

The image and idea of the Negro was a particularly vexing problem for the dominant liberal, humanitarian thought. The treatment of the Negro in the majority culture casts valuable light on the configurations of that culture, on its dynamics and its tensions.

It was chiefly a one-way process, a matter of whites assimilating the figure of the Negro into a pattern geared to middle-class society. Although Negro folklore and music found their way into popular culture, the Negro as a human being became increasingly obscure. Not that his presence cannot be felt, but rarely does he find a place in popular expression as a fully human and social creature, let alone a figure portending an historical force in American life. Under the unexampled influence of *Uncle Tom's Cabin* (1852) many Americans pictured the Negro as an idealized heroic victim, a simple creature suffering under a cruel system. This version of the black man still had currency during and just after the war, but before long other stereotypes appeared, or reappeared, of the Negro as either a comic Sambo or a ferocious savage.

What was the "true character" of the black, who now threatened, during Reconstruction, to force his way into American society? This was a question often discussed in the journals. James Parton, a popular historian and journalist, wrote in the *North American Review* (1878) that the so-called "color repugnance" maintained by Southern apologists was untrue; there is no such thing as a *natural* "antipathy to the Negro," only a social or political one. But committed though he was to racial justice, Parton himself shared a widespread view of the Negro as essentially backward, primitive, childlike. Interestingly enough this stereotype seemed necessary for Parton to argue for eventual integration, for like all children, the Negro was capable of improving himself; unlike the Indian, "an irreclaimable aristocrat," the Negro "takes readily to the hoe and to spelling book." "He improved under slavery from generation to generation, and nowhere so rapidly as in the Southern states, for nowhere else was he treated so well as there. West Indian slavery was hell; Southern slavery was purgatory, that prepared him for the paradise of freedom."

But neither paradise nor freedom were to be taken too literally. At the end of the war a sanguine Northern view was that the liberated blacks "now are rising to the trials and blessings of freedom." And yet by the 1870's, as Reconstruction began to threaten the hegemony of whites in the South, many Northern "friends of the Negro" would have agreed with Parton that "the cruelest stroke ever dealt the Negro, since the time when he was torn from his native land, was hurling him all unprepared into politics." Paradise seemed acceptable—as long as it lay somewhere in the future. Premature equality, Parton argued, only increased the "antipathy" felt by Southerners. Better that Southern society be returned to its "natural chiefs," and, he proposed with the confidence of the "gilded age," "when, in some fair and rational manner, undeveloped races and immature individuals have been withdrawn from the reach of the politician, with the glad consent of the industrious poor man, whose life has been made wellnigh insupportable by their conjunction, we shall soon cease to hear of a color-line." Too much paradise all at once, it seems, might be bad for the system.

The ease with which insincere liberal rhetoric accommodated itself to the Southern point of view is satirized in the following conversation between the sanctimonious crook, Senator Dilworthy, and Colonel Sellers, in *The Gilded Age.*

> "Providence," he said, "has placed them in our hands, although you and I, General, might have chosen a different destiny for them, under the Constitution, yet Providence knows best."
>
> "You can't do much with 'em," interrupted Col. Sellers. "They are a speculating race, sir, disinclined to work for white folks without security, planning how to live by only working for themselves. Idle, sir, there's my garden just a ruin of weeds. Nothing practical in 'em."
>
> "There is some truth in your observation, Colonel, but you must educate them."
>
> "You educate the niggro and you make him more speculating than he was before. If he won't stick to any industry except for himself now, what will he do then?"
>
> "But, Colonel, the negro when educated will be more able to make his speculations fruitful."
>
> "Never, sir, never. He would only have a wider scope to injure himself. A niggro has no grasp, sir. Now, a white man can conceive great operations, and carry them out; a niggro can't."
>
> "Still," replied the Senator, "granting that he might injure himself in a worldly point of view, his elevation through education would multiply his chances for the hereafter—which is the important thing after all, Colonel. And no matter what the result is, we must fulfill our duty by this being."
>
> "I'd elevate his soul," promptly responded the Colonel; "that's just it; you can't make his soul too immortal, but I wouldn't touch *him,* himself. Yes, sir! make his soul immortal, but don't disturb the niggro as he is."

In his blindness Colonel Sellers projects his own idleness and impracticality on the Negro, while the Senator utters grave hypocrisies. But, although the novel satirizes willful perversity and cynical manipulation, it also reveals unwittingly how invisible black men had become. It was far easier to expose the ill-treatment of the Negro, to appeal for sympathy toward him as a victim or object, than to portray him as a person in his own right. Mark Twain's high achievement in his characterization of Nigger Jim in *Adventures of Huckleberry Finn* (1886) appears all the more remarkable when set against the few black characters in *The Gilded Age*. Uncle Dan'l ("aged 40") is presented as a grown-up child ("at least in simplicity and broad and comprehensive ignorance")—a condition which, significantly enough, preserves him from an adult world bent on madness and corruption. Like Jim, Uncle Dan'l provides, however brief his appearance in the novel, an antithesis to white behavior in his gentleness, his superstition, and his protective feeling toward children. But after one comic stint he disappears from the book, perhaps to reappear in Jim, who is permitted by a feat of Mark Twain's imagination to transcend his stereotype and present himself as an adult, at least for a spell.

Another suggestive appearance of a Negro is hardly comic and points to additional complexities. Ruth Bolton and a girl friend, both medical students, discover a black corpse under the "white covering" of a dissecting table. The "black face" of the cadaver seems "to defy the pallor of death," and to scowl repulsively: " 'Haven't you yet done with the outcast, persecuted black man, but you must now haul him from his grave, and send even your women to dismember his body?' " The scene has fascinating dramatic possibilities which remain unrealized, but the rhetoric into which it dissolves suggests a process of sublimation.

While the act of imagining the dead man's defiant remark is itself an expression of self-reproach, the effect is comforting; it appeases the initial anxiety, as Ruth's "fear and disgust" turn into a look of "pity in her sweet face." Pity makes it possible for her to accept the presence of the otherwise terrifying black body. But the emotion is at bottom melodramatic and sentimental. The scene continues with "pulsations" of music and laughter entering the room from a dance hall next door. In this setting the accusing cadaver is even further reduced by becoming an occasion for the experience of the "awful sense of life itself." The specific fear and guilt aroused by the black man are thus successfully replaced by a sentimental "awe" about "life itself." Or almost successfully. The final sentence of the scene gives away some notion of what has been suppressed in this process of replacing social guilt with benevolent sentiment: "When, at length, they went away, and locked the dreadful room behind them, and came out into the street, where people were passing, they, for the first time, realized, in the relief they felt, what a nervous strain they had been under." The locked door and the dreadful room behind it evoke a latent wish to repress and to exclude. These, together with the "nervous strain," point to the authors' unresolved ambivalence toward the place of the Negro in majority culture.

IV

Ambivalence toward the place of woman is also a feature of *The Gilded Age*. Anxiety about the propriety of sweet young girls being in the presence of uncovered male bodies, especially black ones, is surely a component of the "nervous strain." What is at stake is the genteel ideal of the "maiden," an ideal under attack by a rising feminist movement in the period. In their treatment of female characters, Mark Twain and Warner reveal the tenacity of the hold of genteel standards. Their plot, as flagrantly trite and at odds with the satire as it is, reinforces these standards. This makes the novel especially useful as an introduction to the forces at work in the formation of a national middle-class culture. A comic novel of disenchantment, it satirizes the worst features of the age, its hypocrisy, double-dealing, and exploitation of false emotion. But in the end the book fails to escape the clutches of the same deceptions it excoriates.

In "The Genteel Tradition in American Philosophy" (1911), George Santayana commented that American humorists like Mark Twain "only half escape the genteel tradition; their humor would lose its savour if they had wholly escaped it." The humorists ridicule the tradition of ideality by showing how it contradicts reality, but they do not attack it in order to abandon it, "for they have nothing solid to put in its place." "So," he writes, "when Mark Twain says, 'I was born of poor but dishonest parents,' the humour depends on the parody of the genteel Anglo-Saxon convention; but to hint at the hollowness of it would not be amusing if it did not remain at bottom one's habitual conviction."

The central trope in *The Gilded Age* is just such a comic discrepancy between appearance and reality, with no clear alternative to the deceptive values. Inflated language in the form of fantasies of sudden wealth and the clichés of popular romance act like inflated stock, to cheat people of their most generous desires. The speculative spirit which pervades most of the book is based on the wish that reality will conform to a plot, such as a get-rich-quick scheme. The greatness of Colonel Sellers as a literary character lies in the fact that he is a pure expression of this self-deluding spirit; the gulf between his schemes and reality is absolute. His blindness is itself a form of comic vision. " 'There is no country in the world, sir, that pursues corruption as inveterately as we do,' " he says, missing the pun entirely. He banks most of his hopes on a scheme to market a wonderfully apt nonexistent product—"Beriah Sellers' Infallible Imperial Oriental Optic Liniment and Salvation for Sore Eyes."

The genteel conception of woman was one "habitual conviction" which troubled the entire age. In his notes for his remarkable novel of the period, *The Bostonians* (1886), Henry James wrote in 1883 that "the most salient and peculiar point in our social life" was "the situation of women, the decline of the sentiment of sex, the agitation on their behalf." Although they would probably disagree on a desirable concept of woman, Whitman concurs with James on the salience of the problem. He cites "the appalling depletion of women in their powers of sane athletic maternity," he cites as a central feature of the age, and adds: "I have sometimes thought, indeed, that the sole avenue and means of a reconstructed sociology depended, primarily, on a new birth, elevation, expansion, invigoration of woman." He includes in *Vistas* portraits of several women who express dignity, self-respect, independence—"that indescribable perfume of genuine woman-hood"—and admits that they are out of line with the current model, "the stock feminine characters of the current novelists . . . which fill the envying dreams of so many poor girls, and are accepted by our men, too." One mark of the democratic culture he appeals to in his essay will be "the entire redemption of woman" from the hold of these popular stereotypes.

The model contained two essential features: the subordination of women to men in matters of work and practicality, and their elevation in matters of moral ideals (thus the importance of chastity), cultivation, and non-utilitarian "grace." The split between men and women in regard to work and "culture," as Santayana explains, is the essential core of the genteel tradition. "The American Will inhabits the sky-scraper; the American Intellect inhabits the colonial mansion. The one is the sphere of the American man; the other, at least predominantly, of the American woman. The one is all aggressive and enterprise; the other is all genteel tradition."

"Woman," said Henry Ward Beecher, who championed women's rights on the ambiguous grounds of pity for the weak, "is appointed for the refinement of the race. Man is said to have been made a little lower than the angels; woman needs no such comparison; she was made full as high." Such sentiments infuriated feminists like Mrs. Stanton, Lucretia Mott and Susan Anthony, but these notions seemed necessary of the self-esteem of men, especially in the business and professional classes. The prospect of a "liberated" woman—and more than a few feminists dared to speak publicly against marriage and for "free love"—was a threat to masculinity, let alone to the middle-class household.

Certain characteristic strategies appear in *The Gilded Age*. Of the two heroines in the book, Laura Hawkins possesses far more vitality than the Quaker medical student, Ruth Bolton. But, as throughout his fiction, Mark Twain draws back from the sexual implications of his heroine, makes her a "fallen woman," and in the end puts her safely away in a death scene flooded with "official" pity. The authors place much of the blame for Laura's sordid adventures on "the most exaggerated notions of life" in the popular romances and fiction which fed her imagination. "From these stories she learned what a woman of keen intellect and some culture joined to beauty and fascination of manner might expect to accomplish in society as she read of it; and along with these ideas she imbibed other very crude ones in regard to the emancipation of woman." But in the end Twain and Warner resort to similar clichés of popular fiction to guarantee the downfall of their heroine.

A similar tactic is at work in regard to Ruth, who not only has imbibed the ideas of emancipation, but also acts on them. Ruth, a medical student, is a prototype of the middle-class career woman, a figure more subject to ridicule than respect in much popular fiction. " 'I want to be something, to make myself something, to do something,' " she tells her father. " 'Why should I rust, and be stupid, and sit in inaction because I am a girl?' " She wants to "break things and get loose," and the paces she is sent through by her creators indicate both grudging admiration for and uneasiness with there rebellious emotions. On the whole she is treated with indulgence, as if her feelings were signs of youth and immaturity. Held in reserve is the idea that she is still a girl—a "maiden"—and that when the chips are down, she will return to the fold; she will fall in love and marry.

Her visit with the Montagues, an old, respectable New England family, is a turning point. There, in her friendship with Alice, a consummate New England girl—breeding, books, sewing, picnics, "company"—she begins to sense that there may very well be something "beyond" a career, and she comes away enjoying "a new sort of power which has awakened within her." But it is not until she is honored by the authors with a "fever crisis," one of the tritest of romantic conventions, that she safely reenters the world of genteel femininity. The price of her survival is her fevered confession of love for Philip, who then "drew her back to life." She matures at last, and accepts dependency. "It was a new but a dear joy, to be lifted up and carried back into the happy world, which was now all aglow with the light of love; to be lifted and carried by the one she loved more than her own life." For Alice has of course been secretly in love with Philip all along, and the novel's sanction of genteel womanhood is completed by this revelation: "And the world never knows how many women there are like Alice, whose sweet but lonely lives of self-sacrifice, gentle, faithful, loving souls, bless it continually."

Twain and Warner probably took their flimsy plot no more seriously than we do. Nevertheless the plot is there, and its effect is to enforce attitudes, including some at odds with the novel's satire, which lay at the heart of middle-class culture. Senator Dilworthy's blessings may seduce the ignorant and scandalize the sophisticated, but Alice's are sacred to all. Without such self-sacrificing female love, where would society be? It is not too much to say that a whole structure of civilized values seemed to hang on that continual blessing.

V

From the fountain of idealized female love poured an emotion which saturated popular culture. Sentimental benevolence became a major feature of the creed. For the most part it gave middle-class people a way of accepting themselves as worthwhile, proud of their acquirements, free of guilt about their material and social condition. One of the components of this sentiment was an all-embracing religion of the heart, an ostensibly classless humanitarianism which had evolved out of Calvinism in a process begun in the revivals earlier in the century. The famous children of the old school Calvinist, Lyman Beecher—Harriet Beecher Stowe and Henry Ward Beecher—were prominent popularizers of both the content and the cloying style of a sentimental and unshakably optimistic religion of humanity.

The tenacity of such desanctified religion can be understood as an attempt to keep hold of certain virtues which many Americans thought of as "traditional" or pre-industrial. One of the most effective uses of sentimentality appeared in popular fiction dealing with the regional and the local. The spread of mechanization as well as the surge of nationalist feeling after the Civil War began a process of washing away regional cultural differences—a process accompanied by a remarkable outburst of nostalgic affection for what was disappearing. Much of this fiction—Bret Harte's and Mark Twain's are cases in point—was set in the 1840's and 1850's, before the great change of war and industrialization. It served as the American equivalent of British fiction of the pre-industrial countryside, and its dominant mode was sentimental. At its best, as in the work of Sarah Orne Jewett, regional fiction attempted to seize hold of something of genuine value in the way of a distinct style of life. But what is known as local color fiction was another matter. Based on regional stereotypes and drenched in nostalgia, it served to bring the unique into a familiar frame of reference; through the religion of the heart it served to translate the local into the national.

By and large local color fiction employed an extremely effective convention, popularized by Bret Harte as the "heart of gold" formula. This was a device whereby local characters, especially westerners, are first identified as disreputable (gamblers, miners, prostitutes, immigrants), and then through a manipulation of plot, are shown to be decent folk after all, deserving of our sympathy. The plot thus reconciled the assumed respectable reader with the "outcasts" on a revealed common ground— the goodness of the heart. The social function of such fiction was crucial to an evolving middle-class culture. It allowed the reader, in the comfort of his drawing room, to feel superior and democratic at the same time. An important element in the process which brought a national culture into being through the mass media, local color helped stamp that culture with predominantly middle-class, humanitarian values. Above all it established an ideal of "culture," of a cultivated style of life, as the perspective both of the writer, who usually distinguished his own class standing from that of his characters by the use of an "educated" style on one hand and dialect on the other, and the reader, upon whose flood of sympathy and nostalgia the plot depends.

If local color owed its existence, at least indirectly, to the effects of an increasingly mechanized system of communication and transportation which threatened to destroy the regional, another important force in national culture was a more direct response to the machine itself. The religion of the heart was based on a belief, muddled as it may have been, in "nature" as the source of moral values. But a good deal of doubt in the period arose from uncertainty or uneasiness about the nature of modern technology. The machine had a complicated status in the minds of many Americans, and once more, *The Gilded Age* can serve to illustrate this theme.

In the opening chapter Squire Hawkins has a vision in his decaying backwoods village of the coming of steamboats and railroads. " 'They're going to make a revolution in this world's affairs that will make men dizzy to contemplate.' " In his dizziness he envisions all the products of the land, timber and iron ore, corn and wild game, converted into crisp greenbacks. Hoping to cash in, he buys a plot of worthless land, and bequeaths what turns out to be a disastrous, even murderous burden to his children. It is interesting that the failure of his scheme is actually anticipated symbolically by an event which occurs shortly after the purchase—a steamboat explosion of horrible proportions. The jury which investigates the accident "returned the inevitable American verdict . . . 'NOBODY TO BLAME.' "

The accident and the verdict, and the debacle regarding the plot of land later in the novel, all point to the authors' underlying uneasiness with the machine, an uneasiness which had appeared earlier in American literature, in Hawthorne and Thoreau and Melville, but which assumes a more furtive and covert character in this period. In 1867, the New England clergyman and essayist Samuel Osgood, in "New Aspects of the American Mind" (*Harper's New Monthly Magazine*), had accounted for his continuing confidence in America by citing the following curious episode during the Civil War:

> I remember one day, after a good deal of depression at public disaster, visiting a large cluster of work-shops that gathered round a huge steam-engine, not far from Harper's printing-house. I went down into the basement, and there saw the giant power lifting and dropping his ponderous shaft, and turning all those machines by his great force. The workmen in a mood of grim humor had put little flags upon his great head and arms and the monster seemed to be alive with patriotism. The sight was most suggestive and encouraging. I could have cried for joy or sung hallelujahs to the Lord of Hosts, for all was clear then. There, and every where through the loyal States, was that same mighty force working for us—the Providential arm of the nineteenth century.

William Dean Howells, in his description of the Corliss engine at the 1876 Centennial Exposition, conveys a similar note in his celebration of the "lifelike" qualities of the giant machine, its athletic grace and strength. But in the carefully constructed ambiguities of his account, one detects a crucial shift in emphasis. The very qualities which inspire the animating metaphor also portend a threat. The engineer who sits quietly in the midst of the moving parts, "as in a peaceful bower," is "like some potent enchanter," and the engine itself a "prodigious Afreet," a Frankenstein "who could crush him past all semblance of humanity with his lightest touch." Howells concedes the threat in the lovely contraption, but the temple is no place in which to curse the gods: "It is, alas! what the Afreet has done to humanity too often, where his strength has superseded men's industry; but of such things the Machinery Hall is no place to speak."

Howells, at this point, was able to salvage his optimism unruffled. He would have a more difficult time of it later, for example in his novel of 1890, *A Hazard of New Fortunes,* where the sight and sound of an elevated train raise the fear that the universe may be controlled by a mindless mechanism after all. In 1876 he could count on the good readers of *Atlantic* to sigh along with his "alas!" In the same decade other writers, less popular to be sure, were making even more troubled observations. D. A. Wasson, a former Unitarian minister, wrote in the *North American Review* (1874), under the ominous title "The Modern Type of Oppression," that the same social forces which now "enrich" the age also represent a danger; progress was likely to become "its own plague." Anticipating Henry Adams, Wasson feared that "a ruling order adequate to the new conditions," a system of control commensurate with the "magnificent and incomparable achievements" of the age, had yet to appear. "Mr. Jefferson's ideal of a moral and pastoral life"—an ideal still the source of much patriotic rhetoric—had long since died and we now have a society of cities. "Our former rural civilization, with its simple manners, moderate desires, and autonomous life, has as good as disappeared; the country is now just the suburb of the city."

Wasson focused on the means of communication as his evidence. The telegraph system, the railroad, the underground and underwater cables, are like a powerful nervous system, able to propagate instantaneous influence. Several years later the physician George M. Beard, in *American Nervousness* (1881), argued from the same analogy that the spread of technology was an unprecedented assault on the human nervous system. The perfection of the railroad and telegraph, and of clocks, takes its toll by enforcing a nervous desire to be punctual. "From the standpoint only of economy of nerve-force all our civilization is a mistake." Wasson was more concerned with effects upon the social order and on social morale. He felt American society to be "in one of those immature, expectant stages," on the threshold of "such a future as had no antitype in the past." The word "progress" held out no comfort for him. The new mechanical forces, the dynamos and engines, gave society the power to "tame the tropics," but without regulation the system results in oppression, demoralization, and social war. Reaching for a final image he wrote that American society resembled "a coachman who has learned well how to guide a team of horses, but suddenly finds himself in charge of a locomotive-engine, and knows not which way to turn."

VI

How to comprehend the spectacle of runaway forces and collapsing values was a major inner drama of the period. It was a drama performed most urgently—and poignantly—by the class into which Henry Adams was born, a class, he writes in *The Education of Henry Adams* (1907), which felt itself "ruthlessly stamped out" by "the whole mechanical consolidation of force." Adams described American society as an earthworm, blindly trying to understand itself, "to catch up with its own head and to twist about in search of its tail." The figure has a canny resemblance to a railroad turning a sharp, dangerous curve.

One of the ideas Adams' class seized upon was the idea of "culture" as a distinct value. "Wherever men of cultivation looked," writes Richard Hofstadter in *Anti-Intellectualism in American Life* (1964), "they found themselves facing hostile forces and an alien mentality." There emerged, he adds, "a peculiar American underground of frustrated aristocrats, a type of genteel reformer whose very existence dramatized the alienation of education and intellect from significant political and economic power." Francis Parkman was typical. "Two enemies, unknown before," he wrote in "The Failure of Universal Suffrage" (*North American Review*, 1878), "have risen like spirits of darkness on our social and political horizon—an ignorant proletariat and a half-taught plutocracy." "Culture," he writes, "is no friend of vulgar wealth, and most of the mountains of gold and silver we have lately seen are in the keeping of those who are very ill fitted to turn them to the profit of civilization." Neither was "culture" a friend of the "dangerous classes," the "greedy and irresponsible crowds," the "barbarism . . . ready to overwhelm us." Arguing that universal suffrage and the theory of inalienable rights are "an outrage to justice and common sense," he called for a crusade of the liberally educated, the cultivated, even the "literary feller"—"those that find their exercise in the higher fields of thought and action"—against the menace of democracy.

What did such champions of cultivation mean by "culture"? No native theory of high culture was ready at hand, but in its place echoes of Matthew Arnold appeared throughout the writing of this period. Arnold lent himself to easy quotation, and as often as not, his carefully reasoned and humane defense of culture was distorted in the service of class snobbery. In *Culture and Anarchy* (1867), which, as Lionel Trilling points out, was designed to allay upper-class fears about the extension of suffrage in the 1867 Reform Bill, Arnold presented "culture" as a process of searching after perfection, a process of *becoming* rather than having. He proposed beauty and knowledge ("sweetness and light") as superior values, and insisted, perhaps not strongly enough, on the socially beneficent character of "culture." While it is true that Arnold spoke of it as "a certain ideal centre of correct information, taste, and intelligence," "culture" was ultimately classless, and he offered it as "a principle of authority, to counteract the tendency to anarchy"—a tendency implicit in the commitment to "machinery" as a solution to human problems. This account is, of course, a simplification—it leaves out of the picture the role of Oxford in fostering Arnold's conception of the good life—but it is important to stress that at the outset of his argument he disclaimed the version of "culture" which is "valued either out of sheer vanity and ignorance or else as an engine of social and class distinction, separating its holder, like a badge or title, from other people who have not got it."

Arnold remarked elsewhere that certain upper-class Americans over-valued the English aristocratic ideal of the gentleman. For some "frus-trated aristocrats" this ideal was identical with "culture," and as such, a defense against the threats from above and below. In *The Gilded Age*, for example, Twain and Warner describe a group called the "Middle Ground"; an aristocracy of education and refinement, they exist apart from the political corruption, the frenzied speculations, and the hypocrisy of the age. They move "serenely in their wide orbit," with "no troublesome appearances to keep up, no rivalries which they cared to distress them-selves about, no jealousies to fret over." These people, who are "beyond reproach," preserve the only positive values in the book. A portrait of the household of Squire Oliver Montague, retired New England lawyer, reveals some of their identifying appurtenances. "Just a plain, roomy house," it displayed "evidences of culture, of intellectual activity and of a zest in the affairs of all the world."

> Every room had its book-cases or book-shelves, and was more or less a library; upon every table was liable to be a litter of new books, fresh periodicals and daily newspapers. There were plants in the sunny windows and some choice engravings on the walls, with bits of color in oil or watercolors; the piano was sure to be open and strewn with music; and there were photographs and little souvenirs here and there of foreign travel.

The house expresses to perfection an official image, enforced by numerous magazine articles and stories and illustrations, of how the older, literary, responsible families live—refinement, self-confidence, ease with ideas— and the sources of wealth well hidden.

A similar image, with a much blunter political message, appears in John Hay's novel of strikers and aristocrats, *The Breadwinners* (1883). Hay, a close friend of Henry Adams, served as Lincoln's private secretary, and later in many diplomatic posts; he was an architect of the "open door policy" in China at the end of the century. He was also a writer, whose *Pike County Ballads* (1871) have a place in local color literature.

The Breadwinners is set in Cleveland at the time of the 1877 railroad strike. The issue in the strike and in the novel's thin plot are defined culturally: the hero is a gentleman, a model of correctness (though with a taste for lower-class girls, which adds a bit of luster to the plot), while the villains, the strikers, are misfits, blind to art, ill-mannered, vaguely foreign. The lower orders have been corrupted by romantic fiction, by popular fantasies of love and power, and are thus too easily manipulated by agitators. The novel diagrams faithfully a vision of society exalting the gentleman, the lady, the fine parlor—all the emblems of genteel culture—as a last line of defense against barbarism. The gentleman-hero is the only figure in the novel capable of resisting the strikers; he organizes a private militia, comprised of faithful yeoman-types, to protect his own property—and his lady's. He shows no reluctance in using violence himself, in fact gets himself wounded, and survives a "fever crisis," during which the lady in question pours out the love and devotion she had earlier withheld. What the plot tries to show is that gentility is, after all, the best source of values for all Americans, including the "good" workers, the immigrant politicians, the parvenu industrialists.

John Hay was not alone in identifying genteel culture with property. Jonathan Baxter Harrison, a zealous Protestant reformer, took the same line in *Certain Dangerous Tendencies in American Life* (1880), several chapters of which appeared initially in the *Atlantic*. Harrison used an excited prose to try to awaken his readers to the fact that "we are in the earlier stages of a war upon property, and upon everything that satisfies what are called the higher wants of life." Workers are taught by agitators to regard art and culture "as causes and symbols of the laborer's poverty and degradation, and therefore as things to be hated." Self-protection requires, then, a program for the diffusion of values which honor property, and in his unambiguous call for action, Harrison argues for culture as an instrument of class control.

> The people who believe in culture, in property, and in order, that is, civilization, must establish the necessary agencies for the diffusion of a new culture. Capital must protect itself by organized activities for a new object—the education of the people. Those who possess property, and those who value it as one of the great forces and supports of civilization, will be obliged to learn that legislation, even if laws are properly enforced, is not an adequate means for the protection of property and the repression of the disorderly and destructive elements in our society. Legislation itself is fast becoming a weapon in the hands of the hostile forces; and even if it were always the work of wise men it is only one factor of civilization, and would not give us security without a great advance in the culture and character of the people.

Similar ideas appeared in journals throughout the period. In some cases the peril was vaguely identified with the nature of the industrial system, but in all cases the necessity for a wider diffusion of culture had a pointed political appeal. Edward Atkinson, himself a member of an old Boston family and an influential industrialist, viewed the cultural gap as an unfortunate effect of industrialization. His contribution to *The First Century of the Republic* (1876), a collection of essays reprinted from *Harper's Magazine*, was on the whole enthusiastic about machines, progress, and *laissez faire*. But his comments convey a dawning suspicion that not all the effects of industrialization are benign.

> Where the operation of the machine tends to relieve the operative of all thought, the man or woman who tends it risks becoming a machine, well oiled and cared for, but incapable of independent life. The culture of the past was more diffused, but it was obtained by means of the very toil that was needed to gain subsistence, because the work itself called upon all the faculties, and was not a matter of routine; the culture and refinements of to-day come from leisure and opportunity more than from the development of men in the necessary work of their lives. May it not be possible that one of the causes of the great demand which exists for bad and sensational books and for exciting amusements comes from the dreary monotony of many of the necessary occupations of men and women, and that one of the most essential developments of commerce or of mutual service in the future will be in the direction of more ample provision for wholesome amusements? . . . How to provide cheap and wholesome amusements for those who toil is one of the greatest problems of commerce which must be solved.

Atkinson's conclusion may be suspiciously paternalistic, but within a framework of confidence in capitalism, modern technology and progress, he does evince a sound concern for the quality of life. "It is not sufficient to have achieved only the means of living: life must be made worth living to each and all." His striking admission that modern industrial work fails to provide satisfaction leads him, as it did others, to the notion that "The capability for enjoyment which all covet but few attain . . . must come from culture and education, and not in the work itself." He sees the divergence of culture from work as a new historical condition, an inevitable consequence of industrialism. For the first time, "instruction in what constitutes the true use of leisure" is necessary for the security of society.

The notion that industrialism left the "higher wants of life" unfulfilled was widespread. It was supported by two English writers influential in America, Thomas Carlyle and Matthew Arnold. But no one, possibly excepting Whitman, recognized that in large measure the idea of "higher wants"—an idea which gave form to feelings of dislocation and anxiety— was itself a product of industrialism. Industrialism separated large sections of people from their traditional culture—either rural or "old world"—and in its narrow, confining conditions of work, created needs chiefly for distraction and passive entertainment. It also created specialization, requiring more and more exacting training to fulfill precise functions. Indeed, culture itself increasingly became a specialization of its own, a product of elite education and training. The effect was, we now understand more clearly, a dangerous fragmentation of society. Industrialism threatened to rend the fabric of social life into distinct and hostile units. Mass produced cheap diversions rushed in to fill the vacuum caused by the loss of traditional ways of life, particularly in industrial cities. And literary culture, as if to compensate for the destruction of its roots in the life of our society, invented for itself a separate realm, a world of "higher wants" and spiritual values.

Those who spoke of culture in this period referred almost exclusively to this realm of spirit. By failing to generate a satisfying culture of its own, industrialism heightened the appeal of the traditional and the genteel—especially since the degraded sensationalism of mass culture seemed the only alternative. And with intensifying class conflict, the notion of "higher wants" served another function. By definition these wants were universal; they belonged to human nature. They could serve as the basis of a national culture in which conflicts might be submerged in common spiritual experience.

The idea of universal values based upon "high" culture had wide and subtle appeal. It appears in a curiously convoluted way in a letter in *The Nation* (September 1867), titled "A Plea for the Uncultivated." The writer, who signs himself "A Philistine," begins by identifying himself with "the great mass of workers" who are deprived of "the culture which is the chief good to be attained in life." In part, especially by his tone, the writer seems to question whether the conventional idea of culture is indeed the "chief good" of life. But his argument is split in two directions. First he attacks the invidious distinction by which some persons are admitted to the status of "cultivated," and others, by the nature of their vocation (men of science and business, and workers), are excluded. The laboring classes create the leisure which permits the scholar to brood over dead languages, and in turn the scholar—the symbol of genteel culture—despises the worker. Is this just? "We must work, we must be Philistines whether we will or not, else there can be no culture either for us or for our critics who abuse us."

But what seems to be an assault on the class system takes a significant turn in the second part of the argument. Here the writer extends himself as a defender of all of the "uncultivated"—businessmen and manufacturers along with workers. He now questions the relevance of the scholar's culture. "Is it not time for the manufacturers, the merchants, the traders, and the artisans to assert their claim? to prove that any culture which does not include them is incomplete?" After all, what does the "man of pure culture" contribute to the world? Usually he cannot even answer the question "What is a dollar?" Selfish accumulation of culture is no worthier than avaricious accumulation of capital, and probably less useful.

The writer seems to signal a rebellion of his newly-defined underclass, the uncultivated. We sense below the surface of his prose a surging resentment of deprivation, of denial of worth—a hatred for the intellectual who sneers at "philistines." But before he completes his argument the writer makes still another shift which exposes a sag in his position. What, after all, does it mean to be "included" in culture? He urges the alleged uncultivated to cease accepting philistinism as "their doom," or "weakly attempting to evade it by a smattering of literature or art." Instead they should start claiming "a position as high as that of others who now look down upon them; and claiming this position by virtue of a clear perception of the fact that by their work the abundance of things is increased, the comfort of humanity promoted, the leisure of the scholar made possible, and true culture, or, as it has been well defined by Arnold, sweetness and light, diffused among all, and not monopolized by a few." To be included in culture means, in the end, no more than an equitable share of "true culture," of the fruits of leisure. The split between culture and work remains his premise.

Charles Dudley Warner could very well have had this letter in mind as he addressed the alumni of Hamilton College in 1872 on the question "What Is Your Culture to Me?" "The question which the man with the spade asks about the use of your culture to him," he warned, "is a menace." But it is also an opportunity. The problem of the day, he said, was "the reconciliation of the interests of classes," and culture could be its instrument. Drawing on Matthew Arnold's definition of culture as "sweetness and light," as "the best which has been thought and said in the world," Warner recognized that the question of the man with the spade, "What is your culture to me?" had to be answered. The values of culture are universal; culture is "the light which ennobles common things." And as an example of the beneficent influence of art he offered a painting, "a charming, suggestive, historical scene," the original of which hangs in a rich man's house; through new processes of reproduction, it can now be made available to all—to this effect:

> All the world, in its toil, its hunger, its sordidness, pauses a moment to look on it—that grey sea-coast, the receding *Mayflower*, the two young Pilgrims in the foreground regarding it—all the world looks on it perhaps for a moment thoughtfully, perhaps tearfully, and is touched with the sentiment of it, is kindled into a glow of novelness by the sight of that faith, and love, and resolute devotion, which have tinged our early history with the faint light of romance. So art is no longer the enjoyment of the few, but the help and solace of the many.

An official picture, an official creed, and official emotions—these constituted Warner's conception of the value of culture. It appeals to "the higher part of man's nature," the common ground of humanity. "Unless the culture of the age finds means to diffuse itself, working downward and reconciling antagonisms by a commonness of thought and feeling and aim in life, society must more and more separate itself into jarring classes, with mutual misunderstandings and hatred and war." The alternative to culture, to "the light which ennobles common things," was plainly disaster.

VII

"The writers of a time hint the mottoes of its gods," wrote Walt Whitman in *Democratic Vistas*, and "the word of the modern, say these voices, is the word Culture." With this word, he continues, "we find ourselves abruptly in close quarters with the enemy." Troubled by many of the same phenomena as the upholders of culture, Whitman uses the word as a pivot on which he sharply and decisively departs from their leading assumptions. He, too, rejects the notion that America's material progress is sufficient in itself; he rejects as well the sensationalism and cheapness of mass-produced culture. But he reserves the brunt of his attack for the polite cultivation offered as an alternative and for the motive of social control implicit in it. In place of the Arnoldian view of culture as the inheritance of the best that has been said and thought, and the personal ideal of harmonious individual perfection which follows from it, Whitman proposes "a radical change of category, in the distribution of precedence." Instead of a culture delivered to the people, he calls for one delivered from the people themselves.

His conception of "the People" as a new historical force, a coherent social category brought into existence by the democratic revolutions of the nineteenth century, is the crux of Whitman's argument. On this point he stands virtually alone among articulate thinkers of his period. "The great word Solidarity has arisen," he writes, and insists that it is America's purpose to put the word into practice. If not, America "means nothing more, and does nothing more, than any other land." So far the prospect is clouded: "Of all dangers to a nation, as things exist in our day, there can be no greater one than having certain portions of the people set off from the rest by a line drawn—they not privileged as others, but degraded, humiliated, made of no account." The failure to realize "Solidarity" in the fabric of social life is accentuated, moreover, by the remarkable political and material progress of American society. Whitman's purpose in the essay is to reaffirm the egalitarian ideal, as an alternative to polite culture and as the only justification for material prosperity. The stakes are clear: "The United States are destined either to surmount the gorgeous history of feudalism, or else prove the most tremendous failure of time."

Democratic Vistas may strike the reader at first as a loose and baggy meditation, drifting casually from jeremiads of complaint to an often overblown rhetoric of affirmation. But underlying the apparently erratic and ill-shaped movements is a firm argument in the form of an inner dialogue in which opposite perceptions and ideas confront and test each other. Whitman admits that the essay "may be open to the charge of one part contradicting another—for there are opposite sides to the great question of democracy," but asks that the essay be read "in such oneness, each page and each claim and assertion modified and temper'd by the others." Opposition or dialectic is the essay's method; it is also a clue to its meaning. For at the heart of Whitman's thinking is a commitment to process, to activity, to ebb and flow, as the essential rhythm of both personal and social life.

Without a clear sense of its procedure through contradiction, the reader might be deceived by any number of the essay's apparently conflicting assertions. There is no equivocation, however, about ultimate meanings: the keynote of the argument is that the test of democratic society is found, not in political arrangements nor material prosperity, but in a total way of life: "democracy can never prove itself beyond cavil, until it founds and luxuriantly grows its own forms of art, poems, schools, theology, displacing all that exists, or that has been produced anywhere in the past, under opposite influences." Whitman calls for a kind of "Cultural Revolution," the unseating of all inherited forms, with a class of "native authors, literatuses" as vanguard.

But how does he reach this conclusion, and why does he assign the critical role to poets? His meaning cannot be understood without some reconstruction of the dialectic of his thought.

Much of the essay is denunciatory and can be read as a gloss on *The Gilded Age*. At the outset Whitman makes a concession to public discussion regarding the dangers of universal suffrage. He admits the "appalling dangers," and addresses himself to those "within whose thought rages the battle, advancing, retreating, between democracy's convictions, aspirations, and the people's crudeness, vices, caprices." Much of his criticism resembles that of the cultivated groups. He finds some appeal in the notion that a locomotive is a more pregnant work of art than a pyramid but replies, like Atkinson, that "the soul of man will not with such only—nay, not with such at all—be finally satisfied." Like Wasson he sees signs of disease everywhere amidst material abundance: society is "canker'd, crude, superstitious, and rotten"; "everywhere, in shop, street, church, theatre, barroom, official chair, are pervading flippancy and vulgarity, low cunning, infidelity—everywhere the youth puny, impudent, foppish, prematurely ripe—everywhere an abnormal libidinousness, unhealthy forms, male, female, painted, padded, dyed, chignon'd, muddy complexions." With Twain and Warner he agrees that society is "this fantastic farce" enacted "in an atmosphere of hypocrisy." Scoundrelism rules the day. The golden calf is worshiped everywhere. "In business (this all-devouring modern word, business), the one sole object is, by any means, pecuniary gain. The magician's serpent in the fable ate up all the other serpents; and money-making is our magician's serpent, remaining to-day sole master of the field."

It is true, then, that much of Whitman's criticism seems to fall into conventional patterns of assault against "materialism." "It is," he writes, "as if we were somehow being endow'd with a vast and more and more thoroughly appointed body, and then left with little or no soul." But just as "abnormal libidinousness" implies the opposite image of sexual health, "materialism" contains its own inner contradiction. The following passage is typical:

> In the highly artificial and materialistic bases of modern civilization, with the corresponding arrangements and methods of living, the force-infusion of intellect alone, the depraving influences of riches just as much as poverty, the absence of all high ideals in character—with the long series of tendencies, shapings, which few are strong enough to resist, and which now seem, with steam-engine speed, to be everywhere turning out the generations of humanity like uniform iron castings—all of which, as compared with the feudal ages, we can yet do nothing better than accept, make the best of, and even welcome, upon the whole, for their oceanic practical grandeur, and their restless wholesale kneading of the masses—I say all of this tremendous and dominant play

of solely materialistic bearings upon current life in the United States, with the results as already seen, accumulating, and reaching far into the future, that they must either be confronted and met by at least an equally subtle and tremendous force-infusion for purposes of spiritualization, for the pure conscience, for genuine esthetics, and for absolute and primal manliness and womanliness—or else our modern civilization, with all its improvements, is in vain, and we are on the road to a destiny, a status, equivalent, in its real world, to that of the fabled damned.

In the sweep of this oceanic sentence, Whitman attempts to depict a historical process. Like Hawthorne a generation earlier, he has a premonition of damnation in a society which turns itself over to the steam engine. But he also recognizes that there is no turning back, that "we can yet do nothing better than accept, make the best of, *and even welcome*" the new forces. True, modern society may be grinding mankind into "uniform iron castings," but at the same time it is also "kneading" the masses. The historical situation, then, is contradictory, and it is precisely in the tension between the leveling and the liberating forces of modern life that Whitman identifies the possibilities for a new culture. "For," he writes, "how can we remain divided, contradicting ourselves, this way?"

Whitman's fundamental departure from the cultural assumptions of other critics arises from his conception of "the masses" as a historical force. His idea of history is based on a "stages of civilization" theory. Stage one is political—"the planning and putting on record of the political foundation rights of immense masses of people," a plan "not for class but for universal man." This was the work of the French and American revolutions. Stage two is economic; it "relates to material prosperity, wealth, produce, labor-saving machines, iron, cotton . . . "—in sum, the material basis for abundance. This is the stage at which he finds America in the 1870's. Stage three, which he now proclaims, will be the work of "a native expression-spirit, getting into form, . . . to be evidenced by original authors and poets to come . . . by a sublime and serious Religious Democracy . . . from its own interior and vital principles, reconstructing, democratizing society." This is the stage in which democracy enters culture, in which "universal man" is realized in the entire fabric of the social order.

The relevance of the masses for culture begins, in his argument, with the relation between mass and individual. "The two are contradictory," he writes in one of his principal formulations, "but our task is to reconcile them." Democracy rests upon the uniqueness of the individual, which may very well be threatened by the masses in their present condition. But at the same time, the masses represent a necessary condition for the individual's self-realization. The appearance of "the People," he argues, was essential to the democratic concept of the individual, for it permitted a definition of the person characterized "not from extrinsic acquirements or position, but in the pride of himself or herself alone."

Thus, the existential basis of individualism, of "completeness in separatism," must be the universal opportunity for all humans to achieve this condition. Any restriction based on class, or more important, any restriction resulting from education or culture, which subordinates some individuals to others, will restrict the self-realization of all people. The transcendent justification of political democracy (freedom for "all") is that it provides the opportunity for the individual to "become a law, and a series of laws, unto himself, surrounding and providing for, not only his own personal control, but all his relations to other individuals." Thus, "to be a voter with the rest is not so much. . . . But to become an enfranchised man, and now, impediments removed, to stand and start without humiliation, and equal with the rest; to commence, or have the road clear'd to commence, the grand experiment of development, whose end (perhaps requiring several generations) may be the forming of a full-grown man or woman—that *is* something."

This is perhaps Whitman's most difficult and most often misunderstood idea. He is frequently represented as an idealizer of "the People." It must be granted that he lays himself open to the charge with a sometimes vapid rhetoric of "brotherhood." In part the resort to rhetorical flourish is a result of the slipperiness of the concept, which lends itself to the simplification of slogan. But Whitman should be taken seriously when he denies any sentimental regard for the masses: "We do not (at any rate I do not) put it either on the ground that the People, the masses, even the best of them, are, in their latent or exhibited qualities, essentially sensible and good—nor on the grounds of their rights." "Leaving the rest to the sentimentalists," he adds, democracy is "the only safe and preservative" formula for the time—not for the sake of the masses alone but "for community's sake."

This argument points to Whitman's anticipation of one of the most disturbing tendencies of modern society, the polarization of self and society, the retreat of the self from community. In response to what might be called a crisis in a culture of fragmented selves, he wishes to evoke, as a balance to "individualism, which isolates," another force, which he calls "adhesiveness or love, that fuses, ties and aggregates." A major argument for democracy is, then, that it prevents the menacing loss of social love or "Solidarity" as an extra-legal adhesive force. And it is precisely for its failure to cultivate such emotions—to project an image of social love which might provide "proper regulation and potency" to the "mass, or lump character"—that Whitman rejects genteel culture.

"Man, viewed in the lump, displeases," he writes "and is a constant puzzle and affront to the merely educated classes." But his entire argument is that "mere" education is not enough. "Taste, intelligence and culture (so-called) have always been against the masses, and remain so." What is needed is a culture which not only is addressed to the people but takes its life from them. Instead, American society is "already becoming stifled and rotten." "To prune, gather, trim, conform, and ever cram and stuff, and be genteel and proper, is the pressure of our days." Gentility has set in with a gilded display surpassing its sources in aristocratic Europe. "Never, in the Old World, was thoroughly upholster'd exterior appearance and show, mental and other, built entirely on the idea of caste, and on the sufficiency of mere outside acquisition—never were glibness, verbal intellect, more the test, the emulation—more loftily elevated as head and sample—than they are on the surface of our republican States this day."

While the official creed of culture is "rapidly creating a class of supercilious infidels, who believe in nothing," the instruments of mechanization are mass-producing an equally pernicious kind of distraction, "like an endless supply of small coin," the main object of which is "to amuse, to titillate, to pass away time, to circulate the news, and rumours of news." The threat to democratic culture from mechanization and the marketplace is just as serious as the threat from gentility. "To-day, in books . . . success (so-called) is for him or her who strikes the mean flat average, the sensational appetite for stimulus, incident, persiflage, etc., and depicts, to the common calibre, sensual, exterior life. To such, or the luckiest of them, as we see, the audiences are limitless and profitable."

Thus, neither traditional "high" culture nor marketplace art will serve the democratic purpose. Both project unacceptable, debased images of man. In their place Whitman calls for a "radical change of category," a culture which has for "its spinal meaning the formation of a typical personality or character, eligible to the uses of the high average of men—and not restricted by conditions ineligible to the masses." The expression "high average," as opposed to the "mean flat average" of mass art, is the clue to Whitman's program, and to his continuing relevance as a critic of culture. Underlying this distinction is the argument that culture resides in character rather than in objects, in the style and quality of being rather than in possessions. From this it follows that the value of a culture lies in its projected image of human possibility, an image which, to serve a democracy, must emerge from the concrete lives of people and foster their "grand experiment of development." Solidarity is to be based on the highest possibilities of man.

And it is in this regard that Whitman reaches his extraordinary conclusion that the future of American culture is in the hands of its poets. Thinking of figures like Homer and Shakespeare, he argues that poets provide a nation with "original archetypes." "They only put a nation in form." They serve a culture by creating models of character. "They furnish the materials and suggestions of personality for the men and women of that country, and enforce them in a thousand effective ways."

This notion of the supremacy of the poet can be traced to sources in German Romantic thought, particularly in Herder, and it might be dismissed as anachronistic in an age of mechanical communications. This point is not really at issue here. The significant feature of Whitman's program for national poets is its insistence on the value of the *activity* of poetry, its manner of enforcement. More important than his call for a sacred class of "bards" in his account of their work:

> Books are to be call'd for, and supplied, on the assumption that the process of reading is not a half-sleep, but, in the highest sense, an exercise, a gymnast's struggle; that the reader is to do something for himself, must be on the alert, must himself or herself construct indeed the poem, argument, history, metaphysical essay—the text furnishing the hints, the clue, the start or frame-work. Not the book needs so much to be the complete thing, but the reader of the book does. That were to make a nation of supple and athletic minds, well-trained, intuitive, used to depend on themselves, not on a few coteries of writers.

Implicit in this passage is Whitman's major indictment of both genteel and mass culture: both require nothing more of the audience than passive reception of prescribed ideas and feelings. Against what André Malraux has called "the appeasing arts," Whitman proposes a literature of strenuous activity, in which writer and reader complement each other. The performance is valuable as an exchange, an activity of mind and feeling—an idea profoundly at odds with the notion that the masses must be elevated through art to a preferred level of taste. Under the ethos of the "divine average," the artist gives expression and form to the inchoate life of his audience, and in that act, the "getting into form" of the life of the audience, Whitman locates the source of an authentic democratic culture.

VIII

Nothing is so clear in the history of American life since the Civil War as the failure of Whitman's hopes for an authentically democratic popular culture. Major writers—Whitman himself is a case in point—have not been taken to the bosom of the people; a "great audience" has so far not emerged to meet the artist on his own ground. Relations between artists and audience have come to be controlled by a system of mass communication far more powerful in its influence than Whitman or anyone else in the early industrial age imagined. Moreover, in the service of an economy remarkably able to produce material abundance, the mass media have propagated values of consumption above all else. The predominance of these values and their implied society of middling owners and consumers have led to a situation in which, several years ago, Michael Harrington felt compelled to call attention to "the other Americans," perhaps one third of the nation, who live beyond the pale of these values, whose lives are not expressed in popular culture, and who are therefore "invisible" to most Americans.

Since the Civil War, the marriage of the media and affluence has worked to further the polarization between a culture of the "mass"—comprised of a "mean flat average" of best sellers and hit parades and box-office successes—and a culture of an anti-middle-class elite. In the world of mass culture, success or popularity is measured quantitatively, in dollars or points on a rating system, and the effect of this has been to make the artist into a manipulator, often a cynical one who holds his own work in contempt, and the audience into spectators. It is still true that "for him or her who strikes the mean flat average . . . the audiences are limitless and profitable"—only on a scale which would have staggered Whitman's imagination. And this "average" has absorbed features of both gentility and sentimental benevolence—and in our day, even avant-garde modernism and rebelliousness—in the service of middle-class values.

On the other hand, especially in this century, the spread of higher education, particularly in the liberal arts, has made the university experience one path of escape from the hold of mass culture; that experience has created a cultural style of its own, one based on a regard for historical and literary values, a humanistic style with sources in Western civilization as a whole. Ironically enough, Whitman so far has found his most devoted audience in this group, where he is appreciated first for his poetry and then, often grudgingly, for his social vision. In the face of the coarsening and vulgarization of mass culture, the literary elite, even in cases where it is informed by a radical political vision, has tended to turn its back on the "mean flat average," so that the split between literary culture and the culture of "the People" often seems an insuperable gulf.

It is to Whitman's credit that, virtually alone in the post Civil War years, he sensed the disastrous implications of this split and tried to overcome it by proposing an organically whole culture which expresses rather than imposes upon the life of the people. But it must be admitted that *Democratic Vistas* gives few clues to the actual shape of this alternative. How is it to come about? How is it to resist the standardizing and fragmenting forces of industrialism? How is it to deal with specialization?

Whitman can be charged with underestimating the conformist pressures of American society, of failing to provide a social analysis commensurate with his cultural program. He accepts, for example, the major social idea of the nineteenth century, shared by conservative and radical alike, that material well-being must precede culture, that abundance, even leisure, is a prerequisite for "the main thing." "My theory includes riches, and the getting of riches," he writes, and adds that "democracy looks with suspicious, ill-satisfied eye upon the very poor, the ignorant, and on those out of business." But what he failed to take into account—indeed how could he in the early days of industrial society?—is that abundance offered itself as a very persuasive end in its own right. Whitman certainly did not hold that material well-being was by itself a sufficient condition for culture, and he was aware of the dynamic within materialism to spread itself throughout American society. He seemed to sense that an alternative culture needs to be linked to an alternative social order, but when he imagined a society within which egalitarianism might flourish, it took the form of a familiar pastoral vision, already nostalgic in an age of machines and cities:

> I can conceive a community, to-day, in which, on a sufficient scale, the perfect personalities, without noise meet; say in some pleasant western settlement or town, where a couple of hundred of the best men and women, of ordinary worldly status, have by luck been drawn together, with nothing extra of genius or wealth, but virtuous, chaste, industrious, cheerful, resolute, friendly and devout. I can conceive such a community organized in running order, powers judiciously delegated—farming, building, trade, courts, mail, schools, elections, all attended to; and then the rest of life, the main thing, freely branching and blossoming in each individual, and bearing golden fruit.

A Jeffersonian golden age—and not a railroad or factory in sight.

The absence of social analysis and a program for social change can be counted as a limitation in Whitman's argument: are egalitarianism and industrialism at bottom compatible? But also fundamental is a challenge we might bring to Whitman from a reading of a conservative position such as T. S. Eliot's in *Notes Toward a Definition of Culture.*

Is it possible to bring a culture into existence on the basis of a *principle,* even such a fine one as egalitarianism? Can culture be brought about by an act of will? Eliot argues it cannot—though the social conditions necessary for the flourishing of a culture can be. Eliot insists that culture takes time to evolve, that it is a complex fabric of tradition and ceremony; even if we discard his requirement of a stable class structure and an established church, a valuable sense of the inseparability of culture and history remains.

While Eliot wants to preserve traditional patterns, Whitman of course speaks to the future—but can the matter of historical continuity be set aside as easily as he implies? Eliot, moreover, insists on the importance of locale, of customs and values held in common in a specific place over a long period of time. Rapid mechanization after the Civil War, the dislocation of regional societies, and the sudden expansion of an urban proletariat made such development difficult if not impossible in America. The decline of New England literary culture, which was rooted in a traditional religious outlook and a common history, is a case in point. Except for a glance at the Far West as a source of new energy and rudeness, Whitman ignores regional, ethnic and class differences as possible sources of vitality for a national culture. He proposes the sophisticated urban concept of "universal man" rather than plural ways of life.

Finally there is the question of Whitman's instrument of culture, the bardic poet. Whitman asks his poet to do the work of both tradition and a social order; he is the chief culture-bringer, the Theseus of the democratic ethos. But is this notion, derived in large part from Herder's studies of folk society, applicable to an urban, industrial society? Whitman fails to recognize the elitist features of his poet. In one sense, it is true, the function of his bard might be served by popular folk artists like Woody Guthrie or Bob Dylan. But Whitman's own poetry was considerably more sophisticated, more self-conscious, more literary in that, for all his denial, it implied a relation to a tradition which included Homer, Shakespeare, Wordsworth, and even Tennyson. Do Guthrie or Dylan, for all their force and beauty, require of their audience the "exercise," the "gymnast's struggle," Whitman insisted upon? True, the folk singer's traits make for popularity, even in the best sense. But poets like Hart Crane, William Carlos Williams, and Wallace Stevens, who in their own ways have claimed to follow Whitman, appeal chiefly to small trained audiences. In competition with the mass media, is it possible for a "difficult" writer to find a large audience?

Whitman, in short, seems caught in a genuine dilemma. Like his pastoral vision of a communal society, his concept of the poet may be anachronistic

—and already nostalgic. Still, what choice did he have? On one hand, polite gentility; on the other, the "mean flat average." The problem was tortured by the fact that his poet shared certain features of sensibility with the first, and certain desires for popularity with the second. The idea of a "*divine* average" is a solution, but, as Whitman himself understood, it had only hypothetical force in American life. Could it be evoked without a radical transformation of American society? And even then, could it resist the cloying ability of the mass media to convert almost all ideas and ideals into a syrupy "message"?

Eliot wrote in 1949 that the "real revolution" in the United States "was not what is called the Revolution in the history books, but is a consequence of the Civil War; after which arose a plutocratic elite; after which the expansion and material development of the country was accelerated; after which was swollen that stream of mixed immigration, bringing (or rather multiplying) the danger of development into a *caste* system which has not yet been quite dispelled." This states quite well the situation Whitman faced in *Democratic Vistas*. His program may fall short, but who else among his contemporaries grappled with the problems as strenuously, and with such penetration to the underlying issues? The essay tries to find a generalized theoretical form for democracy under the conditions of modern society. Written on the threshold of our own age, it still poses questions that await our response.

PART ONE

PROSPECT
AND RETROSPECT

1. The Union Dead

The meaning of the Civil War is still hidden in American experience. A basic confusion arises from the overlapping of two issues in the stated aims of both sides—the issue of nationalism vs. sectionalism, and the issue of slavery. In the Southern position, slavery seemed to be subordinate to the ideal of sectional independence, supported by reference to the Constitution and the Declaration of Independence; slavery was simply the fact upon which the social order was based. But this fact made it possible for Northerners to conceive of their aims as benevolent as well as nationalistic: the moral idealism of defending the Union was even more exalted in light of the secondary aim of abolishing slavery.

The effects of the war—particularly the liberation of four million slaves—were not immediately assimilated by Americans. After a brief period of public mourning, given a remarkable focus in the ritual of Lincoln's funeral, America seemed to bury the trauma of what is still its most destructive war. More than half a million people were killed, many more maimed for life, and much of the South lay in ruins. How could such an outpouring of blood be explained? It seemed necessary, in the days immediately after Appomattox, to imagine a cause noble enough to justify such devastation, a cause in light of which the dead might appear as heroic sacrifices.

It is not surprising that New England supplied many of the fervent and lofty thoughts on commemorative occasions in 1865. New England was the home of a traditional literary culture, closely bound to, even when at odds with, a virtually established church, Congregationalism. Abolitionism as well as nationalism had a strong following among New England writers and clergy. And the region contributed to the cause the lives of many of its most promising young men from the colleges. In his "Ode Recited at the Harvard Commemoration, July 21, 1865," James Russell Lowell celebrated the "sacred dead," and described "that leap of heart whereby a people rise/ Up to a noble anger's height," in order to "certify to earth a new imperial race." Although the poet conveys deeply felt sorrow, his dominant emotion is an almost defiant nationalism: the "rescued" nation's victory shout "tingling Europe's sullen ears." "Be proud!" he writes, "for she is saved." That same July, Horace Bushnell, an influential Congregational minister, sounded a similar note in his commemorative oration at Yale, his own *alma mater*. In particular he looked forward to a greater American literature emerging from the war. But Bushnell's emphasis was more emphatically upon the war as a tragic experience which could be turned to wisdom if Americans gained from it a more mature sense of history, and a unifying national identity.

Our Obligations to the Dead
HORACE BUSHNELL

Brethren of the Alumni:

To pay fit honors to our dead is one of the fraternal and customary offices of these anniversaries; never so nearly an office of high public duty as now, when we find the roll of our membership starred with so many names made sacred by the giving up of life for the Republic. We knew them here in terms of cherished intimacy; some of them so lately that we scarcely seem to have been parted from them; others of them we have met here many times, returning to renew, with us, their tender and pleasant recollections of the past; but we meet them here no more: they are gone to make up the hecatomb offered for their and our great nation's life. Hence it has been specially desired on this occasion, that we honor their heroic sacrifice by some fit remembrance. Had the call of your committee been different, I should certainly not have responded.

Horace Bushnell, *Building Eras in Religion* (New York, 1881), 319–355.

And, yet, over-willing as I have been to assume an office so entirely grateful, it is a matter none the less difficult to settle on the best and most proper way of doing the honors intended. I think you will agree with me, that it cannot be satisfactorily done by preparing a string of obituary notices of our dead; that would be more appropriate to some published document, and no wise appropriate to a public discourse. Besides, to withdraw them from the vaster roll of the dead, in which it was their honor to die, and set them in a circle of mere literary clanship, bounding our testimony of homage by the accident of their matriculation here with us, would be rather to claim our honors in them, than to pay them honors due to themselves. We should seem not even to appreciate the grand public motive to which they gave up their life. They honored us in dying for their country, and we fitly honor them, when we class them with the glorious brotherhood in which they fell. Reserving it therefore as my privilege, to make such reference specially to them as befits the occasion, I propose a more general subject in which due honors may be paid to all, viz., *The obligations we owe to the dead,*—all the dead who have fallen in this gigantic and fearfully bloody war.

There are various ways in which a people, delivered by great struggles of war, may endeavor to pay their testimony of honor to the men who have fallen. They may do it by chanting requiems for the repose of their souls; which, though it may not have any great effect in that precise way, is at least an act of implied homage and gratitude. The same thing is attempted more frequently by covering the dead benefactors and heroes with tributes of eulogy; only here it is a disappointment, that none but a few leaders are commemorated, while the undistinguished multitude, who jeoparded their lives most freely, are passed by and forgot. The best thing therefore to be done, worthiest both of the dead and the living, is, it seems to me, that which I now propose,—to recount our obligations to the dead in general; what they have done for us, what they have earned at our hands, and what they have put it on us to do for the dear common country to which they sold their life.

First of all then, we are to see that we give them their due share of the victory and the honors of victory. For it is one of our natural infirmities, against which we need to be carefully and even jealously guarded, that we fall so easily into the impression which puts them in the class of defeat and failure. Are they not dead? And who shall count the dead as being in the roll of victory? But the living return to greet us and be with us, and we listen eagerly to the story of the scenes in which they bore their part.

We enjoy their exultations and exult with them. Their great leaders also return, to be crowded by our ovations, and deafened by our applauses. These, these, we too readily say, are the victors, considering no more the dead but with a certain feeling close akin to pity. If, sometime, the story of their fall is told us, the spot described, far in front or on the rampart's edge, where they left their bodies with the fatal gashes at which their souls went out, we listen with sympathy and sad respect, but we do not find how to count them in the lists of victory, and scarcely to include them in the general victory of the cause. All our associations run this way, and before we know it we have them down, most likely, on the losing side of the struggle. They belong, we fancy, to the waste of victory,—sad waste indeed! but not in any sense a part of victory itself. No, no, ye living! It is the ammunition spent that gains the battle, not the ammunition brought off from the field. These dead are the spent ammunition of the war, and theirs above all is the victory. Upon what indeed turned the question of the war itself, but on the dead that could be furnished; or what is no wise different, the life that could be contributed for that kind of expenditure? These grim heroes therefore, dead and dumb, that have strewed so many fields with their bodies,—these are the price and purchase-money of our triumph. A great many of us were ready to live, but these offered themselves, in a sense, to die, and by their cost the victory is won.

Nay, it is not quite enough, if we will know exactly who is entitled to a part in these honors, that we only remember these dead of the war. Buried generations back of them were also present in it, almost as truly as they. Thus, if we take the two most honored leaders, Grant and Sherman, who, besides the general victory they have gained for the cause, have won their sublime distinction as the greatest living commanders of the world, it will be impossible to think of them as having made or begotten their own lofty endowments. All great heroic men have seeds and roots, far back it may be, out of which they spring, and apart from which they could not spring at all; a sublime fatherhood and motherhood, in whose blood and life, however undistinguished, victory was long ago distilling for the great day to come of their people and nation. They knew it not; they sleep in graves, it may be, now forgot. But their huge-grown, manful temperament, the fights they waged and won in life's private battle, the lofty prayer-impulse which made inspirations their element, their brave self-retaining patience, and the orderly vigor of their household command were breeding in and in, to be issued finally in a hero sonship, and by that fight themselves out into the grandest victory for right and law the future ages shall know. So that if we ask who are the dead that are to be counted in our victory, we must pierce the sod of Wethersfield and Stratford, of Woodbury and Norwalk, and find where the Honorable Sherman, the Deacon Sherman, the Judge Sherman, and all the line of the Shermans and their victor wives and mothers lie; and then, if we can guess what they were and how they lived, we shall know who fought the great campaigns at Atlanta, Savannah and Raleigh. So again, if we begin at the good Deacon Grant in Mr. Warham's church at Windsor; descending to the historic Matthew Grant of Tolland, fellow-scout with Putnam and captain of a French war company; then to the now living Joel Root Grant, who removed to Pennsylvania, afterwards also to Ohio, afterwards finally, I believe, to Illinois, whose wanderings appear to be commemorated in the classic name of Ulysses; we shall see by what tough flanking processes of life and family the great Lieutenant-General was preparing, who should turn the front of Vicksburg, and march by Lee and Richmond, and cut off, by the rear, even the Great Rebellion itself. O, if we could see it, how long and grandly were the victories of these great souls preparing! The chief thing was the making of the souls themselves, and when that was done the successes came of course.

And from these two examples you may see by what lines of private worth, and public virtue, and more than noble blood, the stock of our great patriotic armies has been furnished. For how grand a pitch of devotion has been often shown by the private soldiers of these armies! There was never embodied, in all the armies of the world, a public inspiration so remarkable. Really the grandest heroes are these, who have neither had, nor wanted, any motive but the salvation of the Republic. And do you think there was nothing back of them to make them what they were? What but an immense outgrowth were they of whole ages of worth, intelligence, and public devotion? And for what more honorable distinction should we here and always pay our thanks to God? O, it is these generations of buried worth that have been fighting in our battles, and if we will pay our obligations to the dead, it is this nameless fatherhood and motherhood, before whose memory we shall bare our head in the deepest homage and tenderest reverence. . . .

But I pass to a point where the dead obtain a right of honor that is more distinctive, and belongs not to the living at all; or if in certain things partly to the living, yet only to them in some less sacred and prominent way. I speak here of the fact that, according to the true economy of the world, so many of its grandest and most noble benefits have and are to have a tragic origin, and to come as outgrowths only of blood. Whether it be that sin is in the world, and the whole creation groaneth in the necessary throes of its demonized life, we need not stay to inquire; for sin would be in the world and the demonizing spell would be upon it. Such was, and was to be, and is, the economy of it. Common life, the world's great life, is in the large way tragic. As the mild benignity and peaceful reign of Christ begins at the principle: "without shedding of blood, there is no remission," so, without shedding of blood, there is almost nothing great in the world, or to be expected for it. For the life is in the blood,—all life; and it is put flowing within, partly for the serving of a nobler use in flowing out on fit occasion, to quicken and consecrate whatever it touches. God could not plan a Peace-Society world, to live in the sweet amenities, and grow great and happy by simply thriving and feeding. There must be bleeding also. Sentiments must be born that are children of thunder; there must be heroes and heroic nationalities, and martyr testimonies, else there will be only mediocrities, insipidities, common-place men, and common-place writings,—a sordid and mean peace, liberties without a pulse, and epics that are only eclogues.

And here it is that the dead of our war have done for us a work so precious, which is all their own,—they have bled for us; and by this simple sacrifice of blood they have opened for us a new great chapter of life. We were living before in trade and commerce, bragging of our new cities and our census reports, and our liberties that were also consciously mocked by our hypocrisies; having only the possibilities of great inspirations and not the fact, materialized more and more evidently in our habits and sentiments, strong principally in our discords and the impetuosity of our projects for money. But the blood of our dead has touched our souls with thoughts more serious and deeper, and begotten, as I trust, somewhat of that high-bred inspiration which is itself the possibility of genius, and of a true public greatness. Saying nothing then for the present of our victors and victories, let us see what we have gotten by the blood of our slain.

And first of all, in this blood our unity is cemented and forever sanctified. Something was gained for us here, at the beginning, by our sacrifices in the fields of our Revolution,—something, but not all. Had it not been for this common bleeding of the States in their common cause, it is doubtful whether our Constitution could ever have been carried. The discords of the Convention were imminent, as we know, and were only surmounted by compromises that left them still existing. They were simply kenneled under the Constitution and not reconciled, as began to be evident shortly in the doctrines of state sovereignty, and state nullification, here and there asserted. We had not bled enough, as yet, to merge our colonial distinctions and make us a proper nation. Our battles had not been upon a scale to thoroughly mass our feeling, or gulf us in a common cause and life. Against the state-rights doctrines, the logic of our Constitution was decisive, and they were refuted a thousand times over. But such things do not go by argument. No argument transmutes a discord, or composes a unity where there was none. The matter wanted here was blood, not logic, and this we now have on a scale large enough to meet our necessity. True it is blood on one side, and blood on the other,—all the better for that; for bad bleeding kills, and righteous bleeding sanctifies and quickens. The state-rights doctrine is now fairly bled away, and the unity died for, in a way of such prodigious devotion, is forever sealed and glorified.

Nor let any one be concerned for the sectional relations of defeat and victory. For there has all the while been a grand, suppressed sentiment of country in the general field of the rebellion, which is bursting up already into sovereignty out of the soil itself. There is even a chance that this sentiment may blaze into a passion hot enough to utterly burn up whatever fire itself can master. At all events it will put under the ban, from this time forth, all such instigators of treason as could turn their peaceful States into hells of desolation, and force even patriotic citizens to fight against the homage they bore their country. However this may be, the seeds of a true public life are in the soil, waiting to grow apace. It will be as when the flood of Noah receded. For the righteous man perchance began to bethink himself shortly, and to be troubled, that he took no seeds into the ark; but no sooner were the waters down, than the oaks and palms and all great trees sprung into life, under the dead old trunks of the forest, and the green world reappeared even greener than before; only the sections had all received new seeds, by a floating exchange, and put them forthwith into growth together with their own. So the unity now to be developed, after this war-deluge is over, is even like to be more cordial than it ever could have been. It will be no more thought of as a mere human compact, or composition, always to be debated by the letter, but it will be that bond of common life which God has touched with blood; a sacredly heroic, Providentially tragic unity, where God's cherubim stand guard over grudges and hates and remembered jealousies, and the sense of nationality becomes even a kind of religion. How many would have said that the Saxon Heptarchy, tormented by so many intrigues and feuds of war, could never be a nation! But their formal combination under Egbert, followed by their wars against the Danes under Alfred, set them in a solid, sanctified unity, and made them, as a people, one true England, instead of the seven Englands that were; which seven were never again to be more than historically remembered. And so, bleeding on together from that time to this in all sorts of wars; wars civil and wars abroad, drenching the land and coloring the sea with their blood; gaining all sorts of victories and suffering all kinds of defeats; their parties and intestine strifes are no more able now to so much as raise a thought that is not in allegiance to their country. In like manner,—let no one doubt of it,— these United States, having dissolved the intractable matter of so many infallible theories and bones of contention in the dreadful menstruum of their blood, are to settle into fixed unity, and finally into a nearly homogeneous life.

Passing to another point of view, we owe it to our dead in this terrible war, that they have given us the possibility of a great consciousness and great public sentiments. There must needs be something lofty in a people's action, and above all something heroic in their sacrifices for a cause, to sustain a great sentiment in them. They will try, in the smooth days of peace and golden thriftiness and wide-spreading growth, to have it, and perhaps will think they really have it, but they will only have semblances and counterfeits; patriotic professions that are showy and thin, swells and protestations that are only oratorical and have no true fire. All the worse if they have interests and institutions that are all the while mocking their principles; breeding factions that can be quieted only by connivances and compromises and political bargains, that sell out their muniments of right and nationality. Then you shall see all high devotion going down as by a law, till nothing is left but the dastard picture of a spent magistracy that, when everything is falling into wreck, can only whimper that it sees not any thing it can do! Great sentiments go when they are not dismissed, and will not come when they are sent for. We cannot keep them by much talk, nor have them because we have heard of them and seen them in a classic halo. A lofty public consciousness arises only when things are loftily and nobly done. It is only when we are rallied by a cause, in that cause receive a great inspiration, in that inspiration give our bodies to the death, that at last, out of many such heroes dead, comes the possibility of great thoughts, fired by sacrifice, and a true public magnanimity.

In this view, we are not the same people that we were, and never can be again. Our young scholars, that before could only find the forms of great feeling in their classic studies, now catch the fire of it unsought. Emulous before of saying fine things for their country, they now choke for the impossibility of saying what they truly feel. The pitch of their life is raised. The tragic blood of the war is a kind of new capacity for them.

They perceive what it is to have a country and a public devotion. Great aims are close at hand, and in such aims a finer type of manners. And what shall follow, but that, in their more invigorated, nobler life, they are seen hereafter to be manlier in thought and scholarship, and closer to genius in action.

I must also speak of the new great history sanctified by this war, and the blood of its fearfully bloody sacrifices. So much worth and character were never sacrificed in a human war before. And by this mournful offering, we have bought a really stupendous chapter of history. We had a little very beautiful history before, which we were beginning to cherish and fondly cultivate. But we had not enough of it to beget a full historic consciousness. As was just now intimated in a different way, no people ever become vigorously conscious, till they mightily do, and heroically suffer. The historic sense is close akin to tragedy. We say it accusingly often,—and foolishly,—that history cannot live on peace, but must feed itself on blood. The reason is that, without the blood, there is really nothing great enough in motive and action, taking the world as it is, to create a great people or story. If a gospel can be executed only in blood, if there is no power of salvation strong enough to carry the world's feeling which is not gained by dying for it, how shall a selfish race get far enough above itself, to be kindled by the story of its action in the dull routine of its common arts of peace? Doubtless it should be otherwise, even as goodness should be universal; but so it never has been, and upon the present footing of evil never can be. The great cause must be great as in the clashing of evil; and heroic inspirations, and the bleeding of heroic worth must be the zest of the story. Nations can sufficiently live only as they find how to energetically die. In this view, some of us have felt, for a long time, the want of a more historic life, to make us a truly great people. This want is now supplied; for now, at last, we may be said to have gotten a history. The story of this four years' war is the grandest chapter, I think, of heroic fact, and tragic devotion, and spontaneous public sacrifice, that has ever been made in our world. The great epic story of Troy is but a song in comparison. There was never a better, and never so great a cause; order against faction, law against conspiracy, liberty and right against the madness and defiant wrong of slavery, the unity and salvation of the greatest future nationality and freest government of the world; a perpetual state of war to be averted, and the preservation for mankind of an example of popular government and free society that is a token of promise for true manhood, and an omen of death to old abuse and prescriptive wrong the world over; this has been our cause, and it is something to say that we have borne ourselves worthily in it. Our noblest and best sons have given their life to it. We have dotted whole regions with battle-fields. We have stained how many rivers, and bays, and how many hundred leagues of railroad, with our blood! We have suffered appalling defeats; twice at Bull Run, at Wilson's Creek, in the great campiagn of the Peninsula, at Cedar Mountain, at Fredericksburg, at Chancellorsville, at Chickamauga, and upon the Red River, leaving our acres of dead on all these fields and many others less conspicuous; yet, abating no jot of courage and returning with resolve unbroken, we have converted these defeats into only more impressive victories. In this manner too, with a better fortune nobly earned, we have hallowed, as names of glory and high victory, Pea Ridge, Donelson, Shiloh, Hilton Head, New Orleans, Vicksburg, Port Hudson, Stone River, Lookout Mountain, Resaca, Atlanta, Fort Fisher, Gettysburg, Nashville, Wilmington, Petersburg and Richmond, Bentonville, Mobile Bay, and, last of all, the forts of Mobile city. All these and a hundred others are now become, and in all future time are to be, names grandly historic. And to have them is to be how great a gift for the ages to come! By how many of the future children of the Republic will these spots be visited, and how many will return from their pilgrimages thither, blest in remembrances of the dead, to whom they owe their country!

Among the fallen too we have names that will glow with unfading lustre on whatever page they are written; our own brave Lyon, baptizing the cause in the blood of his early death; our Sedgwick, never found wanting at any point of command, equal in fact to the very highest command, and only too modest to receive it when offered; the grandly gifted young McPherson, who had already fought himself into the first rank of leadership, and was generally counted the peerless hope and prodigy of the armies; Reynolds also, and Kearney, and Reno, and Birney; and how many brilliant stars, or even constellations of stars, in the lower degrees of command, such as Rice, and Lowell, and Vincent, and Shaw, and Stedman, and a hundred others in like honor, for the heroic merit of their leadership and death! And yet, when I drop all particular names, dear as they may be, counting them only the smoke and not the fire, letting the unknown trains of dead heroes pack and mass and ascend, to shine, as by host, in the glorious Milky Way of their multitude,—men that left their business and all the dearest ties of home and family to fight their country's righteous war, and fought on till they fell,—then for the first time do I seem to feel the tide-swing of a great historic consciousness. God forbid that any prudishness of modesty should here detain us. Let us fear no more to say that we have won a history and the right to be a consciously historic people. Henceforth our new world even heads the old, having in this single chapter risen clean above it. The wars of Cæsar, and Frederic, and Napoleon, were grand enough in their leadership, but there is no grand people or popular greatness in them, consequently no true dignity. In this war of ours it is the people, moving by their own decisive motion, in the sense of their own great cause. For this cause we have volunteered by the million, and in three thousand millions of money, and by the resolute bleeding of our men and the equally resolute bleeding of our self-taxation, we have bought and sanctified consentingly all these fields, all that is grand in this thoroughly principled history.

Again, it is not a new age of history only that we owe to the bloody sacrifices of this war, but in much the same manner the confidence of a new literary age; a benefit that we are specially called, in such a place as this, and on such an occasion, to remember and fitly acknowledge. Great public throes are, mentally speaking, changes of base for some new thought-campaign in a people. Hence the brillant new literature of the age of Queen Elizabeth; then of another golden era under Anne; and then still again, as in the arrival of another birth-time, after the Napoleonic wars of George the Fourth. The same thing has been noted, I believe, in respect to the wars of Greece and Germany. Only it is in such wars as raise the public sense and majesty of a people that the result is seen to follow. For it is the high-souled thought, and puts the life of genius in the glow of new-born liberty. This we are now to expect, for the special reason also that we have here, for the first time, conquered a position. Thus it will be seen that no great writer becomes himself, in his full power, till he has gotten the sense of position. Much more true is this of a people. And here has been our weakness until now. We have held the place of cliency, we have taken our models and laws of criticism, and to a great extent our opinions, from the English motherhood of our language and mind. Under that kind of pupilage we live no longer; we are thoroughly weaned from it, and become a people in no secondary right. Henceforth we are not going to write English, but American. As we have gotten our position, we are now to have our own civilization, think our own thoughts, rhyme in our own measures, kindle our own fires, and make our own canons of criticism, even as we settled the proprieties of punishment for our own traitors. We are not henceforth to live as by cotton and corn and trade, keeping the downward slope of thrifty mediocrity. Our young men are not going out of college, staled, in the name of discipline, by their carefully conned lessons, to be launched on the voyage of life as ships without wind, but they are to have great sentiments, and mighty impulsions, and souls alive all through in fires of high devotion.

We have gotten also now the historic matter of a true oratoric inspiration, and the great orators are coming after. In the place of politicians we are going to have, at least, some statesmen; for we have gotten the pitch of a grand, new, Abrahamic statesmanship, unsophisticated, honest and real; no cringing sycophancy, or cunning art of demogogy. We have also facts, adventures, characters enough now in store, to feed five hundred years of fiction. We have also plots, and lies, and honorable perjuries, false heroics, barbaric murders and assassinations, conspiracies of fire and poison,—enough of them, and wicked enough, to furnish the Satanic side of tragedy for long ages to come; coupled also with such grandeurs of public valor and principle, such beauty of heroic sacrifice, in womanhood and boyhood, as tragedy has scarcely yet been able to find. As to poetry, our battle-fields are henceforth names poetic, and our very soil is touched with a mighty poetic life. In the rustle of our winds, what shall the waking soul of our poets think of, but of brave souls riding by? In our thunders they may hear the shocks of charges, and the red of the sunset shall take a tinge in their feeling from the summits where our heroes fell. A new sense comes upon every thing, and the higher soul of mind, quickened by new possibilities, finds inspirations where before it found only rocks, and ploughlands, and much timber for the saw. Are there no great singers to rise in this new time? Are there no unwonted fires to be kindled in imaginations fanned by these new glows of devotion? We seem, as it were in a day, to be set in loftier ranges of thought, by this huge flood-tide that has lifted our nationality, gifted with new sentiments and finer possibilities, commissioned to create, and write, and sing, and, in the sense of a more poetic feeling at least, to be all poets. . . .

Again, it is another of the sacred obligations we owe to the dead, that we sanctify their good name. Nothing can be more annoying to the sense of honor, than the mischievous facility of some, in letting down the merit and repute of the fallen by the flippant recollection of their faults, or, it may be, of their former vices. Who have earned immunity from this petty kind of criticism, if not they who have died for their country? How great a thing has it been for many in this war, to spring into consciously new life, in the ennobling discovery that they could have a great feeling! And what, in the plane of mere nature, will so transform a man, as to be caught by the heroic impulse, and begin to have the sense of a cause upon him? Indeed I am not sure that some specially heroic natures do not flag and go down under evil, just because the storm they were made for has not begun to blow. Some such were greater souls perhaps than we thought, and if they were not perfectly great, who but some low ingrate would now dim their halo by a word? And what if it should happen, that even a Congressional Committee may so far turn themselves in to a committee of scandal, as to assail with unrighteous facility the military merit of the dead? If the dead cannot answer, what shall we do but answer for the dead?

A great work also is due from us to the dead, and quite as much for our own sakes as theirs, in the due memorizing of their names and acts. Let the nation's grand war monument be raised in massive granite, piercing the sky. Let every State, honored by such names as Sedgwick, and Lyon, and Mansfield, claim the right to their honors for the future ages, by raising, on some highest mountain top, or in some park of ornament, the conspicuous shaft or pillar, that will fitly represent the majesty of the men. The towns and villages will but honor themselves, when they set up their humbler monuments inscribed with the names of the fallen. Let the churches also, and the college halls and chapels, show their mural tablets, where both worship and learning may be quickened by the remembrance of heroic deeds and deaths. In this way, or some other, every name of our fallen Alumni should be conspicuously recorded in the College; that our sons coming hither may learn, first of all, that our mother gives her best to die for their country. . . .

But there is one other yet higher duty that we owe to these dead; viz., that we take their places and stand in their cause. It is even a great law of natural duty that the living shall come into the places and works of the dead. The same also is accepted and honored by Christianity, when it shows the Christian son, and brother, and friend, stepping into the places made vacant by the dead, to assume their blessed and great work unaccomplished, and die, if need be, in the testimony of a common martyrdom. They challenged, in this manner, if the commentators will suffer it, the vows of baptism, and "were baptized for the dead,"—consecrated upon the dead, for the work of the dead. God lays it upon us in the same way now, to own the bond of fealty that connects us with the fallen, in the conscious community and righteous kinship of their cause. And then, as brothers baptized for the dead,—Alumni, so to speak, of the Republic,— we are to execute their purpose and fulfill the idea that inspired them. Neither is it enough at this point to go off in a general heroic, promising, in high rhetoric, to give our life for the country in like manner. There is no present likelihood that we shall be called to do any such thing. No, but we have duties upon us that are closer at hand; viz., to wind up and settle this great tragedy in a way to exactly justify every drop of blood that has been shed in it. Like the blood of righteous Abel it cries both to us and to God, from every field, and river, and wood, and road, dotted by our pickets and swept by the march of our armies.

First of all we are sworn to see that no vestige of state sovereignty is left, and the perpetual, supreme sovereignty of the nation established. For what but this have our heroes died? Not one of them would have died for a government of mere optional continuance; not one for a government fit to be rebelled against. But they volunteered for a government in perfect right, and one to be perpetual as the stars, and they went to the death as against the crime of hell. Tell me also this,—if a government is good enough to die *for*, is it not good enough to die *by*, when it is violated? Not that every traitor is, of course, to be visited by the punishment of treason. It is not for me to say who, or how many or few, shall suffer that punishment. But I would willingly take the question to the dead victims of Belle Isle, and Salisbury, and Andersonville, and let them be the judges. There is no revenge in them now. The wild storms of their agony are laid, and the thoughts which bear sway in the world where they are gathered are those of the merciful Christ, and Christ is the judge before whose bar they know full well that their redress is sure. And yet I think it will be none the less their judgment that something is due to law and justice here. As, too, it was something for them to die for the law, I can imagine them to ask whether it is not something for the law to prove its vindicated honor in the fit punishment of such barbarities? May it not occur to them also to ask, whether proportion is now an everlasting attribute of justice? And if punctual retribution is to follow the sudden taking off of one, whether the deliberate and slow starvation of so many thousands is to be fitly ignored and raise no sword of judgment? Neither is it any thing to say, that the awful ruin of the rebellious country is itself a punishment upon the grandest scale, and ought to be sufficient; for the misery of it is, that it falls on the innocent and not on the leaders and projectors, who are the chief criminals. Our liberal friends abroad conjure us to follow the lead of their despotisms, and cover up gently all these offenses, because they are only political. Ah! there is a difference which they need to learn. Doubtless governments may be bad enough to make political offenses innocent; nay, to make them even righteous. But we have not fought this dreadful war to a close, just to put our government upon a par with their oppressive dynasties! We scorn the parallel they give us; and we owe it even to them to say, that a government which is friendly, and free, and right, protecting all alike, and doing the most for all, is one of God's sacred finalities, which no hand may touch, or conspiracy assail, without committing the most damning crime, such as can be matched by no possible severities of justice. We are driven in thus on every side, upon the conclusion that examples ought to be and must be made. Only they must be few and such as can be taken apart from all sectional conditions; for we have sections to compose, and the ordinary uses of punishment in cases of private treason do not pertain where the crime is nearly geographic, and is scarcely different from public war.

One thing more we are also sworn upon the dead to do; viz., to see that every vestige of slavery is swept clean. We did not begin the war to extirpate slavery; but the war itself took hold of slavery on its way, and as this had been the gangrene of our wound from the first, we shortly put ourselves heartily to the cleasing, and shall not, as good surgeons, leave a part of the virus in it. We are not to extirpate the form and leave the fact. The whole black code must go; the law of passes, and the law of evidence, and the unequal laws of suit and impeachment for crime. We are bound, if possible, to make the emancipation work well; as it never can, till the old habit of domination, and the new grudges of exasperated pride and passion, are qualified by gentleness and consideration. Otherwise there will be no industry but only jangle; society in fact will be turned into a hell of poverty and confusion. And this kind relationship never can be secured, till the dejected and despised race are put upon the footing of men, and allowed to assert themselves somehow in the laws. Putting aside all theoretic notions of equality, and regarding nothing but the practical want of the emancipation, negro suffrage appears to be indispensable. But the want is one thing, and the right of compelling it another. Our States have always made their own laws of suffrage, and if we want to resuscitate the state rights doctrine, there is no so ready way as to rouse it by state wrongs. But there is always a way of doing what wants to be done,—pardon me if I name it even here; for our dead are not asking mere rhetoric of us, but duty. They call us to no whimpering over them, no sad weeping, or doling of soft sympathy, but to counsel and true action. I remember too, that we have taken more than a hundred thousand of these freedmen of the war to fight our common battle. I remember the massacre of Fort Pillow. I remember the fatal assault of Fort Wagner and the gallant Shaw sleeping there in the pile of his black followers. I remember the bloody fight and victory on the James, where the ground itself was black with dead. Ah, there is a debt of honor here! And honor is never so sacred as when it is due to the weak. Blasted and accursed be the soul that will forget these dead! If they had no offices or honors, if they fought and died in the plane of their humility,—Thou just

God, forbid that we suffer them now to be robbed of the hope than inspired them!

Do then simply this, which we have a perfect constitutional right to do,—pass this very simple amendment, that the basis of representation in Congress shall hereafter be the number, in all the States alike, of the free male voters therein. Then the work is done; a general free suffrage follows by consent, and as soon as it probably ought. For these returning States will not be long content with half the offices they want, and half the power allowed them in the Republic. Negro suffrage is thus carried without naming the word.

Need I add, that now, by these strange fortunes of the rebellion rushing on its Providential overthrow, immense responsibilities are put upon us, that are new. A new style of industry is to be inaugurated. The soil is to be distributed over again, villages are to be created, schools established, churches erected, preachers and teachers provided, and money for these purposes to be poured out in rivers of benefaction, even as it has been in the war. A whole hundred years of new creation will be needed to repair these wastes and regenerate these habits of wrong; and we are baptized for the dead, to go forth in God's name, ceasing not, and putting it upon our children never to cease, till the work is done.

My task is now finished; only, alas! too feebly. There are many things I might say, addressing you as Alumni, as professors and teachers, and as scholars training here for the new age to come. But you will anticipate my suggestions, and pass on by me, to conceive a better wisdom for yourselves. One thing only I will name, which is fitting, as we part, for us all; viz., that without any particle of vain assumption, we swear by our dead to be Americans. Our position is gained! Our die of history is struck! Thank God we have a country, and that country has the chance of a future! Ours be it henceforth to cherish that country, and assert that future; also, to invigorate both by our own civilization, adorn them by our literature, consolidate them in our religion. Ours be it also, in God's own time, to champion, by land and sea, the right of this whole continent to be an American world, and to have its own American laws, and liberties, and institutions.

2. A Plea for Freedom

In Lincoln's mind, the overriding issue of the Civil War was the idea of "Union" —the preservation of the national state. Slavery was subordinate to nationalism, as he made clear in his well-known remark to Horace Greeley: "My paramount object in this struggle is to save the Union, and is *not* either to save or to destroy slavery." He delayed emancipation until it became an urgent political and military necessity, to bolster the flagging support of influential antislavery Northerners, to deprive the South of a large section of its homefront manpower, and to recruit Negro troops for the Union cause. But how much the Union cause was also the cause of complete freedom for Negroes remained a troubling uncertainty. Lincoln saw the problem of political and social integration as monumental, and was unable to conceive of a better solution than resettlement of Negroes outside the country.

The failure of the federal government to insist on full civil rights for the freedmen or to undertake a program of wholesale reform of Southern society indicates clearly the higher value placed on Union rather than on social and racial justice. "By 1877," writes one historian, "the political, social, and economic systems of the South had become remarkably similar to what they had been in 1860, except that now the Negro was a landless laborer rather than a legally bound slave."

For Frederick Douglass the two issues of Union and slavery were inseparable, and throughout the war he campaigned for emancipation and for the use of Negro troops. He argued that emancipation should be the main Union aim, that because the power of the South rested upon slavery, to defeat the rebellion the North had to destroy its underlying cause. Distressed with Lincoln's reluctance to proclaim the end of slavery as the fundamental issue, and to prescribe a program for the total removal of the remains of slavery, Douglass hesitated to support him in the election of 1864, until the Democratic Party nominated General McClellan on a program of peace at any price. The following speech was intended to suggest a position for Negroes in that election, a position based on the demand for complete abolition of slave society and the full enfranchisement of blacks.

Douglass was a remarkable figure—tall, light brown in color with an imposing leonine head. Born a slave, the son of an unknown white man, he escaped in 1838. By 1841 he had become associated with the New England Anti-Slavery Society, and before long, one of the most respected and effective spokesmen for Abolitionism. In 1845 he wrote an autobiography, *The Narrative of the Life of Frederick Douglass, an American Slave*, and in 1847 he established a newspaper which he continued to edit and publish throughout the Civil War. Highly regarded for the force of his writings and especially for the eloquence of his speech—which fused the styles of political and pulpit oratory with intense personal passion—he held several government positions, including that of marshall of the District of Columbia and U. S. Minister to Haiti, before his death in 1895 at the age of seventy-eight.

The Cause of the Negro People
FREDERICK DOUGLASS

Fellow-Citizens:
The members of the Colored National Convention, assembled in Syracuse, State of New York, October the 4th, 1864, to confer with each other as to the complete emancipation, enfranchisement, and elevation of our race, in essaying to address you on these subjects, warmly embrace the occasion to congratulate you upon the success of your arms, and upon the prospect of the speedy suppression of the slaveholders' rebellion. Baptized in the best blood of your noblest sons, torn and rent by a strife full of horrors,— a strife undertaken and prosecuted for aims and objects the guiltiest that can enter the wicked hearts of men long in the practice of crime,—we ardently hope with you that our country will come out of this tremendous conflict, purer, stronger, nobler, and happier than ever before. Having shared with you, in some measure, the hardships, perils, and sacrifices of this war for the maintenance of the Union and Government, we rejoice with you also in every sign which gives promise of its approaching termination, and of the return of our common country again to those peaceful, progressive, and humanizing activities of true national life, from which she has been so wantonly diverted by the insurrection of slaveholders.

Philip S. Foner (ed.), *The Life and Writings of Frederick Douglass*, Vol. III (New York, 1952), 408–422.

In view of the general cheerfulness of the national situation, growing brighter every day; the rapid dispersement of the heavy clouds of dismal terror, which only a few weeks ago mantled our land with the gloomiest forebodings of national disaster and ruin,—we venture to hope that the present is a favorable moment to commend to your consideration the subject of our wrongs, and to obtain your earnest and hearty co-operation in all wise and just measures for their full redress.

When great and terrible calamities are abroad in the land, men are said to learn righteousness. It would be a mark of unspeakable national depravity, if neither the horrors of this war, nor the dawning prospect of peace, should soften the heart, and dispose the American people to renounce and forsake their evil policy towards the colored race. Assuming the contrary, we deem this a happily chosen hour for calling your attention to our cause. We know that the human mind is so constituted, that all postponement of duty, all refusal to go forward when the right path is once made plain, is dangerous.

After such neglect of, and disobedience to, the voice of reason and conscience, a nation becomes harder and less alive than before to high moral considerations. If won to the path of rectitude at all, thereafter, it must be by means of a purer light than that which first brought right convictions and inclinations to the national mind and heart. We speak, then, fellow-citizens, at an auspicious moment. Conviction has already seized the public mind. Little argument is needed. We shall appeal rather than argue; and we may well implore an attentive hearing for our appeal. The nation is still in tears. The warm blood of your brave and patriotic sons is still fresh upon the green fields of the Shenandoah. Mourning mingles everywhere with the national shout of victory; and though the smoke and noise of battle are rolling away behind the southern horizon, our brave armies are still confronted in Georgia and Virginia by a stern foe, whose haughtiness and cruelty have sprung naturally from his long and undisputed mastery over men. The point attained in the progress of this war is one from which you can if you will view to advantage the calamities which inevitably follow upon long and persistent violation of manifest duty; and on the other hand, the signs of final triumph enable you to anticipate the happy results which must always flow from just and honorable conduct. The fear of continued war, and the hope of speedy peace, alike mark this as the time for America to choose her destiny. Another such opportunity as is now furnished in the state of the country, and in the state of the national heart, may not come again in a century. Come, then, and let us reason together.

We shall speak, it is true, for our race,—a race long oppressed, enslaved, ignored, despised, slandered, and degraded; but we speak not the less for our country, whose welfare and permanent peace can only result from the adoption of wise and just measures towards our whole race, North and South.

Considering the number and the grievous character of the wrongs and disabilities endured by our race in this country, you will bear witness that we have borne with patience our lot, and have seldom troubled the national ear with the burden of complaint. It is true that individuals among us have constantly testified their abhorrence of this injustice; but as a people, we have seldom uttered, as we do this day, our protest and remonstrance against the manifold and needless injustice with which we are upon all sides afflicted. We have suffered in silence, trusting that, though long delayed, and perhaps through terrible commotions, the hour would come when justice, honor, and magnanimity would assert their power over the mind and heart of the American people, and restore us to the full exercise and enjoyment of the rights inseparable from human nature. Never having despaired of this consummation so devoutly wished, even in the darkest hours of our history, we are farther than ever from despairing now. Nowhere in the annals of mankind is there recorded an instance of an oppressed people rising more rapidly than ourselves in the favorable estimation of their oppressors. The change is great, and increasing, and is viewed with astonishment and dread by all those who had hoped to stand forever with their heels upon our necks.

Nevertheless, while joyfully recognizing the vast advances made by our people in popular consideration, and the apparent tendency of events in our favor, we cannot conceal from ourselves, and would not conceal from you, the fact that there are many and powerful influences, constantly operating, intended and calculated to defeat our just hopes, prolong the existence of the source of all our ills,—the system of slavery,—strengthen the slave power, darken the conscience of the North, intensify popular prejudice against color, multiply unequal and discriminating laws, augment the burdens long borne by our race, consign to oblivion the deeds of heroism which have distinguished the colored soldiers, deny and despise his claims to the gratitude of his country, scout his pretensions to American citizenship, establish the selfish idea that this is exclusively the white man's country, pass unheeded all the lessons taught by these four years of fire and sword, undo all that has been done towards our freedom and elevation, take the musket from the shoulders of our brave black soldiers, deny them the constitutional right to keep and bear arms, exclude them from the ballot-box where they now possess that right, prohibit the extension of it to those who do not possess it, overawe free speech in and out of Congress, obstruct the right of peaceably assembling, reenact the Fugitive-slave Bill, revive the internal slave-trade, break up all diplomatic relations with Haiti and Liberia, reopen our broad territories to the introduction of slavery, reverse the entire order and tendency of the events of the last three years, and postpone indefinitely that glorious deliverance from bondage, which for our sake, and for the sake of the future unity, permanent peace, and highest welfare of all concerned, we had fondly hoped and believed was even now at the door.

In surveying our possible future, so full of interest at this moment, since it may bring to us all the blessings of equal liberty, or all the woes of slavery and continued social degradation, you will not blame us if we manifest anxiety in regard to the position of our recognized friends, as well as that of our open and declared enemies; for our cause may suffer even more from the injudicious concessions and weakness of our friends, than from the machinations and power of our enemies. The weakness of our friends is strength to our foes. When the "Anti-slavery Standard," representing the American Anti-slavery Society, denies that that society asks for the enfranchisement of colored men, and the "Liberator" apologizes for excluding the colored men of Louisiana from the ballot-box, they injure us more vitally than all the ribald jests of the whole pro-slavery press.

Again: had, for instance, the present Administration, at the beginning of the war, boldly planted itself upon the doctrine of human equality as taught in the Declaration of Independence; proclaimed liberty to all the slaves in all the Slave States; armed every colored man, previously a slave or a freeman, who would or could fight under the loyal flag; recognized black men as soldiers of the Republic; avenged the first act of violence upon colored prisoners, in contravention of the laws of war; sided with the radical emancipation party in Maryland and Missouri; stood by its anti-slavery generals, instead of casting them aside,—history would never have had to record the scandalous platform adopted at Chicago, nor the immeasurable horrors at Fort Pillow. The weakness and hesitation of our friends, where promptness and vigor were required, have invited the contempt and rigor of our enemies. See that, while perilling everything for the protection and security of our country, our country did not think itself bound to protect and secure us, the rebels felt a license to treat us as outlaws. Seeing that our Government did not treat us as men, they did not feel bound to treat us as soldiers. It is, therefore, not the malignity of enemies alone we have to fear, but the deflection from the straight line of principle by those who are known throughout the world as our special friends. We may survive the arrows of the known Negro-haters of our country; but woe to the colored race when their champions fail to demand, from any reason, equal liberty in every respect!

We have spoken of the existence of powerful reactionary forces arrayed against us, and of the objects to which they tend. What are these mighty forces? and through what agencies do they operate and reach us? They are many; but we shall detain by no tedious enumeration. The first and most powerful is slavery; and the second, which may be said to be the shadow of slavery, is prejudice against men on account of their color. The one controls the South, and the other controls the North. Both are original sources of power, and generate peculiar sentiments, ideas, and laws concerning us. The agents of these two evil influences are various; but the chief are, first, the Democratic party; and second, the Republican party. The Democratic party belongs to slavery; and the Republican party is largely under the power of prejudice against color. While gratefully recognizing a vast difference in our favor in the character and composition of the Republican party, and regarding the accession to power of the Democratic party as the heaviest calamity that could befall us in the present juncture of affairs, it cannot be disguised, that, while that party is our bitterest enemy, and is positively and actively reactionary, the Republican party is negatively and passively so in its tendency. What we have to fear from these two parties,—looking to the future, and especially to the settlement of our present national troubles,—is, alas! only too obvious. The intentions, principles, and policy of both organizations, through their platforms, and the antecedents and the recorded utterances of the men who stand upon their respective platforms, teach us what to expect at their hands, and what kind of a future they are carving out for us, and for the country which they propose to govern. Without using the word *"slavery,"* or *"slaves,"* or *"slaveholders,"* the Democratic party has none the less declared, in its platform, its purpose to be the endless perpetuation of slavery. Under the apparently harmless verbiage, *"private rights," "basis of the Federal Union,"* and under the language employed in denouncing the Federal Administration for *"disregarding the Constitution in every part," "pretence of military necessity,"* we see the purpose of the Democratic party to restore slavery to all its ancient power, and to make this Government just what it was before the rebellion,—simply an instrument of the slave-power. *"The basis of the Federal Union"* only means the alleged compromises and stipulations, as interpreted by Judge Taney, by which black men are supposed to have no rights which white men are bound to respect; and by which the whole Northern people are bound to protect the cruel masters against the justly deserved violence of the slave, and to do the fiendish work of hellhounds when slaves make their escape from thraldom. The candidates of that party take their stand upon its platform; and will, if elected,—which Heaven forbid!—carry it out to the letter. From this party we must look only for fierce, malignant, and unmitigated hostility. Our continued oppression and degradation is the law of its life, and its sure passport to power. In the ranks of the Democratic party, all the worst elements of American society fraternize; and we need not expect a single voice from that quarter for justice, mercy, or even decency. To it we are nothing; the slave-holders everything. We have but to consult its press to know that it would willingly enslave the free colored people in the South; and also that it would gladly stir up against us mob-violence at the North,—re-enacting the sanguinary scenes of one year ago in New York and other large cities. We therefore pray, that whatever wrath, curse, or calamity, the future may have in store for us, the accession of the Democratic party to the reins of power may not be one of them; for this to us would comprise the sum of all social woes.

How stands the case with the great Republican party in question? We have already alluded to it as being largely under the influence of the prevailing contempt for the character and rights of the colored race. This is seen by the slowness of our Government to employ the strong arm of the black man in the work of putting down the rebellion; and in its unwillingness, after thus employing him, to invest him with the same incitements to deeds of daring, as white soldiers; neither giving him the same pay, rations, and protection, nor any hope of rising in the service by meritorious conduct. It is also seen in the fact, that in neither of the plans emanating from this party for reconstructing the institutions of the Southern States, are colored men, not even those who had *fought* for the country, recognized as having any political existence or rights whatever.

Even in the matter of the abolition of slavery,—to which, by its platform, the Republican party is strongly committed, as well by President Lincoln's celebrated Proclamation of the first of January, 1863, and by his recent letter, "To whom it may concern,"—there is still room for painful doubt and apprehension. It is very evident, that the Republican party, though a party composed of the best men of the country, is not prepared to make the abolition of slavery, in all the Rebel States, a consideration precedent to the re-establishment of the Union. However anti-slavery in sentiment the President may be, and however disposed he may be to continue the war till slavery is abolished, it is plain that in this he would not be sustained by his party. A single reverse to our arms, in such a war, would raise the hands of the party in opposition to their chief. The hope of the speedy and complete abolition of slavery, hangs, therefore, not upon the disposition of the Republican party, not upon the disposition of President Lincoln; but upon the slender thread of Rebel power, pride, and persistence. In returning to the Union, slavery has a fair chance to live; out of the Union, it has a still better chance to live; but, fighting against the Union, it has no chance for anything but destruction. Thus the freedom of our race and the welfare of our country tremble together in the balance of events.

This somewhat gloomy view of the condition of affairs—which to the enthusiastic, who have already convinced themselves that slavery is dead, may not only seem gloomy, but untruthful—is nevertheless amply supported, not only by the well-known sentiment of the country, the controlling pressure of which is seriously felt by the Administration; but it is sustained by the many attempts lately made by the Republican party press to explain away the natural import of the President's recent address "To whom it may concern," in which he makes the abolition of Slavery a primary condition to the restoration of the Union; and especially is this gloomy view supported by the remarkable speech delivered only a few weeks ago at Auburn, by Hon. William H. Seward, Secretary of State. Standing next to the President in the administration of the government, and fully in the confidence of the Chief Magistrate, no member of the National Cabinet is better qualified than Mr. Seward to utter the mind and policy of the Administration upon this momentous subject, when it shall come up at the close of the war. Just what it will do in the matter of slavery, Mr. Seward says,—

"When the insurgents shall have disbanded their armies, and laid down their arms, the war will instantly cease; and all the war measures then existing, including those which affect slavery, will cease also; and all the moral, economical, and political questions, as well affecting slavery as others, which shall then be existing between individuals and States and the Federal Government, whether they arose before the civil war began, or whether they grew out of it, will, by force of the Constitution, pass over to the arbitrament of courts of law, and the counsels of legislation."

These, fellow-citizens, are studied words, full of solemn and fearful import. They mean that our Republican Administration is not only ready to make peace with the Rebels, but to make peace with slavery also; that all executive and legislative action launched against the slave-system, whether of proclamation or confiscation, will cease the instant the Rebels shall disband their armies, and lay down their arms. The hope that the war will put an end to slavery, has, according to this exposition, only one foundation; and that is, that the courts and Congress will so decree. But what ground have we here? Congress has already spoken, and has refused to alter the Constitution so as to abolish Slavery. The Supreme Court has yet to speak; but what it will say, if this question shall come before it, is very easily divined. We will not assert positively what it will say; but indications of its judgment are clearly against us. What then have we? Only this, as our surest and best ground of hope; namely, that the Rebels, in their madness, will continue to make war upon the Government, until they shall not only become destitute of men, money, and the munitions of war, but utterly divested of their slaves also.

But, fellow-citizens, the object of this Address is not merely to state facts, and point out sources of danger. We would distinctly place our whole cause before you, and earnestly appeal to you to make that cause practically your cause; as we believe it is the cause of justice and of our whole country. We come before you altogether in new relations. Hitherto we have addressed you in the generic character of a common humanity, only as men; but today, owing to the events of the last three years, we bring with us an additional claim to consideration. By the qualities displayed, by the hardships endured, and by the services rendered the country, during these years of war and peril, we can now speak with the confidence of men who have deserved well of their country. While conscious of your power and of our comparative weakness, we may still claim for our race those rights which are not less ours by our services to the country than by the laws of human nature. All, therefore, that justice can demand, and honor grant, we can now ask, without presumption and without arrogance, of the American people.

Do you, then, ask us to state, in plain terms, just what we want of you, and just what we think we ought to receive at your hands? We answer: First of all, the complete abolition of the slavery of our race in the United States. We shall not stop to argue. We feel the terrible sting of this stupendous wrong, and that we cannot be free while our brothers are slaves. The enslavement of a vast majority of our people extends its baleful influence over every member of our race; and makes freedom, even to the free, a mockery and a delusion; we therefore, in our own name, and in the name of the whipped and branded millions, whose silent suffering has pleaded to the humane sentiment of mankind, but in vain, during more than two hundred years for deliverance, we implore you to abolish slavery. In the name of your country, torn, distracted, bleeding, and while you are weeping over the bloody graves of more than two hundred thousand of your noblest sons, many of whom have been cut down, in the midst of youthful vigor and beauty, we implore you to abolish slavery. In the name of peace, which experience has shown cannot be other than false and delusive while the rebellious spirit of Slavery has an existence in the land, we implore you to abolish slavery. In the name of universal justice, to whose laws great States not less than individuals are bound to conform, and the terrible consequences of whose violation are as fixed and certain as the universe itself, we implore you to abolish slavery; and thus place your peace and national welfare upon immutable and everlasting foundations.

Why would you let slavery continue? What good thing has it done, what evil thing has it left undone, that you should allow it to survive this dreadful war from the same cause? Are you so rich in men, money, and material, that you must provide for future depletion? Or do you hope to escape the consequences of wrong-doing? Can you expect any better results from compromises in the future, than from compromises with slavery in the past? If the South fights desperately and savagely to-day for the possession of four millions of slaves, will she fight less savagely and desperately when the prize for which she fights shall become eight instead of four millions? and when her ability to war upon freedom and free institutions shall have increased twofold?

Do you answer, that you have no longer anything to fear? that slavery has already received its death-blow? that it can only have a transient existence, even if permitted to live after the termination of the war? We answer, So thought your Revolutionary fathers when they framed the Federal Constitution; and to-day, the bloody fruits of their mistake are all around us. Shall we avoid or shall we repeat their stupendous error? Be not deceived. Slavery is still the vital and animating breath of Southern society. The men who have fought for it on the battle-field will not love it less for having shed their blood in its defence. Once let them get Slavery safely under the protection of the Federal Government, and ally themselves, as they will be sure to do, to the Democratic party of the North; let Jefferson Davis and his Confederate associates, either in person or by their representatives, return once more to their seats in the halls of Congress,—and you will then see your dead slavery the most living and powerful thing in the country. To make peace, therefore, on such a basis as shall admit slavery back again into the Union, would only be sowing the seeds of war; sure to bring at last a bitter harvest of blood! The sun in the heavens at noonday is not more manifest, than the fact that slavery is the prolific source of war and division among you; and that its abolition is essential to your national peace and unity. Once more, then, we entreat you—for you have the power—to put away this monstrous abomination. You have repeatedly during this wanton slave-holding and wicked Rebellion, in the darkest hours of the struggle, appealed to the Supreme Ruler of the universe to smile upon your armies, and give them victory; surely you will not now stain your souls with the crime of ingratitude by making a wicked compact and a deceitful peace with your enemies. You have called mankind to witness that the struggle on your part was not for empire merely; that the charge that it was such was a gross slander; will you now make a peace which will justify what you have repeatedly denounced as a calumny? Your anti-slavery professions have drawn to you the sympathy of liberal and generous minded men throughout the world, and have restrained all Europe from recognizing the Southern Confederacy, and breaking up your blockade of Southern ports. Will you now proclaim your own baseness and hypocrisy by making a peace which shall give the lie to all such professions? You have over and over again, and very justly, branded slavery as the inciting cause of this Rebellion; denounced it as the fruitful source of pride and selfishness and mad ambition; you have blushed before all Europe for its existence among you; and have shielded yourselves from the execrations of mankind, by denying your constitutional ability to interfere with it. Will you now, when the evil in question has placed itself within your constitutional grasp, and invited its own destruction by its persistent attempts to destroy the Government, relax your grasp, release your hold, and to the disappointment of the slaves deceived by your proclamations, to the sacrifice of the Union white men of the South who have sided with you in this contest with slavery, and to the dishonor of yourselves and the amazement of mankind, give new and stronger lease of life to slavery? We will not and cannot believe it.

There is still one other subject, fellow-citizens,—one other want,—looking to the peace and welfare of our common country, as well as to the interests of our race; and that is, political equality. We want the elective franchise in all the States now in the Union, and the same in all such States as may come in to the Union hereafter. We believe that the highest welfare of this great country will be found in erasing from its statute-books all enactments discriminating in favor or against any class of its people, and by establishing one law for the white and colored people alike. Whatever prejudice and taste may be innocently allowed to do or to dictate in social and domestic relations, it is plain, that in the matter of government, the object of which is the protection and security of human right, prejudice should be allowed no voice whatever. In this department of human relations, no notice should be taken of the color of men; but justice, wisdom, and humanity should weigh alone, and be all-controlling.

Formerly our petitions for the elective franchise were met and denied upon the ground, that, while colored men were protected in person and property, they were not required to perform military duty. Of course this was only a plausible excuse; for we were subject to any call the Government was pleased to make upon us, and we could not properly be made to suffer because the Government did not see fit to impose military duty upon us. The fault was with the Government, not with us.

But now even this frivolous though somewhat decent apology for excluding us from the ballot-box is entirely swept away. Two hundred thousand colored men, according to a recent statement by President Lincoln, are now in the service, upon field and flood, in the army and the navy of the United States; and every day adds to their number. They are there as volunteers, coming forward with other patriotic men at the call of their imperilled country; they are there also as substitutes filling up the quotas which would otherwise have to be filled up by white men who now remain at home; they are also there as drafted men, by a certain law of Congress, which, for once, makes no difference on account of color; and whether they are there as volunteers, as substitutes, or as drafted men, neither ourselves, our cause, nor our country, need be ashamed of their appearance or their action upon the battle-field. Friends and enemies, rebels and loyal men,—each, after their kind,—have borne conscious and unconscious testimony to the gallantry and other noble qualities of the colored troops. . . .

It is quite true, that some part of the American people may, with a show of plausibility, evade the force of this appeal and deny this claim. There are men in all countries who can evade any duty or obligation which is not enforced by the strong arm of the law. Our country is no exception to the rule. They can say in this case, "Colored men, we have done you no wrong. We have purchased nothing at your hands, and owe you nothing. From first to last, we have objected to the measure of employing you to help put down this rebellion, foreseeing the very claim you now set up. Were we to-day invested with the power and authority of this Government, we would instantly disband every colored regiment now in front of Richmond, and everywhere else in the Southern States. We do not believe in making soldiers of black men." To all that, we reply, There need be no doubt whatever. No doubt they would disband the black troops if they had the power; and equally plain is it that they would disband the white troops also if they had the power.

They do not believe in making black men soldiers; but they equally do not believe in making white men soldiers to fight slaveholding rebels. But we do not address ourselves here to particular parties and classes of our countrymen; we would appeal directly to the moral sense, honor, and magnanimity of the whole nation; and, with a cause so good, cannot believe that we shall appeal in vain. Parties and classes rise and fall, combine and dissolve; but the national conscience remains forever; and it is that to which our cause is addressed. It may, however, be said that the colored people enlisted in the service of the country without any promise or stipulation that they would be rewarded with political equality at the end of the war; but all the more, on this very account, do we hold the American people bound in honor thus to reward them. By the measure of confidence reposed in the national honor and generosity, we have the right to measure the obligation of fulfilment. The fact, that, when called into the service of the country, we went forward without exacting terms or conditions, to the mind of the generous man enhances our claims.

But, again, why are we so urgent for the possession of this particular right? We are asked, even by some Abolitionists, why we cannot be satisfied, for the present at least, with personal freedom; the right to testify in courts of law; the right to own, buy, and sell real estate; the right to sue and be sued. We answer, Because in a republican country, where general suffrage is the rule, personal liberty, the right to testify in courts of law, the right to hold, buy, and sell property, and all other rights, become mere privileges, held at the option of others, where we are excepted from the general political liberty. What gives to the newly arrived emigrants, fresh from lands governed by kingcraft and priestcraft, special consequence in the eyes of the American people? It is not their virtue, for they are often depraved; it is not their knowledge, for they are often ignorant; it is not their wealth, for they are often very poor; why, then, are they courted by the leaders of all parties? The answer is, that our institutions clothe them with the elective franchise, and they have a voice in making the laws of the country. Give the colored men of this country the elective franchise, and you will see no violent mobs driving the black laborer from the wharves of large cities, and from toil elsewhere by which he honestly gains his bread. You will see no influential priest, like the late Bishop Hughes, addressing mobocrats and murderers as "gentlemen"; and no influential politician, like Governor Seymour, addressing the "misguided" rowdies of New York as his "friends." The possession of that right is the keystone to the arch of human liberty; and, without that, the whole may at any moment fall to the ground; while, with it, that liberty may stand forever,—a blessing to us, and no possible injury to you. If you still ask why we want to vote, we answer, Because we don't want to be mobbed from our work, or insulted with impunity at every corner. We are men, and want to be as free in our native country as other men.

Fellow-citizens, let us entreat you, have faith in your own principles. If freedom is good for any, it is good for all. If you need the elective franchise, we need it even more. You are strong, we are weak; you are many, we are few; you are protected, we are exposed. Clothe us with this safeguard of our liberty, and give us an interest in the country to which, in common with you, we have given our lives and poured out our best blood. You cannot need special protection. Our degradation is not essential to your elevation, nor our peril essential to your safety. You are not likely to be outstripped in the race of improvement by persons of African descent; and hence you have no need of superior advantages, nor to burden them with disabilities of any kind. Let your Government be what all governments should be,—a copy of the eternal laws of the universe; before which all men stand equal as to rewards and punishments, life and death, without regard to country, kindred, tongue, or people.

But what we have now said, in appeal for the elective franchise, applies to our people generally. A special reason may be urged in favor of granting colored men the right in all the rebellious States.

Whatever may be the case with monarchical governments; however they may despise the crowd, and rely upon their *prestige*, armaments, and standing armies, to support them,—a republican government like ours depends largely upon the friendship of the people over whom it is established, for its harmonious and happy operation. This kind of government must have its foundation in the affections of the people; otherwise the people will hinder, circumvent, and destroy it. Up to a few years of the rebellion, our government lived in the friendship of the masses of the Southern people. Its enemies were, however, numerous and active; and these at last prevailed, poisoned the minds of the masses, broke up the government, brought on the war. Now, whoever lives to see this rebellion suppressed at the South, as we believe we all shall, will also see the South characterized by a sullen hatred towards the National Government. It will be transmitted from father to son, and will be held by them "as sacred animosity." The treason, mowed down by the armies of Grant and Sherman, will be followed by a strong undergrowth of treason which will go far to disturb the peaceful operation of the hated Government.

Every United States mail-carrier, every custom-house officer, every Northern man, and every representative of the United States Government, in the Southern States, will be held in abhorrence; and for a long time that country is to be governed with difficulty. We may conquer Southern armies by the sword; but it is another thing to conquer Southern hate. Now what is the natural counterpoise against this Southern malign hostility? This it is: give the elective franchise to every colored man of the South who is of sane mind, and has arrived at the age of twenty-one years, and you have at once four millions of friends who will guard with their vigilance, and, if need be, defend with their arms, the ark of Federal Liberty from the treason and pollution of her enemies. You are sure of the enmity of the masters,—make sure of the friendship of the slaves; for, depend upon it, your Government cannot afford to encounter the enmity of both.

If the arguments addressed to your sense of honor, in these pages, in favor of extending the elective franchise to the colored people of the whole country, be strong, that which we are prepared to present to you in behalf of the colored people of rebellious States can be made tenfold stronger. By calling them to take part with you in the war to subdue their rebellious masters, and the fact that thousands of them have done so, and thousands more would gladly do so, you have exposed them to special resentment and wrath; which, without the elective franchise, will descend upon them in unmitigated fury. To break with your friends, and make peace with your enemies; to weaken your friends, and strengthen your enemies; to abase your friends, and exalt your enemies; to disarm your friends, and arm your enemies; to disfranchise your loyal friends, and enfranchise your disloyal enemies,—is not the policy of honor, but of infamy. . . .

3. A July 4, (1876) Oration

In an essay in 1868 James Parton characterized the "fashionable" Fifth Avenue churches as richly furnished parlors with Sunday services offered to lull and to comfort. They were "a kind of exclusive ecclesiastical club, designed for the accommodation of persons of ten thousand dollars a year, and upward," persons who preferred not to have their moral sense ruffled on Sunday. It may be, he went on, that the divisions in modern life rule out the older conception of a church "where all sorts and conditions of men came together to dwell upon considerations interesting to all equally." Among these divisions he referred to differences in knowledge even greater now than those between king and peasant. Who could preach to both the man saturated in Mill, Emerson, Spencer, and Humboldt and the man whose only reading is the dime novel? "What form of service can be even imagined, that could satisfy Bridget, who cannot read, and her mistress, who comes to church cloyed with the dainties of half a dozen literatures?"

The question reverberates with implications for American culture at large, and the reply which Parton goes on to describe in the preaching of Henry Ward Beecher at the Plymouth Church in Brooklyn Heights is significant as much for cultural as for church history. By contrasts with the fashionable church, the Plymouth congregation "is simply the most characteristic thing of America. . . . The New Testament, Plymouth Rock, and the Fourth of July,— *this* is what they have brought us to." A plain brick building, the church offered an interior designed in the old-fashioned style to bring the multitude into direct relation with their spiritual leader. It was that relation which was the most conspicuous feature of the career of Beecher, who in two decades with the Plymouth Church had made himself into perhaps the most conspicuous public figure in America. "It is perfect," Beecher himself had said of the church interior, its curving gallery of seats and its platform in the midst of the audience, "because it is built on a principle—the principle of social and personal magnetism, which emanates reciprocally from a speaker and from a close throng of hearers. . . . I want them to surround me, so that they will come up on every side, and behind me, so that I shall be in the center of the crowd, and have the people surge all about me!" As Constance Rourke has pointed out (*Trumpets of Jubilee*, 1927), his extraordinary success as a speaker flowed from his sensitivity to the changing moods and responses of his audience. This son of the embattled New England Calvinist, Lyman Beecher, and brother of Harriet Beecher Stowe, seemed to "compose within his own magnified person the larger emotional elements of his time."

Parton shrewdly placed Beecher's significance in his relation to an essentially middle-class audience. Who understood better than Beecher the nature of that audience? "Here were a number of people,—parents, businessmen, and others,—most of them heavily burdened with responsibility, having notes and rents to pay, customers to get and keep, children to rear,—busy people, anxious people, of extremely diverse characters, but united by a common desire to live nobly." And Beecher gave them the freedom to enjoy nature, books, arts, themselves, which the older doctrines had denied. Religion became a matter of educating the heart in right feelings and noble living, in love of beauty and benevolence. Against the intellectual discipline of the fathers, Beecher offered simple universal axioms. It is not hard to see the fitness of his role in the nationwide celebrations of July Fourth, 1876, even though at that time Beecher was still involved in the bizarre public furor over a charge that he had committed adultery with a parishioner. "The great problem of civilization," Parton wrote, "is how to bring the higher intelligence of the community, and its better moral feeling, to bear upon the mass of people, so that the lowest grade of intelligence and morals shall be always approaching the higher. . . . A church purified of superstition solves part of this problem, and a good school system does the rest." As for Beecher, "He is a bridge over which we are passing from the creed-enslaved past to the perfect freedom of the future."

The Advance of a Century

HENRY WARD BEECHER

I

Of all the places on this continent where, from political considerations, vast assemblies should gather to-day, there is no place that can equal Philadelphia, where that orator and statesman and civilian, Evarts, is holding in rapt attention the great crowds. But if it be not a question of political interest, but of military, I know of no other point throughout the

Henry Ward Beecher, "The Advance of a Century," *The [New York] Tribune*, Extra No. 33, Independence Day Orations, July 4, 1876, 37–44.

land where the people may more fitly assemble for retrospect and for pride than in this goodly place of Peekskill. [Applause] For we stand in the very center of the military operations that were conducted in the northern part of our then country. The great ferry—the King's Ferry—by which chief communication was had between all New-England and New-Jersey and Pennsylvania, in which bounds there was the greatest part of the population of the country, lies right opposite to us. This is the center of that sphere, of that vast drama. (At this point the cannon on the adjacent hill was fired. Mr. Beecher stopped for an instant, but he immediately said "I have spoken very often, but I have never been punctuated with the cannon before.") [Great laughter and applause.] But as I was saying, around this region was that great drama played—the treachery of Arnold and the sad recompense upon André. In these streets our armies have trod; in this town Washington dated, indeed, the commission which was last received by Arnold at the hands of his countrymen. Off upon this bay hovered the British fleet. (The cannon again gave a deafening report, causing Mr. Beecher to say, "I have no objection to being canonized, but don't like to be cannonaded.") [Great laughter.]

A hundred years have passed since this region was the theater of such stirring scenes and vicissitudes. A hundred years is a long period in the life of a man—a short period in the life of a nation. A hundred years! It is 1,800 since the Advent; a thousand years scarcely take us back beyond the beginning of European nations in their modern form. A hundred years is scarcely the "teen" to which nations come. And it seldom happens that any nation has for its thousand such a hundred years as that which has been vouchsafed to us. From a population of scant 3,000,000, including the slave population, we have swelled to more than 40,000,000. Behind a small strip of settled territory lining the Atlantic coast almost no one except the pioneers's foot had trod the mountain path, had pressed the soil of the country beyond. Now the Atlantic and the Pacific are joined by the iron road, and that has come to pass in reality which in the Scripture is spoken of in poetry—"deep answers unto deep," and the ocean breaks upon one shore to be answered by the other; and all the way across are thickly-settled communities, towns, and cities innumerable. And yet this is but small as compared with the augmentation of material interests. The wealth that scarcely now is computable, the industries that thrive, the inventions, the discoveries, the organizations of labor and of capital, the vast spread of the industries over the valleys and hills—who can estimate that of the early day which was but as a seed compared with that of our day which moves like Lebanon? And yet what are the sheen and ships and rails, and what are granaries and roads and canals, what are herds upon a thousand hills, what are all these in comparison with man! All labor and the products of labor are valuable only as they promote the virtue and the comfort of man—are valuable only as they promote the manhood which is in man. Though we had a quadrupled wealth, yet if the people were decayed or enfeebled, what would our property be worth? Not worth the assembling here to look back upon, or to look forward to. The value of our material growth is to be estimated by its effect upon the people.

What has been the history of a hundred years in regard to the people of America? Are they as virtuous as they were a hundred years ago? Are they as manly as they were a hundred years ago? Are they as intelligent, are they as religious as they were a hundred years ago? Not only that— are these individuals that are perhaps, as we shall examine, more or less religious, moral, intelligent, happy—have they learned anything in the highest of all arts, the art of man to live with man, the art of organizing society, of conducting government, the promotion of the common weal through broad spaces and through vast multitudes? What is the history of the people? What are we to-day? What our fathers were we know. Their life was splendid; their history was registered. We read what they were, and form an estimate of them with gratitude to God; but what are we, their sons? Have we shrunk? Are we unworthy of their names, and places, and functions, which have been transmitted from their hands to ours? What are the laws, what are the institutions, what is the Government, what are the policies of this great nation, redeemed from foreign thrall to home independence? Are they committed to puny hands, or is manhood broadened and strengthened and ennobled? Look then at our population, what it is, spread abroad through all the land. It might be said that America represents every nation on the globe better than the nation represents itself. We have the best things they have got in Ireland, for we have stripped her almost bare. We have the canny Scotchman in great numbers among us, though not enough for our good. We have the English-man among us, and are suspected ourselves of having English blood in our veins. We have also those from Norway, Sweden, Denmark, Russia even, Germany, Austria and Hungary, Italy, Spain, France, Switzerland. We can cull from all these nations out of our population many members of whom they are not ashamed and for whom we are grateful. We have our fields tilled by foreign hands, our roads built by them. This is a matter of political economy, but the question which I propose to you is, What are they as component elements of a new American stock? Do you believe in stock; do you believe in blood? I do. Do you believe in crossing judiciously? Do you believe that the best blood of all nations will ultimate by and by in a better race than the primitive and the uncomplex race, mixing new strength and alliances? We have fortified our blood, enriched our blood; we have called the world to be our father and the father of our children and posterity, and there never was a time in the history of this nation when the race-stock had in it so much that was worth the study of the physiologist and philanthropist as to-day. We are enriched beyond the power of gratitude. I for one regard all the inconveniences of foreign mixtures, of difference of language, the difference of customs, the difference of religion, the difference in domestic arrangement—I regard all these inconveniences as a trifle; but the augmentation of power, of breadth of manhood, the promise of the future, is past all computation, and there never was, there never began to be in the early day such promise for physical vigor and enriched life as there is to-day upon this continent.

II

CONDITIONS OF EXISTENCE AND HAPPINESS

And now consider that not only is this race-stock for these reasons made a better one than that which existed a hundred years ago, but consider that the conditions of existence among the whole population are better than they were a hundred years ago. We not only wear better heads, but we have better bellies [great laughter], with better food in them. We have also better clothes now. In other words, the art of living healthily has advanced immensely, and though cities have enlarged, and though the causes of dangers to sanitary conditions are multiplied, science has kept pace, and there never was a time, I will not say in our own history, but in the history of any nation on the globe, when the conditions of life were so wholesome, the conditions of happiness so universally diffused, as they are to-day in this great land. We grumble—we inherit that from our ancestors; we often mope and vex ourselves with melancholy prognostications concerning this or that danger. Some men are born to see the devil of melancholy; they would see him sitting in the very door of heaven, methinks. Not I; for though there be mischiefs and troubles, yet when we look at the great conditions of human life in society, and they have been augmented favorably, they never were so favorable as they are to-day. More than that; if you will look at the diversity of the industries by which men ply their hands, if we look at the accumulating power of the average citizen, you will find that it is in the power of a man to earn more in a single ten years of his life to-day than for our ancestors in the whole of their life. The heavens are nearer to us than to them, for we have learned the secrets of the storm and the sweep of the lightning. The earth itself is but just outside our door. We can now call to Asia and the distant parts of the earth easier than they could to Boston or Philadelphia a hundred years ago; and all the fleets of the world bring hither the tribute of the globe, and that not for the rich man and the sumptuous liver, but for the common folks of the land to which we all belong. The houses in which we live are better; better warmed in Winter—and our Summers are very well warmed too. The implements by which the common man works are multiplied; the processes which he can control, and which are organized in society that he gets the reflex benefit of them, are incalculable. And all that the soil has, and all that the sea has, and all that the mountain locks up, and all that is invisible in the atmosphere, are so many servitors working in this great democratic land for the multitude, for the great mass of the common people. We are in that regard advanced far beyond the days of our fathers; for then they had not escaped from the hereditary notions, or aristocratic thoughts, the aristocratic classes, or the aristocratic tendencies even in government. But the progress of democracy—which is not merely political, but which is religious, in literature, art, even in mechanics—the wave of democratic influence has been for a hundred years washing in further and further toward the feet of the common people. And to-day there is not on the face of the globe another forty millions that have such amplitude of sphere, such strength of purpose, such instruments to their hand, such capital for them, such opportunity, such happiness. And that leads me to speak—going aside from the common people individually or as in classes—of their institutions, and let me begin where you began, in the household.

III

CHANGES IN THE HOUSEHOLD

What is the family and household to-day as compared with the family and household a hundred years ago? Time is a great magnifying medium. We look back a hundred years and think that influences of the household and of society must have been better, purer, than they are to-day. No, no. If there be one thing that has grown in solidity and grandeur, in richness and purity and refinement, it has been the American household. Oh, there were here and there notable mansions, here and there notable households of intelligence and virtue in the olden day. But we are concerned with the averages; and the average American household is wiser, there is more material for thought, for comfort, for home love, to-day, in the ordinary workman's house, than there was a hundred years ago in one of a hundred rich men's mansions and buildings. For no man among us is so poor—unless he drinks whisky too much—no man that is well born among us—and to be well born it is necessary first to have been born at all, and secondly, to have been born out of virtuous parents, who set him a good example—no man has been well born in this land who needs to stand at the bottom of the ladder 20 years. The laborer ought to be ashamed of himself—or to find fault with Providence that stinted him when he was endowed—who in 20 years does not own the ground on which his house stands, and that, too, an unmortgaged house; who has not in that house provided carpets for the rooms, who has not his China plates, who has not his chromos, who has not some picture or portrait hanging upon the walls, who has not some books nestling on the shelf, who has not there a household that he can call his home, the sweetest place upon the earth. This is not the picture of some future time, but the picture of to-day, a picture of the homes of the workingmen of America. The average workingman lives better now in the household and in the family than he did a hundred years ago. But we have come to it steadily, without record or observation. Yet it is none the less true that the average condition of the household for domestic comfort has gone up more than one per cent for every year of the last 100 years.

But that is not all. The members of the household have also developed, and chiefly she into whose hand God put the rudder of time. For if Eve plucked the apple that Adam might help her to eat it, she has been beforehand with him ever since and steered him. The household that has a bad woman may have an angel for a husband, but he is helpless. The household that has a brute for a husband is safe if the woman be God's own woman. Franklin said that a man is what his wife will let him be. It is more than a proverb that the children are what the mother makes them. She is the legislator of the household; she is the judge that sits upon the throne of love. All severity comes from love in a mother's hand; she is the educator; she also is the atonement when sins and transgressions have brought children to shame. The altar of penitence is at the mother's knee, and not the heart of God knows better how to forgive than does she. If womanhood has gone down, woe be to us; the richer we are, the stronger we are, the worse we are. And if woman has gone up in intelligence, in influence, in virtue, and in religion, then the country is safe, though its fleets were sunk and its cities were burned, though its crops were mildewed and blasted. For easy is recovery where the head forces are sound; but where there is corruption at the central point of power all outward helps are in vain. I declare that in the last one hundred years woman, who before had brooded and blossomed in aristocratic circles, has now come to blossom through democratic circles, and is in America to-day undisputed and uncontradicted what before she has been allowed to be only when she had a coronet upon her brow, or some scepter of power in her hand. Not only is she unvailed, not only is she permitted to show her face where men do most congregate, not only is she a power in the silence of the house, but in the church a teacher. Paul from a thousand years ago may in vain now say, "Let not your women teach in the church." They cannot come there without being teachers and silent letters. They are the books and epistles known and read of all men. They have come to that degree of knowledge, they have come to that breadth of intellect and power, they have learned how to dispose of that primary and highest gift, moral intuition, which God gave to them in excess, cheating man, they have come to such influence and grandeur that never before in any land, certainly never in our own, has womanhood attained such authority and eminence as at the present day. That power which is now latent and applied indirectly, is soon to fill the channels that shall be direct and initial. You may die too soon, as many have before they saw the beatific vision, but you that live long enough will see woman vote, and when you see woman vote, you will see less fraud, less selfishness, less brutality, and more public spirit and rectitude and harmony in the administration of public affairs. I do not propose to discuss the question at any length with you, but I cannot without thanksgiving, I cannot fail to recognize that steady advance which is sure to make woman a voter in this generation.

IV

EXTENSION OF THE SUFFRAGE

In the beginning of our history no man could vote that was not a member of the church; and, by the way, the deacons, to relieve the church members from the trouble of calling at the ballot-boxes, took their hats and went around and collected the votes from house to house; but deacons in those days were trustworthy. After a little a man was allowed to vote if a white man and owned property to a certain amount, though he did not belong to the church, and that was the augmentation of suffrage in that respect. After a time it became necessary to knock down even that exception. Franklin labored with might and main to this end, and employed that significant argument: If a man may not vote unless he is a property-holder to the amount of $100, and he owns an ass which is worth $100, and to-day the ass is well and he votes, but to-morrow the ass dies, and so he cannot vote—which votes, the ass or the man? The property qualification disappeared before this argument, and the power of voting became free. Then came the question of foreigners voting, and they were not to be allowed to vote except upon probation. Like many of your fences, one rail after another fell down, until the fence was so low that anything could jump it when it wanted to, and in New-York they jump it now quite easily. But the day is coming, and that very soon, in which this pretense of limitation be thrown down, and every man that means in good faith to settle here shall have it proclaimed to him, "If you wish to settle here you shall have the protection of the laws if you undertake to be responsible for those laws." I would allow a man to vote the very moment he touches the soil.

The next step was the admission of the colored race to vote. This was the boldest thing ever done. It was said it was a war measure; it was necessarily connected with it in such a manner as to come under that general designation. During the war a million of black men were taken from the plantation—they could not read the Constitution or the spelling-book, they could hardly tell one hand from the other—and they were allowed to vote, in the sublime faith that liberty which makes a man competent to vote would render him fit to discharge the duty of the voter. And when these colored men, these unwashed black men were allowed to vote, although much disturbance occurred—as disturbance always occurs upon great changes—I am bound to say that the black man has proved himself worthy of the trust confided to him. Before emancipation the black man was the most docile laborer that ever the world saw. During the war, and when he knew that liberty was the gage, when he knew that the battle was whether he should or should not be true, although the country for hundreds of miles was stripped bare of able-bodied white men, and when property was at the mercy of the slave, arson or rapine or conspiracy was saved to the country, and no uprising took place. They stood still, conscious of their power, and said: "We will see what God will do for us." Such a history has no parallel. And since they began to vote, after their emancipation, I beg to say, in closing on this subject, that they have voted just as wisely and patriotically as did their late masters before emancipation.

And now there is but one step more—there is but one step more. We permit the lame, the halt, and the blind to go to the ballot-box; we permit the foreigner and the black man, the slave and the freedman, to partake of the suffrage; there is but one thing left out, and that is the mother that taught us, and the wife that is thought worthy to walk side by side with us. It is woman that is put lower than the slave, lower than the ignorant foreigner. She is put among the paupers whom the law won't allow to vote, among the insane whom the law won't allow to vote. But the days are numbered in which this can take place, and she too will vote. As in a hundred years suffrage has extended its bounds until it now includes the whole population, in another hundred years everything will vote, unless it be the power of the loom, and locomotive, and watch, and I sometimes think, looking at these machines and their performances, that they too ought to vote.

V

AUGMENTATION IN INTELLIGENCE

More than that, what has been the progress of the country during this time in intelligence and the means of intelligence? A hundred years ago, I had almost said, schoolhouses could be counted, certainly upon the hairs of your head, if not upon the fingers of your hand, in New-England and throughout the country. As I remember them, they were miserable, unpainted buildings, that roasted you in Winter and stunk in Summer, with slabs for seats, with old Webster for the spelling-book, with Daboll for the arithmetic, with three months of school in the Winter, and with one, two, or three in Summer. Compare them with the high schools, the graded schools, and the primary schools that are now the pride of every populous neighborhood. Has there been no augmentation in the instruments of intelligence?

Then there were perhaps 20 newspapers in the United States. Alas! how they have increased since then! These are said to be the leaves of the tree for the healing of the nations; and often in this regard that comes to pass which comes to pass in sickness—that men who take the leaves are made sicker than they were before. But every man reads the newspapers to-day. The drayman, at his nooning, divides the time between his little tin kettle and his newspaper. A man, though he goes home tired, yet must know what the news is. The vast majority of laboring men—not to speak of professional men, and men whose business requires that they shall read— know before the setting of the sun, on any given day, what is being done in Asia, what is being done in Turkey, what is being done in California, what is being done in the world around—for this is a pocket world now, which every man can carry round for himself, in his newspaper.

Consider how cheap books are. Consider how wide is the diffusion of knowledge through essays, through treatises of various kinds, through lectures, through all manner of instruments of enlightenment. Consider how our political organizations are turning themselves into great educating conventions, in which the best men discourse on their theories of government. I hold that no German university ever had in its halls such legists or judicial men as were turned out by the wholesale in this country during the late war, and for years preceding that war, for the discussion of questions relating to the rights of the individual, the nature of the State, the duty of the citizen, and the functions and prerogatives of the Legislature and the Government. Never were a people so educated as this people were during the twenty-five years which preceded the present. For, let me tell you, in 1776 there were 29 public libraries in the United States; or, there were about one and two-thirds volumes for each 100 of the people in the country. In 1876 there are 3,632 public libraries in the United States, not including the libraries of the common schools, of the Church, or the Sunday-school, numbering in the aggregate 12,276,000 volumes, or about 30 volumes to one hundred persons. Between 1775 and 1800—a period of twenty-five years—there were 20 public libraries formed. During another period of twenty-five years—between 1800 and 1825—there were 179 public libraries formed. During the next period of twenty-five years—between 1825 and 1850—there were 551 public libraries formed. During the twenty-five years intervening between 1850 and 1875, there were 2,240 public libraries formed. And in all the history of America there has not been a period when the brain of the population has teemed with such fertility as it did during the 25 years last past, in which the great and agitating discussions of slavery took place. During the war when there was such a subsoiling of this country, there was displayed such energy and activity of its people as they had never before displayed. Never before were there 25 years in which there were such tremendous agents employed for instruction; never before were there such instruments of enlightenment brought to bear upon us.

And that which is indicated in the increase of books is carried out in the increase of newspapers and magazines not only, but in the increase of machinery and agriculture and art and the mechanical business of life. The impulse toward power and fruitfulness was never so eminent as it was during those 25 years in which the rights of men were the fundamental questions that were discussed, and in which we proved the sincerity of the North and the weakness of the South.

VI

RELIGIOUS INFLUENCE

Thus far we have spoken of the condition of the common people and their various institutions. Let me say in passing one word on that subject which from my very profession it might be thought that I would mention first, and which on that very account I only glance at lest I should seem to give undue prominence to that profession. The state of religious feeling in this country is more advanced to-day by many and many degrees than it has been in any period anterior to this. When the Ohio River, the mountain snow melting swells up to the measure of its banks, begins to overflow and overflow, the big Miami bottoms are one sheeted field of water, and where I once lived—in Lawrenceburg, Indiana—I could take a boat and go 25 miles straight across the country, so vast was the volume. Now, suppose a man had taken a skiff and gone out over the fields and plumbed the depth and found only five feet of water, and had said, "Ah! only five feet of water, and the Ohio had forty feet." Well, the Ohio has not shrunk one inch. There are forty feet there and there are five feet everywhere else. Religion used to be in the church pretty much and men used to have to measure the church in order to know how deep it was, but there has been rain on the mountains and the moral feeling that exists in the community and in the world has overflowed the bounds of the church, and you can't measure the religious life or the religious impulse of this people unless you measure their philanthropy, their household virtue, and the general good will that prevails between classes and communities. The church is not less than it has been, it is more than it ever was, but outside of it also there is a vast volume of that which can be registered under no head so well as under that of religious influence, which never existed in old days gone by to the extent to which it exists now. I am one who, although I am a servant of the Church, a minister within her bounds, whenever I look out of her windows and see hundreds of good men outside, am not sorry. I thank God when I see a better man in a denomination that is not my own than I see in my own denomination. I thank God when I see virtue and true piety existing outside of the church, as well as when I see it existing inside of the church. I recognize the hand of God as being as bountiful, and I recognize His administration as being as broad, as are the rains or as is the sunshine. God does not send to Peekskill just as much sunshine as you want for your corn and rye and wheat. It shines on stones and sticks and worms and bugs. It pours its light and heat down upon the mountains and rocks and everywhere. God rains not by the pint nor by the quart, but by the continent. Whether things need it or not, He needs to pour out His bounty, that He may relieve Himself of His infinite fullness.

And so it is in the community. Never before was there so much conscience or so many subjects as there is to-day. I know there is not enough conscience to go around always. I know there are men whose consciences are infirm on certain sides. I know that in the various professions there are many places where there are gaps, or where the walls are too low. But the cultivation of conscience is an art. Conscience is a thing that is learned. No man has much more conscience than he is trained to. So the minister has his conscience; it is according to the training that he has had; and it is thought to be fair for him to hunt a brother minister for heresy, though it would not be fair for him to hunt him for anything else. A lawyer has his conscience. It is sometimes very high, and sometimes it is very low. As an average, it is very good. The doctor has his conscience, and his patients have theirs. Everybody has his conscience, and everybody's conscience acts according to certain lines to which he has been drilled and trained. Right and wrong are to the great mass of men as letters and words. We learn how to spell, and if a man spells wrong, and was taught in that way, nevertheless it is his way of spelling. And so it is with men's consciences. Now, I aver that mere legislative conscience is genius. Not one man in a million has a sense of what is right and wrong except as the result of education and experience. No man in complex circumstances has a conception of justice and rectitude by a legislative conscience. The great mass of men—teachers and the taught—are obliged to depend upon the revelations of experience to enable them to determine what is right and wrong. They have to set their consciences by the rule of the experiences which they have gone through.

Now I aver not that the conscience of this people is a perfect conscience and not that it does not need a great deal of education, but that, such as it is, it is better and higher and more universal that it was at any other period of the hundred years that have just gone by. I would rather trust the moral sentiment of the community now on any question of domestic policy, or on any question of legislative policy, than at any period anterior in the history of America. I would, within the bounds of their knowledge, rather trust the moral judgment and common sense of the millions of the common people than the special knowledge of any hundred of the best trained geniuses that there are in the land. This is not true in respect to those departments of knowledge which the common people have never reached. There is no common sense in astronomy, because there is no common knowledge in astronomy. The same is also true of engineering; but in that whole vast realm of questions which do come down to men's board and bosoms, the moral sentiment of the great mass of the common people is more reliable than the judgment of the few. In all those questions there is a common conscience and a common moral sense; and I say that the average moral sense and conscience of the community never were so high as they are to-day—and to-day at such a height in the common people as to be safer in them than in any class in the community. This is a great gain in the last hundred years.

VII

THE COUNTRY'S ELEMENTS OF GROWTH

Let me once more call your attention to some of the elements of growth that have taken place in this nation. I was one of those whose courage never failed except in spots. Before the war I did have some dark days, in which I felt as though this nation was going to be raised up merely to be the manure of some after nation, being plowed under. It seemed to me as though all the avenues of power were in the hands of despotism, as though a great part of humanity was trodden under foot; as though every element that could secure to despotism a continuance of its power had been seized and sealed; and I did not see any way out—God forgive me—for those very steps which made the power and despotism of Slavery dangerous were in the end its remedy and its destruction. And this great North had so long, partly from necessity, and partly from a misguided and romantic patriotism, encouraged and promoted that which was the *caries* of free institutions, the bane of liberty, and the danger which threatened the continent in all after times.

But when at last the nation was aroused, it smote not once, not twice, but, according to the old prophet, seven times; and then deliverance was prompt. The power of a nation is to be judged by its resistance to disease. All nations are liable to attack, but the real power of a nation is shown in its ability to throw off disease—in its resiliency. The power of recovery is better than all soundness of national constitution. It is better than anything else can be. America has arisen from a fifth-rate power; but she looks calmly and modestly over the ocean, and is a first-rate power among the nations to-day. She was a democracy; the people made their own laws;

they levied and collected their own taxes; and it was said, "Of course they will not allow themselves to be taxed more than they want to be." They were not a military people; Europe told us so. Great Britain told us so. They told me so to my face; and I said, on many a platform, with an audience like this, "You do not understand what democratic liberty means. Wait till this game is played out, and see what the issue is." And what is the issue of the game? To a certain extent, the political economy of the South gave her aid in the beginning; and the political economy of the North gave her inexhaustible resources. The genius of the Northern people is slow to get on fire, and is hard to put out; so that we had to learn the trade of war. We had learned every trade of peace already, but when once we had learned the trade of war, the power of the North was manifest, to the honor and glory of our religion, of our political faiths, and of the whole training of our past history.

But there was something more dangerous than war. An insidious serpent is more dangerous than a roaring lion—if the lion does not jump before he roars. Repudiation threatened more damnation to the morals of this nation than ever war did with all its mischiefs; and I want to record, to the honor of our foreign population, of whom it is often said, "When you come to a great stress, when questions are to be settled on principles of rectitude and truth, they will be found wanting"—I want to record to the honor of the population that we have borrowed from Europe, the fact that when the question came, "Shall this nation pay every dollar which it promised, and by which it put the boys in blue in the field," it was, through the West and the North-West, the foreign vote together with the vote of our own people, that carried the day for honesty and for public integrity. Now, for a Democratic nation that owns everything—the government, the law, the policy, the magistrate, the ruler; that can change, that can make and unmake, that has in its hands almost the power of the Highest to exalt one and to put down another—for such a nation to stand before the world and show that this great people, swarming through our valleys and over our mountains and far away to either shore, and without the continuity necessary to the creation of a common public sentiment, were willing to bear the brunt of a five years' war and to be severely taxed, down to this day, and yet refuse to lighten its burdens in a way that would be wrong and dishonorable—that will weigh more in Europe than any test that any nation is able to put forth, for its honor, its integrity, its strength, and its promise of future life.

Look back, then, through the hundred years of our national history. They are to me like the ascending of stairs, some of which are broader, some narrower, some with higher rising, and some with less than the others, but on the whole there has been a steady ascent in intelligence, in conscience, in purity, in industry, in happiness, in the art of living well individually, and in the higher art of living well collectively, and we stand to-day higher than at any other time. Our burdens are flea-bites. We have some trouble about money. I never saw a time when the most of the population did not. We have our trouble, because there is too much in some places and too little in others. The trouble with us is like the trouble in Winter, when the snow has fallen and drifted, and leaves one-half of the road bare, while it is piled up in the other half, so that you cannot get along for the much nor for the little. But a distribution will speedily bring all things right—and I think we are not far from the time when that will take place. So soon as we can touch the ground of universal confidence, so soon as we stand on a basis of silver and gold—then, and not an hour before then, will this nation begin to move on in the old prosperity of business.

I determined not to say anything that could be construed as an allusion to party politics, and what I have said cannot be so construed, for both sides around here say they are for resumption. The only difference is, that one party say that they are for resumption, and the other say that they are for resumption *as soon as we can have it.* Well, I do not see how anybody can say anything more. You cannot resume before you *can.*

Fellow citizens, in looking back upon the past, it is not right that we should leave the sphere and field of our remarks without one glance at the future. In another hundred years not one of us will be here. Some other speaker, doubtless, will stand in my place. Other hearers will throng —though not with more courtesy, nor with more kindly patience than you have—to listen to his speech. Then on every eminence from New-York to Albany there will be mansions and cottages, and garden will touch garden along the whole Eden of the Hudson River Valley. But it does not matter so much to us, who come and go, or what takes place in the future, except so far as our influence is concerned. When a hundred years hence the untelling sun, that saw Arnold, and André, and Washington, but will not tell us one word of history, shall shine on these enchanted hills and on this unchanging river—then it is for us to have set in motion, or to have given renewed impulse to those great causes, intellectual, moral, social, and political, which have rolled our prosperity to such a height.

To every young man here that is beginning life, let me say, Listen not to those insidious teachers who tell you that patriotism is a sham, and that all public men are corrupt or corrupters. Men in public or private life are corrupt here and there, but let me say to you, no corruption in government would be half so bad as to have the seeds of unbelief in public administration sown in the minds of the young. If you teach the young that their Chief Magistrates, their Cabinets, and their representatives are of course corrupt, what will that be but to teach them to be themselves corrupt? I stand here to bear witness and say that publicity may consist with virtue and does. There are men that serve the public for the public, though they themselves thrive by it also. I would sow in your minds a romance of patriotism and love of country that shall be necessary to the love which you have for your own households, and I would say to every mother that teaches her child to pray, next to the petition, "Our Father which art in heaven," and let it learn this petition: Our Fatherland, and so let our children grow up to love God, to love man, and to love their country, and to be glad to serve their country as well as their God and their fellow-men, though it may be necessary that they should lay down their lives to serve it.

I honor the unknown ones that used to walk in Peekskill and who fell in battle. I honor, too, every armless man, every limping soldier, that through patriotism went to the battle-field and came back lame and crippled, and bears manfully and heroically his deprivation. What though he find no occupation? What though he be forgotten? He has in him the imperishable sweetness of this thought: "I did it for my country's sake." For God's sake and for your country's sake, live, and you shall live forever.

4. America Among the Nations

The international, or better known as the "universal," exhibitions were a special product of the nineteenth century. They were elaborately theatrical displays of the fruits of world culture, displays undertaken in the confidence that industrialization was indeed a harbinger of a new age. Many of these fairs served to whet the taste for the future by fanciful presentations of new styles of building, new forms of technology. They were, as one critic of the Centennial Exhibition in Philadelphia in 1876 put it, "generalizations" of world progress in technology and the arts.

The same critic remarked that the Philadelphia show was decidedly more commercial than earlier expositions in London and Paris. Financed by local businessmen, housed in a hundred and eighty buildings in a site along the Schuylkill River in Fairmount Park, the Centennial drew eight million visitors. It was, as the art historian Oliver Larkin writes, "the oddest collection of buildings that had ever been assembled in America." A Swiss chalet turned out to be the New York State building; minarets and Gothic towers stood incongruously side-by-side. Gaucheries of style were matched by such displays as a Sleeping Iolanthe carved in butter and the largest ceramic piece ever made, showing *America* astride a bison. As Howells' essay shows, critics of art and culture had in one compressed compass an epitome of the age and the nation.

He portrayed the exhibition as characteristic of American life as a whole, and pointed to the superiority of American machines to its art. As interesting as his observations, however, is Howells' style, especially the mild irony which invites the reader to share his point of view, pleased with and even proud of national achievements, yet wishing for more in the way of quality. At bottom his style persuades the reader of his sympathy with common American life.

Howells, Editor-in-Chief of the *Atlantic Monthly* since 1871, was already considered a major literary figure—a Midwesterner who had found acceptance in the country's most influential and respected literary group, the New England Brahmins, which included Longfellow, Lowell, and Emerson. Although the major phase of Howells' career as a novelist did not begin until he left the

Atlantic in the 1880's, he was already being praised in The Californian in 1880 for the agreeable sociability, the "naturalness" and "moral purity" of his writings. The critic singled out as his high service to the public the elevation of the "commonplace"—"He is ennobling the tiresome routine of humdrum lives." His work in the 1870's and 1880's seemed to fill the need for social encouragement and self-respect among middle-class Americans.

A Sennight of the Centennial
WILLIAM DEAN HOWELLS

The Centennial is what every one calls the great fair now open at Philadelphia. "Have you been at the Centennial?" "How do you like the Centennial?" Some politer and more anxious few struggle for logical precision, reflecting that you cannot go to a Centennial, any more than you can go to a Millennial. These entangle themselves in International Exhibition, or talk of the Exposition. The English, who invented it, and have a genius for simplicity (in some things), called the first international exhibition the World's Fair. But this simple and noble name does not quite serve for us, since our World's Fair means the commemoration of our hundredth national anniversary; and so, at last, Centennial is the best name, in spite of its being no name at all.

The Centennial is so far peculiar in other ways that one may fitly give one's self the benefit of a doubt whether it is wholly advantageous to have seen other world's fairs in order to the intelligent appreciation of this; whether, in fact, it were not better never to have seen anything of the sort before. We will assume, for the present writer's purpose, that this is so. We may even go a step further and suppose that one's acquaintance with the Centennial is to be most fortunately formed upon a dull, drizzling day, somewhat cold and thoroughly unpleasant, like the 17th of May, for example. On that day, a week after the opening of the show, the first impression was certainly that of disorder and incompleteness, and the Centennial had nothing to do but to grow upon the visitor's liking. The paths were broken and unfinished, and the tough, red mud of the roads was tracked over the soft asphalt into all the buildings. Carts employed in the construction came and went everywhere, on easy terms alike with the trains of the circular railway whose engines hissed and hooted at

William Dean Howells, "A Sennight of the Centennial," Atlantic Monthly, XXXVIII (1876), 92–107.

points above the confusion, and with the wheeled-chairs in which ladies, huddling their skirts under their umbrellas, were trundled back and forth among the freight cars of the Pennsylvania Railroad. At many points laborers were digging over the slopes of the grounds and vigorously slapping the sides of the clayey embankments with the flat of their spades; and ironical sign-boards in all directions ordered you to keep off the grass on spaces apparently dedicated to the ceramic arts forever. Even if these grassless spots had been covered with tender herbage, there seemed not enough people present to justify the vigilance that guarded them; but I think this was an illusion, to which the vastness of the whole area and its irregular shape and surface contributed. There were probably fifteen thousand visitors that day, but many thousands more dispersed over the grounds and scattered through the different buildings would have given nowhere the impression of a crowd. With my simple Bostonian experiences as ground of comparison, I had been diffidently thinking that Mr. Gilmore's Jubilees possibly afforded some likeness to the appearance of the spectators at the Centennial; I am bound to say now that the Centennial at no time and in no place gave any such notion of multitudes. From day to day the crowd sensibly increased, but it never struck one as a crowd, and it hardly ever incommoded one, except perhaps in the narrow corridors of the Art Hall, and the like passages of the Annex to that building; these were at times really thronged. . . .

We had time that first day for hardly more than a glance at the different buildings. We went next to the Machinery Hall, through the far extent of which we walked, looking merely to the right and left as we passed down the great aisle. Of that first impression the majesty of the great Corliss engine, which drives the infinitely varied machinery, remains most distinct. After that is the sense of too many sewing-machines. The Corliss engine does not lend itself to description; its personal acquaintance must be sought by those who would understand its vast and almost silent grandeur. It rises loftily in the centre of the huge structure, an athlete of steel and iron with not a superfluous ounce of metal on it; the mighty walking-beams plunge their pistons downward, the enormous fly-wheel revolves with a hoarded power that makes all tremble, the hundred life-like details do their office with unerring intelligence. In the midst of this ineffably strong mechanism is a chair where the engineer sits reading his newspaper, as in a peaceful bower. Now and then he lays down his paper and clambers up one of the stairways that cover the framework, and touches some irritated spot on the giant's body with a drop of oil, and goes down again and takes up his newspaper; he is like some potent enchanter there, and this prodigious Afreet is his slave who could crush him past all semblance of humanity with his lightest touch. It is, alas! what the Afreet has done to humanity too often, where his strength has superseded men's industry; but of such things the Machinery Hall is no place to speak, and to be honest, one never thinks of such things here. One thinks only of the glorious triumphs of skill and invention; and wherever else the national bird is mute in one's breast, here he cannot fail to utter his pride and content. It would be a barren place without the American machinery. All that Great Britain and Germany have sent is insignificant in amount when compared with our own contributions; the superior elegance, aptness, and ingenuity of our machinery is observable at a glance. Yes, it is still in these things of iron and steel that the national genius most freely speaks; by and by the inspired marbles, the breathing canvases, the great literature; for the present America is voluble in the strong metals and their infinite uses. I have hinted already that I think she talks too much in sewing-machines, but I dare say that each of these patents has its reason for being, and that the world would go mostly unclad without it. At least I would not like to try to prove the contrary to any of those alert agents or quick young lady attendants. Nevertheless, a whole half-mile of sewing-machines seems a good deal; and *is* there so very much difference between them?

Our first general impressions of the different buildings were little changed by close acquaintance. What we found interesting in the beginning, that we found interesting at the end, and this is an advantage to those whose time is short at the Centennial. You know and see continually more and more, but it is in the line of your first enjoyment. This is peculiarly the case in the Main Building, where the contrasts are sharpest, and the better and worse most obvious. In the case of some of the nations (notably Russia, Turkey, and Spain) no judgment could be formed, for there was as yet nothing to look at, when we first came, in the spaces allotted to them. A few amiable young Spanish workmen loitered smiling about, but neither Turk nor Russ was visible. Before the end of the week the Muscovite had developed a single malachite table, but the Ottoman had still done nothing. But by this time the vigor of Spain was surprising: her space was littered with unpacking goods, and already many things were in place, though the display had not yet the order that could make it easily enjoyed. The people who had been most forward were the Norwegians, the Swedes, the Danes, the Egyptians; and to the last I found pleasure in this superior readiness of the departments. The Chinese, whom we found in disorder and unreadiness, pushed rapidly forward during our stay, and before we left, the rich grotesquery of their industries had satisfactorily unfolded itself. We were none the less satisfied that there should be still a half-score of their carpenters busy about the showcases; their looks, their motions, their speech, their dress, amidst the fantastic forms of those bedeviled arts of theirs, affected one like the things of a capricious dream. It would be interesting to know what they thought of us spectators. We saw but one Jap in his national costume: a small, lady-handed carpenter, who wrought with tools of eccentric uses upon one of the showcases, and now and then darted a disgusted look through his narrow eye-slits at the observer; he had his name neatly lettered on the back of his coat, and it is the fault of my ignorance that I cannot give it here. The other Japanese were in our modification of the English dress; they all had that gentlemanly air of incurious languor which we know in students of their nation at the Cambridge law-school, and that unease in our dress, which they had evidently but half subdued to their use. It is a great pity not to see them in their own outlandish gear, for picturesqueness' sake; the show loses vastly by it; and if it is true that the annoyances they suffered from the street crowds forced them to abandon it, we are all disgraced by the fact. It would have been better to give each Jap a squad of soldiers for his protection everywhere, than lose his costume from our fair for such a reason. There is a lamentable lack of foreignness in the dress at the Centennial. The costumed peoples have all put on European wear. To be sure, the still, sphinx-eyed young Egyptian whom we saw scorning our recentness from a remote antiquity in his department wore a fez, but a fez is very little; at the Hungarian wine-booth the waiters wore the superb Hungarian dress, but this seemed somehow in the way of trade, and I suspect their name was Schulze, they spoke German so well. One Turk we did indeed see, in most consoling bagginess of trousers, crimson jacket, and white stockings, but we liked quite as well the effect that so many Quaker bonnets on dear old Quaker ladies gave the crowd. One hears that you find nothing characteristically Quaker at Philadelphia, any more, and perhaps these ladies were from the country. At any rate they were frequently to be seen in their quaint bonnets and dresses of drab, often with quiet old gentlemen in boad-brims and shad-bellied coats, who would have been perfect if their cloth was drab instead of black, though one must still thank them for the cut of it.

We saw them not only at the Centennial, but also on the trains going to and from the lovely country-place in which our favored lines were cast during our sojourn. New England has so many other advantages that one may freely own she is but a barren stock in comparison with the fertile Pennsylvanian country. With us, even Nature is too conscientious to waste anything, and after our meagreness the frolic abundance of that landscape was not less than astonishing. The density of the foliage, the heavy succulent richness of the herbage, the look of solid comfort and content about the farms, spoke of both pleasure and profit in the country life; whereas our farmers seem (and with reason) to hate their thankless and grudging acres. There were great barns and substantial homesteads of brick and stone, kept with a scrupulous neatness; the pretty, tasteful stations were of stone, and all day long and all night long the incessant trains came and went upon that wonderful Pennsylvania Railroad, bearing the prosperity of the most prosperous commonwealth to and fro. From the passenger's point of view it is the best managed road in the country. I have heard Mr. Scott spoken of as a railroad despot, and I have felt it my duty to hate him. I now make him my apology—if it is he who has been able to teach all those amiable and efficient young men in charge of his trains to treat the public not only with civility but respect; to be polite, to be prompt, to call out intelligibly the name of the next station after that you have just left; to be cleanly uniformed, and to be a joy instead of an abomination to travel. I say from a conscience blameless of free passes that such a man has a right to enslave the public, and I wish that all the conductors and brakemen throughout the land might go and sit at the feet of his employees, and learn their kindness and quickness. Perhaps, however, they must all be Pennsylvanians to do this. Nothing at the Centennial strikes you more agreeably than the good manners of the public functionaries of every grade and service. They listen patiently and answer clearly (in that Philadelphian accent which has its charm), and one may accost them without the least fear of being snubbed out of countenance. They might not improve on acquaintance, but I came away friends with all the Philadelphians I saw in any sort of office. When one thinks of how many officials in other parts of the country he has (in imagination) lain in wait to destroy, this seems a good deal to say.

Our second day at the Centennial began in the Main Building, where after a glance at the not very satisfactory Italian department we found ourselves presently amid the delicate silver-work, the rich furs, the precious and useful metals, the artistic representations of national life of Norway. It was by far the completest department in the building, and for that little country, winter-bound in paralyzing cold and dark for so great a part of the year, the display of tasteful and industrial results was amazing.

The Viking race is not extinct, but the huge energies are refined and directed by the modern spirit to the production of things that may take the mighty West and the delicate South equally with surprise. The silver jewelry was as airily pretty and elegant in device and workmanship as the famous filigree of Genoa, which it so much resembled; and the iron-workers had indulged their stalwart poetry in an iron ship, fashioned like the old Viking craft, and all equipped with iron, at whose prow stood the effigy of Leif Ericsson:—

> "His helmet was of iron, and his gloves
> Of iron, and his breastplate and his greaves
> And tassets were of iron, and his shield;
> In his left hand he held an iron spear."

And his ship, with a touch of that sentiment painfully lacking in so many of the foreign departments, was called the Vinland. The show of furs and feathers, of luxurious wraps and quilts of eider-down, was surpassingly rich, and the mark of an artistic taste was observable in the preparation and arrangement of these, as in everything else. The most interesting things in this and the Swedish departments were, of course, the life-size figures illustrative of present costumes and usages, the work, I believe, of a distinguished Norwegian sculptor. It was like reading one of Björnson's charming stories, to look at these vividly characteristic groups, all of which were full of curious instruction. In one place an old peasant and his wife sit reading in a cottage room; in another a bereaved family surround the cradle of a dead child; here is a group of Laps; there some Swedish peas-ants stand over a stag which one of the hunters has shot; yonder are a Norwegian bride and groom in their wedding-gear, the bride wearing a crown and ornaments of barbaric gold,—which in this case were actual heirlooms descended from mother to daughter in one peasant family through three hundred years. All was for sale. "We will even separate husband and wife, and sell the bride away from the groom," laughingly explained the commissioner. The very pavilion itself, built of Norse pines, and ornamented in the forms of the old Norse architecture, was to be sold; yet there was nothing of the offensiveness of a mere mart in this, as there was in other departments, notably in the extremely sloppy show of the Austrians. The Norwegians had not merely contributed their wares, but had done us an honor and a pleasure by the thoroughly artistic character of their exhibition. So had the Swedes; so had in less degree the Danes, who showed some interesting figures illustrative of the Danish military service, actual and historic, and whose display of exquisite pottery, shaped and colored in the most delicate spirit of antique art, Greek and Egyptian, was certainly one of the most charming features of the fair. So had the Khedive of Egypt, whose section was in perfect order, and who has commanded, it is said, that nothing shall be returned to him and nothing shall be sold, but that all his contributions shall be appropriately given away in this country: despotic splendor that one could more admire if one did not know that the Khedive's march of improvement has been through the blood and tears of his subjects, and that his prosperity is in reality the pomp of a successful slave-driver. . . .

It was not possible, when we saw it, to judge the French department as a whole, and I ought not perhaps to speak of it at all, since so much of it was incompletely arranged. Yet, with all the richness and infinite variety of material the general effect was of shoppiness. The British show was in a more generous spirit, and it was far more interesting. It represented, of course, in English and colonial exhibits, a whole world of varied arts and industries, among which the æsthetic observer would be most taken with the contributions from the Indian empire, and with that wide and beautiful expression of the artistic feeling in household decoration in which England is now leading the world. We Americans could long ago show machinery whose ingenuity and perfection surpassed anything the insular brain had conceived, and now we show in the utilitarian application of the metals, as in tools, and the like, an easy equality, but we cannot yet approach the English in the subjection of material to the higher purposes of both use and pleasure. Their show of tiles, of brasses, of artistically wrought steel and iron, of pottery, of painted glass, was wonderful. We ought, however, to take credit where it is due; in artificial teeth and all the amiable apparatus of dentistry, nothing could approach us; and I must except from a sweeping confession of inferiority the style and workmanship of several large American displays of gas-fixtures: as the most gas-burning people in the world, we were here fitly first; and we were first too, I thought, in the working of silver. The shapes and ornamentations by the different great silver-working houses did justice to the nation which owns the Nevada mines; it proved our capacity for rising equal to an advantage. In glass, however, after the rich colors and manifold lovely forms of the foreign exhibits, we were cold and gray, and in all manufactured stuffs dull and uninteresting; we may have been honest, but we looked poor. I say nothing of our supremacy in a thousand merely ingenious applications and adaptations: that goes without saying; and I say nothing of the display of the publishing houses: books were the last things I cared to see at the Centennial. But I heard from persons less disdainful of literature that the show of book-making did us great honor.

The Main Building is provided with many fountains of the soda sort, and one large fountain for the unsophisticated element, all of which were pretty, and contributed to that brightness of effect which was so largely owing to the handsomeness of the show-cases and pavilions. The finest of these were American. We were thought to have sometimes dimmed the lustre of our jewels by the brilliancy of the casket, but the general display gained by this error. In the middle of the building a band played many hours every day, and over all, with his *bâton* and both arms extended, perpetually triumphed the familiar person of Mr. Gilmore, whom one fancied partially consoled for his lost Coliseums by the bigness of the edifice and the occasion, though, as I said before, the multitude was in nowise comparable to that of our Jubilees. The sparseness of the visitors was more apparent than real, as seen from the organ loft at the end of the building or from the galleries overlooking the central space, but it was worth while to suffer the illusory regret produced by this appearance in order to enjoy the magnificent *coup d' œil* which was to be gained only from those heights.

In the afternoon we made the tour of the State buildings, of which, generally speaking, it is hard to detect at once the beauty or occasion. Doubtless the use could be discovered by public or representative bodies from the various States. The most picturesque building is that of New Jersey; that of Massachusetts was comfortable and complete, which most of the others were not. The Michigan building promises to be handsome; the Ohio building has some meaning in being of Ohio stones, and it is substantially and gracefully designed; the West Virginia building is observable for its exterior display of native woods. But really the most interesting of these not apparently well-reasoned structures is the Mississippi house, which is wholly built of Mississippi woods, the rough bark logs showing without, and the gables and porch decked with gray streamers of Spanish mosses. A typical Mississippian, young in years but venerable in alligator-like calm, sits on this porch (or did sit on the afternoon of our visit), with his boots on the railing and his hat drawn down over his eyes and sheltering his slowly moving jaws as they ruminate the Virginian weed. He had probably been overquestioned, for he answered all queries without looking up or betraying the smallest curiosity as to the age, sex, or condition of the questioner. Being tormented (I will not name the sex of his tormentress), concerning the uses of a little hole or pouch (it was for letters, really) in the wall near the door, he said that it was to receive contributions for a poor orphan. "I," he added, "am the orphan"; and then at last he looked up, with a faint gleam in his lazy eye which instantly won the heart. This Mississippian was white; another, black, showed us civilly and intelligently through the house, which was very creditable every way to the State, and told us that it was built of seventy different kinds of Mississippi wood. We came away applauding the taste and sense shown in the only State building that seemed to have anything characteristic to say for itself. But in a country where for the most part every State is only more unrepresentative in its architecture than another, it is very difficult for the buildings to be representative. . . .

Massachusetts, through the poetic thoughtfulness of one of her women, had done far better in the erection of the Old Colony House of logs, which we found thronged by pleased and curious visitors. Without, it looks much like the log-cabins with which any dweller in the Middle West is familiar, but it is of three rooms instead of one; and within it aims at the accurate commemoration of Plymouth in its arrangement and furnishing. There are many actual relics of the Pilgrim days, all of which the crowd examined with the keenest interest; there was among other things the writing-desk of John Alden, and at the corner of the deep and wide fire-place sat Priscilla spinning—or some young lady in a quaint, old-fashioned dress, who served the same purpose. I thought nothing could be better than this, till a lovely old Quakeress, who had stood by, peering critically at the work through her glasses, asked the fair spinster to let her take the wheel. She sat down beside it, caught some strands of tow from the spindle, and with her long-unwonted fingers tried to splice the broken thread; but she got the thread entangled on the iron points of the card, and there was a breathless interval in which we all hung silent about her, fearing for her success. In another moment the thread was set free and spliced, the good old dame bowed herself to the work, and the wheel went round with a soft triumphant burr, while the crowd heaved a sigh of relief. That was altogether the prettiest thing I saw at the Centennial.

It was not till our third day that we went to the Woman's Pavilion. Those accustomed to think of women as the wives, mothers, and sisters of men will be puzzled to know why the ladies wished to separate their work from that of the rest of the human race, and those who imagine an antagonism between the sexes must regret, in the interest of what is called the cause of woman, that the Pavilion is so inadequately representative of her distinctive achievement. The show is chiefly saved to the visitor's respect by the carved wood-work done by ladies of the Cincinnati Art School. Even this, compared with great wood-carving, lacks richness of effect; it is rather the ornamentation of the surface of wood in the lowest relief; but it is very good of its kind, full of charming sentiment; it is well intentioned, and executed with signal delicacy and refined skill. It is a thing that one may be glad of as American art, and then, if one cares, as women's work, though there seems no more reason why it should be considered more characteristic of the sex than the less successful features of the exhibition. We did not test the cuisine of the School of Cooking attached to the Woman's Pavilion; the School of Second Work was apparently not yet in operation: if it had been a Man's Pavilion, I should have thought it the dustiest building on the grounds. It seems not yet the moment for the better half of our species to take their stand apart from the worse upon any distinct performance in art or industry; even when they have a building of their own, some organizing force to get their best work into it is lacking; many of those pictures and pincushions were no better than if men had made them; but some paintings by women in the Art Hall, where they belonged, suffered nothing by comparison with the work of their brothers. Woman's skill was better represented in the Machinery Hall than in her own Pavilion; there she was everywhere seen in the operation and superintendence of the most complicated mechanisms, and showed herself in the character of a worker of unsurpassed intelligence.

I sometimes fancied that the Agricultural Hall might reclaim the long-sojourning visitor rather oftener than any other building, if he were of a very patriotic mind. It seems the most exclusively American, and it is absorbingly interesting in traits of its display. There are almost as many attractive show-cases and pavilions as in the Main Building, and they are somehow seen to better advantage. Then there is obviously a freer expression of individual tastes and whims. It was delightful, for example, to walk down the long avenue of mowing and reaping machines, and see those imperfectly surviving forms of "dragons of the prime," resplendent in varnished fine woods and burnished steel, and reposing upon spaces of Brussels carpeting, attended by agents each more firmly zealous than another in the dissemination of advertisements and in the faith that his machine was the last triumph of invention. Their fond pride in their machines was admirable; you could not but sympathize with it, and on a morning after it had rained through the roof upon the carpet and shining metals of one reaper-man, who went about mopping and retouching in an amiable desolation, we partook almost insupportably of his despair. We railed bitterly at the culpable negligence of the management, and were not restored to our habitual mood of uncritical enjoyment till we came to our favorite case of sugar-cured hams: a glass case in which hung three or four hams richly canvased, not in the ordinary yellow linen, but in silk of crimson, white, and gold. These were of course from Cincinnati, and the same pork-packer had otherwise shown a humorous fancy in the management of material which does not lend itself readily to the plastic arts in their serious tempers.

The most artistic use of any material was undoubtedly made by some Louisville tobacco dealers, who had arranged the varieties and colors of their product with an eye to agreeable effect which I never saw surpassed in any Italian market, and who had added a final touch by showing different sorts of tobacco growing in pots. It would be interesting to know whether this most tasteful display was the work of an American. Vastly and more simply impressive was a wholly different exhibition from Iowa, to some of whose citizens the happy thought of showing the depth and quality of the soil in several counties of the State had occurred. Accordingly there it was in huge glass cylinders, in which it rose to a height of four, five and six feet—a boast of inexhaustible fertility which New England eyes could hardly credit. This was one of the inspirations which gave a shock of agreeable astonishment, and revived the beholder even after a day of sight-seeing.

There were fanciful and effective arrangements of farm implements; exhibitions of farm products both foreign and domestic; shows of the manufactured and raw material—literally without number. To remember one was to forget a thousand, and yet each was worthy to be seen. I remember the cotton from India with its satisfying Hindoo names; the pavilion of Brazilian cotton, and the whole array of Brazilian products; the pavilions of American wines and the bacchanal show of Rhine wines, where the vine in leaf and cluster wreathed pillar and cornice, and a little maid sat making more vine-leaves out of paper. The finest of the pavilions seemed to me that of an Oswego starch manufacturer, where an artistic use of the corn and its stalk had been made in the carved ornamention of the structure. But there were many and many cases and pavilions which were tasteful and original in high degree; and when one looked about on the work of preparation still going forward over the whole territory of the building,—as large, almost, as a German principality,—one felt that the tale was but half told.

A beneficent Sunday in our country retreat interrupted our sight-seeing: a Sunday of rural scenes and sounds, when the trains forbore to chuckle to and fro on the Pennsylvania Railroad in exultation at Pennsylvanian prosperity, and the rich landscape throbbed under the gathering heat. The meadow-lark sang everywhere; the redbird's voice was mellow in the dense woods; the masses of the dogwood blossoms whitened through all the heavy foliage. It was a land of blossoms and of waving grass, and a drive over the country roads in the afternoon, past thriving farms and thrifty villages, showed it a land of Sabbath-keeping best clothes, clean faces, neat hair, and domestic peace on innumerable front steps and porches, where children sat with their elders, and young girls feigned to read books while they waited for the young men who were to come later.

Monday was hot and abated our zeal for the Philadelphian spring by giving us a foretaste of what the Philadelphian summer must be. The sun fried the asphalt pavements of the Centennial grounds, and a burning heat reverberated from them, charged with the sickening odor of the cement. That was a day for the stone interior of the Art Hall, but to tell the truth we found none of the buildings so hot as we feared they would be. It was very tolerable indeed both in the Main Building and the Machinery Hall, and in the United States Building we should not have lost patience with the heat if it had not been for the luxurious indifference of that glass case full of frozen fishes there, which, as they reposed in their comfortable boxes of snow, with their thermometer at 30°, did certainly appeal to some of the most vindictive passions of our nature; and I say that during the hot months it will be cruelty to let them remain. There are persons who would go down from Massachusetts to join a mob in smashing that case on the 4th of July, and tearing those fish to pieces. There are also people of culture in this region who would sign a petition asking the government to change the language of the placard on the clothes of the Father of his Country, which now reads, "Coat, Vest, and Pants of George Washington," whereas it is his honored waistcoat which is meant, and his buckskin breeches: pantaloons were then unknown, and "pants" were undreamt-of by a generation which had time to be decent and comely in its speech. This placard is a real drawback to one's enjoyment of the clothes, which are so familiarly like, from pictures, that one is startled not to find Washington's face looking out of the coat-collar. The government had been well advised in putting on view these and other personal relics, like his camp-bed, his table furniture, his sword, his pistols, and so forth. There are also similar relics of other heroes, and in the satisfaction of thus drawing nearer to the past in the realization of those historic lives, one's passion for heroic wardrobes mounts so that it stays at nothing. In one of the cases were an ordinary frock-coat of black diagonal, and a silk hat such as is worn in our own epoch, objects which it is difficult to revere in actual life, but for which in their character of relics we severely summoned what veneration we could, while we searched our mind for association of them with some memorable statesman. We were mortified to think of no modern worthy thus to hand down a coat and hat to the admiration of posterity, and in another moment we should have asked whose they were, if we had not caught sight of a busy attendant, in his shirtsleeves and bare head, just in time to save us from this shame.

We passed on to the interesting exhibition of Indian costumes and architecture, and to those curiously instructive photographs and plaster models of the ancient and modern towns of the Moquis. These rehabilitate to the fancy the material aspect of the old Aztec civilization in a wonderful manner, and throw a vivid light upon whatever one has read of the race whose empire the Spaniards overthrew, but which still lingers, a feeble remnant, in the Pueblos of New Mexico. If the extermination of the red savages of the plains should take place soon enough to save this peaceful and industrious people whom they have harassed for hundreds of years, one could hardly regret the loss of any number of Apaches and Comanches. The red man, as he appears in effigy and in photograph in this collection, is a hideous demon, whose malign traits can hardly inspire any emotion softer than abhorrence. In blaming our Indian agents for malfeasance in office, perhaps we do not sufficiently account for the demoralizing influence of merely beholding those false and pitiless savage faces; moldy flour and corrupt beef must seem altogether too good for them.

I have to leave in despair all details of the government show of army and navy equipments, the varied ingenuity and beautiful murderousness of the weapons of all kinds, the torpedoes with which alone one could pass hours of satisfaction, fancifully attaching them to the ships of enemies and defending our coasts in the most effectual manner; the exquisite models of marine architecture; the figures of soldiers of all arms—not nearly so good as the Danish, but dearer, being our own. Every branch of the administrative service was illustrated, so far as it could be, and the bribes almost sprang from one's pocket at sight of the neat perfection with which the revenue department was represented. There was manufacture of Centennial stamped envelopes, which constantly drew a large crowd, and there were a thousand and one other things which every one must view with advantage to himself and with applause of the government for making this impressive display in the eyes of other nations.

After paying our duty to these objects, we took our first ride on the narrow-gauge railroad, of which the locomotive with its train of gay open cars coughs and writhes about the grounds in every direction, with a station at each of the great buildings. I believe this railroad has awakened loathing in some breasts, and that there has been talk of trying to have it abolished. But I venture to say this will never be done, and in fact I do not see how the public could get on without it. The fare is five cents for the whole tour or from any one point to another; the ride is luxuriously refreshing, and commands a hundred charming prospects. To be sure, the cars go too fast, but that saves time; and I am not certain that the flagmen at the crossings are sufficiently vigilant to avert the accidents whose possibility forms a greater objection to the railroad than mere taste can urge against it. As we whirled along, a gentleman next us on the transverse seat entered into an agreeable monologue, from which we learned, among many other things, that they had in the Agricultural Building the famous war-eagle, Old Abe, whom a Wisconsin regiment carried through the war; and the next morning we made haste to see him. We found him in charge of one of the sergeants who had borne him through thirty battles, and who had once been shot down with the eagle on his perch, and left for dead on the field. The sergeant was a slim young fellow, with gray eyes enough like the eagle's to make them brothers, and he softly turned his tobacco from one cheek to the other while he discoursed upon the bird—his honors from the State government of Wisconsin, which keeps him and a man to care for him at the public charge; his preference for a diet of live chicken; his objection to new acquaintance, which he had shown a few days before by plunging his beak into the cheek of a gentleman who had offered him some endearments. We could not see that Old Abe looked different from other bald eagles (which we had seen in pictures); he had a striking repose of manner, and his pale, fierce eye had that uninterested, remote regard said to characterize all sovereign personages. The sergeant tossed him up and down on his standard, and the eagle threw open his great vans; but otherwise he had no entertainment to offer except the record of his public service,—which we bought for fifty cents.

We were early on the ground that morning, and saw the Centennial in some aspects which I suppose the later visitor misses, when the crowd becomes too great for social ease. The young ladies in charge of pavilions or quiescent machinery, and the various young men in uniforms who superabounded at nine o'clock, gave the Machinery Hall the effect of a vast *conversazione*, amidst which no one could wander unconscious of a poetic charm. I am sure this was blamelessly pleasant, and if the Centennial did nothing but promote all that multitudinous acquaintance, it could not be considered other than a most enormous success. These happy young people neglected no duty to the public; there never was on this continent such civility and patience as that of the guards and policemen and officials of the Centennial, and the young ladies would leave a word half-breathed, half-heard, at the slightest demand of curiosity concerning anything they had in charge. In the midst, the Corliss engine set an example of unwearying application to business, and even while one gazed in fond approval, innumerable spindles began to whirr and shuttles to clack, and a thousand *tête-à-têtes* were broken up as by magic.

It was very pleasing to see the enthusiasm of inventors or agents concerning their wares, and the eagerness with which they met curiosity. I do not now speak so much of young ladies like her in charge of a perfumery stand in the Main Building, who would leave her company with both elbows on the counter and his chin in his hands, to spring away and atomize with odorous extracts any passer who showed signs of loitering near; rather I sing such geniuses as he of the Carriage Hall, who illustrated his cradle attachment to the parental bedstead, and his automaton baby-tender. From how much getting up at night, and how much weary care by day, these inventions had sprung, one could only conjecture; but I am sure that the most profound domestic experience inspired them. The inventor was never weary showing how, with his cradle hung by springs to your bedside, you had but to roll over and rock the most refractory baby to sleep, without losing your temper or your rest; how on simply inserting an infant into the aperture of his wheeled stool, the child walked about all day in perpetual content, a blessing to himself and his parents. The terms of confidence which he established with admiring mothers, the winks he gave, the nudges which I am sure he aspired to give, were all charming, and came from nothing less than a sense of having benefited the whole human race. Almost as serenely confident was the young lady who operated the Radiant Flat Iron in the Machinery Hall, an implement in whose hollow frame burnt a gas-flame blown hotter by a draft of air, the two elements being conveyed thither by India-rubber tubes from reservoirs under the ironing-table. "But what makes the pressure of the gas and air?" "Oh, you see I stand on a sort of bellows, which I work by resting from one foot to the other as one always does in ironing." The world is perhaps not yet prepared for the intricate virtues of the Radiant Flat Iron, but in the mean time we venerated its ingenuity. It is, doubtless, as promising of general usefulness as that beautiful ice-boat which our chair-boy hurried us away to see, and which seems peculiarly popular with the wheelers of chairs; they perhaps envy its capacity for getting over spaces at the rate of a mile a minute, though this need not be, as it is time they should rather desire to annihilate. They are an obliging race, and the chairs are a great help to the enjoyment of the Centennial. They are to be found in each of the principal buildings, and it is best to take them anew in each hall, instead of hiring one for a tour of the whole. If you do that, much time is lost, and in getting out to climb steps and cross broken spaces and railroad tracks, the occupant of the chair shares too actively in the enterprise. The chairs are mainly for ladies; very few men have the self-respect requisite for being publicly trundled about in that manner.

To any one who knows the different American types, the attendants and operatives in the Machinery and Agricultural Halls would afford curious study. The Western face distinguishes itself very easily from that of the Middle States, but in its eagerness is not so readily told from that of New England, which shows how largely New England has character-ized the appearance, while Pennsylvania has prevailed in the accent, of the younger States. Where New England came out with most startling evidence was in the visages of the Waltham watch-makers, who, whether pure Yankees or Yankeeized foreigners, had looks that no one could mistake. They were at work there all day with their life-like machinery, and on every side the thousand creations of American inventive genius were in operation, with an exhilaration and impressiveness in the whole effect which can in no wise be described. Of the huger machinery, the working of some pumps that drove their streams of water far over and across a great tank was the gayest and most strenuous sight. I should hardly know how to justify to the inexperienced the joy I knew in putting my hand over an air-blast, that flung it into the air like a leaf. Neverthe-less, such things are.

I have left the Carriage Hall to the last, though it was one of the first things we saw. I am not a connoisseur of wheeled vehicles, and I dare say I admired not too wisely. The American shapes seemed to me the most elegant; there was a queerness, a grotesqueness, an eccentricity, about the English, when they were not too heavy. But what most seizes the spectator is some one's ghastly fancy of a white hearse. It shows that a black hearse is not the most repulsive thing that can be. There are some exquisite specimens of car-architecture for a Brazilian railroad; a buggy from Indiana is kept—I do not know why—in a glass case; and there is a very resplendent Pullman car through which we walked, for no reason that I can give—probably the mere overmastering habit of sight-seeing. . . .

A very pleasant thing about the exhibition is your perfect freedom there. There are innumerable officials to direct you, to help you, to care for you, but none of them bothers you. If you will keep off those clay slopes and expanses which are placarded Grass, there will be no interfer-ence with any caprice of your personal liberty. This is the right American management of a public pleasure.

The muse at all minded to sing the humors of a great holiday affair could find endless inspiration at the Centennial; but there are space and the reader to be regarded. Yet I must not leave the theme without speaking of the gayety of the approaches and surroundings; the side shows are outside here, and the capacity for amusement which the Centennial fails to fill need not go hungering amid the provision made for it by private enterprise. It is curious to see the great new hotels of solid and flimsy construction near the grounds, and the strange city which has sprung up in answer to the necessities of the world's fair. From every front and top stream the innumerable flags, with which during a day in town we found all Philadelphia also decked. Yet it is an honest and well-behaved liveliness. There is no disorder of any sort; nowhere in or about the Centennial did I see any one who had overdrunk the health of his country.

Not the least prodigious of the outside appurtenances of the Centennial is that space allotted on a neighboring ground to the empty boxes and packing cases of the goods sent to the fair. Their multitude is truly astonishing, and they have a wild desolation amidst which I should think the gentlemen of the Centennial Commission, in case of a very disastrous failure of the enterprise, would find it convenient to come and rend their garments. But no one expects failure now. Every day of our week there saw an increase of visitors, and the reader of the newspapers knows how the concourse has grown since. The undertaking merits all possible prosperity, and whatever were the various minds in regard to celebrating the Centennial by an international fair, no one can now see the fair without a thrill of patriotic pride.

5. The First Century

Illustrations Depicting Ideas
of National Experience

1. *The Fall of Richmond, 1865.*

2. *Ruins on Canal Basin, Richmond, Virginia, April, 1865.*

3. *First Maine Cavalry Skirmishing (drawing).*

4. *Federal Dead, Gettysburg, July, 1863.*

5. *The Soldier's Memorial, 1863.*

6. *One More Shot, 1868.*

7. *Across the Continent.*

8. *American Progress, 1872.*

9. *Brooklyn Bridge, 1870.*

10. *The Stride of a Century, 1876.*

11. *The Centennial, Opening Ceremonies, 1876.*

12. *The Centennial, Agricultural Hall, 1876.*

13. *The Freedman's Bureau, 1868.*

14. *Firing Upon the Mob, 1877 Railroad Strike.*

PART TWO

THEMES AND FORMS IN POPULAR CULTURE

6. A View of Emancipated Negroes

Seven months after the bombardment of Fort Sumter, in November 1861, the United States Navy sailed into Port Royal Sound in the Sea Islands off the coast of South Carolina. Resistance was slight and the islands were occupied by federal troops almost immediately. The entire white population of planters and slave owners fled, leaving behind some ten thousand slaves. Within a few months a group of Northern antislavery young people arrived on a mission to help the liberated Negroes find their way to a new life. Before the end of the war several hundred Northerners were involved in what came to be recognized as a major social experiment, a "rehearsal for Reconstruction." Former slaves on the islands were recruited as the first Negro troops and served under the New Englanders Thomas Wentworth Higginson and Colonel Robert Gould Shaw. The first attempt at formal education of the freedman began here, as well as an experiment in distribution of lands and freehold farming.

The Port Royal experiment was the first concerted effort by antislavery Northerners to establish close ties with Southern Negroes, and the experience was an enlightening introduction to the problems of social life and culture created by slavery. William Channing Gannett, one of the young missionaries, perceived the significance of the Sea Island encounter in its demonstration that the stereotype of the Negro as shiftless and childlike derived entirely from the condition of slavery. In a careful, sober account of the effects of a year of freedom, he wrote in 1865 that the progress in education and self-government "gives the lie to the negro-owner," that the evidence shows that "only common contact with common circumstances is needed to produce with the black the same results as with the white man in America." The effect of independence was that "all stagnancy was broken up, and that a great and increasing momentum had been communicated to the impulse for improvement." Arguing that the treatment of the Negro will appear a hundred years hence as "the permanent result of the war," he insisted that the only method of bringing the former slaves into the main currents of American life is to remove all traces of slavery and racism. The lesson of the Port Royal experiment was that "the great work of the admission of the four million Negroes into our civil society" required that they be assured of the basic rights of religion, education, self-government and self-defense. "No training could be better adapted to stamp out the past, and to lay a solid foundation for the qualities and habits of their new character,—that of the free Southern laborer."

Charlotte Forten's account of her experiences as a teacher in the Sea Islands is far less political and theoretical than Gannett's, but it demonstrates her sensitivity to the way of life of the former slaves. A member of a Philadelphia Negro family prominent in Abolitionist circles, Miss Forten was educated in Philadelphia and in Salem, Massachusetts. Her cultivation was clearly a product of New England intellectual life; she wrote poetry, kept a diary (published in 1953), attended lectures, knew Whittier, Parker, Garrison, and Philips, and taught school. Twenty-five years old when the war broke out, she applied to join the project at Port Royal, and arrived in October, 1862. As an educated Negro woman, she was in a unique situation in the Sea Islands, and her articles in *Atlantic Monthly*, written in a casual impressionistic journal style, show her eye for customs and manners, as well as her gentle regard for the children under her care.

Life on the Sea Islands
CHARLOTTE FORTEN

[*To the Editor of the "Atlantic Monthly."*—The following graceful and picturesque description of the new condition of things on the Sea Islands of South Carolina, originally written for private perusal, seems to me worthy of a place in the "Atlantic." Its young author—herself akin to the long-suffering race whose Exodus she so pleasantly describes —is still engaged in her labor of love on St. Helena Island.—J. G. W.]

It was on the afternoon of a warm, murky day late in October that our steamer, the United States, touched the landing at Hilton Head. A motley assemblage had collected on the wharf,—officers, soldiers, and "contrabands" of every size and hue: black was, however, the prevailing color. The first view of Hilton Head is desolate enough,—a long, low, sandy

Charlotte Forten, "Life on the Sea Islands," *Atlantic Monthly*, XIII (1864), 587–596.

point, stretching out into the sea, with no visible dwellings upon it, except the rows of small white-roofed houses which have lately been built for the freed people.

After signing a paper wherein we declared ourselves loyal to the Government, and wherein, also, were set forth fearful penalties, should we ever be found guilty of treason, we were allowed to land, and immediately took General Saxton's boat, the Flora, for Beaufort. The General was on board, and we were presented to him. He is handsome, courteous, and affable, and looks—as he is—the gentleman and the soldier.

From Hilton Head to Beaufort the same long, low line of sandy coast, bordered by trees; formidable gunboats in the distance, and the gray ruins of an old fort, said to have been built by the Huguenots more than two hundred years ago. Arrived at Beaufort, we found that we had not yet reached our journey's end. While waiting for the boat which was to take us to our island of St. Helena, we had a little time to observe the ancient town. The houses in the main street, which fronts the "Bay," are large and handsome, built of wood, in the usual Southern style, with spacious piazzas, and surrounded by fine trees. We noticed in one yard a magnolia, as high as some of our largest shade-maples, with rich, dark, shining foliage. A large building which was once the Public Library is now a shelter for freed people from Fernandina. Did the Rebels know it, they would doubtless upturn their aristocratic noses, and exclaim in disgust, "To what base uses," etc. We confess that it was highly satisfactory to us to see how the tables are turned, now that "the whirligig of time has brought about its revenges." We saw the market-place, in which slaves were sometimes sold; but we were told that the buying and selling at auction was usually done in Charleston. The arsenal, a large stone structure, was guarded by cannon and sentinels. The houses in the smaller streets had, mostly, a dismantled look. We saw no one in the streets but soldiers and freed people. There were indications that already Northern improvements had reached this Southern town. Among them was a wharf, a convenience that one wonders how the Southerners could so long have existed without. The more we know of their mode of life, the more are we inclined to marvel at its utter shiftlessness.

Little colored children of every hue were playing about the streets, looking as merry and happy as children ought to look,—now that the evil shadow of Slavery no longer hangs over them. Some of the officers we met did not impress us favorably. They talked flippantly, and sneeringly of the negroes, whom they found we had come down to teach, using an epithet more offensive than gentlemanly. They assured us that there was great danger of Rebel attacks, that the yellow fever prevailed to an alarming extent, and that, indeed, the manufacture of coffins was the only business that was at all flourishing at present. Although by no means daunted by these alarming stories, we were glad when the announcement of our boat relieved us from their edifying conversation.

We rowed across to Ladies Island, which adjoins St. Helena, through the splendors of a grand Southern sunset. The gorgeous clouds of crimson and gold were reflected as in a mirror in the smooth, clear waters below. As we glided along, the rich tones of the negro boatmen broke upon the evening stillness,—sweet, strange, and solemn:—

> "Jesus make de blind to see,
> Jesus make de cripple walk,
> Jesus make de deaf to hear.
> Walk in, kind Jesus!
> No man can hender me."

It was nearly dark when we reached the island, and then we had a three-miles' drive through the lonely roads to the house of the superintendent. We thought how easy it would be for a band of guerrillas, had they chanced that way, to seize and hang us; but we were in that excited, jubilant state of mind which makes fear impossible, and sang "John Brown" with a will, as we drove through the pines and palmettos. Oh, it was good to sing that song in the very heart of Rebeldom! Harry, our driver, amused us much. He was surprised to find that we had not heard of him before. "Why, I thought eberybody at de Nort had heard o' me!" he said, very innocently. We learned afterward that Mrs. F., who made the tour of the islands last summer, had publicly mentioned Harry. Some one had told him of it, and he of course imagined that he had become quite famous. Notwithstanding this little touch of vanity, Harry is one of the best and smartest men on the island.

Gates occurred, it seemed to us, at every few yards' distance, made in the oddest fashion,—opening in the middle, like folding-doors, for the accommodation of horsemen. The little boy who accompanied us as gate-opener answered to the name of Cupid. Arrived at the headquarters of the general superintendent, Mr. S., we were kindly received by him and the ladies, and shown into a large parlor, where a cheerful wood-fire glowed in the grate. It had a home-like look; but still there was a sense of unreality about everything, and I felt that nothing less than a vigorous "shaking-up," such as Grandfather Smallweed daily experienced, would arouse me thoroughly to the fact that I was in South Carolina.

The next morning L. and I were awakened by the cheerful voices of men and women, children and chickens, in the yard below. We ran to the window, and looked out. Women in bright-colored handkerchiefs, some carrying pails on their heads, were crossing the yard, busy with their morning work; children were playing and tumbling around them. On every face there was a look of serenity and cheerfulness. My heart gave a great throb of happiness as I looked at them, and thought, "They are free! so long down-trodden, so long crushed to the earth, but now in their old homes, forever free!" And I thanked God that I had lived to see this day.

After breakfast Miss T. drove us to Oaklands, our future home. The road leading to the house was nearly choked with weeds. The house itself was in a dilapidated condition, and the yard and garden had a sadly neglected look. But there were roses in bloom; we plucked handfuls of feathery, fragrant acacia-blossoms; ivy crept along the ground and under the house. The freed people on the place seemed glad to see us. After talking with them, and giving some directions for cleaning the house, we drove to the school, in which I was to teach. It is kept in the Baptist Church,—a brick building, beautifully situated in a grove of live-oaks. These trees are the first objects that attract one's attention here: not that they are finer than our Northern oaks, but because of the singular gray moss with which every branch is heavily draped. This hanging moss grows on nearly all the trees, but on none so luxuriantly as on the live-oak. The pendants are often four or five feet long, very graceful and beautiful, but giving the trees a solemn, almost funereal look. The school was opened in September. Many of the children had, however, received instruction during the summer. It was evident that they had made very rapid improvement, and we noticed with pleasure how bright and eager to learn many of them seemed. They sang in rich, sweet tones, and with a peculiar swaying motion of the body, which made their singing the more effective. They sang "Marching Along," with great spirit, and then one of their own hymns, the air of which is beautiful and touching:—

> "My sister, you want to git religion,
>   Go down in de Lonesome Valley;
> My brudder, you want to git religion,
>   Go down in de Lonesome Valley.
>   *Chorus.*
> "Go down in de Lonesome Valley,
>   Go down in de Lonesome Valley, my Lord,
> Go down in de Lonesome Valley,
>   To meet my Jesus dere!

"Oh, feed on milk and honey,
Oh, feed on milk and honey, my Lord,
Oh, feed on milk and honey,
Meet my Jesus dere!

Oh, John he brought a letter,
Oh, John he brought a letter, my Lord,
Oh, Mary and Marta read 'em,
Meet my Jesus dere!
Chorus.
"Go down in de Lonesome Valley," etc.

They repeat their hymns several times, and while singing keep perfect time with their hands and feet.

On our way homeward we noticed that a few of the trees were beginning to turn, but we looked in vain for the glowing autumnal lines of our Northern forests. Some brilliant scarlet berries—the cassena—were growing along the roadside, and on every hand we saw the live-oak with its moss-drapery. The palmettos disappointed me; stiff and ungraceful, they have a bristling, defiant look, suggestive of Rebels starting up and defying everybody. The land is low and level,—not the slightest approach to a hill, not a rock, nor even a stone to be seen. It would have a desolate look, were it not for the trees, and the hanging moss and numberless vines which festoon them. These vines overrun the hedges, form graceful arches between the trees, encircle their trunks, and sometimes climb to the topmost branches. In February they begin to bloom, and then throughout the spring and summer we have a succession of beautiful flowers. First comes the yellow jessamine, with its perfect, gold-colored, and deliciously fragrant blossoms. It lights up the hedges, and completely canopies some of the trees. Of all the wild-flowers this seems to me the most beautiful and fragrant. Then we have the snow-white, but scentless Cherokee rose, with its lovely, shining leaves. Later in the season come the brilliant trumpet-flower, the passion-flower, and innumerable others.

The Sunday after our arrival we attended service at the Baptist Church. The people came in slowly; for they have no way of knowing the hour, except by the sun. By eleven they had all assembled, and the church was well filled. They were neatly dressed in their Sunday attire, the women mostly wearing clean, dark frocks, with white aprons and bright-colored head-handkerchiefs. Some had attained to the dignity of straw hats with gay feathers, but these were not nearly as becoming nor as picturesque as the handkerchiefs. The day was warm, and the windows were thrown open as if it were summer, although it was the second day of November.

It was very pleasant to listen to the beautiful hymns, and look from the crowd of dark, earnest faces within, upon the grove of noble oaks without. The people sang, "Roll, Jordan, roll," the grandest of all their hymns. There is a great, rolling wave of sound through it all.

"Mr. Fuller settin' on de Tree ob Life,
Fur to hear de ven Jordan roll.
Oh, roll, Jordan! roll, Jordan! roll, Jordan roll!
Chorus.
"Oh, roll, Jordan, roll! oh, roll, Jordan, roll!
My soul arise in heab'n, Lord,
Fur to hear de ven Jordan roll!

"Little chil'en, learn to fear de Lord,
And let your days be long.
Oh, roll, Jordan! roll, Jordan! roll, Jordan, roll!
Chorus.
"Oh, march, de angel, march! oh, march, de angel, march!
My soul arise in heab'n, Lord,
Fur to hear de ven Jordan roll!"

The "Mr. Fuller" referred to was their former minister, to whom they seem to have been much attached. He is a Southerner, but loyal, and is now, I believe, living in Baltimore. After the sermon the minister called upon one man of the elders, a gray-headed old man, to pray. His manner was very fervent and impressive, but his language was so broken that to our unaccustomed ears it was quite unintelligible. After the services the people gathered in groups outside, talking among themselves, and exchanging kindly greetings with the superintendents and teachers. In their bright handkerchiefs and white aprons they made a striking picture under the gray-mossed trees. We drove afterward a mile farther, to the Episcopal Church, in which the aristocracy of the island used to worship. It is a small white building, situated in a fine grove of live-oaks, at the junction of several roads. On one of the tombstones in the yard is the touching inscription in memory of two children,—"Blessed little lambs, and *art thou* gathered into the fold of the only true shepherd? Sweet *lillies* of the valley, and *art thou* removed to a more congenial soil?" The floor of the church is of stone, the pews of polished oak. It has an organ, which is not so entirely out of tune as are the pianos on the island. One of the ladies played, while the gentlemen sang,—old-fashioned New-England church-music, which it was pleasant to hear, but it did not thrill us as the singing of the people had done.

During the week we moved to Oaklands, our future home. The house was of one story, with a low-roofed piazza running the whole length. The interior had been thoroughly scrubbed and whitewashed; the exterior was guiltless of whitewash or paint. There were five rooms, all quite small, and several dark little entries, in one of which we found shelves lined with old medicine-bottles. These were a part of the possessions of the former owner, a Rebel physician, Dr. Sams by name. Some of them were still filled with his nostrums. Our furniture consisted of a bedstead, two bureaus, three small pine tables, and two chairs, one of which had a broken back. These were lent to us by the people. The masters, in their hasty flight from the islands, left nearly all their furniture; but much of it was destroyed or taken by the soldiers who came first, and what they left was removed by the people to their own houses. Certainly, they have the best right to it. We had made up our minds to dispense with all luxuries and even many conveniences; but it was rather distressing to have no fire, and nothing to eat. Mr. H. had already appropriated a room for the store which he was going to open for the benefit of the freed people, and was superintending the removal of his goods. So L. and I were left to our own resources. But Cupid the elder came to the rescue,— Cupid, who, we were told, was to be our right-hand man, and who very graciously informed us that he would take care of us; which he at once proceeded to do by bringing in some wood, and busying himself in making a fire in the open fire-place. While he is thus engaged, I will try to describe him. A small, wiry figure, stockingless, shoeless, out at the knees and elbows, and wearing the remnant of an old straw hat, which looked as if it might have done good service in scaring the crows from a cornfield. The face nearly black, very ugly, but with the shrewdest expression I ever saw, and the brightest, most humorous twinkle in the eyes. One glance at Cupid's face showed that he was not a person to be imposed upon, and that he was abundantly able to take care of himself, as well as of us. The chimney obstinately refused to draw, in spite of the original and very uncomplimentary epithets which Cupid heaped upon it,—while we stood by, listening to him in amusement, although nearly suffocated by the smoke. At last, perseverance conquered, and the fire began to burn cheerily. Then Amaretta, our cook,—a neat-looking black woman, adorned with the gayest of head-handkerchiefs,—made her appearance with some eggs and hominy, after partaking of which we proceeded to arrange our scanty furniture, which was soon done. In a few days we began to look civilized, having made a table-cover of some red and yellow handker-chiefs which we found among the store-goods,—a carpet of red and black woollen plaid, originally intended for frocks and shirts,—a cushion, stuffed with corn-husks and covered with calico, for a lounge, which Ben, the carpenter, had made for us of pine boards,—and lastly some corn-husk beds, which were an unspeakable luxury, after having endured agonies for several nights, sleeping on the slats of a bedstead. It is true, the said slats were covered with blankets, but these might as well have been sheets of paper for all the good they did us. What a resting-place it was! Compared to it, the gridiron of St. Lawrence—fire excepted—was as a bed of roses.

The first day at school was rather trying. Most of my children were very small, and consequently restless. Some were too young to learn the alphabet. These little ones were brought to school because the older children—in whose care their parents leave them while at work—could not come without them. We were therefore willing to have them come, although they seemed to have discovered the secret of perpetual motion, and tried one's patience sadly. But after some days of positive, though not severe treatment, order was brought out of chaos, and I found but little difficulty in managing and quieting the tiniest and most restless spirits. I never before saw children so eager to learn, although I had several years' experience in New-England schools. Coming to school is a constant delight and recreation to them. They come here as other children go to play. The older ones, during the summer, work in the fields from early morning until eleven or twelve o'clock, and then come into school, after their hard toil in the hot sun, as bright and as anxious to learn as ever.

Of course there are some stupid ones, but these are the minority. The majority learn with wonderful rapidity. Many of the grown people are desirous of learning to read. It is wonderful how a people who have been so long crushed to the earth, so imbruted as these have been,—and they are said to be among the most degraded negroes of the South,—can have so great a desire for knowledge, and such a capability for attaining it. One cannot believe that the haughty Anglo-Saxon race, after centuries of such an experience as these people have had, would be very much superior to them. And one's indignation increases against those who, North as well as South, taunt the colored race with inferiority while they themselves use every means in their power to crush and degrade them, denying them every right and privilege, closing against them every avenue of elevation and improvement. Were they, under such circumstances, intellectual and refined, they would certainly be vastly superior to any other race that ever existed.

After the lessons, we used to talk freely to the children, often giving them slight sketches of some of the great and good men. Before teaching them the "John Brown" song, which they learned to sing with great spirit,

Miss T. told them the story of the brave old man who had died for them. I told them about Toussaint, thinking it well they should know what one of their own color had done for his race. They listened attentively, and seemed to understand. We found it rather hard to keep their attention in school. It is not strange, as they have been so entirely unused to intellectual concentration. It is necessary to interest them every moment, in order to keep their thoughts from wandering. Teaching here is consequently far more fatiguing that at the North. In the church, we had of course but one room in which to hear all the children; and to make one's self heard, when there were often as many as a hundred and forty reciting at once, it was necessary to tax the lungs very severely.

My walk to school, of about a mile, was part of the way through a road lined with trees,—on one side stately pines, on the other noble live-oaks, hung with moss and canopied with vines. The ground was carpeted with brown, fragrant pine-leaves; and as I passed through in the morning, the woods were enlivened by the delicious songs of mocking-birds, which abound here, making one realize the truthful felicity of the description in "Evangeline,"—

> "The mocking-bird, wildest of singers,
> Shook from his little throat such floods of de-
> lirious music
> That the whole air and the woods and the
> waves seemed silent to listen."

The hedges were all aglow with the brilliant scarlet berries of the cassena, and on some of the oaks we observed the mistletoe, laden with its pure white, pearl-like berries. Out of the woods the roads are generally bad, and we found it hard work plodding through the deep sand.

Mr. H.'s store was usually crowded, and Cupid was his most valuable assistant. Gay handkerchiefs for turbans, pots and kettles, and molasses, were principally in demand, especially the last. It was necessary to keep the molasses-barrel in the yard, where Cupid presided over it, and harangued and scolded the eager, noisy crowd, collected around, to his heart's content; while up the road leading to the house came constant processions of men, women, and children, carrying on their heads cans, jugs, pitchers, and even bottles,—anything, indeed, that was capable of containing molasses. It is wonderful with what ease they carry all sorts of things on their heads,—heavy bundles of wood, hoes and rakes, everything, heavy or light, that can be carried in the hands; and I have seen a woman, with a bucketful of water on her head, stoop down and take up another in her hand, without spilling a drop from either.

We noticed that the people had much better taste in selecting materials for dresses than we had supposed. They do not generally like gaudy colors, but prefer neat, quiet patterns. They are, however, very fond of all kinds of jewelry. I once asked the children in school what their ears were for. "To put ring in," promptly replied one of the little girls.

These people are exceedingly polite in their manner towards each other, each new arrival bowing, scraping his feet, and shaking hands with the others, while there are constant greetings, such as "Huddy? How's yer lady?" ("How d' ye do? How's your wife?") The hand-shaking is performed with the greatest possible solemnity. There is never the faintest shadow of a smile on anybody's face during this performance. The children, too, are taught to be very polite to their elders, and it is the rarest thing to hear a disrespectful word from a child to his parent, or to any grown person. They have really what the New-Englanders call "beautiful manners."

We made daily visits to the "quarters," which were a few rods from the house. The negro-houses, on this as on most of the other plantations, were miserable little huts, with nothing comfortable or home-like about them, consisting generally of but two very small rooms,—the only way of lighting them, no matter what the state of the weather, being to leave the doors and windows open. The windows, of course, have no glass in them. In such a place, a father and mother with a large family of children are often obliged to live. It is almost impossible to teach them habits of neatness and order, when they are so crowded. We look forward anxiously to the day when better houses shall increase their comfort and pride of appearance.

Oaklands is a very small plantation. There were not more than eight or nine families living on it. Some of the people interested us much. Celia, one of the best, is a cripple. Her master, she told us, was too mean to give his slaves clothes enough to protect them, and her feet and legs were so badly frozen that they required amputation. She has a lovely face,—well-featured and singularly gentle. In every household where there was illness or trouble, Celia's kind, sympathizing face was the first to be seen, and her services were always the most acceptable.

Harry, the foreman on the plantation, a man of a good deal of natural intelligence, was most desirous of learning to read. He came in at night to be taught, and learned very rapidly. I never saw any one more determined to learn. We enjoyed hearing him talk about the "gun-shoot,"—so the people call the capture of Bay Point and Hilton Head. They never weary of telling you "how Massa run when he hear de fust gun."

"Why didn't you go with him, Harry?" I asked.

"Oh, Miss, 'twasn't 'cause Massa didn't try to 'suade me. He tell we dat de Yankees would shoot we, or would sell we to Cuba, an' do all de wust tings to we, when dey come. 'Bery well, Sar,' says I. 'If I go wid you, I be good as dead. If I stay here, I can't be no wust; so if I got to dead, I might's well dead here as anywhere. So I'll stay here an' wait for de "dam Yankees." ' Lor', Miss, I knowed he wasn't tellin' de truth all de time."

"But why didn't you believe him, Harry?"

"Dunno, Miss; somehow we hear de Yankees was our friends, an' dat we'd be free when dey come, an' 'pears like we believe *dat*."

I found this to be true of nearly all the people I talked with, and I thought it strange they should have had so much faith in the Northerners. Truly, for years past, they had had but little cause to think them very friendly. Cupid told us that his master was so daring as to come back, after he had fled from the island, at the risk of being taken prisoner by our soldiers; and that he ordered the people to get all the furniture together and take it to a plantation on the opposite side of the creek, and to stay on that side themselves. "So," said Cupid, "dey could jus' sweep us all up in a heap, an' put us in de boat. An' he telled me to take Patience —dat's my wife—an' de chil'en down to a certain pint, an' den I could come back, if I choose. Jus' as if I was gwine to be sich a goat!" added he, with a look and gesture of ineffable contempt. He and the rest of the people, instead of obeying their master, left the place and hid themselves in the woods; and when he came to look for them, not one of all his "faithful servants" was to be found. A few, principally house-servants, had previously been carried away.

In the evenings, the children frequently came in to sing and shout for us. These "shouts" are very strange,—in truth, almost indescribable. It is necessary to hear and see in order to have any clear idea of them. The children form a ring, and move around in a kind of shuffling dance, singing all the time. Four or five stand apart, and sing very energetically, clapping their hands, stamping their feet, and rocking their bodies to and fro. These are the musicians, to whose performance the shouters keep perfect time. The grown people on this plantation did not shout, but they do on some of the other plantations. It is very comical to see little children, not more than three or four years old, entering into the performance with all their might. But the shouting of the grown people is rather solemn and impressive than otherwise. We cannot determine whether it has a religious character or not. Some of the people tell us that it has, others that it has not. But as the shouts of the grown people are always in connection with their religious meetings, it is probable that they are the barbarous expression of religion, handed down to them from their African ancestors, and destined to pass away under the influence of Christian teachings. The people on this island have no songs. They sing only hymns, and most of these are sad. Prince, a large black boy from a neighboring plantation, was the principal shouter among the children. It seemed impossible for him to keep still for a moment. His performances were most amusing specimens of Ethiopian gymnastics. Amaretta the younger, a cunning, kittenish little creature of only six years old, had a remarkably sweet voice. Her favorite hymn, which we used to hear her singing to herself as she walked through the yard, is one of the oddest we have heard:—

> "What makes ole Satan follow me so?
> Satan got nuttin' 't all fur to do wid me.
> *Chorus.*
> "Tiddy Rosa, hold your light!
> Brudder Tony, hold your light!
> All de member, hold bright light
> On Canaan's shore!"

This is one of the most spirited shouting-tunes. "Tiddy" is their word for sister.

A very queer-looking old man came into the store one day. He was dressed in a complete suit of brilliant Brussels carpeting. Probably it had been taken from his master's house after the "gun-shoot"; but he looked so very dignified that we did not like to question him about it. The people called him Doctor Crofts,—which was, I believe, his master's name, his own being Scipio. He was very jubilant over the new state of things, and said to Mr. H.,—"Don't hab me feelins hurt now. Used to hab me feelins hurt all de time. But don't hab 'em hurt now no more." Poor old soul! We rejoiced with him that he and his brethren no longer had their "feelins" hurt, as in the old time.

On the Sunday before Thanksgiving, General Saxton's noble Proclamation was read at church. We could not listen to it without emotion. The people listened with the deepest attention, and seemed to understand and appreciate it. Whittier has said of it and its writer,—"It is the most beautiful and touching official document I ever read. God bless him! 'The bravest are the tenderest.'"

General Saxton is truly worthy of the gratitude and admiration with which the people regard him. His unfailing kindness and consideration for them—so different from the treatment they have sometimes received at the hands of other officers—have caused them to have unbounded confidence in General "*Saxby*," as they call him.

After the service, there were six couples married. Some of the dresses were unique. One was particularly fine,—doubtless a cast-off dress of the bride's former mistress. The silk and lace, ribbons, feathers and flowers, were in a rather faded and decayed condition. But, comical as the costumes were, we were not disposed to laugh at them. We were too glad to see the poor creatures trying to lead right and virtuous lives. The legal ceremony, which was formerly scarcely known among them, is now everywhere consecrated. The constant and earnest advice of the minister and teachers has not been given in vain; nearly every Sunday there are several couples married in church. Some of them are people who have grown old together.

Thanksgiving-Day was observed as a general holiday. According to General Saxton's orders, an ox had been killed on each plantation, that the people might that day have fresh meat, which was a great luxury to them, and, indeed, to all of us. In the morning, a large number—superintendents, teachers, and freed people—assembled in the Baptist Church. It was a sight not soon to be forgotten,—the crowd of eager, happy dark faces, from which the shadow of Slavery had forever passed. "Forever free! forever free!" those magical words of the Proclamation were constantly singing themselves in my soul. After an appropriate prayer and sermon by Mr. P., and singing by the people, General Saxton made a short, but spirited speech, urging the young men to enlist in the regiment then forming under Colonel Higginson. Mrs. Gage told the people how the slaves in Santa Cruz had secured their liberty. It was something entirely new and strange to them to hear a woman speak in public; but they listened with great attention, and seemed much interested. Before dispersing, they sang "Marching Along," which is an especial favorite with them. It was a very happy Thanksgiving-Day for all of us. The weather was delightful; oranges and figs were hanging on the trees; roses, oleanders, and japonicas were blooming out-of-doors; the sun was warm and bright; and over all shone gloriously the blessed light of Freedom,— Freedom forevermore! . . .

7. Nostalgia for the Old South

Although the notion of an established literary class is associated in most minds exclusively with New England, a separate tradition was developing in the antebellum South. Perhaps more ornate in its rhetoric, more prone to idealizations and romantic masquerades (Mark Twain went so far as to blame the Civil War on the popularity of Walter Scott in the South), Southern literature also included an important strain of vernacular humor based on regional peculiarities. The hold of the regional intensified after the Civil War, mixed with unmistakable nostalgia to be sure. In part the important contributions of Southern writers in the twentieth century, particularly William Faulkner, derive from the persistence of regional loyalties, an attachment, sometimes fierce and chauvinistic, to local history and manners.

George William Bagby's career was typical of the Southern literary class. Son of a Virginia merchant, he was schooled in the North, and was graduated from the University of Pennsylvania in 1849 with a degree in medicine. After his return to Lynchburg he soon gave up his practice to pursue the profession of literature. Beginning as a writer of humorous sketches for local papers, he became an editor of a Lynchburg paper in the 1850's, achieved some fame for his humorous "Letters of Mozis Addums to Billy Ivvins," contributed to Northern periodicals such as *Harper's* and *Atlantic*, and early in 1860, took over the editorship of the prestigious *Southern Literary Messenger*. He served for a brief spell in the Confederate Army until poor health forced him from the field. His patriotic defense of the Southern cause is typified by his popular poem, "The Empty Sleeve," in which he consoles a disfigured veteran: "The arm you lost was worth to me / Every Yankee that ever died."

Bagby left the *Messenger* in 1864, tried his hand at journalism in New York immediately after the war, but soon returned to Virginia and a new career as a lecturer on themes devoted to regional life, some delivered in dialect. These were quite popular in the defeated Old Dominion, and in 1868 he established and edited the *Native Virginian*. "The Old Virginia Gentleman" was one of his best known lectures. It evokes an idyllic country setting, a pre-industrial world based on family values, closeness to nature—and slave labor.

The Old Virginia Gentleman

GEORGE WILLIAM BAGBY

His house was not jammed down within two inches and a half of "the main, plain road." Why? He held, as his father did before him, that it was immodest to expose even his house to the public gaze. Perhaps he had that lack of curiosity, which, the newspaper men tell us, is characteristic of the savage—most of us, you know, are descended from Pocahontas—and, at all events, it would never do to have his headquarters on the very edge of a plantation of one thousand or two thousand acres. What was there to see on the main, plain road? Nothing. Morning and evening the boys dashed by on their colts, hurrying to or from the Academy, so-called. On Sundays, carry-alls, buggies, and wagons, filled with women-folk and children, in split-bottom chairs, wended their way to Mt. Zion, a mile or two farther on in the woods. Twice a week the stage rattled along, nobody inside, a negro in the boot, the driver and the negro-trader, both drunk, on top. Once a month the lawyers, in their stick-gigs or "single-chairs," and the farmers on their plantation mares, chatting and spitting amicably, with switches poised in up-and-downy elbows, jogged on to court. And that was all that was to be seen on the main, plain road, except the doctor and the deputy-sheriff, with their leggings and saddle-bags.

Tramps there were none, unless you call the county idiot who stalked barefoot through the winter snow, fanning himself industriously the while with a turkey-wing fan, a tramp. Once a year the peddler, with his pack, or the plausible oilcloth table-cloth man, put in an appearance; and that was literally all. Why, even the hares played in the middle of the lonesome road! And yet there was a life and animation along the country roads, especially about the country taverns, in the good old days (they *were* good) which we who remember them sadly miss in these times of rapid railroad transit.

A stranger would never dream that the narrow turning out of the main road, scarcely marked by a rut, led to a habitation better than a charcoal-burner's shed. But the drivers of the high-swung, bug-back family carriages of the period knew the turning "mighty well." So did many gentle-

Edwin Anderson Alderman and Joel Chandler Harris (eds.), *Library of Southern Literature* (Atlanta, 1907–1923), Vol. I, 151–162.

men, old and young, in all parts of the Commonwealth. "Oaklands," "Bellefield," "Mt. Airy," whatever it might be named, was the half-way house to "Cousin Tom's," "Uncle Randolph's," or "Grandpa's," twenty or thirty miles farther on. Also it was a convenient place to spend the night and mend the high-swung bug-back from Alpha to Omega when on your way to the White Sulphur, Richmond, or anywhere. Truth to tell, there was no getting around it; it drew like a magnet.

And whenever the road was adorned by a white-haired, florid-faced gentleman astride a blooded horse, with his body-servant in charge of his portmanteau following at respectful distance behind, that party, you may be very sure, turned off the main plain road and disappeared in the depths of the forest. Col. Tidewater had come half the length of the State to try a little more of Judge Piedmont's Madeira, to know what on earth induced Piedmont to influence the Governor in making that appointment, and to inquire if it were possible that Piedmont intended to bring out Jimson—of all human beings, Jimson—for Congress?

"Disappeared in the depths of the forest!" Yes. And why? Because there must be plenty of wood where is no end of negroes, and fifteen or twenty miles of worm-fencing to keep in repair. So there was a forest on this side and on that of the old Virginia gentleman's home; sometimes on all sides; and the more woodland the better. How is a man to get along without clearing new ground every year? The boys must have *some* place to hunt squirrels. Everybody is obliged to have wild indigo to keep flies off his horse's head in summer. If you have no timber, what becomes of your hogs when you turn them out? How about fuel? Where is your plank to come from, and your logs for new cabins and tobacco barns? Are you going to *buy* poles for this, that and the other? There's no use talking— negroes can't be healthy without wood, nor enjoy life without pine-knots when they go fishing at night.

Pleasant it was to trot through these forests on a hot summer day, or any other day, knowing what was to come at your journey's end. Pleasant, too, to bowl along under the arching boughs, albeit the ruts were terrible in places, and there were two or three immemorial holes, made by the butts of saw-logs (you could swear that the great mark in the centre of the road was the tail-trace of an Iguanodon, or some other Greek beast of prehistoric times)—two or three old holes, that made every vehicle, but chiefly the bug-back carriage, lurch and careen worse than a ship in a heavy sea.

But these were useful holes. They educated the young negro driver, and compelled the old one to keep his wrinkled, mealy hand in. They toned, or rather tuned up, the nerves of the young ladies, and gave them an excuse for uttering the prettiest shrieks; whereat the long-legged cousin, leaning to the left at an angle of ninety degrees, with his abominable red head forever inside the carriage window, would display his horsemanship in the most nimble, over-affectionate, and unpleasing manner—unpleasing to the young gentleman from the city, who was not a cousin, did not want to be a cousin, wasn't a bit proud of riding, but had "some sense of decency, and really a very high regard for the sensibilities of the most refined ladies in the whole State of Virginia, Sir!" Many were the short but fervent prayers ejaculated by the old ladies in consequence of these same holes, which came to be provocative of late piety, and on that account were never molested; and they were prized beyond measure by the freckle-face ten-year-old brother, who, standing up behind and hanging back by the carriage-straps, yelled with delight every time the bug-back went "way down," and wished from the bottom of his horrid boy's heart that "the blamed old thing would bust all to flinders and plump the whole caboodle smack into the middle of the mud puddle."

Col. Tidewater declared that Piedmont's forest road was the worst in the world, and enough to bring in jeopardy soul as well as body; to which Piedmont hotly replied that a five-mile stretch in August through the sand in Tidewater's county was eternity in Hades itself.

The forest once passed, a scene not of enchantment, though contrast often made it seem so, but of exceeding beauty, met the eye. Wide, very wide fields of waving corn, billowy seas of green or gold, as the season chanced to be, over which the scudding shadows chased and played, gladdened the heart with wealth far spread. Upon lowlands level as a floor, the plumed and tasseled corn stood tall and dense, rank behind rank in military alignment—a serried army, lush and strong. The rich, dark soil of the gently swelling knolls could scarcely be seen under the broad, lapping leaves of the mottled tobacco. The hills were carpeted with clover. Beneath the tree-clumps, fat cattle chewed the cud or peaceful sheep reposed, grateful for the shade. In the midst of this plenty, half-hidden in foliage over which the graceful shafts of the Lombardy poplar towered, with its bounteous garden and its orchards heavy with fruit near at hand, peered the old mansion, white or dusty-red or mellow-gray by the storm and shine of years.

Seen by the tired horseman, halting at the woodland's edge, this picture, steeped in the intense, quivering summer noonlight, filled the soul with unspeakable emotions of beauty, tenderness, peace, *home*.

—How calm could we rest
In that bosom of shade, with the friends we love best!

Sorrow and cares were there—where do they not penetrate? but oh! dear God, one day in these tranquil homes outweighed a fevered lifetime in the gayest cities of the globe. Tell me nothing; I undervalue naught that man's heart delights in; I dearly love operas and great pageants; but I do know—as I know nothing else—that the first years of human life, and the last, yea, if it be possible, all the years, should be passed in the country. The towns may do for a day, a week, a month at most; but Nature, Mother Nature, pure and clean, is for all time; yes, for eternity itself. What think you of heaven? It is a narrow street, packed full of houses, with a theatre at one end and a beer saloon at the other? Nay! the city of God is under the trees and beside the living waters.

These homes of Virginia are ruins now; not like the ivied walls and towers of European lands, but ruins none the less. The houses, indeed, are still there, little changed, it may be, as to the outside; but the light, the life, the charm are gone for ever. "The soul is fled."

About these Virginia homes there was much that was unlike the houses I have seen in the more populous states of the North and in Canada. A Southerner traveling through Central Pennsylvania and Western New York to the falls of Niagara, and thence down the St. Lawrence, is painfully impressed by the scarcity—the absence, one might say,—of human beings around the houses and in the fields. There are no children playing in the cramped-up yards. The few laborers in the narrow fields make but a pitiful show, even at harvest time. The farms have a deserted look, that is most distressing to one accustomed to the sights and sounds of Virginia country life. For thirty miles below Quebec I watched the houses that thickly line the verdant river banks, but saw no human being—not one. The men were at work in the villages, the women were at the wash-tubs or in the kitchens; and as for the children, I know not where they were.

How unlike Virginia of the olden time! There, people were astir, and something was always going on. The young master, with his troop of little darkies, was everywhere—in the yard, playing horses; in the fields, hunting larks or partridges; in the orchards, hunting for birds' nests; at the barn, sliding down the straw stacks; in the woods, twisting or smoking hares out of hollow trees; in the "branch," fishing or bathing (we call it "washing" in Virginia); in the patch, plugging half-ripe watermelons; or elsewhere, in some fun or mischief. "Young Mistiss," in her sun-bonnet, had her retinue of sable attendants, who, bare-armed and bare-footed, accompanied her in her rambles through the garden, the open woodland near the house, and sometimes as far as the big gate. By the way, whenever you heard the big gate slam, you might know that "comp'ny" was coming. And comp'ny was always coming—beaux to see the grown-up girls, neighbors, friends, strangers, kinsfolk—no end of them. Then some comely negro woman, with bright kerchief on her head, was ever passing to and fro, on business with her mistress; few days passed that did not witness the "drop-shot gang" of small Ethiops sweeping up the fallen leaves that disfigured the broad yard.

Some one was always coming or going. The gig, the double buggy, the carryall, the carriage, were in constant use. Horses, two or a dozen, were seldom wanting at the rack, and the boy of the family was sure to be on the horse-block, begging permission to "ride behind," or to carry the horse to the stable. Bringing in breakfast, dinner, and supper, and carrying the things back to the kitchen, kept three or four servants busy from dawn till long after dark. The mistress had a large provision store at the smoke-house, where there was much to do every day except Sunday. So, too, with the dairy. From the rooms set apart for weaving and spinning came the tireless droning of wheels and the clatter of looms—wonderful machines, that delighted the knots of white and black children gathered at the open doorways. How gracefully Aunt Sooky stepped back and forth with her thread, as it kept growing and lengthening on the spindle! Why, I can smell the wool-rolls now, and see the brooches, and the shucks on which they were wound!

These were the scenes and occupations that gave life to the house. In the fields, from the time that the gangs of ploughers (we never called them ploughmen), moving steadily *en echelon,* turned up the rich sod, until the wheat was shocked, the corn laid by, the tobacco planted, suckered, primed, topped, cut, and hung in the golden sunshine to cure, there was something perpetually afoot to enliven the plantation. But who shall tell of harvest-time, when the field fairly swarmed with cutters, the binders, the shockers, the gleaners, all agog with excitement and joy? A murrain on your modern reapers and mowers! What care I if Cyrus McCormick *was* born in Rockbridge County? These new-fangled "contraptions" are to the old system what the little, dirty, black steam-tug is to the three-decker, with its cloud of snowy canvas towering to the skies— the grandest and most beautiful sight in the world. I wouldn't give Uncle Isham's picked man, "long Billy Carter," leading the field, with one good drink of whiskey in him—I wouldn't give one swing of his cradle and one "ketch" of his straw for all the mowers and reapers in creation.

But what was the harvest-field compared with threshing-time at the barn? Great goodness alive! Do you all remember that huge cog-wheel aloft, and the little cog-wheels, that big post that turned 'round, the thick shafts,—two horses to a shaft; eight or ten horses to a machine—(none of your one-horse, out-o'-door concerns—this was under a large shed, close to the barn), and how we sat on those shafts, and how we drove those horses, and hollered at 'em, and how the dust flew, and what a glorious, glorious racket, hubbub and confusion there was? Surely you do.

Then came beating-cider time. Bless me! how sick "us boys" used to get from drinking sweet cider and eating apple "pommels!" You recollect the cider press? None of your fish-traps, cut in two, and set on end, with an iron crank, but a good, honest beam, a foot and a half thick, and fifteen to twenty feet long, jobbed into a hole cut clean through a stout oak tree, with a wooden trough holding half a ton of rocks, and an affair with holes and pegs, to regulate the prizing. Now that was a press, a real press— not a gimcrack. Don't ask me about corn-shuckings. It would take a separate lecture to describe them; besides, you already know more about them than I can tell you.

If the house, the barn, the fields were alive, so also were the woods. There the axe was ever plying. Timber to cut for cabins (the negroes increased so fast), for tobacco houses, and for fuel, new ground to clear, etc., etc. The crack of the gun was heard continually—the boys were shooting squirrels for Brunswick stew—and when the wild pigeons came there was an endless fusilade. As for sports, besides squirrels, 'coons and 'possums, there were partridges, robins, larks, and even kildees and bull-bats for shooting; but far above all these, was the *fox-hunt!* Ah! who can ever forget it? When the chase swept through the forest and across the hills, the hounds and the beagles in full, eager, piercing, passionate cry, making music for the very gods and driving the huntsmen stark mad. What were staked and ridered fences, tangled underwood, gullies, ditches, banks that were almost precipices, what was life, what was death to the young fellow just out of college, that glorious music ringing in his ears, his horse, a thing all fire and steel, going under him like a thunderbolt, and the fox not five hundred yards away? Tell me Southern country life was monotonous! Bah!

Why, something or somebody was forever stirring. In the dead of night, hours before day-break, some old negro was eternally getting up to chunk his fire, or to cut another stick or two. In the dead of winter, the wagons were busy hauling wood, to keep up the grand old fires in the big old fire-places. And at the worst, the boys could always jump a hare out of a briar-patch, and *then* such "hollering," such whistling, such whooping, such calling of dogs:—"here, here, here! who-eet! whoop! here!" as if Bedlam had broke loose.

Of church-going on Sunday, when the girls kept the carriage waiting;

of warrant-tryings, vendues, election and general muster days, of parties of all kinds, from candy-stews and "infairs" up to the regular country balls at the county-seat, of fun at negro weddings, of fish-fries, barbecues, sailing-parties, sora and duck-shooting, rides and drives—the delights of Tidewater life—of dinings in and dinings out, of the Bishop's visit, of company come for all day in addition to the company regularly domiciled for the week, month or half-year, I need not speak at length. Country life in Virginia tiresome! You are crazy!

The habitation of the old Virginia gentleman—house is too short a word to express it—always large enough, however small it might be, was sometimes stately, like the great, square house of "Rosewell," and others I might name. As a rule, to which, indeed, there were many exceptions, it was neither planned nor built—it grew: and that was its great charm. To be sure, the main structure or body of it had been put up with an eye not to convenience but to elbow-room and breathing space—without which no Virginian can live. But in course of time, as the children came along, as the family connexions increased, and as the desire, the necessity in fact, of keeping a free hotel grew upon him, the old gentleman kept adding a wing here and tacking a shed room there until the original building became mixed up, and, as it were, lost in the crowd of additions. In cold weather the old house was often miserably uncomfortable, but at all other times it was simply glorious. There was, of course, a large hall or passage, a parlor and dining-room, "the chamber" proper for the old lady and for everybody, and a fine old-time staircase leading to the guest-chamber, but the rest of the house ran mostly into nondescript apartments, access to which was not always easy. For the floors were on different levels, as they ought to be in an old country-house. Fail to step up or down at the proper time, and you were sure to bump your head or bruise your shins. Then there were dark closets, cuddies, and big old chests that came mayhap from England, say nothing of the garret, full of mystery, that stretched the whole length of the house. Here was romance for childhood—plenty of it. These irregular rooms, two steps up and three down before you got fairly into them, teemed with poetry; but your modern houses, with square rooms all on a dead level, are prosaic as dry-goods boxes.

A fine old house it was to play hide-and-seek in, to romp with the girls, to cut all sorts of capers without disturbing the old folks. Then these dark passages, these cuddies and closets, that big garret, never failed to harbor some good-natured old hip-shot fool of a family ghost, who was everlastingly "projicking" around at night after the girls had quit their talk, making the floors crack, the doors creak, and whispering his nonsense through the keyhole, as if he could scare you or anybody else! To modernize the old Virginia house would kill that ghost, and if it be a crime to kill a live man, what an enormity it must be to kill one who has been dead a hundred years, who never harmed a living soul, and who, I suspect, was more fretted than sorry when the young ones would persist in hiding their heads under the bed-clothes for fear of him? "You little geese! it's nobody but me," and "whish, whish, whish," he would go on with his idiotic whispering.

The heavy, dark furniture; the huge sideboard; the quaint solid chairs; the more common article, with spraddled legs, scooped seats and stick backs; the diamond-paned book-case; the long horse-hair sofas, with round tasseled pillows, hard as logs of ebony, with nooks to hide them in; the graceful candle-stand; the gilt mirror, with its three compartments; the carved mantel, so high you could hardly reach the silver candlesticks on its narrow top; the bureaux, with swinging brass handles; the dressing tables; the high-post bedstead, with valance and tester; the—

But stay! it suddenly and painfully occurs to me—there are grown-up men and women in this room, actually here, immortal beings, who never laid eyes on a bed-wrench and pin, and who do not so much as know the meaning of cording a bed! Think of it! Yet these people live on. Ah me! the fashion of this world passeth away!

The massive dinner table, never big enough to hold all the dishes, some of which had to go on the hearth to be kept warm; the old-time silver, the heavy cut glassware, the glass pitchers for thick, rich milk—how it foamed, when they "poured it high!" The Canton china, thin as thin biscuit; the plainer blue dinner set for every day use, with the big apples on the little trees, the blue islands in a white sea, the man or woman that was always going over that short bridge, but stopped and stood provokingly in the middle—how they all come back to you! But I "lay" you have forgotten the band-boxes. Think of that again! Band-boxes have fled away from the face of this earth, but not to heaven; for they were much uglier than any sin I'm acquainted with. I recall the very pattern of them —the red brick houses, with many windows, the clumsy trees, and that odd something, more like a pile of rocks than an elephant, but spouting clods of water, like an elephant who had got drunk on mud.

When you were a boy, did you sleep in a low-pitched, dormer-windowed room, with two little gable windows that looked out upon a narrow-necked chimney, just where the neck ended and the shoulder began? You didn't? Then I pity you; you must have had a mighty poor sort of boyhood. Why, I can see the moss growing on that chimney, can see how very thick the old thing is at the bottom, and, by George! there is the identical old toad (frog, we called him) that pops out every night from the slit in the wall at the side of the chimney. How well he looks! Hasn't changed a hair in forty years! Come! Let's "ketch" some lightning-bugs and feed him, right now!

Surely, you haven't forgotten the rainy days at the old country house? How the drops kept dropping, dropping from the eaves, and popping, popping up from the little trough worn into the earth below the eaves; how draggled and miserable the rooster looked, as you watched him from your seat in the deep window-sill; and how (tired of playing in-doors) you wondered if it would never, never stop raining. How you wandered from room to room, all over the house, upstairs and downstairs, eating cakes and apples, or buttered bread and raspberry jam; how at last you settled down in the old lady's chamber and held a hank till your arms ached, and you longed for bed-time to come. If you have never known such days, never seen the reel the hanks were placed on, nor the flax-wheels that clacked when the time came to stop winding, then you have neither seen nor known anything. You don't know how to "skin the cat," or to play "Ant'ny over"; you don't know how to drop a live coal in a little puddle of water, and explode it with an axe; you "don't know nothin',"— you have never been a Virginia boy.

Yes, your arms arched, poor little fellow, pining for out-door fun; they were sure to ache if you held the hank for Miss Mehaly Sidebottom, the poor lady who had lived in the family time out o' mind; but if you held it for a pretty girl—and what Virginia gentleman's house was without one—two—three—half a dozen of them?—then your arms didn't give out half so soon, and you didn't know what it was to get hungry or sleepy. When you grew older, a rainy day in the country was worth untold money, for then you had the pretty girl all to yourself the livelong day in the drawing room. What music the rain made on the roof at night, and how you wished the long season in May would set in, raise all the creeks past fording, wash away all the bridges, and keep you there for ever.

And such girls! They were of a piece with the dear old house; they belonged to it of right, and it would not, and it could not have been what it was without them. Finer women, physically, I may have seen, with much more bone, a deal more of muscle and redder cheeks; but more grace, more elegance, more refinement, more guileless purity, were never found the whole world over, in any age, not even that of the halcyon. There was about these country girls—I mean no disparagement of their city sisters, for all Virginia girls were city girls in winter and country girls in summer, so happy was our peculiar social system—there was about these country girls I know not what of sauce—the word is a little too strong—of mischief, of spirit, of fire, of archness, coquetry, and bright winsomeness—tendrils these of a stock that was strong and true as heart could wish or Nature frame; for in essentials their character was based upon a confiding, trusting, loving, unselfish devotion—a complete, immaculate world of womanly virtue and home piety was theirs, the like of which, I boldly claim, was seldom approached, and never excelled, since the Almighty made man in His own image.

8. Housekeeping for Ladies

Like her brother, Harriet Stowe was a representative figure in American culture, a reflector as much as a formulator of changing values. A product of the intellectual life of New England, daughter of a militant evangelist who upheld orthodoxy, Mrs. Stowe embodied the transition in the middle of the nineteenth century to a religion of love and moral uplift. In her literary work, moral fervor and benevolence appears as keynotes of popular culture. In addition to her most famous novel, the work which made her a virtual symbol of Northern repugnance for slavery, *Uncle Tom's Cabin* (1852), Mrs. Stowe produced a number of works dealing with New England village life—the delineation of regional manners and character. Such works as *The Minister's Wooing* (1859), *The Pearl of Orr's Island* (1862), *Oldtown Folks* (1869) and *Poganuc People* (1878) convey lovingly the homely details of a passing culture. Much of the importance of these works lies in their introduction of "the commonplace" into literature, along with a benevolent regard for "the common man." In *Oldtown Folks* she writes: "It has always been a favorite idea of mine, that there is so much of the human in every man, that the life of any one individual, however obscure, if really and vividly perceived in all its aspirations, struggles, failures, and successes, would command the interest of all others."

Mrs. Stowe's regionalist fiction after the war celebrated old-fashioned virtues, particularly domestic virtues centered in the figure of the wife and mother. In a number of little essays, collected as *Chimney Corner Papers* and *House and Home Papers*, she attempted to reassert the value of a traditional New England femininity in changed social circumstances. Domesticity took on the guise of a moral force. "There has been a slow and gradual reaction against household labor," she wrote. But the figure of the resourceful and devoted little woman—a true "lady"—wore the aspect of salvation. "The women of America can, if they choose, hold back their country from following in the wake of an old, corrupt, worn-out, effeminate European society, and make America the leader of the world in all that is good." Arguing for simplicity and absence of ostentation, for the virtue of work, the *House and Home Papers*, while hardly her most important contributions to letters, does demonstrate an effort to maintain a link with tradition in a society fast entering a mechanized age.

The Lady Who Does Her Own Work

HARRIET BEECHER STOWE

"My dear Chris," said my wife, "isn't it time to be writing the next 'House and Home Paper'?"

I was lying back in my study-chair, with my heels luxuriously propped on an ottoman, reading for the two-hundredth time Hawthorne's "Mosses from an Old Manse," or his "Twice-Told Tales," I forget which,—I only know that these books constitute my cloud-land, where I love to sail away in dreamy quietude, forgetting the war, the price of coal and flour, the rates of exchange, and the rise and fall of gold. What do all these things matter, as seen from those enchanted gardens in Padua where the weird Rappaccini tends his enchanted plants, and his gorgeous daughter fills us with the light and magic of her presence, and saddens us with the shadowy allegoric mystery of her preternatural destiny? But my wife represents the positive force of time, place, and number in our family, and, having also a chronological head, she knows the day of the month, and therefore gently reminded me that by inevitable dates the time drew near for preparing my—which is it now, May or June number?

"Well, my dear, you are right," I said, as by an exertion I came head-uppermost, and laid down the fascinating volume. "Let me see, what was I to write about?"

"Why, you remember you were to answer that letter from the lady who does her own work."

"Enough!" said I, seizing the pen with alacrity; "you have hit the exact phrase:—

" 'The *lady* who *does her own work.*' "

America is the only country where such a title is possible,—the only country where there is a class of women who may be described as *ladies* who do their own work. By a lady we mean a woman of education, cultivation, and refinement, of liberal tastes and ideas, who, without any very material additions or changes, would be recognized as a lady in any circle of the Old World or the New.

What I have said is, that the existence of such a class is a fact peculiar

Harriet Beecher Stowe, *House and Home Papers* (Boston, 1872), 125–147.

to American society, a clear, plain result of the new principles involved in the doctrine of unversal equality.

When the colonists first came to this country, of however mixed ingredients their ranks might have been composed, and however imbued with the spirit of feudal and aristocratic ideas, the discipline of the wilderness soon brought them to a democratic level; the gentleman felled the wood for his log-cabin side by side with the ploughman, and thews and sinews rose in the market. "A man was deemed honorable in proportion as he lifted his hand upon the high trees of the forest." So in the interior domestic circle. Mistress and maid, living in a log-cabin together, became companions, and sometimes the maid, as the more accomplished and stronger, took precedence of the mistress. It became natural and unavoidable that children should begin to work as early as they were capable of it. The result was a generation of intelligent people brought up to labor from necessity, but turning on the problem of labor the acuteness of a disciplined brain. The mistress, outdone in sinews and muscles by her maid, kept her superiority by skill and contrivance. If she could not lift a pail of water, she could invent methods which made lifting the pail unnecessary,—if she could not take a hundred steps without weariness, she could make twenty answer the purpose of a hundred.

Slavery, it is true, was to some extent introduced into New England, but it never suited the genius of the people, never struck deep root, or spread so as to choke the good seed of self-helpfulness. Many were opposed to it from conscientious principle,—many from far-sighted thrift, and from a love of thoroughness and well-doing which despised the rude, unskilled work of barbarians. People, having once felt the thorough neatness and beauty of execution which came of free, educated, and thoughtful labor, could not tolerate the clumsiness of slavery. Thus it came to pass that for many years the rural population of New England, as a general rule, did their own work, both out doors and in. If there were a black man or black woman or bound girl, they were emphatically only the *helps*, following humbly the steps of master and mistress, and used by them as instruments of lightening certain portions of their toil. The master and mistress with their children were the head workers.

Great merriment has been excited in the Old Country, because years ago the first English travellers found that the class of persons by them denominated servants were in America denominated *help* or helpers. But the term was the very best exponent of the state of society. There were few servants, in the European sense of the word; there was a society of educated workers, where all were practically equal, and where, if there was a deficiency in one family and an excess in another, a *helper*, not a servant, was hired. Mrs. Browne, who has six sons and no daughters, enters into agreement with Mrs. Jones, who has six daughters and no sons. She borrows a daughter, and pays her good wages to help in her domestic toil, and sends a son to help the labors of Mr. Jones. These two young people go into the families in which they are to be employed in all respects as equals and companions, and so the work of the community is equalized. Hence arose, and for many years continued, a state of society more nearly solving than any other ever did the problem of combining the highest culture of the mind with the highest culture of the muscles and the physical faculties.

Then were to be seen families of daughters, handsome, strong females, rising each day to their in-door work with cheerful alertness,—one to sweep the room, another to make the fire, while a third prepared the breakfast for the father and brothers who were going out to manly labor; and they chatted meanwhile of books, studies, embroidery, discussed the last new poem, or some historical topic started by graver reading, or perhaps a rural ball that was to come off the next week. They spun with the book tied to the distaff; they wove; they did all manner of fine needlework; they made lace, painted flowers, and, in short, in the boundless consciousness of activity, invention, and perfect health, set themselves to any work they had ever read or thought of. A bride in those days was married with sheets and tablecloths of her own weaving, with counterpanes and toilet-covers wrought in divers embroidery by her own and her sisters' hands. The amount of fancy-work done in our days by girls who have nothing else to do will not equal what was done by these, who performed besides, among them, the whole work of the family.

For many years these habits of life characterized the majority of our rural towns. They still exist among a class respectable in numbers and position, though perhaps not as happy in perfect self-satisfaction and a conviction of the dignity and desirableness of its lot as in former days. Human nature is above all things—lazy. Every one confesses in the abstract that exertion which brings out all the powers of body and mind is the best thing for us all; but practically most people do all they can to get rid of it, and as a general rule nobody does much more than circumstances drive him to do. Even I would not write this article, were not the publication-day hard on my heels. I should read Hawthorne and Emerson and Holmes, and dream in my arm-chair, and project in the clouds those lovely unwritten stories that curl and veer and change like mist-wreaths in the sun. So, also, however dignified, however invigorating, however really desirable are habits of life involving daily physical toil, there is a constant evil demon at every one's elbow, seducing him to evade it, or to bear its weight with sullen, discontented murmurs.

I will venture to say that there are at least, to speak very moderately, a hundred houses where these humble lines will be read and discussed, where there are no servants except the ladies of the household. I will venture to say, also, that these households, many of them, are not inferior in the air of cultivation and refined elegance to many which are conducted by the ministration of domestics. I will venture to assert, furthermore, that these same ladies who live thus find quite as much time for reading, letter-writing, drawing, embroidery, and fancy-work as the women of families otherwise arranged. I am quite certain that they would be found on an average to be in the enjoyment of better health, and more of that sense of capability and vitality which gives one confidence in one's ability to look into life and meet it with cheerful courage, than three quarters of the women who keep servants,—and that on the whole their domestic establishment is regulated more exactly to their mind, their food prepared and served more to their taste. And yet, with all this, I will *not* venture to assert that they are satisfied with this way of living, and that they would not change it forthwith, if they could. They have a secret feeling all the while that they are being abused, that they are working harder than they ought to, and that women who live in their houses like boarders, who have only to speak and it is done, are the truly enviable ones. One after another of their associates, as opportunity offers and means increase, deserts the ranks, and commits her domestic affairs to the hands of hired servants. Self-respect takes the alarm. Is it altogether genteel to live as we do? To be sure, we are accustomed to it; we have it all systematized and arranged; the work of our own hands suits us better than any we can hire; in fact, when we do hire, we are discontented and uncomfortable,— for who will do for us what we will do for ourselves? But when we have company! there's the rub, to get out all our best things and put them back,—to cook the meals and wash the dishes ingloriously,—and to make all appear as if we didn't do it, and had servants like other people.

There, after all, is the rub. A want of hardy self-respect,—an unwillingness to face with dignity the actual facts and necessities of our situation in life,—this, after all, is the worst and most dangerous feature of the case. It is the same sort of pride which makes Smilax think he must hire a waiter in white gloves, and get up a circuitous dinner-party on English principles, to entertain a friend from England. Because the friend in England lives in such and such a style, he must make believe for a day that he lives so too, when in fact it is a whirlwind in his domestic establishment equal to a removal or a fire, and threatens the total extinction of Mrs. Smilax. Now there are two principles of hospitality that people are very apt to overlook. One is, that their guests like to be made at home, and treated with confidence; and another is, that people are always interested in the details of a way of life that is new to them. The Englishman comes to America as weary of his old, easy, family-coach life as you can be of yours; he wants to see something new under the sun,—something American; and forthwith we all bestir ourselves to give him something as near as we can fancy exactly like what he is already tired of. So city-people come to the country, not to sit in the best parlor, and to see the nearest imitation of city-life, but to lie on the haymow, to swing in the barn, to form intimacy with the pigs, chickens, and ducks, and to eat baked potatoes exactly on the critical moment when they are done, from the oven of the cooking-stove,—and we remark, *en passant,* that nobody has ever truly eaten a baked potato, unless he has seized it at that precise and fortunate moment.

I fancy you now, my friends, whom I have in my eye. You are three happy women together. You are all so well that you know not how it feels to be sick. You are used to early rising, and would not lie in bed, if you could. Long years of practice have made you familiar with the shortest, neatest, most expeditious method of doing every household office, so that really for the greater part of the time in your house there seems to a looker-on to be nothing to do. You rise in the morning and despatch your husband, father, and brothers to the farm or wood-lot; you go sociably about chatting with each other, while you skim the milk, make the butter, turn the cheeses. The forenoon is long; it's ten to one that all the so-called morning work is over, and you have leisure for an hour's sewing or reading before it is time to start the dinner preparations. By two o'clock your house-work is done, and you have the long afternoon for books, needle-work, or drawing,—for perhaps there is among you one with a gift at her pencil. Perhaps one of you reads aloud while the others sew, and you manage in that way to keep up with a great deal of reading. I see on your book-shelves Prescott, Macaulay, Irving, besides the lighter fry of poems and novels, and, if I mistake not, the friendly covers of the "Atlantic." When you have company, you invite Mrs. Smith or Brown or Jones to tea; you have no trouble; they come early, with their knitting or sewing; your particular crony sits with you by your polished stove while you watch the baking of those light biscuits and tea-rusks for which you are so famous, and Mrs. Somebody-else chats with your sister, who is spreading the table with your best china in the best room. When tea is over, there is plenty of volunteering to help you wash your pretty India teacups, and get them back into the cupboard. There is no special figure or exertion in all this, though you have taken down the best things and put them back, because you have done all without anxiety or effort, among those who would do precisely the same, if you were their visitors.

But now comes down pretty Mrs. Simmons and her pretty daughter to spend a week with you, and forthwith you are troubled. Your youngest, Fanny, visited them in New York last fall, and tells you of their cook and chambermaid, and the servant in white gloves that waits on table. You say in your soul, "What shall we do? they never can be contented to live as we do; how shall we manage?" And now you long for servants.

This is the very time that you should know that Mrs. Simmons is tired to death of her fine establishment, and weighed down with the task of keeping the peace among her servants. She is a quiet soul, dearly loving her ease, and hating strife; and yet last week she had five quarrels to settle between her invaluable cook and the other members of her staff, because invaluable cook, on the strength of knowing how to get up state-dinners and to manage all sorts of mysteries which her mistress knows nothing about, asserts the usual right of spoiled favorites to insult all her neighbors with impunity, and rule with a rod of iron over the whole house. Anything that is not in the least like her own home and ways of living will be a blessed relief and change to Mrs. Simmons. Your clean, quiet house, your delicate cookery, your cheerful morning tasks, if you will let her follow you about, and sit and talk with you while you are at your work, will all seem a pleasant contrast to her own life. Of course, if it came to the case of offering to change lots in life, she would not do it; but very likely she *thinks* she would, and sighs over and pities herself, and thinks sentimentally how fortunate you are, how snugly and securely you live, and wishes she were as untrammelled and independent as you. And she is more than half right; for, with her helpless habits, her utter ignorance of the simplest facts concerning the reciprocal relations of milk, eggs, butter, saleratus, soda, and yeast, she is completely the victim and slave of the person she pretends to rule.

Only imagine some of the frequent scenes and rehearsals in her family. After many trials, she at last engages a seamstress who promises to prove a perfect treasure,—neat, dapper, nimble, skilful, and spirited. The very soul of Mrs. Simmons rejoices in heaven. Illusive bliss! The new-comer proves to be no favorite with Madam Cook, and the domestic fates evolve the catastrophe, as follows. First, low murmur of distant thunder in the kitchen; then a day or two of sulky silence, in which the atmosphere seems heavy with an approaching storm. At last comes the climax. The parlor-door flies open during breakfast. Enter seamstress, in tears, followed by Mrs. Cook with a face swollen and red with wrath, who tersely introduces the subject-matter of the drama in a voice trembling with rage.

"Would you be plased, Ma'am, to suit yerself with another cook? Me week will be up next Tuesday, and I want to be going."

"Why, Bridget, what's the matter?"

"Matter enough, Ma'am! I niver could live with them Cork girls in a house, nor I won't; them as likes the Cork girls is welcome for all me; but it's not for the likes of me to live with them, and she been in the kitchen a-upsettin' of me gravies with her flat-irons and things."

Here bursts in the seamstress with a whirlwind of denial, and the altercation wages fast and furious, and poor, little, delicate Mrs. Simmons stands like a kitten in a thunder-storm in the midst of a regular Irish row.

Cook, of course, is sure of her victory. She knows that a great dinner is to come off Wednesday, and that her mistress has not the smallest idea how to manage it, and that, therefore, whatever happens, she must be conciliated.

Swelling with secret indignation at the tyrant, poor Mrs. Simmons dismisses her seamstress with longing looks. She suited her mistress exactly, but she didn't suit cook!

Now, if Mrs. Simmons had been brought up in early life with the experience that *you* have, she would be mistress in her own house. She would quietly say to Madame Cook, "If my family arrangements do not suit you, you can leave. I can see to the dinner myself." And she *could* do it. Her well-trained muscles would not break down under a little extra work; her skill, adroitness, and perfect familiarity with everything that is to be done would enable her at once to make cooks of any bright girls of good capacity who might still be in her establishment; and, above all, she would feel herself mistress in her own house. This is what would come of an experience in doing her own work as you do. She who can at once put her own trained hand to the machine in any spot where a hand is needed never comes to be the slave of a coarse, vulgar Irishwoman.

So, also, in forming a judgment of what is to be expected of servants in a given time, and what ought to be expected of a given amount of provisions, poor Mrs. Simmons is absolutely at sea. If even for one six months in her life she had been a practical cook, and had really had charge of the larder, she would not now be haunted, as she constantly is, by an indefinite apprehension of an immense wastefulness, perhaps of the disappearance of provisions through secret channels of relationship and favoritism. She certainly could not be made to believe in the absolute necessity of so many pounds of sugar, quarts of milk, and dozens of eggs, not to mention spices and wine, as are daily required for the accomplishment of Madam Cook's purposes. But though now she does suspect and apprehend, she cannot speak with certainty. She cannot say, "*I* have made these things. I know exactly what they require. I have done this and that myself, and know it can be done, and done well, in a certain time." It is said that women who have been accustomed to doing their own work become hard mistresses. They are certainly more sure of the ground they stand on,— they are less open to imposition,—they can speak and act in their own houses more as those "having authority," and therefore are less afraid to exact what is justly their due, and less willing to endure impertinence and unfaithfulness. Their general error lies in expecting that any servant ever will do as well for them as they will do for themselves, and that an untrained, undisciplined human being ever *can* do house-work, or any other work, with the neatness and perfection that a person of trained intelligence can. It has been remarked in our armies that the men of cultivation, though bred in delicate and refined spheres, can bear up under the hardships of camp-life better and longer than rough laborers. The reason is, that an educated mind knows how to use and save its body, to work it and spare it, as an uneducated mind cannot; and so the college-bred youth brings himself safely through fatigues which kill the unreflective laborer. Cultivated, intelligent women, who are brought up to do the work of their own families, are labor-saving institutions. They make the head save the wear of the muscles. By fore-thought, contrivance, system, and arrangement, they lessen the amount to be done, and do it with less expense of time and strength than others. The old New England motto, *Get your work done up in the forenoon,* applied to an amount of work which would keep a common Irish servant toiling from daylight to sunset.

A lady living in one of our obscure New England towns, where there were no servants to be hired, at last by sending to a distant city succeeded in procuring a raw Irish maid-of-all-work, a creature of immense bone and muscle, but of heavy, unawakened brain. In one fortnight she established such a reign of Chaos and old Night in the kitchen and through the house, that her mistress, a delicate woman, encumbered with the care of young children, began seriously to think that she made more work each day than she performed, and dismissed her. What was now to be done? Fortunately, the daughter of a neighborhing farmer was going to be married in six months, and wanted a little ready money for her *trousseau.*

The lady was informed that Miss So-and-so would come to her, not as a servant, but as hired "help." She was fain to accept any help with gladness. Forthwith came into the family-circle a tall, well-dressed young person, grave, unobtrusive, self-respecting, yet not in the least presuming, who sat at the family-table and observed all its decorums with the modest self-possession of a lady. The new-comer took a survey of the labors of a family of ten members, including four or five young children, and, looking, seemed at once to throw them into system, matured her plans, arranged her hours of washing, ironing, baking, cleaning, rose early, moved deftly, and in a single day the slatternly and littered kitchen assumed that neat, orderly appearance that so often strikes one in New England farm-houses. The work seemed to be all gone. Everything was nicely washed, brightened, put in place, and stayed in place; the floors, when cleaned, remained clean; the work was always done, and not doing; and every afternoon the young lady sat neatly dressed in her own apartment, either quietly writing letters to her betrothed, or sewing on her bridal outfit. Such is the result of employing those who have been brought up to do their own work. That tall, fine-looking girl, for aught we know, may yet be mistress of a fine house on Fifth Avenue; and if she is, she will, we fear, prove rather an exacting mistress to Irish Biddy and Bridget; but *she* will never be threatened by her cook and chambermaid, after the first one or two have tried the experiment.

Having written thus far on my article, I laid it aside till evening, when, as usual, I was saluted by the inquiry, "Has papa been writing anything to-day?" and then followed loud petitions to hear it; and so I read as far, reader, as you have.

"Well, papa," said Jenny, "what are you meaning to make out there? Do you really think it would be best for us all to try to go back to that old style of living you describe? After all, you have shown only the dark side of an establishment with servants, and the bright side of the other way of living. Mamma does not have such trouble with her servants; matters have always gone smoothly in our family; and if we are not such wonderful girls as those you describe, yet we may make pretty good housekeepers on the modern system, after all."

"You don't know all the troubles your mamma has had in your day," said my wife. "I have often, in the course of my family-history, seen the day when I have heartily wished for the strength and ability to manage my household matters as my grandmother of notable memory managed hers. But I fear that those remarkable women of the olden times are like the ancient painted glass,—the art of making them is lost; my mother was less than her mother, and I am less than my mother."

"And Marianne and I come out entirely at the little end of the horn," said Jenny, laughing; "yet I wash the breakfast cups and dust the parlors, and have always fancied myself a notable housekeeper."

"It is just as I told you," I said. "Human nature is always the same. Nobody ever is or does more than circumstances force him to be and do. Those remarkable women of old were made by circumstances. There were, comparatively speaking, no servants to be had, and so children were trained to habits of industry and mechanical adroitness from the cradle, and every household process was reduced to the very minimum of labor. Every step required in a process was counted, every movement calculated; and she who took ten steps, when one would do, lost her reputation for 'faculty.' Certainly such an early drill was of use in developing the health and the bodily powers, as well as in giving precision to the practical mental faculties. All household economies were arranged with equal niceness in those thoughtful minds. A trained housekeeper knew just how many sticks of hickory of a certain size were required to heat her oven, and how many of each different kind of wood. She knew by a sort of intuition just what kinds of food would yield the most palatable nutriment with the least outlay of accessories in cooking. She knew to a minute the time when each article must go into and be withdrawn from her oven; and if she could only lie in her chamber and direct, she could guide an intelligent child through the processes with mathematical certainty. It is impossible, however, that anything but early training and long experience can produce these results, and it is earnestly to be wished that the grandmothers of New England had only written down their experiences for our children; they would have been a mine of maxims and traditions, better than any other traditions of the elders which we know of."

"One thing I know," said Marianne,—"and that is, I wish I had been brought up so, and knew all that I should, and had all the strength and adroitness that those women had, I should not dread to begin housekeeping, as I now do. I should feel myself independent. I should feel that I knew how to direct my servants, and what it was reasonable and proper to expect of them; and then, as you say, I shouldn't be dependent on all their whims and caprices of temper. I dread those household storms, of all things."

Silently pondering these anxieties of the young expectant housekeeper, I resumed my pen, and concluded my paper as follows.

In this country, our democratic institutions have removed the superincumbent pressure which in the Old World confines the servants to a regular orbit. They come here feeling that this is somehow a land of liberty, and with very dim and confused notions of what liberty is. They are for the most part the raw, untrained Irish peasantry, and the wonder is, that, with all the unreasoning heats and prejudices of the Celtic blood, all the necessary ignorance and rawness, there should be the measure of comfort and success there is in our domestic arrangements. But, so long as things are so, there will be constant changes and interruptions in every domestic establishment, and constantly recurring interregnums when the mistress must put her own hand to the work, whether the hand be a trained or an untrained one. As matters now are, the young housekeeper takes life at the hardest. She has very little strength,—no experience to teach her how to save her strength. She knows nothing experimentally of the simplest processes necessary to keep her family comfortably fed and clothed; and she has a way of looking at all these things which makes them particularly hard and distasteful to her. She does not escape being obliged to do house-work at intervals, but she does it in a weak, blundering, confused way, that makes it twice as hard and disagreeable as it need be.

Now what I have to say is, that, if every young woman learned to do house-work and cultivated her practical faculties in early life, she would, in the first place, be much more likely to keep her servants, and, in the second place, if she lost them temporarily, would avoid all that wear and tear of the nervous system which comes from constant ill-success in those departments on which family health and temper mainly depend. This is one of the peculiarities of our American life which require a peculiar training. Why not face it sensibly?

The second thing I have to say is, that our land is now full of motorpathic institutions to which women are sent at great expense to have hired operators stretch and exercise their inactive muscles. They lie for hours to have their feet twigged, their arms flexed, and all the different muscles of the body worked for them, because they are so flaccid and torpid that the powers of life do not go on. Would it not be quite as cheerful and less expensive a process, if young girls from early life developed the muscles in sweeping, dusting, ironing, rubbing furniture, and all the multiplied domestic processes which our grandmothers knew of? A woman who did all these, and diversified the intervals with spinning on the great and little wheel, never came to need the gymnastics of Dio Lewis or of the Swedish motorpathist, which really are a necessity now. Does it not seem poor economy to pay servants for letting our muscles grow feeble, and then to pay operators to exercise them for us? I will venture to say that our grandmothers in a week went over every movement that any gymnast has invented, and went over them to some productive purpose too.

Lastly, my paper will not have been in vain, if those ladies who have learned and practise the invaluable accomplishment of doing their own work will know their own happiness and dignity, and properly value their great acquisition, even though it may have been forced upon them by circumstances.

9. Working Girls

The discovery of the poor, particularly in crowded, disease-infested slums in the cities, posed a major problem for middle-class America, a problem chiefly of point of view: how to explain poverty and pauperism, and how to reconcile them with ideals of equality and benevolence. One solution was to sentimentalize the poor, especially homeless children; magazine fiction and engravings abound with melodramatic images of sweet-faced starving youngsters and work-weary mothers, frequently presented against a scene of affluent and comfortable family life. The feeling aroused by such a contrast derives from a sentimental religion of the heart and serves in effect to deflect criticism of the social order by appealing to charitableness. Although the traditional Calvinist condemnation of poverty as springing from vice and idleness still had some appeal, the dominant feeling was that the poor simply did not have a chance and thus deserved pity as well as charity.

One note which jarred with the sentimental view was struck by Charles Loring Brace in *The Dangerous Classes of New York* (New York, 1872). A humanitarian crusader and founder of the Children's Aid Society, which provided cheap lodging, schools and work for more than 100,000 of the city poor, Brace presented the case for philanthropy as a form of self-defense. Rather than gloss over the brutalizing effects of poverty, he called attention to the menace of socially alienated groups harbored in the city. About New York he wrote: "Certain small districts can be found in our metropolis with the unhappy fame of containing more human beings packed to the square yard, and stained with more acts of blood and riot, within a given period, than is true of any other equal space of earth in the civilized world." The anti-Negro draft riots during the Civil War were one sign of the peril; the desperate poor "are ready for any offense or crime," and New York has yet to feel "the full effect of the nurture of these youthful ruffians as she will one day." Recognizing that to the destitute "Capital . . . is the tyrant," he warned: "Let but Law lift its hand from them for a season, or let the civilizing influences of American life fail to reach them, and, if the opportunity offered, we should see an explosion from this class which might leave this city in ashes and blood." To avoid this, Brace offered a form of charity based on self-help, in order to prevent a permanent class of paupers from taking root.

For his part, Wirt Sikes was less troubled by the public menace of pauperism than by the complacency of the comfortable classes. Born in Watertown, New York, Sikes was early in life caught up in the temperance movement, but his enthusiasm soon shifted to literature and to social reform. He wrote tales and poems, contributed to the major journals, founded the Authors' Union after the war, and wrote two novels on social themes, *The World's Broad Stage* (1868) and *One Poor Girl* (1869), both of which try, as he indicates in the following essay on working girls, to bring a sympathetic view of the poor and the downtrodden into fiction. His outrage against an unfair system, and his portrait of vice as a last resort for working girls, suggest he may be, in however minor a way, a forerunner of writers like Stephen Crane and Theodore Dreiser. Sikes was the husband of the actress and lecturer, Olive Logan.

Among the Poor Girls

WIRT SIKES

It is half-past five o'clock in the morning, and I stand at your bedside and bid you get up. It is bitter cold, and the wind is blowing razors, which cut keenly. It is a winter morning that I choose on which to show you the poor girls; for the summer is more kind to them—more gentle, that is, though not less deathly. The winter is to them a terrible thing; and you must see their woes at their worst, if you look with my eyes. This is not the charity which labors with great, throbbing heart, that will not look at misery's direst, or which says, "I know a score of poor girls who do not suffer greatly." It were enough that I replied, I know a score who do. But I reply, that I know *thousands* who do. They suffer most in winter; therefore let it be on a winter morning that I call you from your comfortable bed to look at them.

Wirt Sikes, "Among the Poor Girls," *Putnam's Magazine,* I (1868), 432–443.

Where the Bowery runs into Chatham-street, we pause, and from within our close-buttoned overcoats look out over our mufflers at the passing throng. There are many novel features in it, but let them pass. Note these thinly-clad creatures who hurry shivering past, while the keen wind searches with icy fingers through their scanty garments, and whirls the blinding snow in the pitiful, wearied faces. We count them by tens, by scores, by hundreds, as we stand patiently here—all bearing the same general aspect of countenance, all hurrying anxiously forward, as if this morning's journey were the most momentous one of their whole lives. But they take the same journey every morning, year in and year out, whether the sun shines or the rain falls, or the bleak winds whistle and the snow sweeps in their faces with a pain like the cutting of knives. The same faces go past in this dreary procession month after month. Occasionally one will be missing; she is dead. Another; she is worse than dead— *her* face had beauty in it. Thus one by one I have seen them drop away, caught by disease born of their work and their want, bringing speedy end to the weary, empty life—caught by temptation, and drawn into the giddy maelström of sin, to come out no more forever.

To-morrow morning, take your stand at Fulton or Catherine ferry, and you shall see much such another procession go shivering by. The next day, station yourself somewhere on the West side—say in Canal-street, a few blocks from Broadway; here it is again. If, Asmodeus-like, you could hover in the air above the roofs of the town, and look down upon its myriad streets at this hour, you would see such processions in every quarter of the metropolis. The spectacle would help you to form some idea of the vastness of the theme now on our hands. . . .

Is it no matter what perils beset the paths of these poor creatures? If you think it is, it must be that you need to know the subject better.

The sewing-girls of New York are of two classes—those who work at home, and those who work in rooms provided by their employers. The former class is smaller than the latter. Where girls sew at home, it is generally a special necessity that keeps them there. They are cripples, unable to go out; or they have a bed-ridden father, mother, sister, or brother to look after. Are you surprised? Many a poor girl, to whom life is a deathly struggle with starvation and cold, keeps a heart warm with such love as might win the plaudits of angels. I have known more than one case, in which was exhibited the most wonderful abnegation of self, amounting to a devotion of the girl's very life on the altar of filial affection. One such case will tell you the story of the whole.

The case of a gentle Mary, who ekes out a miserable existence in Mulberry-street. This is one of the vilest of the Five-Points-streets; but Mary's home is not in the Five-Points part of it, being above Canal-street. It is a dismal abode for human beings, nevertheless, this forgotten rookery where Mary dwells. Let us look into this girl's daily life a little. With her needle alone she earns the money that pays for all they (herself and her father, who is dying with consumption) have—and very little that is. Put a few questions to Mary; you have earned the right, she feels, by the trifles you have brought her—trifles to us, but ah, what value they possess to her! They represent two good weeks of toil to the poor girl—of such toil, pray God, as your daughter and mine may never know!

"What rent do you pay for this room, Mary?"

"Four dollars a-month, sir."

That is a little more than thirteen cents a-day, you will observe.

"What do you get for making such a shirt as that?"

"Six cents, sir."

"What! You make a whole shirt for six cents?"

"Yes, sir, *and furnish the thread.*"

Does not this almost stagger credulity? But there is truth in the girl's face; it is impossible to disbelieve her. If, however, my reader is incredulous, I can assure him that Mary does not tell a falsehood; I know that this price is paid by some of the most "respectable" firms in New York.

"Can't you get work to do at higher prices?"

"Sometimes, sir. But these folks are better than many others, and pay regularly. Some who offer better prices will cheat, or they won't pay when the work is carried home. These folks give me plenty of work, and I never have to wait; so I don't look around for better. I can't afford to take the risk, sir; so many will cheat us." . . . .

So you see that, in order merely to pay her rent, Mary must make two shirts a day. That being done, she must make more to meet her other expenses. She has fuel to buy—and a pail of coal costs her fifteen cents. She has food to buy—but she eats very little, her father still less. She has not tasted meat of any kind for over a year, she tells us. What, then, does she eat? Bread, and potatoes, principally; she drinks a cup of cheap tea, without milk or sugar, at night—provided she has any, which she frequently has not. She has also to buy (I am not painting fancy pictures; I am stating facts, which are not regulated by any rules known to our experience) "a trifle of whiskey." Mary's father was not reared a teetotaller; and though I was, and have no taste for liquor, I am not unable to see how a little whiskey may be the last physical solace possible to this miserable man, whose feet press the edge of a consumptive's grave.

"It's more than victuals to him, sir," says poor Mary, her eyes filling with tears; "and how can I refuse him, and he so nigh his end?"

It is nine o'clock when we say "goodby" to this poor girl. By the dim light of the tallow candle that stands upon the window-sill, she will sit patiently stitching, hours after we are gone. We shall be in our beds, asleep, and still Mary will be sitting there at work—the weary, dreary work in which

> "the weary thread
> Along the garments' even hem
> And winding seam is led."

Her father asleep beside her; dead stillness all about her; the tallow candle flickering feebly with its long wick, which she hardly dares to snuff, because that will make it burn the faster; midnight passed, and the morning hours creeping on—still she sits and sews, with heavy eyes, making shirts at six cents a-piece.

This is one poor girl's life. It has a hundred parallels in the city. Whoso looks, will find them without difficulty. I have looked, and I have found them. Making no pretensions to the title of philanthropist—being merely a *littérateur*, who have looked in low life for some of my themes—I "say what I see," and have the satisfaction of knowing that I have, in some cases, guided the philanthropist to his object.

Perhaps you think that it cannot be any of our first and wealthiest firms that pay poor girls starvation-prices for their work. But you are mistaken. If my publishers did not deem it unwise to do so, I should give the names of some of our best-known Broadway houses as among the offenders against these poor girls. . . .

And just here we come to the unanswerable argument of the men who hire poor girls at these prices, to wit, that there are plenty who need the work, and will do it at such prices *because* they need it. Once, when I said a plain word to one such employer, taking the liberty of a friend, he replied good-naturedly, "My dear fellow, what are you talking about? You forget that those girls *must have* work. They are thankful enough to get what I pay them. You men who want to set the world right in a day, don't know what you are doing, half the time. If any girl that works for me wants to stop working at those prices, she's *perfectly* welcome to stop; there's a dozen want it, where one gets it. Why, I'm a philanthropist myself, in one sense. *I* grind the poor girls! They'd starve if I didn't give 'em work. Keep your indignation for those scamps that *cheat* the poor girls out of their earnings; the city's full of 'em." "Never mind them, just now. The gist of your argument is, that you take advantage of the necessities of the poor girl. If she did not need your work so badly, you would pay better prices. Suppose you could sell girls' fingers for gold. Suppose a girl was starving, and offered to sell you her fingers. You would take them, wouldn't you? What! not if she needed the money? She might starve, you know!" "Pooh, that's nonsense!" "No, it is only putting the case figuratively. These girls sell you their health, their very lives; sometimes they grow weary of that, and prefer to sell their chastity." . . .

There is a certain big rascal, whose "place of business" is so frequently changed that it would be useless to name its locality, upon whom I should dearly like to see the thumbscrews put. The law does not often reach him; but there is no blackleg known to the police who is more notorious for his peculiar rascality than this fellow. I should like to put the thumbscrews on him, and gently press him to unburden his conscience—to give a few of the interesting details of his private business. Not that he could tell any thing particularly new—for I know all about him already. Here is his confession, phonographically reported prior to delivery:

"I keeps a shirt-shop. I don't keep any hands. I have a large amount of work did from week to week, hows'ever. The way I does it is this 'ere. I advertises in the 'Herald' or the 'Sun' for gals to work on shirts, at good prices. There's allers gals a-plenty, bless yer—the supply of gals never do gin out. I offers 'em big pay for makin' my shirts. But I makes 'em leave a han'some deposit. They takes away the shirts to make 'em up. They brings 'em back, and I pays 'em—(agh!—*please* don't screw this here right thumb so hard!)—I *don't* pay 'em. I looks at the shirts, and I says, 'What do you call this? What's this here? Do you call that sewin'? Who do you think I am? Say! What do you take me for now? What? That scares 'em, you see. —'Is the work done bad?'—Oh, that don't signify; not at all—it's all bad work as comes to my shop, don't you see? So I pays 'em back their deposit-money—(agh! *do* ease that left screw jest a mite!)—but really, now, really, I *do* sometimes give 'em their deposit-money back.—'Not always?' —No, not always; some days I feel the value of money more than I do others, and them days perhaps I don't pay the deposit back. Then, sometimes, I ketch a Tartar—one of them black-eyed little snappers as says she'll have me up to the police-court, you know—and of course *that* won't do; so I not only pays her back her deposit, but, if she is *very* abusive onto me, I pays her somethin' for her work, too. But they ain't often took that way. They generally goes off a-cryin', and I ain't troubled with 'em no more. There's allers a fresh set comin' on as the last lot is a'goin' off. Lor! you've no idee what a quantity of gals they be in New York. Where the fresh ones keeps a-comin' from every day, *I* can't imagine, I'm sure. But I don't see what would become of me without 'em.—'Am I a-gettin' rich?'

—Not me; oh, no—(ugh! that hurts!)—I mean, yes; I've got considerable together, by industry and strict attention to business.—'How do I suppose those girls live—how they get food and clothing—when I rob them of the money they earn?'—Now, really, don't ask me; you shouldn't expect a man to answer such questions, really. *Some* things mustn't be talked about, you know. I *can't* say what they does. It ain't my look-out."

It is our look-out, however.

Let us follow one of these poor girls, as she comes out of the den of this beast of prey, and moves off, wringing her hands in an agony of distress. Day and night, with wearing industry, she had been working upon the dozen shirts he had given her to make. She had been looking forward—with what eagerness you can hardly realize—to the hour when she could carry him her work and get her pay, and recover her deposit-money or receive more shirts to do. Now she is turned into the street with nothing! She dares not return to her miserable boarding-place in Delancey-street, for her Irish landlady is clamorous for the two weeks' board now due. Six dollars! The sum is enormous to her. She had expected that to-night she could hand the Irish woman the money she had earned, and that it, with a promise of more soon, might appease her. But now, she has nothing for her—nothing. Despair settles down upon her. Hunger is its companion, for she has had no supper. Where shall she go?

Night has come down since she left Delancey-street, carrying the heavy bundle of new-made shirts. The streets are lighted up, and are alive with bustle. Heedless what course she takes, unnoticed, uncared-for by any in the great ocean of humanity whose waves surge about her, she wanders on, and by-and-by turns into Broadway. Broadway, ever brilliant with shop-windows where wealth gleams in a thousand rare and beautiful shapes; Broadway, with its crowding omnibuses and on-pouring current of life, its Niagara roar, its dazzle—its utter loneliness to her. The fiery letters over the theatre entrances are glowing in all the colors of the rainbow. Gayly-attired ladies, girls of her own age blest with lovers or brothers, are streaming in at the portal beyond which she imagines every delight—music, and beauty, and perfume of flowers, and *warmth*. She looks in longingly, hugging her shivering shoulders under her sleazy shawl, till a policeman bids her "move on." Out of restaurants there float delicious odors of cooking meats, making her hungrier still. Her eyes rest, with a look half wild and desperate, on the painted women who pass, in rustling silks, and wearing the *semblance* of happiness. At least they are fed—they are clothed—they can sit in bright parlors, though they sit with sin. It is easy to yield to temptation. So many do! You little know how many. In Paris, she might perhaps go and throw herself into the

Seine. In New York, such suicides are not common; but there is a moral suicide, which is common. Thousands on thousands of poor girls have thrown themselves into this stream in the last agony of desperation, sinking down in the dark current of sin, to be heard of no more.

But this poor wanderer has memories of a home, and a mother, under whose protection she has been taught to shudder at sin. She cannot plunge into this ghastly river with wide-open eyes—at least, not yet. She walks on.

He ear is caught by sounds of music and laughter, songs and bursts of applause, that come up out of these basement-haunting concert-saloons. She has heard of the "pretty waiter-girls," the fine clothes they wear, the gay lives they lead, their only labor to wait upon the patrons of the saloon, and chat with them as they sit about the tables listening to the music. "It is a life of Paradise," she murmurs, "to this life I lead!" At least, she thinks, there is no actual sin in being a waiter-girl. She perceives a wide distance between the descent of these basement-stairs to solicit employment, and that other dreadful resource.

"They get good pay in these concert-saloons," said to me a benevolent lady who has done much for the poor working-girls. "They dress well, and feed well, and their work is comparatively nothing."

The lady knew very little about them, it would seem.

The poor girls who work in these underground hells do not get good pay, and their work is not light. They are confined in these noisome places, thick with tobacco-smoke and foul with poisonous odors, till two o'clock in the morning; in some places till five o'clock. Their pay is four dollars to six dollars a week; higher figures, certainly, than thousands of working-girls get, but, for two reasons, lower, in effect. The first of these two reasons is, that the waiter-girl must dress with some degree of attractiveness. The second, and the most weighty, is, that she must pay a high price for board. Going home long after midnight, she must live somewhere in the vicinity of the saloon. Then, the woman who, having taken a girl to board, finds that she comes home after two o'clock every night, draws her own conclusions at once. That girl must pay *well* for her board, if, indeed, she be not turned out of the house without a word. It will scarcely help the matter, if the girl explains that she is employed at a concert-saloon. The woman knows very well what "pretty waiter-girls" are. "Those creatures" must pay for what they have, and pay roundly. The result is, that the waiter-girl's occupation will not support her. The next result is, that there are no virtuous girls in the concert-saloons of Broadway—unless they be such girls as this we are following to-night, as she wanders the streets, pausing to look down into this fancied half-Paradise, only to enter it at last, in search of "good pay."

Let us go down with her. She pushes open the green-baize door, and walks timidly to the bar. A girl who is passably pretty can almost always get a situation here. The big-armed prize-fighter-looking brute behind the bar reads our wanderer's history at once. "Fresh" girls are rare in that quarter. She is assisted to improve her dress a little—in some cases, these girls are provided with a fancy costume à la Turque, which they don at coming, and doff at leaving each night—and she commences her work. A crowd of half-drunk rowdies enter, and call on her to serve them, attracted by her sweet face. The grossest insults are put upon her, her character being taken for granted; infamous liberties are taken with her person, and her confusion laughed at. She would fly from the place at once, if she dared; but she does not dare—she is afraid of the man behind the bar. Her experience with men has taught her to expect nothing but brutality from them, if she offend them in any way. When the weary hours have dragged along to the end, and the place is closed, she goes out into the street again, with a bevy of other girls. The street is still and lonely; the long lines of lamps twinkle in silence; the shop-windows are all shrouded in darkness; there are no rumbling wheels, save when an occasional hack passes with slow-trotting horses.

Now she must decide upon her course. This is the critical moment. Will she adhere to her new-found employment? If she do, one of her companions will volunteer to take her to a boarding-place—and from that hour she is lost. But perhaps she breaks away; a policeman saunters by, and she appeals to him, begging to be taken to a station-house to sleep— a common resource with the homeless poor girl—and on the morrow resumes her deathly struggle for existence. How long it will last—how long she will fight her almost inevitable fate—no one can tell. . . .

Until you have lived the life of the working-girl, lady, reading this page, you cannot know what their temptation is—how hard it is to keep away sin and shame. By all the doors at which temptation can enter to you, it enters to them; and by many other doors of which you know nothing by experience. It comes in the guise of friendship to them, who are utterly friendless in the world. It comes in the guise of love—and do you think the poor girl never yearns for the caressing touch of love's palm on her aching brow? never longs to be folded in the comforting embrace of love's strong arms? Ah, *she* knows the worth of love! It comes, too, through womanly vanity, as it does to her happier sisters, who sit higher in the social scale. But, in addition to these, temptation comes to the poor girl through the tortures of a hunger which gnaws upon the vitals—of a cold which chills the young blood with its ice—of a weariness under which the limbs tremble, the head reels, the whole frame sinks prostrate.

If you were starving, and could not otherwise get food, possibly you would steal it. I would. If hunger will rouse strong men to active crime, how easy must it be for it to lead the poor girl to a merely passive sin! Yet she struggles with a bravery which few would give her credit for— with this, as with all her temptations. There was Agnes ——, a beautiful girl of 17, who resisted the temptation that came to her through her own employer. He discharged her. Unable to pay her board, she was turned into the streets. It was a bitter day in January. For *four days* she wandered the streets, looking for work—only for work. "I envied the boys who shovelled snow from the side-walks. I would gladly have done their work for half they got." Hungry, she pawned her shawl. When that was gone, she went twenty-four hours without a crumb, shivering through the streets. At night she slept in the station-house—without a bed, thankful for mere shelter. Again and again she was tempted; but she did not yield. She found work at last, and leads her cruel life still, patiently and uncomplainingly. There was Caroline G——, who came from the West to New York, fancying the great city would have plenty of work to give her. She, too, wandered the streets, and slept at night in the station-house. On the third day—which was the Christian Sabbath—mercy seemed to have found her. A gentlemanly-appearing person spoke to her, and, learning her want, offered to give her a place as seamstress in his family. He lived a short distance in the country, he said, and took her to a hotel to stay till next day, when they would take the cars for his home. The hotel was an elegant one; the room given her was hung with silk and lace, but she preferred the hard floor of the station-house that night to its luxurious state, for her "protector" was a wolf in sheep's clothing.

It is very dreadful to soil literature with such matters as these, is it not? "Really, now, *really*—there's *some* things mustn't be talked about, you know," says the beast of prey we had in the thumb-screws.

There are worse things to be done in this world than soiling literature. It is a worse thing to shut our dainty eyes to the terrible evils that beset the path of the poor girl. It is a worse thing to confine charity to curing, forgetting the charity of preventing. There are two or three institutions in New York devoted wholly and exclusively to the rescue and reformation of fallen women. I cannot think of them without the dreariest of heartaches. The work they accomplish is smaller, in proportion to the efforts put forth and the money employed, than that of any other charity in the world. One at a time, with weary labor and care—as one might dip spoonfuls of water from the East River—a few abandoned women are gathered under its roof, of whom a minority are saved, while the majority slip back into their old paths. The whole work suggests nothing so much as the stone of Sisyphus. Back-sliding is so fatally easy in that direction!

I yield to no man in the leniency with which I look on error, the sympathy I feel for the erring one—generally "more sinned against than sinning," more weak than wicked. But *prevention* is more needed in this corner than cure. While you are rescuing one from out this slough, a score are entering it from the ranks of the poor girls, tempted as no other creatures on earth are tempted. They are at the entrance of the ghastly avenue of sin, which, with all its tawdry attractions, is drawing them with a fatal enchantment; while the fiends of Starvation, Cold, Cruelty, second and assist that enchantment by their goadings. Why do you stand far down this avenue, waiting to pick up, with painful effort, here and there one of the victims? Why do you not stand at the entrance instead? Here, a dollar will do more good than will a hundred there. Here, no coaxings are necessary; the poor girls will fly to your protection with eagerness, with tears of gratitude; and here your work of salvation is a permanent one. Fifteen thousand, they tell us, is the number of fallen women in New York, among whom you can occasionally find one, less hardened than the rest, who is willing to be coddled into a renewal of a virtuous life. You take this one, shelter her, feed her, clothe her, teach her a remunerative trade, and get her a good situation—after all of which, ten to one, she goes back to her life of vice. The poor girls are at least double the number of these women—perhaps triple; and nine tenths of them more than willing to retain their virtue, and to work hard and faithfully. When this throng no longer besets you, give all your efforts to the fallen. Till then, is not your work a wasteful extravagance? It is certainly humane, in its relation to the fallen; but is it just, in its relation to the poor girls? To reach your kind offices, they, too, must first fall! Let us bar the entrance, before all else.

The giddy life of the town spins on unchecked; the spring comes, and the streets are alive with bustle; the summer, and the country wooes with its flowers; the autumn, and the air is laden with balm; the winter, with its merry parties in gay *salons*, its carousals, its carnivals; and still the poor girl leads on her dismal life, dreading each day as it comes with its burden, asking her heart if in the future there is to be for her nothing but this— nothing but toil, nothing but struggle, nothing but weariness. Still the demon of Want hovers over her with its dark wings, watching for the stumble, the touch of sickness, which shall bid him descend upon his victim with destruction. And little the great city thinks of her—little it cares what becomes of her. *Nos quoque tela sparsimus.* We are all in some sense blamable for every wrong.

10. A View of the Working Class

Jonathan Baxter Harrison represented a widespread conservative viewpoint among Unitarian ministers in this period. He shared with many clergymen a premonition of social crisis in the extremes of wealth and poverty, the rising agitation of labor militants, and the loosening of the hold of traditional Christian values. Like other conservative clergymen with a social concern, he was especially fearful that the secular doctrine of socialism would gain a foothold among alienated workers at the expense of Christianity, and a note of alarm and militancy marks his writings. He also displays what Henry May has described as typical *noblesse oblige* in the attitude toward reform of many Unitarians, an attitude which reflects the social and economic positions of many members of that church. Harrison's account of his investigations of working-class life in a New England industrial town is a good example of his somewhat condescending yet sympathetic attitude toward the masses.

Born in Ohio, Harrison made his home in Franklin Falls, New Hampshire. In addition to this work he also published *Notes on Industrial Conditions* (1886), *A Note on Labor Agitations* (1887), and *The Latest Studies on Indian Reservations* (nd).

Study of a New England Factory Town

JONATHAN BAXTER HARRISON

The place has about fifty thousand inhabitants. It has one great industrial occupation, the making of cotton cloth of various kinds. There are more than forty mills used for this manufacture,—great buildings, some of them hundreds of feet in length, and six stories high; most of them are of granite, but a few are of brick. They do not occupy any particular region in the city, but are found in nearly every part of it,—in the central squares and principal business streets, and even in those in which the most substantial and elegant dwellings are situated, as well as in the poorer quarters and in the suburbs.

I visited the place recently, and saw something of the life of the operatives and of other portions of the population. Various friends had offered me letters of introduction to prominent citizens and owners of the mills; but I have long been aware that when one wishes to see things directly, and for himself, introductions are not always helpful. They are apt to commit an observer to certain lines and methods of investigation, and they necessitate the adoption, at the outset, of some plan of operations; and this, whether it is adhered to or discarded, is commonly a disadvantage. A man who is capable of making valuable observations of the life around him can usually obtain access to all those persons who possess knowledge or information which is essential to his objects; and he can do this most successfully by making his plans as he goes on,—that is, by leaving himself free to adapt his methods, at every step, to circumstances and conditions which could not possibly be foreseen.

I employed one day in leisurely sauntering about the city, in the course of which I saw nearly all its streets and by-ways, its nooks and out-of-the-way corners. During the day the noise of the machinery of the mills fills the air of the whole city with a muffled humming sound, which is not unmusical, but rather soft and dreamy; inside of the mills the shrill buzz and clatter are at first rather painful to unaccustomed ears. In the evening I saw the mill people on their way to their homes. When I walked in the direction opposite to theirs, so as to meet them and see their faces, I noted

Jonathan Baxter Harrison, *Certain Dangerous Tendencies in American Life* (Boston, 1880), 157–202.

that they all regarded me with alert, searching glances, and they were plainly at once aware that I was a stranger. A group of children came first, laughing and chattering. They were about twelve or fourteen years old. One of the girls gave me a critical look, and remarked to her companions, "He's a detective." I heard that exclamation many times during the first few days of my sojourn, but the operatives soon recognized me everywhere. I often walked in the same direction with them, going a little more slowly than they, so as to hear their talk. It did not differ greatly from that of young people of about the same age of any class with which I am acquainted: "what Jane said about you;" "what Ned told Delia Smith;" and animated remarks about the "new things" which some of the girls had bought lately, with grave talk of the sickness of some of their companions; all this accompanied and interrupted by frequent careless, noisy laughter. It was rather pleasant and encouraging. The young people of the mills appeared to be very much like other young people when in a crowd together in the street.

When I inquired at the hotels whether one could see the mills, the answer was, "Yes, most of them; but at a few of the largest the rules forbid the admission of visitors. The officers are very strict, and if you are a stranger you cannot go in." In the shops and business houses which various errands led me to visit, and in which I always met gentlemen who were ready to talk about the trade and manufactures of their city, this information about the mills from which visitors were excluded was often repeated, and the same mills were always named. I therefore decided to begin by looking through the places which were thus reported to be difficult of access. I encountered no obstacle anywhere that was not easily surmounted. I passed through more than half a dozen of the largest mills, inspecting all the processes and details of the manufacture, from the boiler room in the cellar, where the smooth, resistless swing of the gigantic Corliss engines made one feel as if he were watching the motion of a planet in its path, to the enormous tubs of sizing, high up in the attic.

In all the mills which I visited, far more than half the operatives were girls and women. I saw very few children who appeared to be under twelve years of age, though I heard much criticism, among some of my new acquaintances in the city, of the cruelty of the laws and usages relating to the employment of young children in the mills. As to nationality or descent, the English, Scotch, and Irish operatives, with their children born here, constitute the most numerous classes, but there are also many French Canadians. I had often heard and read the assertion that very few Americans, or, more strictly, descendants of American families, now work in the mills. But I found among the operatives a considerable proportion of young women who are the children of families that have lived in this country for one hundred and fifty or two hundred years, and I have since learned that the same thing is true of several other factory towns.

All the mill people looked as if they had enough to eat, but some of them showed in their faces indications of the effects of poor cookery. Some had the peculiar look which comes from living in impure air, and this result is produced chiefly, as I was convinced by what I saw in the mills and in the homes of the people, by the foulness of the air in the rooms in which the operatives eat and sleep. In many, probably in most, of their homes the cooking is done in the "sitting-room;" that is, the apartment in which the members of the family pass the evening together until bed-time. The cost of fuel is one of the principal expenditures and burdens of the household, and economy in its use is one of the most important means of saving; so the room is kept closely shut to prevent the escape of heat and the entrance of cold air from the outside. The impurity of the air in these rooms during cold weather is very great, and this is one of the most unwholesome features of the life of the operatives.

The cotton is brought to the mills in the bale, "just as it comes from the fields in Indiana, or wherever it grows," as an obliging overseer in one of the largest mills explained to me, and all the processes of picking, cleaning, carding, spinning, weaving, dressing, and finishing are performed in the same building. Nearly all this work is done by machinery, and the labor of the operatives consists almost entirely in attendance upon the machinery. There are a few things, such as the drawing of the threads of the warp through the "harness," which are done with the fingers, but the wonderful capabilities of the machines leave very few things to be done by human hands. Many of the looms are so constructed that they stop at once if a thread breaks, and do not go on till it is mended. Each girl tends four, five, or six looms. A few of the most skillful can manage eight looms each, as many as the best hands among the men.

There is not much work that requires great muscular strength or exertion, not much lifting or handling heavy materials or articles of any kind. Most of it requires alertness and exactness of attention, the concentration of the faculties and their constant application to the processes going on under one's hand, rather than severe muscular effort. Such work usually exhausts the nervous vitality quite as rapidly as many occupations which appear to be more difficult and toilsome. Most of the operatives are necessarily on their feet nearly all the time, and this feature of their work has an unfavorable effect upon the health of the women and girls. They all appear to be tired at the end of their day's toil, though I saw no signs of extreme weariness or exhaustion. It is very hard for any one who is not well, or who is "nervous" and sensitive. The noise of the machinery then becomes insufferably irritating and torturing.

No part of the work in the mills appeared to me so severe, or so unwholesome, for girls and women as is the toil of those who run sewing-machines in city shops; yet it is work which requires good health and high average vitality. The high temperature which is necessary for some of the processes of cotton manufacture renders the operatives specially liable, during the winter, to injury by taking cold when they pass into the open air, unless they use some precautions against it by putting on extra clothing when they leave the mills. But I observed that most of them were careless in this respect, though not more so, probably, than is usual among the pupils of the high-schools in every part of our country. I noted considerable coughing, and some complained of sore throats. In several departments of a mill the air is always filled by fine flying fibres and particles of cotton. Some of these are drawn into the lungs, and this produces injurious effects. When the lungs are at all sensitive or inclined to disease, this dust increases the irritation. Even for persons who are strong and well it is of course unwholesome, and it probably causes greater injury to health than any other feature or condition of mill work.

A group or company of the young people of the mills, when approached by a stranger, always exhibits the peculiar instinctive shrinking and drawing together for self-defense which is shown by wild animals in similar circumstances. In the mill people it is a feeling of distrust, suspicion, and hostility regarding all who do not belong to their class. The first question asked of a stranger is always, "Do you wish to get work in the mill?" Of course I was simply a stranger, who wished to see the mills and the work which was done in them. During the hour at noon, when the machinery is at rest, is a favorable time for forming some acquaintance with the operatives. Many of them have brought their dinner with them, and they eat it sitting on the floor, or standing in groups together. One scarcely knows when or how the eating is done in some of these little companies, for the talk and chatter and laughter are incessant. The presence of a stranger is at first a restraint, and excites their caution when he approaches or addresses them. Unless a man knows how to penetrate and disarm this reserve, he will learn little from them of their thought or life. They soon became merry and communicative with me. Some of the younger girls were then inclined to be forward and impudent, but they were checked and controlled by the older ones.

The girls and young women in the mills "learn to take care of themselves," to use a phrase which one often hears among them; that is, they are not at all ignorant of evil or vice. They know what are the dangers that beset and threaten young girls in their circumstances, among men many of whom are coarse and sensual. In such conditions the delicacy and modesty of thought, deportment, and speech which are so precious and lovely in the character of young women are almost impossible, and we have no right to require or expect them. But these girls are not so liable to be led into actual vice or immorality as are some of the pupils in our Sunday-schools, whose very ignorance of evil, and of the need of avoiding or resisting it, sometimes exposes them to temptation unwarned and unprepared. The mill girls are familiar with coarse and vile language, and can hear it unabashed and without blushing; they can answer in like terms. But these facts are not, in their case, marks of extreme depravity or immorality. They afford no evidence of unchastity. I do not believe that this vice prevails to any considerable extent among the young women of the mills. Some of the older women, especially among the English and Irish, have not always been successful in self-protection, or in repelling temptation, as one can plainly see. But there is, as I am thoroughly convinced, far less of sexual vice among the factory operatives than is usually attributed to them. I am certain that working-people in general, of both sexes, are more pure and free from this vice than most moralists and clergymen think them. Their toil represses passion. Their time is filled by their regular occupations, and they have little leisure for vicious thoughts, for nourishing mischievous and profligate desires. It is among idle men and women that this evil finds most of its recruits. No system of morals or of religious culture has yet been devised which provides any effective safeguard against licentiousness for those who are exempt from toil.

In studying the life of any class of people, an observer soon distinguishes the persons who can be of use to him, who represent or possess something which he wishes to learn or understand. When I had found several men and women who could thus be of service to me, the next step was to visit their homes, which I did upon their invitation. I saw their food and their methods of preparing it, examined the books and papers which they read, and listened to their accounts of their own life and work and experience.

There are but few "tenement houses" in this place owned by the mill proprietors. Most of the operatives find homes or apartments wherever they prefer, and many of them live in small buildings where there are only two or three families under the same roof. I think this much better than the system of large tenement houses, unless these could be superior in design and arrangement to the buildings of this class which are ordinarily found in American cities. There are, however, a few large buildings here belonging to the mill owners, and each is occupied by a large number of families. I examined two or three of them, and am compelled to say that their construction is not what it should be. In some cases the cellars are not properly secured against the ingress of surface water, and the water-closets are inadequate and unsuitable. The city government should give this matter immediate attention. The tenants should be required by the proprietors to keep the yards surrounding these houses in a more wholesome and cleanly condition than that in which I found them.

The cookery in the homes of the operatives, if judged by what I saw and learned in several families, is not usually very good. They fry too much of their food, and many do not know how to extract the nutritive elements from beef-bones by long boiling. They throw out to their dogs what would give them the basis for a valuable and delicious soup. (The operatives keep a great many dogs, as is the custom among poor people generally, in this country.) If the women had sufficient knowledge in regard to the best methods of preparing it, they could have better food and more of it without additional expense. Much good might be done by an arrangement for instructing these women and girls in economical methods of preparing wholesome and appetizing food. Perhaps the good women of the city who possess the advantages of wealth and culture can do something to aid their less fortunate sisters among the operatives in this matter.

The young people of the mills generally read the story papers, published (most of them) in New York city, and devoted to interminably "continued" narratives, of which there are always three or four in process of publication in each paper. I have read some of these stories. They have usually no very distinct educational quality or tendency, good or bad. They are simply stories,—vapid, silly, turgid, and incoherent. As the robber-heroes are mostly grand-looking fellows, and all the ladies have white hands and splendid attire, it may be that some of the readers find hard work more distasteful because of their acquaintance with the gorgeous idlers and thieves, who, in these fictions are always so much more fortunate than the people who are honest and industrious. But usually, as I am convinced by much observation, the only effect of this kind of reading is that it serves "to pass away the time," by supplying a kind of entertainment, a stimulus or opiate for the mind, and that these people resort to it and feel a necessity for it much the same way that others feel they must have whisky or opium. The reading is a narcotic, but it is less pernicious than those just named.

Many hundreds of the older operatives, especially foreigners, of two or three nationalities, were reading a paper which is devoted to the liberation of the working-people of America. Its principal literary attraction at this time was a very long serial story of the overthrow of the republic in 1880. This is written as if the events which form the subject of the narrative had already occurred. It introduces General Grant as dictator, and describes elaborately the character and effects of the terrible despotism which he establishes, in that year, upon the ruins of popular government. He "suppresses Congress," seizes New York city at the head of an armed force and by the assistance of the capitalists or "money power" of the country, and is about to make himself emperor, when the working-people rise in arms, under the direction of a nameless leader, "a man with the executive intellect of Cæsar, Napoleon, and Bismarck, and the lofty impulses of Leonidas, Cincinnatus, and Washington." (To continue the description of this personage, "he was a man of huge bulk and brawn. His head was the size and shape of Daniel Webster's, whom he greatly resembled, except in being of the blonde type. His awful gray eyes had a power in them far beyond that of the orbs of the indolent Webster.")

The workingmen, soldiers of the new revolution, are instructed by this hero to supply their own needs from the abundant stores of their neighbors, giving them receipts in the name of the revolution for the property thus forcibly appropriated. They accordingly seize the national banks, and help themselves to as much money as they desire. This story was read with deep interest by many of the older operatives, especially those who were interested in labor reform. The paper containing it prints each week a declaration of principles, which affirms that the government should hold all the land of the nation; that it should be without price (the free use of as much of it as he can cultivate being secured to every man); that ground rents of towns and cities should be controlled by government; that gold and silver should be demonetized, and that in their stead absolute paper money should be issued by the government; that interest on money should be forbidden; that all mines, railroads, and highways should be owned and controlled by the government; that the government ought not to interfere for the collection of debts between individuals, but that the payment of debts should be left entirely to the honor of the debtor. There should be an income tax on all incomes above one thousand dollars, growing heavier for larger sums. Eight hours' labor should be a legal day's work, and the senate of the United States should be abolished. Recently the paper has devoted much space to the advocacy of "the right of the people to free travel:" the government should own the railroads, and tax capitalists to obtain means for operating them, and people who do not wish to pay fares should be permitted to ride free. This paper has a large circulation among operatives, miners, and city mechanics, in nearly all parts of the country. It is a large sheet, and is conducted with much ability. It always contains two or three serial stories by popular writers, which are designed to "float" the heavier articles devoted to the propagation of the doctrines of the agitators, who seek to establish a universal, international sovereignty of workingmen upon principles and methods which contradict and oppose every essential of civilization. The tone and spirit of the paper are indescribably bitter, and expressive of intense hostility against the possessors of property and culture. It represents capitalists as a class of cruel and inhuman oppressors, and instructs the working-people that the time is at hand for them to seize the rights of which they have been so long deprived. All its teaching is opposed to the spirit and principle of nationality, and tends, so far as it has any effect, to produce social and political disintegration.

There is a labor-reform newspaper published in this city of mills, and I had much conversation with the editor. He thinks the mill owners and capitalists of the city are thoroughly selfish and heartless; that they have no regard for the interests or welfare of the operatives, and care only to obtain the greatest possible amount of labor from them for the least possible pay. He was engaged, when I saw him, in the promotion of a movement having for its object the reduction of the hours of labor in the mills. The legal day's work is now ten hours, but my friend the editor informed me that the mill agents often disregard the law and work the hands ten and a half, and even eleven hours per day. He said that the largest mill in the city was run nearly seventy hours one week, and that the agent of this mill was "determined to be king of devils."

I asked the editor what change he regarded as, at present, most important and necessary for the emancipation of labor and the improvement of the condition of the working-people; and he replied, "The next great step is the reduction of the hours of labor."

"What should be the length of a day's work?"

"We are working now to obtain more stringent legislation against running the mills more than ten hours, but six hours a day would be enough for people to work."

I asked him if he could give me any information regarding the amount of deposits by operatives in the savings-banks of the city. This is his reply, in a note which he kindly sent me not long ago, and which is now before me: "I have no exact means of stating the precise amount, but it is practically nothing. There is no city where the operatives own fewer bankbooks than here. The operatives of this city are very poor indeed, perhaps no place poorer, and the per cent who own their homes is a great deal smaller. Factory life has almost reached serfdom."

I thought my friend a well-meaning, sincere man, but extreme in his bitterness against capitalists. He could give me little information regarding the most important features of the life of the operatives of his city, but I am grateful to him for the opportunity for acquaintance with his opinions and the aims of his fellow-reformers.

I am obliged to say that I found few signs of interest among the work people in reforms of any kind. Most of them appeared to be entirely indifferent to such matters, and to political subjects in general. But there is a considerable number of men, especially among the spinners, who are discontented under what they deem tyranny and oppression on the part of the mill owners and agents. These operatives have an organization, or society, for the promotion of their aims, and they employ a secretary with a salary sufficient to enable him to devote his time to their interests. I met this secretary, and had a long conversation with him. He is a foreigner, and seemed a very good-natured fellow. He thought that in cases of dissatisfaction on the part of the operatives, the employers were usually ready to hear and consider any statement which the working-people might wish to present through a committee of their own choosing. He appeared to regard the owners and agents as reasonable men, who were disposed to deal justly with the laborers; and I thought that he, more than any other of the reformers whom I met, understood that both capitalists and laborers in this country are suffering from the operation of causes which no legislation or reform could at once remove.

The operatives are paid by the piece, and not by the day or hour; that is, it is the quantity of goods manufactured, and not the amount of time employed, which determines the amount of wages paid. The reformers complained that when a new mill is opened the agent stimulates the operatives to the highest possible performance and production for the first few days, and then adjusts the wages-rate upon the basis of what the best hands have thus been able to do for a short time. As only a few operatives are capable of such a pace, and even they cannot maintain it permanently, the arrangement has the effect of establishing a low rate of wages. (That is, if we represent by one hundred the amount of work performed in a day by the best hands when spurred to unusual activity, the average daily performance will not rise above eighty-five or ninety; but the amount of pay is regulated upon the assumption that the average daily work will reach one hundred.)

The reformers thought the average pay of the operatives of the city, at the time of my visit, was considerably less than one dollar per day for "full hands," that is, for those who can do a full day's work; but the mill owners and agents assured me that the average pay was above one dollar per day. I visited the agents and managers of several of the largest mills, and asked them for their view of the condition of the operatives and of the situation and prospects of the cotton manufacture in the city. They answered my inquiries with ready, quiet courtesy. Here is the substance of the notes which I made as we talked:—

"The women weavers are paid a little more than one dollar per day. Any boy of thirteen or fourteen years old can make two dollars and a half per week. Operatives pay for rent, for four rooms, from three and a half dollars to six dollars per month. The owners and managers are satisfied with the ten-hour law, and do not think any additional legislation necessary (in this State) for the proper regulation of the relations between capital and labor, or the working-people and their employers. We prefer ten hours per day, but as the machinery is run by steam-power we have to start it a little before the hour, and some of the hands always go to work at once, in order to add a little to the day's production, and so to their wages. At present rates of pay, the average operatives can save something from their wages. If we compare the cost of living and wages of the times before the war, say in 1860, with the cost of living and wages now, we shall find that operatives are better paid now than they were then. All of us, operatives and employers, have lived more extravagantly since the war than ever before. All wars make waste, and we are all of us suffering from the consequences of the waste caused by our civil war, and especially by the unwise expenditure of money since 1865. When wages were very high, a few years ago, the operatives wasted nearly all that they received. Few of them saved anything. We must all learn and practice economy. Many people who are regarded as being rich are living more carefully and economically than most of the working-people, because they have more foresight and a clearer understanding of the absolute necessity of keeping their expenditures within their income. . . ."

The capitalists and mill owners of the city with whom I conversed attributed the prevailing depression of business and industry in large measure to the waste of capital necessarily produced by our civil war, and in still greater degree to the extravagance of expenditure which was so general among our people a few years ago. They thought that the principal means of recovery must be economy and wisdom in expenditure; that capitalists and employers have come to understand this necessity more fully than the operatives do, as a class; and that those who belong to the capitalist class are at present really more saving and economical in their methods of living than the operatives.

I was greatly interested in learning about the amusements or diversions of the mill people. My first step was to ask a great many of the young women what they did in the evening, after working hours were over. The French Canadian girls, who are Catholics, nearly all replied, "We stay at home. We have to sew, and mend our clothes, and wash them. We do not know anybody, and so we have no place to go in the evening." At times the answer was, "My mother" or "my sister will not let me go out." Most of the other young women said, "Oh, we go out with our fellers, and with some of the other girls." "And where do you go?" "Oh, along the streets, down town; to the post-office, or the candy-store, if the boys will shout." "If they will shout,—what is that?" "Oh, don't you know? Why, that means if they will treat,—if they will buy some candy for us." "And do you drink something, too?" To this the younger women always answered, "No, we don't drink anything, unless it's soda-water, sometimes, in warm weather." But they usually pointed to some older companion, and said, "She drinks,— she drinks beer." Then the woman thus spoken of would laugh, and toss her head, and say, "Ain't you goin' to shout?" And when I met the same group in the street in the evening, the question would be repeated, with a smile of recognition.

I do not think these girls and younger women have usually any habitual amusement, except this walking out with their friends which I have just mentioned. Once or twice during the winter many of them go to a ball. To go more frequently would be regarded by their own class as an extravagance, as an indication of unsteadiness and a tendency to dissipation. I found many young people in the mills who "belonged," as they said, to the Methodist church, and some who were Baptists. Probably there were, among the operatives, members of other religious societies, but I did not happen to meet them.

The young people whom I have thus far been describing appeared to be rather steady and well-behaved. They looked and acted as if they kept good hours, and had no marks of anything wild or irregular about them. But I saw others, both young men and women, whom I knew at once to be of a different type. Every class, every type of character, has a rhythm of its own, which runs through all bodily movements, through the tones of the voice; which is accented in glances and changes of expression, and is revealed in all spontaneous mental action. I knew that some of these young people would have other amusements than those I have described. I did not think it wise to ask any of them how they passed their evenings. I thought there might be better ways of acquiring this knowledge.

I had observed in various parts of the city such signs as "Harmony Hall," "The Avon Arms," "St. George's Hall," etc. I sauntered into one of these places, one evening, about nine o'clock. It was on the second floor, and was reached by an open stair-way running up from the street. I found a hall about fifty feet long and twenty-five wide. At one end was a bar for the sale of liquors, and at the other a curtained recess and a small stage or platform elevated two or three steps from the floor. There were about fifty persons present, grouped around eight or ten tables. About one fourth of them were young women. Some of the young men were smoking. There were glasses on the tables, and some of the young people were drinking beer. As I went up the stairs, I heard the clang of a piano much out of tune and the clapping of hands, and a young man was just descending from the stage, while he smiled and bowed in acknowledgment of the applause. He sat down with one of the groups nearest the stage, and some one at the table called for "four beers." The four glasses were taken away by a pleasant-looking English girl, and brought back filled. There were similar requests from various parts of the room, and after she had responded to them the young waitress approached the place where I sat alone, and civilly inquired, "Is there anything you wish for?" I gave her an order that would bring her back to my table now and then.

When most of the glasses had been emptied once or twice, some one said, quietly, "Mr. Lee will oblige," and there was a general clapping of hands. A young Englishman ascended the stage, and sang, in tolerable accord with the weary, protesting piano, a melancholy song about a sailor lover who sailed away from his mistress and never returned. Both hearts were true: one lies "in his long, last sleep, a thousand fathoms deep, where the wild monsoons do sweep" forever above his rest; the other "watched her life away, looking seaward o'er the bay," from a New England hill-top, and hoping to the end for one who came no more. At the close there was more applause and more beer, and for some time busy, chattering talk. There was nothing loud or boisterous. One of the girls, who was a little tipsy, came across the room, in a rather demonstrative way, and asked me if I was not "going to shout"; but a young man at the

table she had left reproved her sharply, and one of the young women
from the same company came over and led her back to her place.

By this time I had noted most of those present as persons whom I had
met before, in the mills and on the streets. They were nearly all operatives,
or had at some time belonged to that class. But I observed at one of the
tables, with half a dozen young men and women around him, a young
colored man whom I had never seen until now. He was more silent than
any other member of the company, but was evidently the object of general attention and respect. He was the only person of his color in the hall,
but was plainly as welcome there as any one. He seemed obviously
superior to his neighbors, and I was interested at once, and felt that I
must know something about him. Presently there was another invitation
to the stage, and when the young colored man rose to comply with it there
was unusually hearty applause. He sang one song after another till he
seemed tired, but the audience was still impatient for more. The songs
were of many kinds, comic, sentimental, pathetic, and silly. One had these
stanzas:—

> "Sampson was a strong man,
>   He was not counted lazy;
> He took the jaw-bone of a shark
>   And slewed the gates of Gazy.
>
> "It rained forty days and forty nights
>   Exactly by the countin',
> And landed Noah and his ark
>   On the Alleghany mountain."

When he sang "I got a mammy in the promised land," with a strange,
wailing refrain, the English waiter-girl, who was sitting at my table, wiped
her eyes with her apron, and everybody was very quiet. He sang and
acted with a kind of suppressed intensity of manner and expression, and I
thought that to him the dusty hall and its somewhat squalid appointments
had given place to a grand theatre, thronged by an admiring, applauding
audience. He seemed rapt and inspired. His face was black, and the
features African in type, but not at all repulsive or unpleasant. When he
left the stage, I sent the waiter-girl to tell him I wished to see him. He
came down the hall with a dignified courtesy of manner; we were introduced, and had a little conversation. I found him very intelligent. He
talked well, but quietly and deliberately. His speech was that of cultivated
New England people, and had none of the peculiarities which usually
mark the language and utterance of colored persons.

It would not do to show too much curiosity or interest there, as this was my first visit to the hall; but I arranged to meet my colored friend next day, and took my leave, assured of a welcome there whenever I might return. I visited half a dozen similar places before midnight. They were all much alike. I spent several hours, at various times, in these music halls, calling sometimes in the afternoon, because the attendants had more time then than in the evening. Some of them had stories to tell which I wished to hear, but I had to wait till I had established such relations between us as would inspire them with the willingness to talk to me.

All the attendants at these places had worked in the mills. The young man who plays the piano is usually paid four or five dollars per week, besides his board. The young men who sing receive one dollar per night, but most of them board themselves. The real business at all these places is the sale of liquor. They all keep cigars, and most of them have pies and a few other articles of food, but the profits come from the drinking. The piano, the singing, the recitations attract and entertain visitors. These resorts are sustained almost entirely by the operatives, besides a great many other places where there is no music or entertainment of any kind, except the drink. At the city clerk's office I learned from the official records that there are in the city two hundred and fifty-seven houses licensed to sell liquors, and many of the leading citizens expressed the opinion that the unlicensed drinking places (where liquor is sold unlawfully) were at least equal in number. Last year there were 5,400 voters in the city; so there was a licensed drinking saloon for every twenty-one voters. The city's revenue from these licenses last year was $38,782. This large sum, and a great deal besides, the liquor dealers received from the working-people,—a very large proportion of it from the mill hands. At one of these music halls the woman in charge informed me that "the expenses of the establishment" averaged two hundred dollars per month, and I visited several places which did a much larger business than this one.

The editor of the labor-reform newspaper told me that the most usual course for a man who for any reason falls out of the ranks of mill workers (if he loses his place by sickness, or is discharged) is the opening of a liquor saloon or drinking place. He takes up this business for a living and rarely quits it for any other occupation. At first, he buys a very small stock,—a keg of beer, or a few gallons of low-grade whisky. He hires a little corner or closet in some shop or basement, or he begins in his own cellar, and is soon able to lay in a larger and more varied supply. After much observation and study of the subject in most of the States of our country, I believe there is no other kind of business or employment which can be entered upon or engaged in with so little capital, or which will yield so large a return in proportion to the amount invested. There is greater profit and less risk of loss than in any other occupation which is open to so many people. Its principal support comes from the classes engaged in manual labor. Many men will buy intoxicating liquors when they and their families are suffering for food. Whatever degree of poverty may prevail among the working-people, those who sell liquor to them still find the business profitable. The great causes of the drinking habit among the working-people are poor cookery, living in impure air, and the lack of any dramatic entertainment or amusement for their evenings or times of leisure.

I met the young colored man several times, and found him a person to give one a sad kind of interest in him. He was just then doing more to amuse and entertain the mill people than any one else in the city, so I gave a little time to conversation with him. I like average and ordinary men and women best, and have not commonly found what is unusual or extraordinary in human life or character best worth study or acquaintance. But this man was not precisely what I was looking for. On one occasion I asked him who was the author of a song he had just sung. Looking at me keenly, he asked, "Do you like it?" "Yes," I said; "it is simple and tender and natural." "Well," he replied, "it is mine, such as it is." "Do you mean that you wrote the words?" "Yes, the words and the music." "Have you written others?" "Oh, yes; I have quite an income from my songs." "Where are they published?" He gave me the name of a well-known music-publishing house in Boston, and when I came home I ordered specimens of my friend's compositions. They were sent to me, and I found everything as he had told me.

I asked him if he had been singing at these places in the city very long. "Nearly a year," he replied; and then he told me that his business was negro minstrelsy and theatricals. He had traveled with the principal companies in this country, and had a permanent engagement at a good salary. But about a year ago his mother died. He was greatly attached to her, was with her in her last illness, and was "too heart-broken to be making money. I did not feel like acting, and thought it would show more respect to my mother, if she knows about it, if I did not appear in public for a year. I sing a little in this private way to accommodate my friends here, and because it is not good to be doing nothing." He acknowledged that he drank too much, and that his life was not what it should be. I asked him if anybody had ever encouraged him to cultivate his mind and make a man of himself. "No," said he; "the only encouragement anybody ever gave me was, 'Bill, go another dollar on this!'" But many people would probably find this man's story more interesting if it were not true.

At the principal hotel I met many salesmen and book-keepers from the shops and stores of the city, and when there was opportunity I sometimes made inquiries regarding the mill people,—their character and ways of living. These gentlemen always appeared to be surprised that I should be interested about the operatives, or suppose there was anything in their life that was worthy of attention. At one time there was considerable excitement among my friends at the hotel, on account of the announcement that a certain "celebrated star troupe" of actors would appear "for one night only" at the Academy of Music. It was to be a "variety entertainment," to comprise a play in two acts, songs, dances, a trapeze performance, etc.,—all of the very highest character. My companions at the table courteously advised me to go. It would be a good opportunity to see the people of the city, as the attendance would be very large. "Will the mill people be there?" I inquired. "Oh, no [with impatience]; they are not capable of appreciating anything of this kind. They have their own low amusements, but this is first-class." I went. The house was filled with well-dressed people of both sexes. The feature of the entertainment which was most to the mind of the audience was a song. A rather pretty girl came out in spangled tights, and sang half a dozen stanzas with this refrain:—

> "So, boys, keep away from the girls, I say,
>   And give them plenty of room;
>   For when you are wed they will bang till you're dead
>   With the bald-headed end of a broom."

This was "received with great enthusiasm," as the play-bills said it would be, and was encored again and again. I looked around over the applauding multitude; the mill people were not there.

The mills were running on full time, and were worked to their utmost capacity, with all the hands the machinery would employ. They require about fifteen thousand hands. But there were, as I judged from all I could learn about the matter, between fifteen hundred and two thousand persons of the operative class in the city in excess of the number which the mills could employ. These were destitute of work, except when, now and then, the temporary illness of some hand left a place vacant, and so gave the opportunity of work to one of these superfluous laborers for a day or two. There was much hardship among these people. Many had families, and their children suffered for food. In some of the worst cases the city gave assistance; the labor unions sustained others in part; and neighborly kindness among the operatives was more helpful than either. The labor-reform agitation, in all its stages, from vague discontent to violent denunciation, was reinforced and sustained chiefly by the presence of this unemployed class. Their life was a daily struggle against the inevitable,—a long and useless waiting for what could not come. Every morning some hundreds of these seekers after employment presented themselves at the doors of the mills, in the hope, almost always a vain one, that a few of them might be wanted.

The overseers at the mills kindly allowed persons seeking work to put down their names in application for the opportunity of filling vacancies when they should occur. In visiting one of these unemployed families, I saw a fine-looking, capable young man, who had been idle for months. His name was on the list at one of the principal mills, but there were twenty-eight names before his, and it was not probable that his turn would ever come. This young man bears a well-known name, and his ancestors have lived in the State more than two hundred years. The presence of so large number of superfluous hands in any place is a matter of grave importance. There were too many laborers there already, but every day there were new arrivals from other manufacturing towns. Some, on learning that the mills were crowded, resumed their quest in new directions. Others had not means to go farther, and remained to swell the number of the unemployed and discontented. Is it impossible to devise some plan which would prevent this migration of crowds of laborers to places where there is no demand for labor and no prospect of their finding employment? We already map the course of the winds and the state of the weather for the whole country each day. Would it be much more difficult to map the state of the labor market for the whole country every week or every month, or less valuable in its results? The impotence of society in the presence of such evils is more apparent than real.

I found several large Catholic temperance societies among the mill people. They were working vigorously and with excellent effect. The Catholic Church is doing more than any other, I think, for the moral guidance and improvement of the operatives. The Methodist Church comes next, and its work is important and salutary. I saw evidences, now and then, among the young Methodist converts, of strong sectarian feeling, a disposition to employ social pressure as a means of increasing the influence of the church. As this was, under the circumstances, a sign of earnestness and vitality, it was a less evil than indifference. The Baptist Church has also a considerable share in the religious culture of the mill people; and it is probable that other religious bodies, besides those which I have named, are at work with noticeable energy and success among the operatives, but I had no opportunity of observing their activities. The Unitarian pastor informs me that his church has some influence among the young mill people, "but it reaches very few, as you might naturally expect it would. It is not fitted to their appreciation, nor, perhaps, to their wants." He adds, "Being brought little into contact with the operative class, I can in general speak only from hearsay in regard to them, and therefore should not presume to give an opinion to one who is searching for facts."

Many of the older operatives, especially among the English, Scotch, and Americans, are strongly influenced by what is called modern scientific thought, and have come to regard religion as something outgrown and antiquated for all intelligent persons, but still useful and necessary for the ignorant inferior classes,—the common people. The strongest separative and unfraternal influence which I have encountered or observed in American life and thought is this tendency of "scientific thought" to produce a feeling of contempt for those who do not share it,—for "the unenlightened masses."

Several of the mill corporations of this city are embarrassed by indebtedness out of all proportion to their financial strength or available assets. Some of them have recently been forced to suspend payment, and it is probable that others will soon have a similar experience. These difficulties have been caused in part by embezzlements and defalcations, of which the city has had its share, within a few years, in common with most other places in our country; but the popular judgment attributes far too large a proportion of the financial troubles of the mills to this source. Most of them have resulted from the effects upon business and industry produced by our civil war, and from the peculiar intellectual and psychological conditions which prevailed among our people for a few years after that convulsion. Usually these evils or embarrassments are the result of false or erroneous thinking. There was too much money invested in machinery for the manufacture of cotton goods, more than was required for all the business that could be done. More mills were built and equipped than could be employed with profit. These excessive and abnormal investments of capital in a particular branch of business were made because capitalists and manufacturers depended upon imaginary markets, upon a demand for cotton goods which was supposed to be practically unlimited.

The labor reformers insist that there can be no overproduction while any human want remains unsupplied. This is pure sentimentalism, worthy of the political economy of Rousseau, and has no scientific or practical quality whatever. What is more to be regretted is, that many of the writers of our time who are trying to aid the development of rational ideas on these subjects are themselves influenced, and much of their work is vitiated, by the same illusions which have made the sentimentalists their prey. When we declare, in poems, sermons, and optimistic essays, that men everywhere should be able to possess and enjoy whatever can add to the comfort, refinement, and happiness of life, it has a delightfully generous and philanthropic sound, and we are disposed to feel that we have done something to hasten "the good time coming." But the simple fact, of inexpugnable strength, upon which the whole matter depends in actual business is that overproduction occurs whenever a manufacturer produces so many more goods than he can sell that the amount left upon his hands absorbs the profits of his business, or such a proportion of the profits as gradually to impair and lessen his productive capital. Men do not manufacture cotton cloth, or grow corn and wheat, or make newspapers, from motives of generosity or sentimental philanthropy. They produce all these articles to sell them; and fraternal justice to the laborers employed, and the use of whatever means can be applied for their education, will give increasing productiveness, security, and permanence to all these branches of industry. But it will not do to make any kind of goods merely because people ought to have them. We might insist that life must be a condition of squalid misery in every family where there is not a seven-octave piano; but the manufacturer who should therefore undertake to make pianos for all who do not now possess them would soon be in a position to give lessons to our political economists on the real nature of overproduction. It is not true philanthropy to employ men to make goods which cannot be sold. To do so must always result in the destruction of capital and the injury of the laborer. Of course, there are chances of loss by the production of unsalable goods which cannot be foreseen, but this only makes all possible foresight the more necessary. We have built many mills and bought much costly machinery for the manufacture of cotton and iron goods which nobody would buy. Some of these enterprises have already come to an end in necessary ruin. Others are deferring their fate by adding to an indebtedness which is already greater than the present value of the entire property or investment. Much of the capital thus invested is lost, and can never be recovered by any possible skill or ingenuity.

My friend the editor of the labor-reform newspaper holds that the best means for securing the rights of the laboring people, and obtaining a just remuneration for their labor, is the multiplication of their wants; that is, they should be taught to live more and more expensively. He says that civilization consists in this constant increase in the number of the wants of human beings, and that we must encourage the working-people to demand and use so many things as necessaries of life for them that employers will be compelled to give them higher wages. But I think that all the facts which have any relation to the subject indicate that this particular element or tendency of civilization has already an excessive development, and that most persons in this country have already more wants than can possibly be satisfied. It would tend to greater clearness of thinking if people would remember that there is no evidence of any provision in the nature of things which assures us the possession of everything we may want. It does not appear that the earth contains materials for unlimited wealth, or that it will ever be possible for everybody to be rich and live in luxury. The earth does contain materials for subsistence for human beings, as long as there are not too many of them. But the overproduction of human beings is a frequently recurring fact in the history of the race. It is a possibility in nearly all civilized countries, and though it may not require attention here for a long time to come, it is certain that its recognition is already necessary in all systematic treatment of the chief subjects connected with political economy and national welfare.

I believe the labor reformers are in error in thinking that the continued and indefinite reduction of the hours of labor would be a benefit to the working-people; but I am aware that they have the support, in this view of the matter, of nearly all the political economists of every school. Most writers upon the subject eulogize the effect of labor-saving machinery upon the interests of the workingman, affirming that any inconvenience resulting from it is but temporary, and that the permanent effects are necessarily beneficial. It is constantly assumed, as if it were an indisputable certainty, that the less men have to work the better for them. I cannot discover any necessity or provision in the nature of things which renders it thus certain that all devices and inventions which result in dispensing with human labor are to work advantage to mankind. It is time to challenge this assumption. It is entirely a question of fact, and a priori reasoning is here out of place. The most positive proof that labor-saving machinery is beneficial up to some certain point or degree of development and application cannot be safely accepted as evidence that its development and application can be profitably extended without limit.

I believe that for most men more than eight hours' work per day is required for the maintenance of physical, mental, and moral health. I think that for most men, including operatives, mechanics, farmers, and clergymen, more than eight hours' labor per day is necessary, in order to keep down and utilize the forces of the animal nature and passions. I believe that if improvements in machinery should discharge men from the necessity of laboring more than six hours a day, society would rot in measureless and fatal animalism. I have worked more than ten hours per day during most of my life, and beli ;ve it is best for us all to be compelled to work. It would be well, I think, :f we could make it impossible for an idler to live on the face of the earth. Religious teachers are not without responsibility for having taught that the necessity of labor is a curse. The world owes most of its growth hitherto to men who tried to do as much work as they could. Its debt is small to the men who wished to do as little as possible.

The principal thing required in connection with these interests of our national life is, I think, that the operatives and other working-people shall have a better education,—an education which shall include some more adequate safeguards or defenses against illusion that are provided by the methods of culture and training now in common use in this country. As things are, it can scarcely be said that any effort is made to teach the working-people anything regarding their duties, rights, and interests as citizens, as Americans, except by the churches and the labor reformers. As religion is at present usually understood by its teachers in this country, it does not habitually give great prominence or emphasis to the cultivation of feelings of attachment, responsibility, and obligation to our country. It is commonly regarded as dealing with men only as individuals, and as accomplishing the elevation of society by improving the character of the units of which it is composed. Few, even of our best people, have now any vital feeling or sense of nationality, of our position and duties as Americans. Nor have I been able to find anywhere a clear exposition of the claims which our country has upon us all, of any service which the nation rightly demands of its children, except what is required in time of war.

I think the time will come (and should come soon) when the preparation and supply of suitable reading matter, as an instrument for the education and guidance of the working-people, will be regarded as a necessary part of the equipment of the manufacturers in a town like this. It is so now, but the prevailing optimism, being essentially unintelligent, and therefore wanting in flexibility, is not yet aware of the new conditions and tendencies in our industrial, social, and national life. The capitalists, manufacturers, and cultivated people of every town where there are one thousand operatives should unite in the publication of a small, low-priced newspaper for circulation among the working-people,—a paper conducted by some one who understands that the elements and tendencies of our national life cannot be adequately dealt with by the subjective method which most of our teachers now employ; by a man who sees clearly that the knowledge and recognition of the objective facts of human experience supply the only sufficient basis for wise action.

The use of such means for the education and guidance of the working-people would cost far less, in money even, than the present plan of letting things take their course. The confident expectation that an improvement or revival of business will soothe the discontent of the working classes, and relieve the country from anxiety regarding their action, which has become general within the last few months is, in part, the result of a hasty and superficial judgment of the facts of the time. There are many working-men and teachers of workingmen in this country, believing in the absolute sovereignty of the laboring classes, who would not be rendered less active or determined in their campaign against the existing order of things by any possible degree of industrial prosperity. They believe in a different order of society, and hope to organize the wage laborers of the United States, and unite them in a persistent endeavor to modify the existing social and political order. They have more impulse and endurance than most of the supporters of our existing civilization, and also a better under-standing of the necessity of adapting means to ends. They have also a measure of truth on their side, for the existing order and civilization cannot be defended as complete, or wholly just; they need improvement.

I wish to deal gently with the impenetrable inapprehension which thinks it a sufficient answer to all such pleas for an increase of activity on the part of cultivated people to say that the ignorant and visionary schemers who would like to overthrow our institutions can never succeed. Sarcasm here would be a waste of force. But intelligence can understand that some things short of absolute ruin are still so undesirable and injurious that it is worth while to try to prevent them. The force by which the world has chiefly grown hitherto is the love of excellence for its own sake, the feeling of obligation to try to make things better, to remedy injustice, and to remove hurtful, enslaving ignorance whenever we can do so. But it is to be confessed that these are considerations of little weight with the optimism of our time.

It is not enough that people who have money and culture pay the operatives their wages. That is not all that justice requires. It is my belief that, in the city of which I have here written, the manufacturers were paying the laborers, at the time of my visit, all that they could pay, and that in some cases their wages absorbed the entire profits of the business. But the working-people are ignorant, and they are not taught as they should be. They are among the most valuable and indispensable of all the children of our country. Our national industry and prosperity would be impossible without them. Their life is at best rather hard and uninviting, with little room or means for the ameliorating, refining, and sustaining influences which vary and brighten life for many others. There is far too little fraternal interest in them,—too little disposition to share their burdens, and to help them to make the best of their life and of themselves that its inevitable conditions will allow. We do not know as much about them as we should. Most people think and care very little about the operatives, except when they threaten to make trouble. It is not safe or wise to allow so large a class to be so far alien and separate from the influences and spirit of our national life. I do not think the mill people are, as a class, inferior in morality, in the ordinary sense of that word, to any equally numerous class in this country. On the contrary, I believe they are superior in this respect to any class of men and women who do not work.

We ought to know more about this sort of people, about their circumstances, their ways of living, their thought, and the tendencies and effects of such a life as theirs upon character and civilization. As things are, there is nobody to speak for them. . . .

11. Figures and Groups

Illustrations of Social Life

1. *Emancipation, 1865.*

at the Headquarters of the Lincoln Central Campaign Club, Corner of Broadway and Twenty Third Street New York Sept. 22 ᵈ, 1864 being a perfect fac simile of the room &c. &c. (From the New York World Sept. 23 ᵈ, 1864) No sooner were the formal proceedings and speeches hurried through with, than the room was cleared for a 'negro ball,' which then and there took place! Some members of the 'Central Lincoln Club' left the room before the mystical and circling rites of languishing glance and mazy dance commenced. But that MANY remained is also true. This fact WE CERTIFY, *that on the floor during the progress of the ball were many of the accredited leaders of the Black Republican party*, thus testifying their faith by their works in the hall and headquarters of their political gathering. There were Republican OFFICE-HOLDERS, and prominent men of various degrees, and at least one PRESIDENTIAL ELECTOR ON THE REPUBLICAN TICKET.

2. *The Miscegenation Ball, 1864.*

3. *The First Vote, 1867.*

4. *Scene on the Mississippi, 1878.*

5. *Seeing the Circus Pass, 1872.*

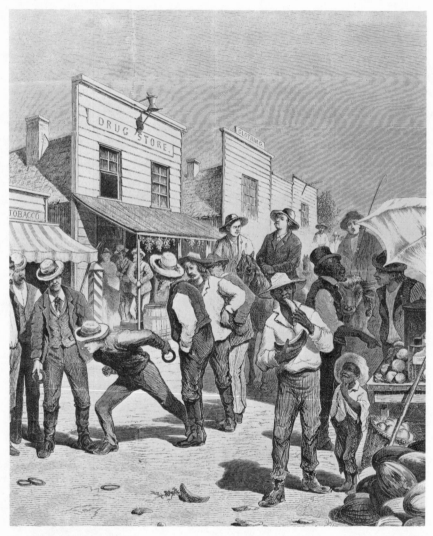

6. *Pitching Quoits, 1874.*

7. *A Sweltering Night in New York, 1883.*

8. *Family Record, Photograph Album, 1873.*

9. *Rush for Rooms at the Philadelphia Hotels, 1876.*

10. *Great Five Mile Rowing Match, 1867.*

11. *Influence of Music, 1869.*

12. *Hunting, Fishing, and Forest Scenes, 1867.*

12 An Excursion Into a New Landscape

From the time of its beginnings in the 1840's, the railroad was viewed with mixed feelings. Remarkably appropriate in its physical aspect as a symbol of concentrated energy and power, the railroad became inseparable from the idea of national destiny and of progress. But a sense of alarm or menace often accompanied the image of the mechanical horse in its leap through the countryside. For good or ill the railroad clearly made a decisive difference in American society, as Henry Adams understood when he wrote that with the opening of the Boston and Albany line in 1838, "the old universe was thrown into the ash-heap and a new one created." The new universe brought with it a new, technological landscape, which, as Leo Marx has shown in *The Machine in the Garden* (1964), seemed to most Americans to be beneficent evidence of progress. But not always: writers like Hawthorne, Melville and Mark Twain expressed in their fictions an undercurrent of fear that the machine would upset the values associated with a pretechnological pastoral idea of landscape.

In the post-Civil War period the machine seemed to enjoy a status virtually free from anxiety; social critics attacked the pathology of the factory system, but were generally sanguine about the potentially healthy benefits of mechanization. There were exceptions, as subsequent selections will show, but in the following excerpt from a cheerful account of an excursion by rail from Washington, D. C. to Niagara Falls, the wonders of technology are applauded in a "polite" style of popular magazine prose. It is interesting, though, that even in such an optimistic and genteel essay, the author cannot avoid certain jarring notes.

Travelling by Telegraph

JAMES RICHARDSON

Morning on Arlington Heights, after a frosty night; season, Indian summer. The broad reach of the Potomac, curving from Georgetown to below the mouth of the Eastern Branch, sleeps under the slant rays of the haze-tempered sun, unreached by the puffs of wind which rustle the crimson foliage that still clings to the oaks on the Heights, or send the fallen leaves chasing each other by fits and starts, like flocks of yellow-birds frollicking over a patch of thistles. The air is crisp and cool; the sunshine just warm enough to be inviting. Both together act like a tonic, filling body and mind with a healthy glow that gives a zest to mere existence. The view from the Heights is not imposing. It is not particularly beautiful. Yet it would be hard to look on it with indifference on a day like this, when all the sunshine of the ripened year seems to have got into the blood,—when the mind dances with the overflow of animal spirits (*pace* Huxley and the rest—"nerve-vibrations!"), and we are eager to find pleasure in everything.

Did you never envy the perfect abandon of some plump little chipmunk, as he lay stretched along the sunny side of a rail, alertly lazy, rippling his tail and chippering from very gladness? We share this careless joy to-day, his utter surrender to the delight of living. A tardy vacation has given us a respite from the rush and worry of every-day life, and we have followed the example of Nature, giving ourselves up to a brief period of æsthetic loafing.

The budding and blooming activity of spring, the panting toil of summer, the hurried ingathering of early fall, are past. Mother Earth has finished her year's work, has put on her holiday garb, and entered upon a fortnight of do-nothing enjoyment. She enjoys herself handsomely. There is no fretting over the mistakes and mishaps of the year, untimely frosts, occasional hail-storms and too frequent droughts; no borrowing trouble from the immeasurable bundle that winter is bringing. "Let by-gones be by-gones," she says: "let the future take care of itself!" It is the holiday of the year, and for the nonce Nature's sole business is to have a good time. We have a chance to do likewise: we will do it!

Thus meditating, we sit at the foot of the old flag-staff and drink in the

James Richardson, "Travelling by Telegraph," *Scribner's Monthly*, IV (1872), 1–23.

influence of the season and the scene. Before us, almost beneath us, lies the ample plain of Washington, rimmed by low hills and a placid river. Through an opening in the trees we look down upon the Heights of Georgetown, but the distance is too great for us to distinguish the handsome dwellings which give that ancient city so honorable a fame. In Washington everything is eclipsed by the magnificent proportions of the national buildings. The Treasury building and the Patent Office gleam in the sunshine like mammoth blocks of marble, and over all rises the noble dome of the Capitol, a mountain of light.

Behind us is that relic of plantation grandeur, Arlington House, an imitation Grecian temple, with a double row of clumsy columns sustaining nothing and shutting out half the view. Behind the house endless rows of painted head-boards mark the resting-places of thousands of boys in blue and boys in grey who lie in peace awaiting the Final Reveille.

Sauntering about the garden, enjoying the sunshine and the flowers, or wandering through the deserted rooms of the old mansion, vainly trying to re-people them as of old, when their walls rang with merriment or glowed with generous hospitality, when culture and comfort, fame and fashion made the old house their abiding-place, we fall in with a party from Baltimore, pilgrims like ourselves to this historic spot. Fortunately, there are no ladies in either party to keep up the bars of formality. We meet, mingle, and by the time the circuit of the grounds is completed, the two parties are merged into one.

At last the doubled party stands on the grassy mound in front of the house. The artist closes his sketch-book, and we begin to speak of returning. Our coachman brought us by a roundabout road through Georgetown. "Why not return by the Long Bridge?"

"Impossible," is the reply of one of our new friends; "it has been torn down. That is the Alexandria and Washington Railroad Bridge," he goes on, noticing our look of surprise toward the long black line crossing the river below us. "By the side of it the Baltimore and Potomac Railroad Company are putting up a splendid bridge, with carriage-ways, on the site of the old Long Bridge, to connect with the Alexandria and Fredericksburg Railroad; but it is not passable yet."

"Baltimore and Potomac! Never heard of that road before. Something new, isn't it?"

"Quite new,—indeed, not completed yet. There has been a great deal of heavy work to do here at Washington and at Baltimore,—tunneling, bridging, and so on. When we get that done the rest of the road can be put through rapidly."

"Some very interesting cuttings at this end of the line," interposes another (railroad men, all of them, it is easy to see). "If you care for such things, you'll find them well worth a visit."

"How deep are they?" eagerly queries our scientific companion, whose geological proclivities are incessantly leading him and us into dirty places.

"Forty or fifty feet, perhaps."

"Splendid! singular formation here at Washington; calico-clay,—very curious, you know—"

"No! we don't know, and don't want to," Artist interrupts, with some acerbity. Artist never did admire clay-banks.

But science carries the day, as it always does, sooner or later, against prejudice. Besides, our business in Washington is to see the sights, and what better sight could be seen—patriotically considered—than a new raid upon our sleepy capital by the army of progress?—particularly when we should have for (volunteer) chaperones such entertaining captains in that army.

The spell of reverent silence that falls on us as we drive slowly past the white field where

> ". . . Glory guards with solemn round
> The bivouac of the dead,"

wears away as we descend the hill, forgetting the sorrowful Present of the old mansion, while our thoughts recur to the happy years gone by, to the joyous companies of the fair and the famous who climbed this historic hill ere the dead took possession of its summit.

"What a glorious place this must have been for lovers' strolls!"

The remark comes from the back seat, as the line of carriages winds round a charming curve through a deeply-shaded dell.

"That shows how your mind runs," is the mild rebuke from the opposite side; and we all look at the offender as if shocked by a thought so out of keeping with the character of the place.

"And what were *you* thinking about so seriously?"

"I?—I—I—was thinking what splendid tie-timber these oaks would make."

"Sacrilege! You railroad men would dig the hill down, if it stood in your way, and use the bones to ballast your road!"

"But what is this new road you were telling about? What is the need of it? Isn't the present road sufficient?"

"Quite sufficient."

"Is yours any shorter?"

"A trifle longer, if anything."

To our abject ignorance of railroad matters the idea of building a new road by the side of an old one, when the old road is capable of doing all the work, seems the height of absurdity.

"I see you don't understand these things. The construction of this Baltimore and Potomac road has been compelled by the dog-in-the-manger policy of the Baltimore and Ohio Railroad Company. Controlling the only line between Washington and Baltimore, that corporation has naturally sought to use it so as to send all the travel and traffic between Washington and the West over their main road. It has carried its efforts in this direction so far as to refuse to extend even the ordinary courtesies to other roads, to the great inconvenience of the public."

"How so?"

"Suppose you wish to go to Chicago by way of Harrisburg or the Falls. You go to the station here and call for a through ticket. You can't get it. The Baltimore and Ohio Company will ticket you only to Baltimore. There you are put to the delay and trouble of buying a new ticket, and transferring yourself and baggage across the city to another station before you can fairly begin your journey. Passengers from the West are subjected to the same inconvenience, none of the great East and West lines north of Baltimore being able to check beyond our city.

"The main competition being with the Pennsylvania Central in connection with the Northern Central, these Companies have undertaken the construction of the Baltimore and Potomac line. When it is finished, passengers will be able to check through from Washington to any part of the country, and trains will be run to accommodate them. Besides, the monopoly of the B. and O. Company broken, competition will naturally benefit the public by a reduction of rates, which might be considerably lowered and still give a reasonable profit, as well as by a saving of time and trouble."

"A tender regard your great Railroad corporations have for the dear public, truly,—when it pays!"

"Of course, 'when it pays.' You surely do not imagine that men build railroads and run them from pure benevolence, or for the fun of the thing. Self-interest is at the bottom of every work, except, perhaps, missionary work,—and no one pretends that railroading is of that sort. Under a monopoly, self-interest may be and generally is grasping and unwise. But, with plenty of competition, the truest self-interest is that which studies to give the public the greatest return for its money consistent with legitimate profit. In railroading the main returns are safety, speed, economy, and comfort. The road which excels in these will get the most custom, and presumably will make the most money. Here self-interest compels the study of public interest, and the public reap the benefit of the improvements thus suggested. What those improvements have been you can easily estimate, by comparing the facilities for intercourse enjoyed now with those that existed fifty or even twenty-five years ago." . . .

"You have seen how railroads are made," our chief guide says, as we stand leaning over the fence on the brow of the hill overlooking the Eastern Branch; "would you like to see how we run them?"

"To put the question in another way," he continues, "will you accept the hospitalities of the Northern Central Railway Company, and spend the rest of your vacation on a run through some of the finest scenery in the country?"

"What do you mean?"

"Simply this: it is necessary for certain officers of the company to make a business trip over the road and its branches once or twice a year. We intend to make such an excursion next week. Our custom is to combine pleasure with business, and take a party of friends along. We shall have a special train, and everything to insure a pleasant time, taking the whole week for it. Will you join us?"

Baltimore—Philadelphia—Harrisburg—up the Susquehanna, among the coal mines—over the Alleghanies—through the Glen region—to Niagara Falls! The programme is too tempting to be lightly treated; and there is no mistaking the frank heartiness of the invitation. We talk it over on our way back to our carriages, which have been left half a mile behind.

"Beautiful scenery," says the artist, who has spent a summer along the banks of the Susquehanna. "There's not another river in the country like it."

"Then there are the coal mines," says the geologist. "I've seen pretty much every kind of mining but that."

"And the Alleghany wilderness," says another. "Next to the Adirondacks, I'm told."

"And Watkins' Glen," say we all. "That's the latest rage, and we haven't seen it."

"And the special train!"

The Potomac may have its attractions; but it can offer no "special train." About face! for the North!

"Remember," urge our seductive friends, as we scrape the red and yellow clay from our boots: "Calvert Station, eight o'clock Monday morning. Don't disappoint us!" . . .

"What's our programme for to-day?"

"We run by telegraph—to Harrisburg—shall take the day for it."

All day for a three-hours' ride—by telegraph! The incongruity is a little comical, to say the least. But the Veteran does not appear to be conscious of it.

"Usually a special train is run by special schedule," he explains; "but as we could not tell where or how long we might stop by the way, we have arranged to run by special orders from our office in Baltimore. At each station the conductors will receive a dispatch, telling him what trains to look out for, what to keep out of the way of, how long he can be in making the next station, and so on. If we wish to stop longer at any point, we telegraph the fact, and the road is kept clear for us."

There is a peculiar charm in this free-and-easy railroading, with no other object than to see all there is to be seen, and enjoy one's self generally. The present moment, the present scene, receives undivided attention, regardless of what is to come, and undisturbed by any desire to get anywhere. It has all the freedom of a sauntering tour on foot, with none of the fatigue, and with the delightful ability to hurry over a commonplace region a mile a minute if we want to. As yet we have had no occasion to hurry. . . .

On every side are evidences of our passage into a new State, with a different population, different history, different modes of life. One who had never heard of the famous line of Mason and Dixon, might discover it by the sudden contrast in the appearance of things on either side. In physical characteristics the better portions of the Counties of Baltimore and York are not much unlike; in all that shows the hand of man they are strikingly different.

The well-to-do old-time farmer of Maryland sprang from a high-bred, aristocratic race. The very location of his residence shows it. The first requisite seems to have been a commanding prospect. He shunned the valley, choosing rather the highest point accessible, away from the highway, and overlooking a wide reach of country. Here he built a cream-colored Grecian temple, and surrounded it with trees. The barns and outhouses are in the back ground, secondary, and concealed, if possible, from general view.

The Pennsylvania settler nestled in a hollow on the sunny side of a hill, and as near the highway as possible. He built him a small house of stones or logs, surrounded it with sheds and cattle-yards, cut away all the trees, and spent the rest of his life improving his little farm and erecting an immense barn, which he painted red, and ornamented with as many windows as the frame-work would admit of. What purpose he had in lighting up his hay-mows like a five-story cotton-mill it is impossible to conjecture.

"Perhaps a sash-factory was one of the first manufacturing enterprises in this region—and you know the Pennsylvanians are strong for encouraging home industry."

"Or the fashion once started became a craze, like that of Yankee farmers for lightning-rods," suggests another.

Close by, sometimes attached to, the old homestead, the thrifty descendants of the original settlers have erected a more pretentious, yet comparatively small red-brick house. In some cases the front yard is fenced in and planted with shrubbery, or a few flowers, but as a rule the æsthetics of life appear to be but little regarded. The farms, however, show admirable care and culture, while solid wealth and homely comfort are visible on every side.

"Pennsylvania milk, Robert?"

"No, sah; got dat at a station 'cross the line, sah."

"Very rich milk."

"Have another glass, sah?"

"Thank you, yes. We don't get such milk as that in the city."

"Delightful flavor, don't you think?"

"Delicious. What do they feed the cattle with over there, Robert?"

"C'on, sah, mostly; rye sometimes, sah. Dere's nothing better'n a little ol' rye, sah, for dat purpose."

"Evidently not"; and the man of science empties the second glass abstractly, reconsidering his first impression that the peculiar flavor must have been due to something in the soil. . . .

Awaiting orders at Goldsboro, we admiringly study the new locomotive that has served us so faithfully to-day. Polished, massive, magnificent, it stands a triumph of human genius,—a type of beautiful strength.

"Could we ride with the driver?"

"You won't find it so pleasant as you imagine, but you can try it."

The conductor signals, the engineer grasps one of the mysterious levers which put him *en rapport* with the modern behemoth, and the docile monster whisks away as if rejoicing in the lightness of the play-day train behind him. As our speed increases we become painfully aware that we are not on springs. The easy swing of the car does not pertain to the locomotive, which jumps to its work with a rioting, trampling, trip-hammer energy that disdains the thought of ease and softness. We cannot keep our feet, and find it hard to keep the high and narrow slippery seat, with nothing to hold on to. The speed seems terrific. The country no longer glides away from us with a drifting motion,—it rushes on us like a thunderbolt. The trees and houses have a whirling motion, fierce, tumultuous, maddening, as though hurled towards a vortex from which we are momentarily escaping. Instinctively we shrink as the track cuts under us, and the huge rocks by the wayside seem flying at us.

Ahead is a curve. What is beyond it? We watch the disclosing line with peculiar fascination, for terrible possibilities are ever just out of sight. Gradually our senses become used to their new experience, and we are willing to forego our useless vigilance. On the right the river flows like a river in a vision,—noiseless, swift, and strangely calm. On the left the hills waltz and reel, bearing down on the track like an endless avalanche. Above, the fiery clouds betoken the close of a brilliant day, but it makes us dizzy to look at them. It is pleasanter to study the steady poise of the driver. Alert, self-possessed, unpretending, he sees every inch of the track by flashes of observation, lets out or restrains the heedless energy of his all but living engine, and holds the lives of us all with a grasp as true as it is seemingly unconscious. We plunge into the shadow of Kittatinny Mountain, pierce the point of rocks that projects into the river, and stop amid a confusion of backing trains, shrieking engines, and the shouts of trackmen. We are at Bridgeport, and as soon as the bridge is clear we shall cross to Harrisburg.

"I shall have a realizing sense of my obligation to the engine-driver, after this," remarks the untraveled man, as we climb down from the locomotive; "and a wholesome respect for his skill and courage."

The red flames of the Lochiel iron-works gleam on the water as we roll slowly over the long bridge. The islands opposite are but vague shadows on the smooth surface of the river; and, by contrast with the roaring, tumultuous, headlong speed of the past half-hour, the quiet, gliding motion of the car seems to drift us into the night as into a dream.

Morning finds us in the City of Brotherly Love.

We had a jolly run last night over the road, to be retraced to-day, but it was not by telegraph.

The forenoon is well advanced before our hosts have finished the business that called them hither, and the "special" is headed once more toward the Susquehanna. At the last moment the Executive enters with a representative of the Pennsylvania Railroad,—"the Subscriber."

"And where is the Poet?"

"Could not get away to-day."

A chorus of regrets testifies the disappointment of all at this announcement, for the poet had proved a delightful companion on our midnight run from Harrisburg.

"But he sends these verses in commemoration of our ride last night. I propose that the Quiet Man be appointed reader."

The appointment is made by acclamation, and the charms of Fairmount are forgotten while the reading goes on.

THE RAILWAY RIDE

In their yachts on ocean gliding,
On their steeds Arabian riding,
Whirled o'er snows on tinkling sledges,
   Men forget their woe and pain;
What the pleasure then should fill them—
What the ecstasy should thrill them—
Borne with ponderous speed, and thunderous,
   O'er the narrow iron plain.

Restless as a dream of vengeance,
Mark you there the iron engines
Blowing steam from snorting nostrils,
   Moving each upon its track;
Sighing, panting, anxious, eager,
Not with purpose mean or meager,
But intense intent for motion,
   For the liberty they lack.

Now one screams in triumph, for the
Engine-driver, grimed and swarthy,
Lays his hand upon the lever,
   And the steed is loose once more;
Off it moves, and fast and faster,
With no urging from the master,
Till the awed earth shakes in terror
   At the rumbling and the roar.

Crossing long and thread-like bridges,
Spanning streams, and cleaving ridges,
Sweeping over broad green meadows,
   That in starless darkness lay—
How the engine rocks and clatters,
Showers of fire around it scatters,
While its blazing eye outpeering
   Looks for perils in the way.

To yon tunnel-drift careering,
In its brown mouth disappearing,

Past from sight and passed from hearing,
 Silence follows like a spell;
Then a sudden sound-burst surges,
As the train from earth emerges
With a scream of exultation,
 With a wild and joyous yell.

What the chariot swift of Ares
Which a god to battle carries?
What the steeds the rash boy handled
 Harnessed to the sun-god's wain?
Those are mythic; this is real;
Born not of the past ideal,
But of craft and strength and purpose,
 Love of speed and thirst of gain.

Oh! what wildness! oh! what gladness!
Oh! what joy akin to madness!
Oh what reckless feeling raises
 Us to-day beyond the stars!
What to us all human ant hills,
Fame, fools sigh for, land that man tills,
In the swinging and the clattering
 And the rattling of the cars?

.   .   .

Sweeping over the level river plain near the end of our day's ride, we pass a lofty furnace-stack, which pours its sooty products into the still air. "The Lochiel Iron Mills that we saw from the bridge last night?"

"We haven't come to them yet. These are the Baldwin Steel Works. The most of our rails are made here."

"Have we time to see the operation?"

A hasty consultation among the railroad men ensues. It is decided that our preparations for to-morrow can be made after business hours, and the order is given to return to Baldwin Station, which has been left behind.

Our visit is fortunately timed, for preparations are already making for charging the huge converter. With but a passing glance at the preliminary storm of fire that roars from the mouth of the converter, we follow the superintendent past the hot piles of ingots lately drawn from the moulds; past the great receivers wherein Æolus is imprisoned and forced to do fiery service, past the engines which generate the power used in the Cyclopean operations going on all around, and stop to watch the gigantic steam hammers under which the glowing masses of steel are forged by blows that may be twenty tons or twenty grains as the forger wills. Just beyond the forge is the rolling-mill where the white-hot bars of steel are seized and drawn into rails with a rapidity that bewilders. But it is time for tapping the furnaces, and we hasten back, with scarcely a look at the various piles of rails awaiting shipment.

This is no place for the philosophy of the Bessemer process: no place for describing all the steps by which crude iron is now so quickly converted into steel. Our attention is absorbed by the scenic effect, and that is beyond the power of words to describe. Even the pencil of a Weir would fail to do it justice.

"What are those circular artists driving at over there?" queries the Subscriber, pointing to a number of men on a raised platform, each with his hand on a wheel like that of a car-brake.

The Superintendent explains how their movements control the almost resistless force of the hydraulic presses, and we stand amazed at the magic by which a turn of the wrist is made to manipulate the ponderous converter, with its charge of melted metal, as easily as a man might handle a glass of water.

A whirlwind of sparks pours from the converter's mouth and rolls along the vaulted roof, sending sudden gusts of fire almost into our faces. The converter comes to rest and the fiery blast is turned off. In a moment streams of molten iron creep along the conduits from the row of furnaces, and pour a flood of scintillating metal into the converter. The charge complete, the blast is turned on again with augmented force, and through a hundred openings air is forced into the liquid metal burning out the carbon and sulphur and other impurities, and sending the dross up the chimney— a coruscating metallic fountain. Our eyes are blinded by the brightness, yet fascinated by the play of colors that mark the progress of the purification. The prevailing hue is a rose-tint of exquisite loveliness, lost in the dazzling whiteness when we look steadily, but reappearing as often as the eye is rested by looking away for a moment.

"We have pure iron now," remarks the Superintendent, as the flame suddenly ceases. "In a moment will be added the compound, which is to change the iron into steel."

The converting mixture pours a fiery cascade into the converter, and a magnificent eruption of many-colored scintillations shows the intensity of chemical action going on. It ends abruptly, and as the huge retort is canted over to pour its contents into the moulds below, we follow the Superintendent's suggestion, and look in at its shining mouth.

"You know what white-heat looks like now," he says; and we confess that thus far we have had no adequate conception of its perfect whiteness.

On our way back to our car we stop to look at the crushing-machine for pulverizing the refractory lining of the converter.

"If you only had jaws like that, Subscriber," remarks the Little Man, "you wouldn't have had to send back the chops they offered you at the hotel this morning."

The Subscriber watches the machine a moment, working his mouth with unconscious envy, as the blocks of quartzite crumble to sand in its resistless bite: then keeping time with the machine, he ejaculates,—

"With—a—masticating—apparatus—like—that—a man—might *live*,— yes, sir!—a man might LIVE—in a second-rate boarding-house!"

An express train follows us in to Harrisburg. As we press through the waiting throng that crowds the platform and overruns the road-way,—for the station is sadly lacking in capacity,—a wild-looking son of Ham sweeps down the track, hustling men and women right and left, clearing the way for the approaching locomotive.

"Crazy Dick," says the Executive, as the apparition speeds past, now dashing forward to shoulder from the track some heedless loiterer, now falling into a reckless dog-trot, scarcely a foot ahead of the cow-catcher.

"There seems to be method in his madness."

"Indeed there is, and a useful method too. Dick saves a good many lives in the course of a year."

"In the employ of the road?"

"No, on his own hook. It's a craze he has."

The train passes on, and Dick slouches away, looking as if he never had a thought or a purpose in his life. His whole mind seems absorbed by a single object—to keep people from being run over, and nothing but an approaching train can rouse him to activity. Then his zeal flames out in a magnificent burst of action, to be followed by abject listlessness until the next train is due.

"*Live?* Oh, Dick is one that takes no thought for the morrow. The men about the station see that his board is paid at the lunch-counter; and the engineers, conductors, and other roadmen club together now and then and rig him out with a new suit of clothes. He sleeps anywhere."

Among many incidents in Dick's career, recounted on our way to the Superintendent's office to make arrangements for to-morrow's run up the river, one especially illustrates the intensity of his life-saving instinct.

Two or three years ago a company of Harrisburg firemen succeeded in enticing Dick away from his self-elected duty—not an easy thing to do— and took him off with them on an excursion to Altoona. Arrived there, Dick straightaway forgot his companions and fell to guarding the track, as at home. Like many another public benefactor's, Dick's motives were misjudged. His zeal was attributed to the wrong spirit, and before his friends could explain matters he was marched off to the police-station on the charge of drunkenness. Naturally, the simple-minded fellow took his arrest very much to heart; but that was nothing to his distress on his return to Harrisburg, to find that during his absence a boy had been run over and killed—the first accident of the kind that had occurred since Dick came upon the field.

"I done knowed su'thin' would happen if I went away!" the poor fellow cried, deploring his remissness in a storm of weeping. Since then nothing can induce him to desert his post; and so plainly beneficial is his mania, that he is allowed to pursue his mission unchecked, although it is only too evident that it must some day come to a tragic end.

13. Perils of Mechanization

Virtually a separate American institution, the Adams family of Boston and Quincy had a remarkable record of public service. Conservative and historically self-conscious in its outlook, the family contributed two presidents, John Adams and his son John Quincy Adams, and the statesman Charles Francis Adams, who served in the crucial role of ambassador to England during the Civil War. The tradition of statesmanship and public service was deflected in two of Charles Francis Adams' sons, Brooks and Henry, who, unable to find places for themselves in the new political and social world after the Civil War, turned to teaching and writing, casting somewhat bitter and disillusioned reflections upon the course of American life. But the tradition was carried forward in the career of another brother, Charles Francis Adams, Jr., who, although he never held elected office, was one of the most active public figures of his times.

Adams' career represents the attempt at reconciliation between the conservative New England politics of the gentleman and the new conditions of power. A graduate of Harvard in 1856, a student of law in the office of Richard Henry Dana, a close friend of the older Charles Sumner, Adams enlisted as a regimental officer in the war. While his brother Henry spent the duration with his father in the consulate in London, Charles Francis served three and a half years, saw action at Antietam and Gettysburg, and spent part of his time with a Negro regiment. After the war he left the law and devoted himself to a study of the railroad system, its economic function in the nation's expansion, the role of government aid, and the corruption and recklessness involved in planning and financing roads. He published a series of essays *(Chapters of Erie and Other Essays,* 1871) exposing the schemes of a group of speculators to gain possession of and wreck the Erie Railroad. In 1869 he was appointed to the newly formed Massachusetts Board of Railroad Commissioners, and as chairman produced a series of reports on accidents and faults in the system. In 1884 he became president of the Union Pacific Railroad, and before being ousted by Jay Gould six years later, he brought the system back from the verge of bankruptcy.

But he had had enough of dealing with the new tycoons, from whom he was separated by birth and education as well as principles. He remained active in public life, particularly on the local level—he was largely responsible for reforms in the Quincy school system—and as a member of the Board of Overseers of Harvard, was influential in curricular reform. He devoted himself to historical writings, mainly in local New England history. He also wrote biographies of Richard Henry Dana (1890), and of his father (1900).

The Revere Catastrophe

CHARLES FRANCIS ADAMS, JR.

The history of railroad development in New England now covers a period of more than forty years. During all that time there have been but two accidents within the limits of the six States which have left a deep and lasting impression on the public mind; two only which have become, as it were, names as familiar as household words. The first of these happened at the Norwalk bridge, in Connecticut, on the 8th of May, 1853; the second, in front of the railroad station at Revere, in Massachusetts, on the 26th of August, 1871. The Norwalk disaster was described in The Atlantic for December, and the present paper will relate almost exclusively to that at Revere. This was, properly speaking, not an accident at all; it was essentially a catastrophe, the legitimate and almost inevitable final calamity of an antiquated and insufficient system. As such it should long remain a subject for prayerful meditation to all those who may at any time be entrusted with the immediate operating of railroads. It was terribly dramatic, but it was also frightfully instructive; and while the lesson was by no means lost, it yet admits of further and advantageous study. For, like most other men whose lives are devoted to a special calling, the managers of railroads are apt to be very much wedded to their own methods, and when any new emergency necessitates a new appliance, they not infre-

Charles Francis Adams, Jr., "The Revere Catastrophe," *Atlantic Monthly*, XXXVII (1876), 92–103.

quently, as Captain Tyler well puts it in one of his reports, "display more ingenuity in finding objections than in overcoming them." As the statistics of the subsequent years show clearly enough, the Revere disaster was fruitful of new safeguards to travel in New England; and yet at the same time, in spite of that experience, there are to-day roads in Massachusetts, even, the managers of which cling with an almost touching faith to the simple rules and antiquated appliances of twenty years ago. Their minds, like those of their English brethren, display a truly marvelous fertility in puerile objections.

The Eastern Railroad of Massachusetts connects Boston with Portland, in the State of Maine, by a line which is located close along the sea-shore. Between Boston and Lynn, a distance of eleven miles, the main road is in large part built across the salt marshes, but there is a branch which leaves it at Everett, a small station some miles out of Boston, and thence, running deviously through a succession of towns on the higher ground, connects with the main track again at Lynn; thus making what is known in England as a loop-road. At the time of the Revere accident this branch was equipped with but a single track, and was operated simply by schedule, without any reliance on the telegraph; and indeed there were not even telegraphic offices at a number of its stations. Revere, the name of the station in front of which the accident took place, was on the main line about five miles from Boston and two miles from Everett, where the Saugus branch, as the loop-road was called, began. . . .

The travel over the Eastern Railroad is of a somewhat exceptional nature, varying in a more than ordinary degree with the different seasons of the year. During the winter months the corporation had, in 1871, to provide for a regular passenger movement of about seventy-five thousand a week, but in the summer what is known as the excursion and pleasure travel not infrequently increased the number to one hundred and ten thousand, and even more. As a natural consequence, during certain weeks of each summer, and more especially towards the close of August, it was no unusual thing for the corporation to find itself taxed beyond its utmost resources. It is emergencies of this description, which periodically occur on every railroad, which always subject to the final test the organization and discipline of companies and the capacity of superintendents. A railroad in quiet times is like a ship in steady weather; almost anybody can manage the one or sail the other; it is the sudden stress which reveals the undeveloped strength or the hidden weakness; and the truly instructive feature in the Revere accident lay in the amount of hidden weakness everywhere which was brought to light under that sudden stress. During the week ending with that Saturday evening upon which the disaster occurred, the rolling stock of the road had been heavily taxed, not only to accommodate the usual tide of summer travel, then at its full flood, but also those attending a military muster and two large camp-meetings upon its line. The number of passengers going over it had accordingly risen from about one hundred and ten thousand, the full summer average, to over one hundred and forty thousand; while instead of the one hundred and fifty-two trains a day provided for in the running schedule, there were no less than one hundred and ninety-two. It had never been the custom with those managing the road to place any reliance upon the telegraph in directing the train movement, and no use whatever appears to have been made of it towards straightening out the numerous hitches inevitable from so sudden an increase in that movement. If an engine broke down, or a train got off the track, there had accordingly throughout that week been nothing done, except patient and general waiting, until it was gotten in motion again; each conductor or station-master had to look out for himself, under the running regulations of the road, and need expect no assistance from headquarters. This, too, in spite of the fact that, including the Saugus branch, no less than ninety-three of the entire one hundred and fifteen miles of road operated by the company were supplied only with a single track. The whole train movement, intricate in the extreme as it was, thus depended solely on a schedule arrangement and the watchful intelligence of individual employés. Not unnaturally, therefore, as the week drew to a close the confusion became so great that the trains reached and left the Boston station with an almost total disregard of the schedule; while towards the evening of Saturday the employés of the road directed their efforts almost exclusively to dispatching trains as fast as cars could be procured, thus trying to keep the station as clear as possible of the throng of impatient travelers which continually blocked it up.

According to the regular schedule four trains should have left the Boston station in succession during the hour and a half between 6:30 and eight o'clock P.M.: a Saugus branch train for Lynn at 6:30; a second Saugus branch train at seven; an accommodation train, which ran eighteen miles over the main line, at 7:15; and finally the express train through to Portland, also over the main line, at eight o'clock. The collision at Revere was between these last two trains, the express overtaking and running into the rear of the accommodation train; but it was indirectly caused by the delays and irregularity in movement of the two branch trains. It will be noticed that, according to the schedule, both of the branch trains should have preceded the accommodation train; in the prevailing confusion, however, the first of the two branch trains did not leave the station until about seven o'clock, thirty minutes behind its time, and it was followed forty minutes later, not by the second branch train, but by the accommodation train, which in its turn was twenty-five minutes late. Thirteen minutes afterwards the second Saugus branch train, which should have preceded, followed it, being nearly an hour out of time. Then at last came the Portland express, which got away practically on time, at a few minutes after eight o'clock. All of these four trains went out over the same track as far as the junction of Everett, but at that point the first and third of the four were to go off on the branch, while the second and fourth kept on over the main line. Between these last two trains the running schedule of the road allowed an ample time-interval of forty-five minutes, which, however, on this occasion was reduced, through the delay in starting, to some fifteen or twenty minutes. No causes of further delay, therefore, arising, the simple case was presented of a slow accommodation train being sent out to run eighteen miles in advance of a fast express train, with an interval of twenty minutes between them.

Unfortunately, however, the accommodation train was speedily subjected to another and very serious delay. It has been mentioned that the Saugus branch was a single track road, and the rules of the company were explicit that no outward train was to pass on to the branch at Everett until any inward train then due there should have arrived and passed off it. There was no siding at the junction, upon which an outward branch train could be temporarily placed to wait for the inward train, thus leaving the main track clear; and accordingly, under a strict construction of the rules, any outward branch train while awaiting the arrival at Everett of an inward branch train was to be kept standing on the main track, completely blocking it. The outward branch trains, it subsequently appeared, were often delayed at the junction, but no practical difficulty had arisen from this cause, as the employé in charge of the signals and switches there, exercising his common sense, had been in the custom of moving any delayed train temporarily out of the way on to the branch or the other main track, under protection of a flag, and thus relieving the block. On the day of the accident this employé happened to be sick, and absent from his post. His substitute either had no common sense or did not feel called upon to use it, if its use involved any increase of responsibility. Accordingly, when a block took place, the simple letter of the rule was followed;

and it is almost needless to add that a block did take place on the afternoon of August 26th.

The first of the branch trains, it will be remembered, had left Boston at about seven o'clock, instead of at 6:30, its schedule time. On arriving at Everett this train should have met and passed an inward branch train, which was timed to leave Lynn at six o'clock, but which, owing to some accident to its locomotive, and partaking of the general confusion of the day, on this particular afternoon did not leave the Lynn station until 7:30 o'clock, or one hour and a half after its schedule time, and one half-hour after the other train had left Boston. Accordingly, when the Boston train reached the junction its conductor found himself confronted by the rule forbidding him to enter upon the branch until the Lynn train then due should have passed off it, and so he quietly waited on the outward track of the main line, blocking it completely to traffic. He had not waited long before a special locomotive, on its way from Boston to Salem, came up and stopped behind him; followed presently by the accommodation train, and then by the next branch train, and finally by the Portland express. At such a time, and at that period of railroad development, there was something ludicrous about the spectacle. Here was a road utterly unable to accommodate its passengers with cars, while a succession of trains were standing idle for hours, because a locomotive had broken down ten miles off. The telegraph was there, but the company was not in the custom of putting any reliance upon it. A simple message to the branch trains to meet and pass at any point other than that fixed in the schedule would have solved the whole difficulty; but no! there were the rules, and all the rolling stock of the road might gather at Everett in solemn procession, but until the locomotive at Lynn could be repaired, the law of the Medes and Persians was plain; and in this case it read that the telegraph was a new-fangled and unreliable auxiliary. And so the lengthening procession stood there long enough for the train which caused it to have gone to its destination and come back again to take its place in the block, dragging the disabled locomotive from Lynn behind it.

At last, at about ten minutes after eight o'clock, the long-expected Lynn train made its appearance, and the first of the branch trains from Boston immediately went off the main line. The road was now clear for the accommodation train, which had been standing some twelve or fifteen minutes in the block, but which from the moment of starting again was running on the schedule time of the Portland express. This its conductor did not know. Every minute was vital, and yet he never thought to look at his watch. He had a vague impression that he had been delayed some six or eight minutes, when in reality he had been delayed fifteen; and, though he was running wholly out of his schedule time, he took not a single precaution, so persuaded was he that every one knew where he was.

The confusion among those in charge of the various engines and trains was, indeed, general and complete. As the Portland express was about to leave the Boston station, the superintendent of the road, knowing by the non-arrival of the branch train from Lynn that there must be a block at the Everett junction, had directed the depot-master to caution the engineer to look out for the trains ahead of him. The order was a verbal one, was delivered after the train had started, the station-master walking along by the side of the slowly-moving locomotive, and was either incorrectly transmitted or not fully understood; the engineer supposing it to apply to the branch train which had started just before him, out of both its schedule time and schedule place. Presently, at the junction, he was stopped by the signal-man of this train. The course of reasoning he would then have had to pass through to divine the true situation of affairs was complicated indeed, and somewhat as follows. "The branch train," he should have argued to himself, "is stopped, and it is stopped because the train which should have left Lynn at six o'clock has not yet arrived; but, under the rules, that train should pass off the branch before the 6:30 train could pass on to it; if, therefore, the 'wild' train before me is delayed, not only the 6:30 but all intermediate trains must likewise be delayed, and the accommodation train went out this afternoon after the 6:30 train, so it, too, must be in the block ahead of me; unless, indeed, as is usually the case, the signal-master has got it out of the block under the protection of a flag." This line of reasoning was, perhaps, too intricate; at any rate the engineer did not follow it out, but, when he saw the tail-lights immediately before him disappear on the branch, he concluded that the main line was now clear, and dismissed the depot-master's caution from his mind. Meanwhile, as the engineer of this train was fully persuaded that the only other train in his front had gone off on the branch, the conductor of the accommodation train was equally persuaded that the head-light immediately behind him in the block at the junction had been that of the Portland express, which consequently should be aware of his position. Both were wrong.

Thus when they left Everett the express was fairly chasing the accommodation train, and overtaking it with terrible rapidity. Even then no collision ought to have been possible. Unfortunately, however, the road had no system, even the crudest, of interval signals; and the utter irregularity prevailing in the train movement seemed to have demoralized the employés along the line, who, though they noticed the extreme proximity of the two trains to each other as they passed various points, all sluggishly took it for granted that those in charge of them were fully aware of their relative positions. Thus, as the two trains approached the Revere station, they were so close together as to be on the same piece of straight track at the same time, and a passenger standing at the rear end of the accommodation train distinctly saw the head-light of the express locomotive. The night, however, was not a clear one, for the east wind had prevailed all day, driving a mist in from the sea which lay in banks over the marshes, lifting at times so that distinct objects were quite visible, and then obscuring them in its heavy folds. Consequently it did not at all follow, because the powerful reflecting head-light of the locomotive was visible from the accommodation train, that the dim tail-lights of the latter were also visible to those on the locomotive. Here was another mischance. The tail-lights in use by the company were ordinary red lanterns without reflecting power.

The station-house at Revere stood at the end of a tangent, the track curving directly before it. In any ordinary weather the tail-lights of a train standing at this station would have been visible for a very considerable distance down the track in the direction of Boston, and even on the night of the accident they were probably visible for a sufficient distance in which to stop any train approaching at a reasonable rate of speed. Unfortunately, the engineer of the Portland express did not at once see them, his attention being wholly absorbed in looking for other signals. Certain freight tracks to points on the shore diverged from the main line at Revere, and the engineers of all trains approaching that place were notified by signals at a masthead close to the station whether the switches were set for the main line or for these freight tracks. A red lantern at the masthead indicated that the main line was closed; in the absence of any signal it was open. In looking for this signal as he approached Revere the engineer of the Portland express was simply attending closely to his business, for, had the red light been at the masthead, his train must at once have been stopped. Unfortunately, however, while peering through the mist at the masthead he overlooked what was directly before him, until, when at last he brought his eyes down to the level, to use his own words at the subsequent inquest, "the tail-lights of the accommodation train seemed to spring right up in his face."

When those in charge of the two trains at almost the same moment became aware of the danger, there was yet an interval of some eight hundred feet between them. The express train was, however, moving at a speed of some twenty-five or thirty miles an hour, and was equipped only with the old-fashioned hand-brake. In response to the sharply given signal from the whistle these were rapidly set, but the rails were damp and slippery, so that the wheels failed to catch upon them, and when everything was done which could be done, the eight hundred feet of interval sufficed only to reduce the speed of the colliding locomotive to about ten miles an hour.

In the rear car of the accommodation train there were at the moment of the accident some sixty-five or seventy human beings, seated and standing. They were of both sexes and of all ages; for it was a Saturday evening in August, and many persons had, through the confusion of the trains, been long delayed in their return from the city to their homes at the seaside. The first intimation the passengers had of the danger impending over them was from the sudden and lurid illumination of the car by the glare from the head-light of the approaching locomotive. One of them, who survived the disaster though grievously injured, described how he was carelessly watching a young man standing in the aisle, laughing and gayly chatting with four young girls who were seated, when he saw him turn and instantly his face in the sudden blaze of the head-light assumed a look of frozen horror which was the single thing in the accident indelibly impressed on the survivor's memory; that look haunted him. The car was crowded to its full capacity, and the colliding locomotive struck it with such force as to bury itself two thirds of its length in it. At the instant of the crash a panic had seized upon the passengers, and a sort of rush had taken place to the forward end of the car, into which furniture, fixtures, and human beings were crushed in a shapeless, indistinguishable mass. Meanwhile the blow had swept away the smoke-stack of the locomotive, and its forward truck had been forced back in some unaccountable way until it rested between its driving wheels and the tender, leaving the entire boiler inside of the passenger car and supported on its rear truck. The valves had been so broken as to admit of the free escape of the scalding steam, while the coals from the fire-box were scattered among the *débris*, and coming in contact with the fluid from the broken car lamps kindled the whole into a rapid blaze. Neither was the fire confined to the last car of the train. It had been mentioned that in the block at Everett a locomotive returning to Salem had found itself stopped just in advance of the accommodation train. At the suggestion of the engineer of that train this locomotive had there coupled on to it, and consequently made a part of it at Revere. When the collision took place, therefore, the four cars of which the accommodation train was made up were crushed between the weight of the entire colliding train on one side and that of two locomotives on the other. That they were not wholly demolished was due simply to the fact that the last car yielded to the blow and permitted the locomotive of the express train fairly to imbed itself in it. As it was, the remaining cars were jammed and shattered, and, though the passengers in them escaped, the oil from the broken lamps ignited, and before the flames could be extinguished the cars were entirely destroyed.

This accident resulted in the death of twenty-nine persons, and in more or less severe injuries to fifty-seven others. No person not in the last car of the accommodation train was killed, and one only was seriously injured. Of those in the last car more than half lost their lives; many instantly by crushing, others by inhaling the scalding steam which poured forth from the locomotive boiler into the wreck, and which, where it did not kill, inflicted frightful injuries. Indeed, for the severity of injuries and for the protractedness of agony involved in it, this accident has rarely, if ever, been exceeded. Crushing, scalding, and burning did their work together.

It may with perfect truth be said that the disaster at Revere marked an epoch in the history of railroad development in New England. At the moment it called forth the deepest expression of horror and indignation, which, as usual in such cases, was more noticeable for its force than for its wisdom. An utter absence of all spirit of justice is, indeed, a usual characteristic of the more immediate utterances both from the press and on the platform, upon occasions of this character. Writers and orators seem always to forget that, next to the immediate sufferers and their families, the unfortunate officials concerned are the greatest losers by railroad accidents. For them, not only reputation but bread is involved. A railroad employé in any way implicated in the occurrence of an accident from that moment lives under a stigma. And yet, from the tenor of public comment it might fairly be supposed that they plotted to bring disasters about, and took a fiendish delight in them. Nowhere was this ever illustrated more perfectly than in Massachusetts during the last days of August and the early days of September, 1871. Grave men—men who ought to have known better—indulged in language which would have been simply ludicrous save for the horror of the event which occasioned but could not justify it. A public meeting, for instance, was held at the town of Swampscott on the evening of the Monday evening succeeding the catastrophe. The gentleman who presided over it very discreetly, in his preliminary remarks, urged those who proposed to join in the discussion to control their feelings. Hardly had he ceased speaking, however, when Mr. Wendell Phillips was noticed among the audience, and immediately called to the platform. His remarks were a most singular commentary on the chairman's injunction to calmness. He began by announcing that the first requisite to the formation of a healthy public opinion in regard to railroad accidents, as other things, was absolute frankness of speech, and he then proceeded as follows: "So I begin by saying that to my mind this terrible disaster, which has made the last thirty-six hours so sad to us all, is a deliberate murder. I think we should try to get rid in the public mind of any real distinction between the individual who, in a moment of passion or in a moment of heedlessness, takes the life of one fellow-man, and the corporation that in a moment of greed, of little trouble, of little expense, of little care, of little diligence, takes lives by wholesale. I think the first requisite of the public mind is to say that there is no accident in the case, properly speaking. It is a murder; the guilt of murder rests somewhere." Mr. Phillips's definition of the crime of "deliberate murder" would apparently somewhat unsettle the criminal law as at present understood, but he was not at all alone in this bathos of extravagance. Prominent gentlemen seemed to vie with each other in their display of ignorance. Mr. B. F. Butler, for instance, suggested his view of the disaster and the measure best calculated to prevent a repetition of it, which last was certainly original, inasmuch as he urged the immediate raising of the pay of all enginemen until a sufficiently high order of ability and education should be brought into the occupation to render impossible the recurrence of an accident which was primarily caused by the negligence, not of an engineer, but of a conductor. Another gentleman described with much feeling his observations during a recent tour in Europe, and declared that such a catastrophe as that at Revere would have been impossible there. As a matter of fact the official reports not only showed that the accident was one of a class of most frequent occurrence, but also that sixty-one cases of it had occurred in Great Britain alone during the very year the gentleman in question was journeying in Europe, and had occasioned over six hundred case of death or personal injury. Perhaps, in order to illustrate how very reckless in statement a responsible gentleman talking under excitement may become, it is worth while to quote in his own language Captain Tyler's brief description of one of those sixty-one accidents which "could not possibly" but yet did occur. As miscellaneous reading it is amusing. "As four London & North-Western excursion trains on September 2, 1870, were returning from a volunteer review at Penrith, the fourth came into collision at Penruddock with the third of those trains. An hundred and ten passengers and three servants of the company were injured. These trains were partly in charge of acting guards, some of whom were entirely inexperienced, as well in the line as in their duties; and of engine-drivers and firemen, of whom one, at all events, was very much the worse for liquor. The side-lamps on the hind van of the third train were obscured by a horse-box, which was wider than the van. There were no special means of protection to meet the exceptional contingency of three such trains all stopping on their way from the eastward, to cross two others from the westward, at this station. And the regulations for telegraphing the trains were altogether neglected."

The annals of railroad accidents are indeed full of cases of "rear-end collision," as it is termed. Their frequency may almost be accepted as a very accurate gauge of the pressure of traffic on any given system of lines, and because of them the companies are continually compelled to adopt new and more intricate systems of operation. At first, on almost all roads, trains follow each other at such great intervals that no precautions at all, other than flags and lanterns, are found necessary. Then comes a succeeding period when an interval of time between following trains is provided for, through a system of signals which at given points indicate danger during a certain number of minutes after the passage of every train. Then, presently, the alarming frequency of rear collisions demonstrates the inadequacy of this system, and a new one has to be devised, which, through the aid of electricity, secures between trains an interval of space as well as of time. This last is known as the "block-system," of which so much has of late years been heard. Its essential principle lies in the division of the road into segments or blocks, through the establishment of telegraphic stations at such intervals as may be deemed necessary, varying from a few hundred yards to several miles; and no train is permitted to pass one of these stations until a preceding train has been signaled back as having passed the next station farther on; that is, no two locomotives are allowed to be on one segment of the road at the same time. Yet rear-end collisions occur notwithstanding all the precautions implied in a thoroughly perfected "block-system." There was such a case on the Metropolitan road, in the very heart of London, on the 29th of August, 1873. It happened in a tunnel. A train was stalled there, and an unfortunate signal officer in a moment of flurry gave "line clear" and sent another train directly into it.

A much more impressive disaster, both in its dramatic features and as illustrating the inadequacy of every precaution depending on human agency to avert accident under certain conditions, was afforded in the case of a collision which occurred on the London & Brighton Railway upon the 5th of August, 1861; ten years almost to a day before that at Revere. Like the Eastern Railroad, the London & Brighton enjoyed an enormous passenger traffic, which became peculiarly heavy during the vacation season, towards the close of August; and it was to the presence of the excursion trains made necessary to accommodate this traffic that the catastrophes were in both cases due. In the case of the London & Brighton road it occurred on a Sunday. An excursion train from Portsmouth on that day was to leave Brighton at five minutes after eight A. M., and was to be followed by a regular Sunday excursion train at 8:15 or ten minutes later, and that again, after the lapse of a quarter of an hour, by a regular parliamentary train at 8:30. These trains were certainly timed to run sufficiently near to each other; but, owing to the existing pressure of traffic on the line, they started almost simultaneously. The Portsmouth excursion, which consisted of sixteen carriages, was much behind its time, and did not leave the Brighton station until 8:28; when, after a lapse of three minutes, it was followed by the regular excursion train at 8:31, and that again by the parliamentary train at 8:35. Three passenger trains had thus left the station on one track in seven minutes! The London & Brighton Railway traverses the chalky downs for which that portion of England is noted, through numerous tunnels, the first of which after leaving Brighton is known as the Patcham Tunnel, about five hundred yards in length, while two and a half miles farther on is the Croydon Tunnel, rather more than a mile and a quarter in length. The line between these tunnels was so crooked and obscured that the managers had adopted extraordinary precautions against accident. At each end of the Croydon Tunnel a signal-man was stationed, with a telegraphic apparatus, a clock, and a telegraph bell in his station. The rule was absolute that when any train entered the tunnel the signal-man at the point of entry was to telegraph "train in," and no other train could follow until the return signal of "train out" came from the other side. In fact of such a regulation it was difficult to see how any collision in the tunnel was possible. When the Portsmouth excursion train arrived, it at once entered the tunnel and the fact was properly signaled to the opposite outlet. Before the return signal that this train was out was received, the regular excursion train came in sight. It should have been stopped by a self-acting signal which was placed about a quarter of a mile from the mouth of the tunnel, and which each passing locomotive set at "danger," where it remained until shifted to "safety" by the signal-man, on receipt of the message, "train out." Through some unexplained cause, the Portsmouth excursion train had failed to act on this signal, which consequently still indicated safety when the Brighton excursion train came up. Accordingly the engine driver at once passed it, and went on to the tunnel. As he did so, the signal-man, perceiving some mistake and knowing that he had not yet got his return signal that the preceding train was out, tried to stop him by waving his red flag. It was too late, however, and the train passed in. A moment later the parliamentary train also came in sight, and stopped at the signal of danger. Now ensued a most singular misapprehension between the signal-men, resulting in a terrible disaster. The second train had run into the tunnel and was supposed by the signal-man to be on its way to the other end of it, when he received the return message that the first train was out. To this he instantly responded by again telegraphing "train in," referring now to the second train. This dispatch the signal-man at the opposite end conceived to be a repetition of the message referring to the first train, and he accordingly again replied that the train was out. This reply, however, the other operator mistook as referring to the second train, and accordingly he signaled "safety" and the third train at once got under way and passed into the tunnel. Unfortunately the engineer of the second train had seen the red flag waved by the signal-man, and, in obedience to it, stopped his locomotive as soon as possible in the tunnel and began to back out of it. In doing so, he drove his train into the locomotive of the third train advancing into it. The tunnel was twenty-four feet in height. The engine of the parliamentary train struck the rear carriage of the excursion train, and mounted upon its fragments and then on those of the carriage in front of it, until its smokestack came in contact with the roof of the tunnel. It rested finally in a nearly upright position. The collision had taken place so far within the tunnel as to be beyond the reach of daylight, and the wreck of the trains had quite blocked up the arch, while the steam and smoke from the engines poured forth with loud sound and in heavy volumes, filling the empty space with stifling and scalding vapors. When at last assistance came, and the trains could be separated, twenty-three corpses were taken from the ruins, while one hundred and seventy-six other persons had sustained more or less severe injuries.

A lot less extraordinary accident of the same description, unaccompanied, however, by an equal loss of life, occurred on the Great Northern Railway upon the 10th of June, 1866. In this case the tube of the locomotive of a freight train burst at about the centre of the Welwyn Tunnel, some five miles north of Hatfield, bringing the train to a stand-still. The guard in charge of the rear of the train failed from some cause to go back and give the signal for an obstruction, and speedily another freight train from Midland road entered and dashed into the rear of the train already there. Apparently those in charge of these two trains were in such consternation that they did not think to provide against a further disaster; at any rate, before measures to that end had been taken, an additional freight train, this time belonging to the Great Northern road, came up and plowed into the ruins which already blocked the tunnel. One of the trains had contained wagons laden with casks of oil, which speedily ignited from contact with the coals scattered from the fire-boxes, and there then ensued one of the most extraordinary spectacles ever witnessed on a railroad. The tunnel was filled to the summit of its arch and completely blocked with ruins. These had ignited, and the whole cavity, more than half a mile in length, was converted into one huge furnace, belching forth smoke and flame with a loud roaring sound through its several air shafts. So fierce was the fire that no attempt was made to subdue it, and eighteen hours elapsed before any steps could be taken towards clearing the track. Strange to say, in this disaster the lives of but two persons were lost.

Rear-end collisions have been less frequent in this country than in England, for the simple reason that the volume of traffic has pressed less heavily on the capacity of the lines. Yet here, also, they have been by no means unknown. In 1865 two occurred, both of which were accompanied with a considerable loss of life; though, coming as they did during the exciting scenes which marked the close of the war of the Rebellion, they attracted much less public notice than they otherwise would. The first of these took place in New Jersey on the 7th of March, 1865, just three days after the second inauguration of President Lincoln. As the express train from Washington to New York over the Camden & Amboy road was passing through Bristol, about thirty miles from Philadelphia, at half-past two o'clock in the morning, it dashed into the rear of the twelve o'clock, or "owl train," from Kensington to New York, which had been delayed by meeting an oil train on the track before it. The case appears to have been one of very culpable negligence, for though the owl train was some two hours late, those in charge of it seem to have been so deeply engrossed in what was going on before them that they wholly neglected to guard their rear. The express train accordingly, approaching round a curve, plunged at a high rate of speed into the last car, shattering it to pieces; the engine is even said to have passed completely through the car and to have imbedded itself in the preceding car. It so happened that most of the sufferers by this accident, numbering about fifty, were soldiers on their way home from the army upon furlough. The second of these two disasters occurred on the 16th of August, 1865, upon the Housatonic road, in the State of Connecticut. A new engine was out upon an experimental trip, and in rounding a curve it ran into the rear of a passenger train, which, having encountered a disabled freight train, had coupled on to it and was then backing down with it to a siding in order to get by it. In this case the impetus was so great that the colliding locomotive utterly destroyed the rear car of the passenger train and penetrated some distance into the car next to the last one, where its boiler burst. Fortunately the train was by no means full of passengers; but, even as it was, eleven persons were killed and some seventeen badly injured.

The great peculiarity of the Revere accident, and that which gave a permanent interest to it, lay in the revelation it afforded of the degree in which a system had outgrown its appliances. At every point a deficiency was apparent. The railroads of New England had long been living on their early reputation, and now, when a sudden test was applied, it was found that they were years behind the time. In August, 1871, the Eastern Railroad was run as if it were a line of stage-coaches in the days before the telegraph. Not in one point alone, but in everything, it broke down under the test. The disaster was due not to any single cause but to a combination of causes, running down from the highest official to the meanest subordinate. In the first place the capacity of the road was taxed to the utmost; it was vital, almost, that every wheel should be kept in motion. Yet, under that very exigency, the wheels stopped almost as a matter of necessity. How could it be otherwise? Here was a crowded line, more than half of which was equipped with but a single track, and placing no reliance upon the telegraph. With trains running out of their schedule time and out of their schedule place, engineers and conductors were left to grope their way along as best they could in the light of rules of the essence of which was that when in doubt they were to stand stock still. Then, in the absence of the telegraph, a block occurred almost at the mouth of the central station; and there the trains stood for hours in stupid obedience to a stupid rule, because the one man who, with a simple regard to the dictates of common sense, was habitually accustomed to violate it happened to be sick. Trains commonly left a station out of time and out of place; and the engineer of an express train was sent out to run a gauntlet the whole length of the road with a simple verbal injunction to look out for some one before him. Then, at last, when this express train through all this chaos got to chasing an accommodation train much as a hound might course a hare, there was not a pretense of a signal to indicate the time which had elapsed between the passage of the two, and employés, lanterns in hand, gaped on in bewilderment at the awful race, concluding that they could not at any rate do anything to help matters, but on the whole they were inclined to think that those most immediately concerned must know what they were about. Finally, even when the disaster was imminent, when deficiency in organization and discipline had done its worst, its consequences might yet have been averted through the use of better appliances; had the one train been equipped with the Westinghouse brake, already largely in use in other sections of the country, it might and would have been stopped; or had the other train been provided with reflecting tail-lights in place of the dim hand-lanterns which glimmered on its rear platform, it could hardly have failed to make its proximity known. Any one of a dozen things, every one of which should have been but was not, ought to have averted the disaster. Obviously its immediate cause was not far to seek. It lay in the carelessness of a conductor who failed to consult his watch, and never knew until the crash came that he was leisurely moving along on the time of another. Nevertheless, what can be said in extenuation of a system under which at this late day a railroad is operated on the principle that each employé under all circumstances can and will take care of himself and of those whose lives and limbs are entrusted to his care?

There is, however, another and far more attractive side to the picture. The lives sacrificed at Revere were not lost in vain. Four complete railroad years have now passed by since that catastrophe occurred, and during that time not less than one hundred and thirty millions of persons have been carried by rail within the limits of Massachusetts. Of this vast number the life of not a single one has been lost through causes for which any railroad company was responsible. This certainly is a record of which any community might well be proud; and it is due more than anything else to the great disaster of August 26, 1871. More than once, and on more than one road, have accidents occurred which, but for the improved appliances introduced in consequence of the experience at Revere, could hardly have failed of fatal results. Not that these appliances were in all cases very cheerfully or very eagerly accepted. Neither the Miller platform nor the Westinghouse brake won its way into general use unchallenged. Indeed, the earnestness and even the indignation with which presidents and superintendents then protested that their car construction was better and stronger than Miller's; that their antiquated hand-brakes were the most improved brakes, better, much better, than the Westinghouse; that their crude old semaphores and targets afforded a protection to trains which no block-system would ever equal,—all this certainly was comical enough, even in the very shadow of the great tragedy. Men of a certain type always have protested and will always continue to protest that they have nothing to learn; yet, under the heavy burden of responsibility, learn they still do. They dare not but learn. On this point the figures of the annual returns speak volumes. At the time of the Revere disaster, with one single honorable exception,—that of the Boston & Providence road,—both the atmospheric train-brake and the Miller platform, the two greatest modern improvements in car construction, were practically unrecognized on the railroads of Massachusetts. That was four years ago, in September, 1871. Even a year later, but ninety-three locomotives and four hundred and fifteen cars had been equipped even with the train-brake. In September, 1873, the number had, however, risen to one hundred and ninety-four locomotives and seven hundred and nine cars; and another twelve months carried these numbers up to three hundred and thirteen locomotives and nine hundred and ninety-seven cars. The adoption of the Miller platform and of systems of signals to secure intervals between trains was not less rapid. So the world advances through the lessons of bitter experience; but to-day not a human being is carried on a Massachusetts railroad who does not enjoy an appreciably greater immunity from danger for which he is wholly indebted to those who died or suffered in the terrible experience at Revere in August, 1871.

14. The Uses of Invention

Edison came to public attention in the 1870's with a series of inventions, mainly improvements of electrical systems such as the telegraph and the stock ticker. He established himself in a laboratory in Menlo Park, New Jersey, a sort of "invention factory" or, in current parlance, a research and development center, and by the end of the decade had presented the world with the phonograph and a workable incandescent lamp. At the same time he presented in his person a living embodiment of the figure of the inventor—particularly the American inventor: a homespun, hardworking, stubborn-minded and practical innovator who through perseverance and ingenuity found his way from the obscurity of a country village in Ohio to international fame and wealth. In the numerous articles and illustrations about him at the period of the phonograph invention, he was well on his way toward the fairly mythical status he held the rest of his life.

The myth characterizes him as a down-to-earth "wizard," part otherworldly alchemist, part small-town mechanic and entrepreneur. The period was prepared to receive him in such terms. An article in Scribner's Monthly, "A Night with Edison" (May 1879), finds it appropriate that his inventions and their "moral side," the hope they present that "there may, after all, be a relief for all human ills in the great storehouse of nature," should occur "in a time of more than usual discontent." Edison seemed to possess the very qualities the age required: on one hand he represented the traditional Protestant values of work, self-confidence, thirst for knowledge, and unpretentious success. On the other hand, he had "a radical instinct which goes, in every piece of mechanism, straight to the underlying principle." Accepting nothing on authority, he was "a burning spark of inventiveness, and that only." In his laboratory, with its strange contraptions of jars and cylinders and an apparent chaos of wires—all devoted to recording or amplifying sound—one felt in the presence of "some strange, new rite—a martial chant of rejoicing in the greatness of a new era full of sublime promise and the dissipation of mysteries." It seems that one mystery dissipates another, but in the figure of Edison the age's pure technological spirit became comprehensible in familiar American terms.

In this essay Edison speaks in his own voice, and displays his conception of the vast commercial and recreational implication of his invention. His language expresses firm confidence in the beneficence of the new process of mechanical reproduction.

The Phonograph and Its Future

THOMAS A. EDISON

Of all the writer's inventions, none has commanded such profound and earnest attention throughout the civilized world as has the phonograph. This fact he attributes largely to that peculiarity of the invention which brings its possibilities within range of the speculative imaginations of all thinking people, as well as to the almost universal applicability of the foundation principle, namely, the gathering up and retaining of sounds hitherto fugitive, and their reproduction at will.

From the very abundance of conjectural and prophetic opinions which have been disseminated by the press, the public is liable to become confused, and less accurately informed as to the immediate result and effects of the phonograph than if the invention had been one confined to certain specific applications, and therefore of less interest to the masses. The writer has no fault to find with this condition of the discussion of the merits and possibilities of his invention; for, indeed, the possibilities are so illimitable and the probabilities so numerous that he—though subject to the influence of familiar contact—is himself in a somewhat chaotic condition of mind as to where to draw the dividing line. In point of fact, such line cannot with safety be defined in ordinary inventions at so early a stage of their development. In the case of an invention of the nature and scope of the phonograph, it is practically impossible to indicate it to-day, for to-morrow a trifle may extend it almost indefinitely.

There are, however, certain stages in the developing process which have thus far been actually reached; certain others which are clearly within reach; and others which, though they are in the light of to-day classed as possibilities, may to-morrow become probable, and a little later actual achievements. It is the intention of the writer in this article to confine himself to the actual and the probable, to the end that a clearer conception of the immediate realizations of the phonograph may be had. He concedes to the public press and the world of science the imaginative work of pointing and commenting upon the possible. It is in view of the liberal manner

Thomas A. Edison, "The Phonograph and Its Future," *North American Review*, CXXVI (1878), 527–536.

in which this has already been done, and the handsome treatment he has received at their hands, that he for the first time appears *in propria persona* to discuss and comment upon the merits of one of his own inventions.

In order to furnish a basis upon which the reader may take his stand, and accept or combat the logic of the writer in his presentment of the probabilities of the phonograph, a few categorical questions are put and answers given upon the essential features of the principle involved:

1. Is a vibrating plate or disk capable of receiving a complex motion which shall correctly represent the peculiar property of each and all the multifarious vocal and other sound-waves?

The telephone answers affirmatively.

2. Can such complex movement be transmitted from such plate, by means of a single embossing-point attached thereto, to effect a record upon a plastic material by indentation, with such fidelity as to give to such indentations the same varied and complex form; and, if so, will this embossing-point, upon being passed over the record thus made, follow it with such fidelity as to retransmit to the disk the same variety of movement, and thus effect a restoration or reproduction of the vocal or other sound-waves, without loss of any property essential to producing upon the ear the same sensation as if coming direct from the original source?

The answer to this may be summed up in a statement of the fact that, by the application of power for uniformity of movement, and by attention to many seemingly unimportant and minor details, such as the *form* and material of the embossing-point, the proper *dampening* of the plate, the character of the material embossed, the formation of the mouth-piece over the plate, etc., the writer has at various times during the past weeks reproduced these waves with such degree of accuracy in each and every detail as to enable his assistants to read, without the loss of a word, one or more columns of a newspaper article unfamiliar to them, and which were spoken into the apparatus when they were not present. The only perceptible loss was found to be in the quality of the utterance—a non-essential in the practical application of the apparatus. Indeed, the articulation of some individuals has been very perceptibly improved by passage through the phonograph, the original utterance being mutilated by imperfection of lip and mouth formation, and these mutilations eliminated or corrected by the mechanism of the phonograph.

3. Can a record be removed from the apparatus upon which it was made, and replaced upon a second without mutilation or loss of effective power to vibrate the second plate?

This is a mere mechanical detail, presenting no greater obstacle than having proper regard for the perfect interchangeableness of the various working parts of the apparatus—not so nice a problem as the manufacture of the American watch.

4. What as to facility of placing and removing the record-sheet, and as to its transportation by mail?

But ten or fifteen seconds suffice for such placing or removal. A special envelope will probably be required for the present, the weight and form of which, however, will but slightly increase the cost of postage.

5. What as to durability?

Repeated experiments have proved that the indentations possess wonderful enduring power, even when the reproduction has been effected by the comparatively rigid plate used for their production. It is proposed, however, to use a more flexible plate for reproducing, which, with a perfectly smooth stone point—diamond or sapphire—will render the record capable of from 50 to 100 repetitions, enough for all practical purposes.

6. What as to duplication of a record and its permanence?

Many experiments have been made with more or less success, in the effort to obtain electrotypes of a record. This work has been done by others, and, though the writer has not as yet seen it, he is reliably informed that, very recently, it has been successfully accomplished. He can certainly see no great practical obstacle in the way. This, of course, permits of an indefinite multiplication of a record, and its preservation for all time.

7. What are the requisite force of wave impinging upon the diaphragm and the proximity of the mouth to the diaphragm to effect a record?

These depend in a great measure upon the volume of sound desired in the reproduction. If the reproduction is to be made audible to an audience, considerable force is requisite in the original utterance; if for the individual ear, only the ordinary conversational tone (even a whisper has been reproduced). In both cases the original utterances are delivered directly in the mouthpiece of the instrument. An audible reproduction may, however, be had by speaking at the instrument from a distance of from two to three feet in a loud tone. The application of a flaring tube or funnel to collect the sound-waves and the construction of an especially delicate diaphragm and embossing-point, etc., are the simple means which suggest themselves to effect this. The writer has not as yet given this stage of the development much attention, but sees no practical difficulty in gathering up and retaining a sectional part of the sound-waves diffused about the original source, within a radius of, say, three feet (sufficiently removed not to be annoying to a speaker or a singer).

The foregoing presentment of the stage of development reached by the several essential features of the phonograph demonstrates the following as *faits accomplis:*

1. The captivity of all manner of sound-waves heretofore designated as "fugitive," and their permanent retention.

2. Their reproduction with all their original characteristics at will, without the presence or consent of the original source, and after the lapse of any period of time.

3. The transmission of such captive sounds through the ordinary channels of commercial intercourse and trade in material form, for purposes of communication or as merchantable goods.

4. Indefinite multiplication and preservation of such sounds, without regard to the existence or non-existence of the original source.

5. The captivation of sounds, with or without the knowledge or consent of the source of their origin.

The probable application of these properties of the phonograph and the various branches of commercial and scientific industry presently indicated will require the exercise of more or less mechanical ingenuity. Conceding that the apparatus is practically perfected in so far as the faithful reproduction of sound is concerned, many of the following applications will be made the moment the new form of apparatus, which the writer is now about completing, is finished. These, then, might be classed as actualities; but they so closely trench upon other applications which will immediately follow, that it is impossible to separate them: hence they are all enumerated under the head of probabilities, and each specially considered. Among the more important may be mentioned: Letter-writing, and other forms of dictation books, education, reader, music, family record; and such electrotype applications as books, musical-boxes, toys, clocks, advertising and signaling apparatus, speeches, etc., etc.

Letter-writing.—The apparatus now being perfected in mechanical details will be the standard phonograph, and may be used for all purposes, except such as require special form of matrix, such as toys, clocks, etc., for an indefinte repetition of the same thing. The main utility of the phonograph, however, being for the purpose of letter-writing and other forms of dictation, the design is made with a view to its utility for that purpose.

The general principles of construction are, a flat plate or disk, with spiral groove on the face, operated by clock-work underneath the plate; the grooves are cut very closely together, so as to give a great total length to each inch of surface—a close calculation gives as the capacity of each sheet of foil, upon which the record is had, in the neighborhood of 40,000 words. The sheets being but ten inches square, the cost is so trifling that but 100 words might be put upon a single sheet economically. Still, it is problematical whether a less number of grooves per inch might not be the better plan—it certainly would for letters—but it is desirable to have but one class of machine throughout the world; and as very extended communications, if put upon one sheet, could be transported more economically than upon two, it is important that each sheet be given as great capacity as possible. The writer has not yet decided this point, but will experiment with a view of ascertaining the best mean capacity.

The practical application of this form of phonograph for communications is very simple. A sheet of foil is placed in the phonograph, the clock-work set in motion, and the matter dictated into the mouth-piece without other effort than when dictating to a stenographer. It is then removed, placed in a suitable form of envelope, and sent through the ordinary channels to the correspondent for whom designed. He, placing it upon his phonograph, starts his clock-work and *listens* to what his correspondent has to say. Inasmuch as it gives the tone of voice of his correspondent, it is *identified*. As it may be filed away as other letters, and at any subsequent time reproduced, it is a perfect *record*. As two sheets of foil have been indented with the same facility as a single sheet, the "writer" may thus *keep a duplicate* of his communication. As the principal of a business house, or his partners now dictate the important business communications to clerks, to be written out, they are required to do no more by the phonographic method, and do thereby *dispense with the clerk*, and *maintain perfect privacy* in their communications.

The phonograph letters may be dictated at home, or in the office of a friend, the *presence* of a stenographer *not being required*. The dictation may be as rapid as the thoughts can be formed, or the lips utter them. The recipient may listen to his letters being read at a rate of from 150 to 200 words per minute, and at the same time busy himself about other matters. Interjections, explanations, emphasis, exclamations, etc., may be thrown into such letters, *ad libitum*.

In the early days of the phonograph, ere it has become universally adopted, a correspondent in Hong-Kong may possibly not be supplied with an apparatus, thus necessitating a written letter of the old-fashioned sort.

In that case the writer would use his phonograph simply as a dictating-machine, his clerk writing it out from the phonograph at leisure, causing as many words to be uttered at one time as his memory was capable of retaining until he had written them down. This clerk need not be a stenographer, nor need he have been present when the letter was dictated, etc.

The advantages of such an innovation upon the present slow, tedious, and costly methods are too numerous, and too readily suggest themselves, to warrant their enumeration, while there are no disadvantages which will not disappear coincident with the general introduction of the new method.

Dictation.—All kinds and manner of dictation which will permit of the application of the mouth of the speaker to the mouth-piece of the phonograph may be as readily effected by the phonograph as in the case of letters. If the matter is for the printer, he would much prefer, in setting it up in type, to use his ears in lieu of his eyes. He has other use for them. It would be even worth while to compel witnesses in court to speak directly into the phonograph, in order to thus obtain an unimpeachable record of their testimony.

The increased delicacy of the phonograph, which is in the near future, will enlarge this field rapidly. It may then include all the sayings of not only the witness, but the judge and the counsel. It will then also comprehend the utterances of public speakers.

Books.—Books may be read by the charitably-inclined professional reader, or by such readers especially employed for that purpose, and the record of such book used in the asylums of the blind, hospitals, the sick-chamber, or even with great profit and amusement by the lady or gentleman whose eyes and hands may be otherwise employed; or, again, because of the greater enjoyment to be had from a book when read by an elocutionist than when read by the average reader. The ordinary record-sheet, repeating this book from fifty to a hundred times as it will, would command a price that would pay the original reader well for the slightly-increased difficulty in reading it aloud in the phonograph.

Educational Purposes.—As an elocutionary teacher, or as a primary teacher for children, it will certainly be invaluable. By it difficult passages may be correctly rendered for the pupil but once, after which he has only to apply to his phonograph for instructions. The child may thus learn to spell, commit to memory, a lesson set for it, etc., etc.

Music.—The phonograph will undoubtedly be liberally devoted to music. A song sung on the phonograph is reproduced with marvelous accuracy and power. Thus a friend may in a morning-call sing us a song which shall delight an evening company, etc. As a musical teacher it will be used to enable one to master a new air, the child to form its first song, or to sing him to sleep.

Family Record.—For the purpose of preserving the sayings, the voices, and *the last words* of the dying member of the family—as of great men—the phonograph will unquestionably outrank the photograph. In the field of multiplication of original matrices, and the indefinite repetition of one and the same thing, the successful electrotyping of the original record is an essential. As this is a problem easy of solution, it properly ranks among the probabilities. It comprehends a vast field. The principal application of the phonograph in this direction is in the production of

Phonographic Books.—A book of 40,000 words upon a single metal plate ten inches square thus becomes a strong probability. The advantages of such books over those printed are too readily seen to need mention. Such books would be listened to where now none are read. They would preserve more than the mental emanations of the brain of the author; and, as a bequest to future generations, they would be unequaled. For the preservation of languages they would be invaluable.

Musical-Boxes, Toys, etc.—The only element not absolutely assured, in the result of experiments thus far made—which stands in the way of a perfect reproduction at will of Adelina Patti's voice in all its purity—is the single one of quality, and even that is not totally lacking, and will doubtless be wholly attained. If, however, it should not, the musical-box, or cabinet, of the present, will be superseded by that which will give the voice and the words of the human songstress.

Toys.—A doll which may speak, sing, cry, or laugh, may be safely promised our children for the Christmas holidays ensuing. Every species of animal or mechanical toy—such as locomotives, etc.—may be supplied with their natural and characteristic sounds.

Clocks.—The phonographic clock will tell you the hour of the day; call you to lunch; send your lover home at ten, etc.

Advertising, etc.—This class of phonographic work is so akin to the foregoing, that it is only necessary to call attention to it.

Speech and other Utterances.—It will henceforth be possible to preserve for future generations the voices as well as the words of our Washingtons, our Lincolns, our Gladstones, etc., and to have them give us their "greatest effort" in every town and hamlet in the country, upon our holidays.

Lastly, and in quite another direction, the phonograph will *perfect the telephone,* and revolutionize present *systems of telegraphy.* That useful invention is now restricted in its field of operation by reason of the fact that it is a means of communication which leaves no record of its transactions, thus restricting its use to simple conversational chit-chat, and such unimportant details of business as are not considered of sufficient importance to record. Were this different, and our telephone-conversation automatically recorded, we should find the reverse of the present status of the telephone. It would be expressly resorted to *as* a means of perfect record. In writing our agreements we incorporate in the writing the summing up of our understanding—using entirely new and different phraseology from that which we used to express our understanding of the transaction in its discussion, and not infrequently thus begetting perfectly innocent causes of misunderstanding. Now, if the telephone, with the phonograph to record its sayings, were used in the preliminary discussion, we would not only have the full and correct text, but every word of the whole matter capable of throwing light upon the subject. Thus it would seem clear that the men would find it more advantageous to actually separate a half-mile or so in order to discuss important business matters, than to discuss them verbally, and then make an awkward attempt to clothe their understanding in a new language. The logic which applies to transactions between two individuals in the same office, applies with the greater force to two at a distance who must discuss the matter between them by the telegraph or mail. And this latter case, in turn, is reënforced by the demands of an economy of time and money at every mile of increase of distance between them.

"How can this application be made?" will probably be asked by those unfamiliar with either the telephone or phonograph.

Both these inventions cause a plate or disk to vibrate, and thus produce sound-waves in harmony with those of the voice of the speaker. A very simple device may be made by which the one vibrating disk may be made to do duty for both the telephone and the phonograph, thus enabling the speaker to *simultaneously transmit and record his message*. What system of telegraphy can approach that? A similar combination at the distant end of the wire enables the correspondent, if he is present, *to hear it while it is being recorded*. Thus we have a mere passage of words for the action, but a complete and durable record of those words as the result of that action. Can economy of time or money go further than to annihilate time and space, and bottle up for posterity the mere utterance of man, without other effort on his part than to speak the words?

In order to make this adaptation, it is only requisite that the phonograph shall be made slightly more sensitive to record, and the telephone very slightly increased in the vibrating force of the receiver, and it is accomplished. Indeed, the "Carbon Telephone," invented and perfected by the writer, will already well-nigh effect the record on the phonograph; and, as he is constantly improving upon it, to cause a more decided vibration of the plate of the receiver, this addition to the telephone may be looked for coincident with the other practical applications of the phonograph, and with almost equal certainty.

The telegraph company of the future—and that no distant one—will be simply an organization having a huge system of wires, central and subcentral stations, managed by skilled attendants, whose sole duty it will be to keep wires in proper repair, and give, by switch or shunt arrangement, prompt attention to subscriber No. 923 in New York, when he signals his desire to have private communication with subscriber No. 1001 in Boston, for three minutes. The minor and totally inconsequent details which seem to arise as obstacles in the eyes of the groove-traveling telegraph-man, wedded to existing methods, will wholly disappear before that remorseless Juggernaut—"the needs of man"; for, will not the necessities of man surmount trifles in order to reap the full benefit of an invention which practically brings him face to face with whom he will; and, better still, doing the work of a conscientious and infallible scribe?

15. Strain on the Nervous System

A sense of peril in the new industrial environment was not confined to accidents or mechanical failures. An awareness developed in this period that even a well-functioning industrial system exacts a price from both society and the individual. A *Treatise on Hygiene and Public Health*, a two-volume compendium of studies by medical specialists published in 1879, included a long section on the "hygiene of occupation." An oppressive parade of facts delineated the effects of industrialization upon body and mind. The picture was dreary indeed. Contact with irritating matter, inhalation of offensive and poisonous gases and dust, overuse of certain organs and constrained postures—these seemed unavoidable penalties of industrial production.

George Beard's investigations were directed to the effects of what he called "civilization" upon the nervous system. Son of a New England Congregational minister, graduate of Philips Andover, Yale, and The College of Physicians and Surgeons of New York (1866), Beard perhaps reveals his background and education in his assertion that "civilization" depends on the culture and balance of a relatively few "brainworkers." But his account of the impact of new forms of mechanization, of the strain of the environment upon the nervous system, is clearly relevant to all of American society, and constitutes one of the most telling critiques of mechanization in the period. Beard, a prolific researcher and writer, pioneered in the study of neurasthenia or nervous disorders. *The Medical and Surgical Use of Electricity* (1871) established his international reputation. He was a founder of the "National Association for the Protection of the Insane and the Prevention of Insanity."

Causes of American Nervousness

GEORGE M. BEARD

The causes of American nervousness are complicated, but are not beyond analysis: First of all modern civilization. The phrase modern civilization is used with emphasis, for civilization alone does not cause nervousness. The Greeks were certainly civilized, but they were not nervous, and in the Greek language there is no word for that term. The ancient Romans were civilized, as judged by any standard. Civilization is therefore a relative term, and as such is employed throughout this treatise. The modern differ from the ancient civilizations mainly in those five elements—steam power, the periodical press, the telegraph, the sciences, and the mental activity of women. When civilization, plus these five factors, invades any nation, it must carry nervousness and nervous diseases along with it.

CIVILIZATION VERY LIMITED IN EXTENT

All that is said here of American nervousness refers only to a fraction of American society; for in America, as in all lands, the majority of the people are muscle-workers rather than brain-workers; have little education, and are not striving for honor, or expecting eminence or wealth. All our civilization hangs by a thread; the activity and force of the very few make us what we are as a nation; and if, through degeneracy, the descendants of these few revert to the condition of their not very remote ancestors, all our haughty civilization would be wiped away. With all our numerous colleges, such as they are, it is a rarity and surprise to meet in business relations with a college-educated man.

A late writer, Dr. Arthur Mitchell, has shown that if, of the population of Scotland, a few thousands were destroyed or degenerated and their places unsupplied, the nation would fall downward to barbarism. To a somewhat less degree this is true of all lands, including our own land. Of our fifty millions of population, but a few millions have reached that elevation where they are likely to be nervous. In the lower orders, the classes that support our dispensaries and hospitals, in the tenements of our crowded cities, and even on farms in the country, by the mountain

George M. Beard, *American Nervousness: Its Causes and Consequences* (New York, 1881), 96–113; 133–138.

side—among the healthiest regions, we find, now and then, here and there cases of special varieties of nervous disease, such as hay-fever, neurasthenia, etc.; but the proportion of diseases of this kind among these people is much smaller than among the in-door-living and brain-working classes, although insanity of the incurable kind is more common among the lower or the middle than in the very highest classes.

Edison's electric light is now sufficiently advanced in an experimental direction to give us the best possible illustration of the effects of modern civilization on the nervous system. An electric machine of definite horse-power, situated at some central point, is to supply the electricity needed to run a certain number of lamps—say one thousand, more or less. If an extra number of lamps should be interposed in the circuit, then the power of the engine must be increased; else the light of the lamps would be decreased, or give out. This has been mathematically calculated, so that it is known, or believed to be known, by those in charge, just how much increase of horse-power is needed for each increase in the number of lamps. In all the calculations, however widely they may differ, it is assumed that the force supplied by any central machine is limited, and cannot be pushed beyond a certain point; and if the number of lamps interposed in the circuit be increased, there must be a corresponding increase in the force of the machine. The nervous system of man is the centre of the nerve-force supplying all the organs of the body. Like the steam engine, its force is limited, although it cannot be mathematically measured—and, unlike the steam engine, varies in amount of force with the food, the state of health and external conditions, varies with age, nutrition, occupation, and numberless factors. The force in this nervous system can, therefore, be increased or diminished by good or evil influences, medical or hygienic, or by the natural evolutions—growth, disease and decline; but none the less it is limited; and when new functions are interposed in the circuit, as modern civilization is constantly requiring us to do, there comes a period, sooner or later, varying in different individuals, and at different times of life, when the amount of force is insufficient to keep all the lamps actively burning; those that are weakest go out entirely, or, as more frequently happens, burn faint and feebly—they do not expire, but give an insufficient and unstable light—this is the philosophy of modern nervousness.

The invention of printing, the extension of steam power into manufacturing interests and into means of conveyance, the telegraph, the periodical press, the political machinery of free countries, the religious excitements that are the sequels of Protestantism—the activities of philanthropy, made necessary by the increase of civilization, and of poverty, and certain forms of disease—and, more than all, perhaps, the heightening and extending complexity of modern education in and out of schools and universities, the inevitable effect of the rise of modern science and the expansion of history in all its branches—all these are so many additional lamps interposed in the circuit, and are supplied at the expense of the nervous system, the dynamic power of which has not correspondingly increased.

NECESSARY EVILS OF SPECIALIZATION

One evil, and hardly looked for effect of the introduction of steam, together with the improved methods of manufacturing of recent times, has been the training in special departments or duties—so that artisans, instead of doing or preparing to do, all the varieties of the manipulations needed in the making of any article, are restricted to a few simple exiguous movements, to which they give their whole lives—in the making of a rifle, or a watch, each part is constructed by experts on that part. The effect of this exclusive concentration of mind and muscle to one mode of action, through months and years, is both negatively and positively pernicious, and notably so, when re-enforced, as it almost universally is, by the bad air of overheated and ill-ventilated establishments. Herein is one unanticipated cause of the increase of insanity and other diseases of the nervous system among the laboring and poorer classes. The steam engine, which would relieve work, as it was hoped, and allow us to be idle, has increased the amount of work done a thousand fold; and with that increase in quantity there has been a differentiation of quality and specialization of function which, so far forth, is depressing both to mind and body. In the professions—the constringing power of specialization is neutralized very successfully by general culture and observation, out of which specialties spring, and by which they are supported; but for the artisan there is no time, or chance, or hope, for such redeeming and antidotal influences.

CLOCKS AND WATCHES—NECESSITY OF PUNCTUALITY

The perfection of clocks and the invention of watches have something to do with modern nervousness, since they compel us to be on time, and excite the habit of looking to see the exact moment, so as not to be late for trains or appointments. Before the general use of these instruments of precision in time, there was a wider margin for all appointments; a longer period was required and prepared for, especially in travelling—coaches of the olden period were not expected to start like steamers or trains, on the instant—men judged of the time by probabilities, by looking at the sun, and needed not, as a rule, to be nervous about the loss of a moment, and had incomparably fewer experiences wherein a delay of a few moments might destroy the hopes of a lifetime. A nervous man cannot take out his watch and look at it when the time for an appointment or train is near, without affecting his pulse, and the effect on that pulse, if we could but measure and weigh it, would be found to be correlated to a loss to the nervous system. Punctuality is a greater thief of nervous force than is procrastination of time. We are under constant strain, mostly unconscious, oftentimes in sleeping as well as in waking hours, to get somewhere or do something at some definite moment. Those who would relieve their nervousness may well study the manners of the Turks, who require two weeks to execute a promise that the Anglo-Saxon would fulfil in a moment. In Constantinople indolence is the ideal, as work is the ideal in London and New York; the follower of the Prophet is ashamed to be in haste, and would apologize for keeping a promise. There are those who prefer, or fancy they prefer, the sensations of movement and activity to the sensations of repose; but from the standpoint only of economy of nerve-force all our civilization is a mistake; every mile of advance into the domain of ideas, brings a conflict that knows no rest, and all conquests are to be paid for, before delivery often, in blood and nerve and life. We cannot have civilization and have anything else, the price at which nature disposes of this luxury being all the rest of her domain.

THE TELEGRAPH

The telegraph is a cause of nervousness the potency of which is little understood. Before the days of Morse and his rivals, merchants were far less worried than now, and less business was transacted in a given time; prices fluctuated far less rapidly, and the fluctuations which now are transmitted instantaneously over the world were only known then by the slow communication of sailing vessels or steamships; hence we might wait for weeks or months for a cargo of tea from China, trusting for profit to prices that should follow their arrival; whereas, now, prices at each port are known at once all over the globe. This continual fluctuation of values, and the constant knowledge of those fluctuations in every part of the world, are the scourges of business men, the tyrants of trade—every cut in prices in wholesale lines in the smallest of any of the Western cities, becomes known in less than an hour all over the Union; thus competition is both diffused and intensified. Within but thirty years the telegraphs of the world have grown to half a million miles of line, and over a million miles of wire—or more than forty times the circuit of the globe. In the

United States there were, in 1880, 170,103 miles of line, and in that year 33,155,991 messages were sent over them.

EFFECT OF NOISE ON THE NERVES

The relation of noise to nervousness and nervous diseases is a subject of not a little interest; but one which seems to have been but incidentally studied.

The noises that nature is constantly producing—the moans and roar of the wind, the rustling and trembling of the leaves and swaying of the branches, the roar of the sea and of waterfalls, the singing of birds, and even the cries of some wild animals—are mostly rhythmical to a greater or less degree, and always varying if not intermittent; to a savage or to a refined ear, on cultured or uncultured brains, they are rarely distressing, often pleasing, sometimes delightful and inspiring. Even the loudest sounds in nature, the roll of thunder, the howling of storms, and the roar of a cataract like Niagara—save in the exceptional cases of idiosyncrasy— are the occasions not of pain but of pleasure, and to observe them at their best men will compass the globe.

Many of the appliances and accompaniments of civilization, on the other hand, are the causes of noises that are unrhythmical, unmelodious and therefore annoying, if not injurious; manufactures, locomotion, travel, housekeeping even, are noise-producing factors, and when all these elements are concentred, as in great cities, they maintain through all the waking and some of the sleeping hours, an unintermittent vibration in the air that is more or less disagreeable to all, and in the case of an idiosyncrasy or severe illness may be unbearable and harmful. Rhythmical, melodious, musical sounds are not only agreeable, but when not too long maintained are beneficial, and may be ranked among our therapeutical agencies.

Unrhythmical, harsh, jarring sounds, to which we apply the term noise, are, on the contrary to a greater or less degree, harmful or liable to be harmful; they cause severe molecular disturbance.

In regard to this general subject of the relation of noises to the nerves these three general principles are to be recognized:

1. That what is disagreeable may not of necessity be especially injurious to the health.

2. That it is possible to adapt the system to noises that are at first disagreeable, so that they cease to have any appreciable or at least demontrable effect.

3. That there may be idiosyncrasies against noises as against all other forms of irritation—as there may be idiosyncrasies against certain articles

of food or drink, or against the various stimulants and narcotics or different articles on the materia medica.

Although it is usually assumed that the disagreeable and the unhealthful are identical, although offensive odors in large cities have been regarded as nuisances in the eye of the modern law, yet there is no scientific proof that there is any such necessary correlation. The odor of a tanyard is not only unpleasant, but enormously so; one, at first, wonders that any human being could live, even for a day, in such an atmosphere; and yet investigations that I made a number of years ago convinced me that those who regularly worked in these yards were not in any perceptible way injured in health, and that their longevity compared favorably with that of other muscle-workers in the various trades.

Likewise there are many vile odors in all our cities that are legislated against as nuisances, and for permitting which the members of the Board of Health of the city of New York were lately indicted, but which certainly cannot be proved to be injurious to health; there is no evidence that they directly excite either acute or chronic disease, or that they tend to shorten life, although they are so disagreeable as to subtract largely from the comfort of those who are exposed to them. On the other hand, it is well established that the sewer gas and other poisons that give rise to most serious disease have little or no odor, and only make their presence felt by their effects.

With disagreeable sounds the same principle, up to a certain point at least, applies; the rumble of omnibuses, the jangling of car-bells, and the clatter of many carriages, with the tramping and shuffling of vast multitudes in our crowded streets, all jar on a sensitive frame; but whether they excite, in any considerable number of people, symptoms of either acute or chronic disorder, must be regarded as doubtful. That in connection with the bad air of cities and the confinement, they do tend to increase the nervousness of civilization is quite probable, but any claim more definite than that cannot well be maintained.

In cases of illness or idiosyncrasy, however, it is quite different, for the evil effects of noise on those confined with grave or debilitating disease are oftentimes so speedy, direct, and severe that no doubt can be raised, and the cessation of the nuisance or the removal of the sufferer is an urgent need.

This must without dispute be allowed, that one may have an idiosyncrasy against a certain form of sound just as against a certain odor, taste, or action of food or medicine. How painful the noise of filing a saw may be is well known; but it is not so well known that this is but one of many noises that are specially offensive to individuals. The scraping of the foot on a corn cob or rubber mat is to some as painful as though a pin were stuck into the skin; and at one time, when somewhat exhausted by over-work, the noise of the tearing of a newspaper was to myself unpleasant in the extreme. These peculiarities, however, are not necessarily the result of disease or symptomatic of any recognizable state; they are found in the strongest and hardiest. One who for a number of years has been my guide in the White Mountains, a man of rare endurance and vigor, who in a long and laborious life has never known a day of real illness, tells me that the noise of the filing of a saw has always been exceedingly dis-tressing. A professional gentleman whom I know, says that the noise of the elevated railway trains in New York city are so harassing to him that he never goes on the avenue where these trains run unless compelled to do so; the effect he declares is rasping, exasperating, amounting to positive pain; and yet this man is not only well, but is remarkably tough and wiry, capable of bearing confinement and long and severe application.

This elevated railroad, it may be observed, has been a convenient means of illustrating all the principles here brought forward in regard to the relation of noise to nerves. When first organized, during the heat of summer, while people lived with doors and windows open for the admis-sion of air, the noise of the trains was a source of distress to all or nearly all, who lived on or very near the avenue and streets through which it passed; a new structure usually makes more noise than an old one, and this fact not being understood caused the complaints to be almost as loud as the noise. Those who were so unfortunate as to be confined to the house by any form of sickness in some cases suffered so severely that it was feared their lives would be sacrificed; and some were obliged to dispose of their property and move away.

The majority of the residents, however, in the course of a few months became so used to the din that, except when their attention was specially directed to it, it ceased to be painfully annoying; they had adapted them-selves to their environment; the nervous system had become in a degree benumbed, so that the vibrations striking on the ear gave rise to no con-scious or rememberable sensation. This process of the moulding of the internal to the external was made much easier and shorter by the coming of cold weather, which closed the doors and windows; and by the fact that the structure of the road had been so affected by use that its vibra-tions were less rasping to the nerves. It would appear that the vibrations were both changed in quality and diminished in loudness, although so far as I know no scientific proof of this has ever been offered.

In some cases of idiosyncrasy it is probable that instead of adaptation to environment directly the reverse will take place, and the more the noise is heard the more distressing it will become. The analogy of hay-fever gives us a suggestion of truth on this subject. In this malady there is usually an idiosyncrasy against some one or a number of vegetable or other irritants, as dust or roses, or certain fruits, as strawberries, or peaches, or grapes, or watermelons; and this idiosyncrasy cannot be overcome by any effort of the will, and the sufferer, instead of getting used to any of these irritants by long dwelling among them, becomes thereby worse and worse; and the only relief is to run away and escape the irritation; the effect of a long absence being in some cases to make the sensitiveness less; avoidance of the irritant doing for them just what long subjection to it does for others. To sum up briefly, any irritation constantly or repeatedly acting, may have two precisely opposite effects—it may benumb or it may increase the sensitiveness—this latter effect occurring chiefly in cases of idiosyncrasy.

RAILWAY TRAVELLING AND NERVOUSNESS

Whether railway travelling is directly the cause of nervous disease is a question of not a little interest. Reasoning deductively, without any special facts, it would seem that the molecular disturbance caused by travelling long distances, or living on trains as an employe, would have an unfavorable influence on the nervous system.

In practice this seems to be found; that in some cases—probably a minority of those who live on the road—functional nervous symptoms are excited, and there are some who are compelled to give up this mode of life.

A German physician has given the name "Fear of Railway Travelling," to a symptom that is observed in some who have become nervously exhausted by long residence on trains; they become fearful of taking a journey on the cars mainly from the unpleasant sensations caused by the vibrating motions of the train.

That railway travel, though beneficial to some, is sometimes injurious to the nerve system of the nervous, is demonstrable all the time in my patients; many while travelling by rail suffer from the symptoms of seasickness and with increase of nervousness. . . .

COMPARATIVE SIZE OF THE ANCIENT AND MODERN WORLD

Little account has been made of the fact that the old world is small geographically. The ancient Greeks knew only of Greece and the few outside barbarians who tried to destroy them. The discovery of America, like the invention of printing, prepared the way for modern nervousness; and, in connection with the telegraph, the railway, and the periodical press increased a hundred-fold the distresses of humanity.

The sorrows of any part of the world, many times greater geographically than the old world as known to the ancients, through the medium of the press and the telegraph are made the sorrows of individuals everywhere.

The burning of Chicago—a city less than half a century old, on a continent whose existence was unknown a few centuries ago—becomes in a few hours the property of both hemispheres, and makes heavy drafts on the vitality not only of Boston and New York, but of London, Paris, and Vienna. With the extension and complexity of populations of the globe, with the rise and growth of nations and peoples, these local sorrows and local horrors become daily occasions of nervous disorders.

Our morning newspaper, that we read with our breakfast, has the history of the sorrows of the whole world for a day; and a nature but moderately sympathetic is robbed thereby, consciously or unconsciously, of more or less nervous strength.

LIFE IN ANCIENT ATHENS AND NEW YORK CONTRASTED

When we consider the life of an American child, from its early school-days until the hour it leaves the university or seminary, the many and tiresome hours of study, the endless committing and repeating and reciting, the confinement in constrained positions, the overheated and over-dried atmosphere, the newspapers and novels that he is and must be prepared to criticise, the sermons and lectures which he is compelled to listen to and analyse, the strife and struggle for bread and competence against inflammatory competition, the worry and concentration of work made both possible and necessary by the railway, mail service, and the telegraph; in view of these facts, we wonder not that the Americans are so nervous, but rather wonder at the power of adaptation of the human frame for unfavorable environment. The education of the Athenian boy consisted in play and games and songs, and repetitions of poems, and physical feats in the open air. His life was a long vacation, in which, as a rule, he rarely toiled as hard as the American lad in the intervals of his toil.

All that the world has done for two thousand years—all the history it has made, all its art, science, religion, politics, morals, and social life, the Greek boy could know nothing of, could not even anticipate; the world to him was young, and Greece was all the world. No scholar can graduate with even a moderate stand from one of our public schools, without mastering in a certain way, and after years of labor, many of the good or evil thoughts and deeds that have occupied the human race since the time of Socrates and Aristotle. From all these events of history, which every year are rolling up as an increasing burden for the future, the Athenian scholar was joyously free; education was to him but a delicious union of poetry, philosophy, and art. What they called work, gymnastics, competition games, and conversations on arts and letters, is to us recreation. Equally striking is the contrast in the life of Athenian and American adults. We have our occasional holidays, and a picnic or other pleasure party is cautiously allowed, or some anniversary is celebrated; but the Greek's life was a long holiday, a perpetual picnic, a ceaseless anniversary.

The Greek wife was half a doll, half a slave. Save a few of the more brilliant among the *etairae*—the *demi monde* of the time—they had no more voice in the interests of state, or art, or learning, or even of social life, than the children of to-day; the mental activity of woman is indeed almost all modern. The American mother is not only the acknowledged queen of society, but also aims to lead, and oftentimes does lead, with the highest success, in literature, on the platform, in the pulpit, in philanthropy and reform, and in the practice of the medical art.

The offspring of those whose brains are thus kept in constant motion musts be affected for better or for worse, sometimes in both ways. If the brain of the average American is tenfold more active than the brain of the average Athenian, the contrast in the cerebral activity of the women must be even greater. But waiving all attempts to bring the subject under mathematical law, these contrasts make clear, and bring into strong relief, the fact that in every direction the modern brain is more heavily taxed than the ancient. In accordance with all analogies, therefore, nervous sensitiveness and nervous diseases ought to increase with the progress of modern civilization; and neurasthenia would naturally be more abundant in the present than in the last century.

It might theoretically be objected to this reasoning that the capacity of the brain for work, and of the nerves for endurance, would grow with the growth of culture. This consideration is surely one of import. Up to a certain point work develops capacity for work; through endurance is evolved the power of greater endurance; force becomes the parent of force. But here, as in all animate nature, there are limitations of development which cannot be passed. The capacity of the nervous system for sustained work and worry has not increased in proportion to the demands for work and worry that are made upon it. Particularly during the past quarter of a century, under the press and stimulus of the telegraph and railway, the methods and incitements of brain-work have multiplied far in excess of average cerebral development. It is during this period that various functional nervous disorders have multiplied with a rapidity for which history gives us no analogy. Modern nervousness is the cry of the system struggling with its environment.

16. Life in the Mill

Elizabeth Stuart Phelps wrote *The Gates Ajar* (1869) at the age of twenty-four. The immediate source of the book was her brooding grief at the death of her fiancé in the war, but the book's message and its amazing popularity indicate deeper sources in her culture. The novel is one of several eschatological works popular shortly after the war; it presents a comforting version of heaven as a place of sweetness and love, where the dead are reunited intact with their loved ones. To the great solace of the book's heroine (Miss Phelps addressed herself mainly to women), who had learned of her brother's death in the war the old severe Calvinist universe is domesticated, transmuted into love and light, complete with cookie jars in the heavenly kitchens. As her fellow author and sometimes neighbor Harriet Beecher Stowe said about *Uncle Tom's Cabin*, Miss Phelps humbly confessed that the book was not original with her, but dictated by God himself.

Miss Phelps is another example, then, of the shift in New England from a religion of creed to a religion of heart and love. Born into an old Massachusetts family, she was raised chiefly in Andover where her father was a professor of theology. Her paternal grandfather, a Congregational minister, had left a family record of curious psychic experiences, "manifestations," while her mother's father, Moses Stuart, was a strict New England theologian. From her mother, also a writer on religious themes, she seems to have inherited a nervous susceptibility and proneness to psychic disturbances. The figure of the intense, sensitive, lonely, sacrificing woman dominates her later fiction, and seems to represent a version of herself. A victim of insomnia, she was given to disorders often severe enough to force her into seclusion. Some of this intensity—and her ability to transform it into sentimental fiction with wide popular appeal—is evident in this selection, which, like many of her stories, shows her sympathy with the deprived lives of working women. "The Tenth of January" is based on an actual accident—the collapse of a Lawrence textile mill in 1860, in which nearly ninety employees perished. In 1871 she published a novel, *The Silent Partner*, dealing with conditions in the mills. In both cases her point of view toward industrial labor and its brutalizing effects and physical dangers is based on benevolence, piety, and trust in the open gates of a mild and soothing heaven.

The Tenth of January

ELIZABETH STUART PHELPS

The city of Lawrence is unique in its way.

For simooms that scorch you and tempests that freeze; for sand-heaps and sand-hillocks and sand-roads; for men digging sand, for women shaking off sand, for minute boys crawling in sand; for sand in the church-slips and the gingerbread-windows, for sand in your eyes, your nose, your mouth, down your neck, up your sleeves, under your *chignon*, down your throat; for unexpected corners where tornadoes lie in wait; for "bleak, uncomforted" sidewalks, where they chase you, dog you, confront you, strangle you, twist you, blind you, turn your umbrella wrong side out; for "dimmykhrats" and bad ice-cream, for unutterable circus-bills and religious tea-parties; for uncleared ruins, and mills that spring up in a night; for jaded faces and busy feet; for an air of youth and incompleteness at which you laugh, and a consciousness of growth and greatness which you respect,—it—

I believe, when I commenced that sentence, I intended to say that it would be difficult to find Lawrence's equal.

Of the twenty-five thousand souls who inhabit that city, ten thousand are prisoners,—prisoners of factories perhaps the most healthfully, considerately, and generously conducted of any in this country or in any country, but factories just the same. Dust, whir, crash, clang; dizziness, peril, exhaustion, discontent,—that is what the word means, taken at its best. Of these ten thousand two thirds are girls: voluntary captives, indeed; but what is the practical difference? It is an old story,—that of going to jail for want of bread.

My story is written as one sets a bit of marble to mark a mound. I linger over it as we linger beside the grave of one who sleeps well: half sadly, half gladly,—more gladly than sadly,—but hushed.

The time to see Lawrence is when the mills open or close. So languidly the dull-colored, inexpectant crowd wind in! So briskly they come bound-

Elizabeth Stuart Phelps, "The Tenth of January," *Atlantic Monthly*, XXI (1868), 345–362.

ing out! Factory faces have a look of their own. Not only their common dinginess, and a general air of being in a hurry to find the wash-bowl, but an appearance of restlessness,—often of envious restlessness, not habitual in most departments of "healthy labor." Watch them closely: you can read their histories at a venture. A widow this, in the dusty black, with she can scarcely remember how many mouths to feed at home. Worse than widowed that one: she has put her baby out to board,—and humane people know what that means,—to keep the little thing beyond its besotted father's reach. There is a group who have "just come over." A child's face here, old before its time. That girl—she climbs five flights of stairs twice a day—will climb no more stairs for herself or another by the time the clover-leaves are green. "The best thing about one's grave is that it will be level," she was heard once to say. Somebody muses a little here,—she is to be married this winter. There is a face just behind her whose fixed eyes repel and attract you; there may be more love than guilt in them, more despair than either.

Had you stood in some unobserved corner of Essex Street, at four o'clock one Saturday afternoon towards the last of November, 1859, watching the impatient stream pour out of the Pemberton Mill, eager with a saddening eagerness for its few holiday hours, you would have observed one girl who did not bound.

She was slightly built, and undersized; her neck and shoulders were closely muffled, though the day was mild; she wore a faded scarlet hood which heightened the pallor of what must at best have been a pallid face. It was a sickly face, shaded off with purple shadows, but with a certain wiry nervous strength about the muscles of the mouth and chin: it would have been a womanly, pleasant mouth, had it not been crossed by a white scar, which attracted more of one's attention than either the womanliness or pleasantness. Her eyes had light long lashes, and shone through them steadily.

You would have noticed as well, had you been used to analyzing crowds, another face,—the two were side by side,—dimpled with pink and white flushes, and framed with bright black hair. One would laugh at this girl and love her, scold her and pity her, caress her and pray for her,—then forget her perhaps.

The girls from behind called after her: "Del! Del Ivory! look over there!"

Pretty Del turned her head. She had just flung a smile at a young clerk who was petting his mustache in a shop-window, and the smile lingered.

One of the factory boys was walking alone across the Common in his factory clothes.

"Why, there's Dick! Sene, do you see?"

Sene's scarred mouth moved slightly, but she made no reply. She had seen him five minutes ago.

One never knows exactly whether to laugh or cry over them, catching their chatter as they file past the show-windows of the long-showy street.

"Look a' that pink silk with the figures on it!"

"I've seen them as is betther nor that in the ould counthree.—Patsy Malorrn, let alon' hangin' onto the shawl of me!"

"That's Mary Foster getting out of that carriage with the two white horses,—she that lives in the brown house with the cupilo."

"Look at her dress trailin' after her. I'd like my dresses trailin' after me."

"Well may they be good,—these rich folks!"

"That's so. I'd be good if I was rich; wouldn't you, Moll?"

"You'd keep growing wilder than ever, if you went to hell, Meg Match: yes you would, because my teacher said so."

"So, then, he wouldn't marry her, after all; and she—"

"Going to the circus to-night, Bess?"

"I can't help crying, Jenny. You don't *know* how my head aches! It aches, and it aches, and it seems as if it would never stop aching. I wish— I wish I was dead, Jenny!"

They separated at last, going each her own way,—pretty Del Ivory to her boarding-place by the canal, her companion walking home alone.

This girl, Asenath Martyn, when left to herself, fell into a contented dream not common to girls who have reached her age,—especially girls who have seen the phases of life which she had seen. Yet few of the faces in the streets that led her home were more gravely lined. She puzzled one at the first glance, and at the second. An artist, meeting her musing on a canal-bridge one day, went home and painted a May-flower budding in November.

It was a damp, unwholesome place, the street in which she lived, cut short by a broken fence, a sudden steep, and the water; filled with children,—they ran from the gutters after her, as she passed,—and filled to the brim; it tipped now and then, like an over-full soup-plate, and spilled out two or three through the break in the fence.

Down in the corner, sharp upon the water, the east-winds broke about a little yellow house, where no children played; an old man's face watched at a window, and a nasturtium-vine crawled in the garden. The broken panes of glass about the place were well mended, and a clever little gate, extemporized from a wild grape-vine, swung at the entrance. It was not an old man's work.

Asenath went in with expectant eyes; they took in the room at a glance, and fell.

"Dick hasn't come, father?"

"Come and gone, child; didn't want any supper, he said. You're an hour before time, Senath."

"Yes. Didn't want any supper, you say? I don't see why not."

"No more do I, but it's none of our concern as I knows on; very like the pickles hurt him for dinner; Dick never had an o'er-strong stomach, as you might say. But you don't tell me how it m' happen you're let out at four o'clock, Senath," half complaining.

"O, something broke in the machinery, father; you know you wouldn't understand if I told you what."

He looked up from his bench,—he cobbled shoes there in the corner on his strongest days,—and after her as she turned quickly away and up stairs to change her dress. She was never exactly cross with her father; but her words rang impatiently sometimes.

She came down presently, transformed as only factory-girls are transformed by the simple little toilet she had been making; her thin, soft hair knotted smoothly, the tips of her fingers rosy from the water, her pale neck well toned by her gray stuff dress and cape;—Asenath always wore a cape: there was one of crimson flannel, with a hood, that she had meant to wear to-night; she had thought about it coming home from the mill; she was apt to wear it on Saturdays and Sundays; Dick had more time at home. Going up stairs to-night, she had thrown it away into a drawer, and shut the drawer with a snap; then opened it softly, and cried a little; but she had not taken it out.

As she moved silently about the room, setting the supper-table for two, crossing and recrossing the broad belt of sunlight that fell upon the floor, it was easy to read the sad story of the little hooded capes.

They might have been graceful shoulders. The hand which had scarred her face had rounded and bent them,—her own mother's hand.

Of a bottle always on the shelf; of brutal scowls where smiles should be; of days when she wandered dinnerless and supperless in the streets through loathing of her home; of nights when she sat out in the snowdrifts through terror of her home; of a broken jug one day, a blow, a fall, then numbness, and the silence of the grave,—she had her distant memories; of waking on a sunny afternoon, in bed, with a little cracked glass upon the opposite wall; of creeping out and up to it in her night-dress; of the ghastly twisted thing that looked back at her. Through the open window she heard the children laughing and leaping in the sweet summer air. She crawled into bed and shut her eyes. She remembered stealing out at last, after many days, to the grocery around the corner for a pound of coffee. "Humpback; humpback!" cried the children,—the very children who could leap and laugh.

One day she and little Del Ivory made mud-houses after school.

"I'm going to have a house of my own, when I'm grown up," said pretty Del; "I shall have a red carpet and some curtains; my husband will buy me a piano."

"So will mine, I guess," said Sene, simply.

"*Yours!*" Del shook back her curls; "who do you suppose would ever marry *you?*"

One night there was a knocking at the door, and a hideous, sodden thing borne in upon a plank. The crowded street, tired of tipping out little children, had sent her mother staggering through the broken fence. At the funeral she heard some one say, "How glad Sene must be!"

Since that, life had meant three things,—her father, the mills, and Richard Cross.

"You're a bit put out that the young fellow didn't stay to supper,—eh, Senath?" the old man said, laying down his boot.

"Put out! Why should I be? His time is his own. It's likely to be the Union that took him out,—such a fine day for the Union! I'm sure I never expected him to go to walk with me *every* Saturday afternoon. I'm not a fool to tie him up to the notions of a crippled girl. Supper is ready, father."

But her voice rasped bitterly. Life's pleasures were so new and late and important to her, poor thing! It went hard to miss the least of them. Very happy people will not understand exactly how hard.

Old Martyn took off his leather apron with a troubled face, and, as he passed his daughter, gently laid his tremulous, stained hand upon her head. He felt her least uneasiness, it would seem, as a chameleon feels a cloud upon the sun.

She turned her face softly and kissed him. But she did not smile.

She had planned for little for this holiday supper; saving three mellow-cheeked Louise Bonnes—expensive pears just then—to add to their bread and molasses. She brought them out from the closet, and watched her father eat them.

"Going out again, Senath?" he asked, seeing that she went for her hat and shawl, "and not a mouthful have you eaten! Find your father dull company hey? Well, well!"

She said something about needing the air; the mill was hot; she should soon be back; she spoke tenderly and she spoke truly, but she went out into the windy sunset with her little trouble, and forgot him. The old man, left alone, sat for a while with his head sunk upon his breast. She was all he had in the world,—this one little crippled girl that the world had dealt hardly with. She loved him; but he was not, probably would never be, to her exactly what she was to him. Usually he forgot this. Sometimes he quite understood it, as to-night.

Asenath, with the purpose only of avoiding Dick, and of finding a still spot, where she might think her thoughts undisturbed, wandered away over the eastern bridge, and down by the river's brink. It was a moody place; such a one as only apathetic or healthy natures (I wonder if that is tautology) can healthfully yield to. The bank sloped steeply; a fringe of stunted aspens and willows sprang from the frozen sand: it was a sickening, airless place in summer,—it was damp and desolate now. There was a sluggish wash of water under foot, and a stretch of dreary flats behind. Belated locomotives shrieked to each other across the river, and the wind bore down the current the roar and rage of the dam. Shadows were beginning to skulk under the huge brown bridge. The silent mills stared up and down and over the streams with a blank, unvarying stare. An oriflamme of scarlet burned in the west, flickered dully in the dirty, curdling water, flared against the windows of the Pemberton, which quivered and dripped, Asenath thought, as if with blood.

She sat down on a gray stone, wrapped in her gray shawl, curtained about by the aspens from the eye of passers on the bridge. She had a fancy for this place when things went ill with her. She had always borne her troubles alone, but she must be alone to bear them.

She knew very well that she was tired and nervous that afternoon, and that, if she could reason quietly about this little neglect of Dick's, it would cease to annoy her. Indeed, why should she be annoyed? Had he not done everything for her, been everything to her, for two long, sweet years? She dropped her head with a shy smile. She was never tired of living over these two years. She took positive pleasure in recalling the wretchedness in which they found her, for the sake of their dear relief. Many a time, sitting with her happy face hidden in his arms, she had laughed softly to remember the day on which he came to her. It was at twilight, and she was tired. Her reels had troubled her all the afternoon; the overseer was cross; the day was hot and long. Somebody, on the way home, had said in passing her: "Look at that girl! I'd kill myself if I looked like that": it was in a whisper, but she heard it. All life looked hot and long; the reels would always be out of order; the overseer would never be kind. Her temples would always throb, and her back would ache. People would always say, "Look at that girl!"

"Can you direct me to—" She looked up; she had been sitting on the door-steps with her face in her hands. Dick stood there with his cap off. He forgot that he was to inquire the way to Newbury Street, when he saw the tears on her shrunken cheeks. Dick could never bear to see a woman suffer.

"I wouldn't cry," he said simply, sitting down beside her. Telling a girl not to cry is an infallible recipe for keeping her at it. What could the child do, but sob as if her heart would break? Of course he had the whole story in ten minutes, she his in another ten. It was common and short enough:— a "Down-East" boy, fresh from his father's farm, hunting for work and board,—a bit homesick here in the strange, unhomelike city, it might be, and glad of some one to say so to.

What more natural than, that, when her father came out and was pleased with the lad, there should be no more talk of Newbury Street; that the little yellow house should become his home; that he should swing the fantastic gate, and plant the nasturtiums; that his life should grow to be one with hers and the old man's, his future and theirs unite unconsciously?

She remembered—it was not exactly pleasant, somehow, to remember it to-night—just the look of his face when they came into the house that summer evening, and he for the first time saw what she was, her cape having fallen off, in the full lamplight. His kindly blue eyes widened with shocked surprise, and fell; when he raised them, a pity like a mother's had crept into them; it broadened and brightened as time slid by, but it never left them.

So you see, after that, life unfolded in a burst of little surprises for Asenath. If she came home very tired, some one said, "I am sorry." If she wore a pink ribbon, she heard a whisper, "It suits you." If she sang a little song, she knew that somebody listened.

"I did not know the world was like this!" cried the girl.

After a time there came a night that he chanced to be out late,—they had planned an arithmetic lesson together, which he had forgotten,—and she sat grieving by the kitchen fire.

"You missed me so much then?" he said regretfully, standing with his hand upon her chair. She was trying to shell some corn; she dropped the pan, and the yellow kernels rolled away on the floor.

"What should I have, if I didn't have you?" she said, and caught her breath.

The young man paced to the window and back again. The firelight touched her shoulders, and the sad, white scar.

"You shall have me always, Asenath," he made answer. He took her face

within his hands and kissed it; and so they shelled the corn together, and
nothing more was said about it.

He had spoken this last spring of their marriage; but the girl, like all
girls, was shyly silent, and he had not urged it.

Asenath started from her pleasant dreaming just as the oriflamme was
furling into gray, suddenly conscious that she was not alone. Below her,
quite on the brink of the water, a girl was sitting,—a girl with a bright
plaid shawl, and a nodding red feather in her hat. Her head was bent,
and her hair fell against a profile cut in pink-and-white.

"Del is too pretty to be here alone so late," thought Asenath, smiling
tenderly. Good-natured Del was kind to her in a certain way, and she
rather loved the girl. She rose to speak to her, but concluded, on a second
glance through the aspens, that Miss Ivory was quite able to take care of
herself.

Del was sitting on an old log that jutted into the stream, dabbling in
the water with the tips of her feet. (Had she lived in The Avenue, she
could not have been more particular about her shoemaker.) Some one—
it was too dark to see distinctly—stood beside her, his eyes upon her
face. Attitudes translate themselves. Asenath could hear nothing, but she
needed to hear nothing, to know how the young fellow's eyes drank in
the coquettish picture. Besides, it was an old story. Del counted her
rejected lovers by the score.

"It's no wonder," she thought in her honest way, standing still to watch
them with a sense of puzzled pleasure much like that with which she
watched the print-windows,—"it's no wonder they love her. I'd love her
if I was a man: so pretty! so pretty! She's just good for nothing, Del is;—
would let the kitchen fire go out, and wouldn't mend the baby's aprons;
but I'd love her all the same; marry her, probably, and be sorry all my life."

Pretty Del! Poor Del! Asenath wondered whether she wished that she
were like her; she could not quite make out; it would be pleasant to sit
on a log and look like that; it would be more pleasant to be watched as
Del was watched just now: it struck her suddenly that Dick had never
looked like this at her.

The hum of their voices ceased while she stood there with her eyes
upon them; Del turned her head away with a sudden movement, and the
young man left her, apparently without bow or farewell, sprang up the
bank at a bound, and crushed the undergrowth with quick, uneasy strides.

Asenath, with some vague idea that it would not be honorable to see
his face,—poor fellow!—shrank back into the aspens and the shadow.

He towered tall in the twilight as he passed her,—he was so near that she might have touched him,—and a dull, umber gleam, the last of the sunset, struck him from the west.

Struck it out into her sight,—the haggard struggling face,—Richard Cross's face.

Of course you knew it from the beginning, but remember that the girl did not. She might have known it perhaps, but she had not.

Asenath stood up, sat down again.

She had a distinct consciousness, for the moment, of seeing herself crouched down there under the aspens and the shadow, a humpbacked white creature, with distorted face and wide eyes. She remembered a picture she had somewhere seen of a little chattering goblin in a grave-yard, and was struck with the resemblance. Distinctly, too, she heard herself saying, with a laugh, she thought, "I might have known it; I might have known."

Then the blood came through her heart with a hot rush, and she saw Del on the log, smoothing the red feather of her hat. She heard a man's step, too, that rang over the bridge, passed the toll-house, grew faint, grew fainter, died in the sand by the Everett Mill.

Richard's face! Richard's face, looking—God help her!—as it had never looked at her; struggling—God pity him!—as it had never struggled for her.

She shut her hands into each other, and sat still a little while. A faint hope came to her then perhaps, after all; her face lightened grayly, and she crept down the bank to Del.

"I won't be a fool," she said, "I'll make sure,—I'll make as sure as death."

"Well, where did *you* drop down from, Sene?" said Del, with a guilty start.

"From over the bridge, to be sure. Did you think I swam, or flew, or blew?"

"You came on me so sudden!" said Del, petulantly; "you nearly frightened the wits out of me. You didn't meet anybody on the bridge?" with a quick look.

"Let me see." Asenath considered gravely. "There was one small boy making faces, and two—no, three—dogs, I believe; that was all."

"Oh!"

Del looked relieved, but fell silent.

"You're sober, Del. Been sending off a lover, as usual?"

"I don't know anything about its being usual," answered Del, in an aggrieved, coquettish way, "but there's been somebody here that liked me well enough."

Del curled the red feather about her fingers, and put her hat on over her eyes, then a little cry broke from her, half sob, half anger.

"I might perhaps,—I don't know. He's good. I think he'd let me have a parlor and a door-bell. But he's going to marry somebody else, you see. I sha'n't tell you his name, so you needn't ask."

Asenath looked straight upon the water. A dead leaf that had been caught in an eddy attracted her attention; it tossed about for a minute, then a tiny whirlpool sucked it down.

"I wasn't going to ask; it's nothing to me, of course. He doesn't care for her then,—this other girl?"

"Not so much as he does for me. He didn't mean to tell me, but he said that I—that I looked so—pretty, it came right out. But there! I mustn't tell you any more."

Del began to be frightened; she looked up sideways at Asenath's quiet face. "I won't say another word," and so chattered on, growing a little cross; Asenath need not look so still, and sure of herself,—a mere hump-backed fright!

"He'll never break his engagement, not even for me; he's sorry for her, and all that. I think it's too bad. He's handsome. He makes me feel like saying my prayers, too, he's so good! Besides, I want to be married. I hate the mill. I hate to work. I'd rather be taken care of,—a sight rather. I feel bad enough about it to cry."

Two tears rolled over her cheeks, and fell on the soft plaid shawl. Del wiped them away carefully with her rounded fingers.

Asenath turned and looked at this Del Ivory long and steadily through the dusk. The pretty, shallow thing! The worthless, bewildering thing!

A fierce contempt for her pink-and-white, and tears and eyelashes and attitude, came upon her; then a sudden sickening jealousy that turned her faint where she sat.

What did God mean,—Asenath believed in God, having so little else to believe in,—what did he mean, when he had blessed the girl all her happy life with such wealth of beauty, by filling her careless hands with this one best, last gift? Why, the child could not hold such golden love! She would throw it away by and by. What a waste it was!

Not that she had these words for her thought, but she had the thought distinctly through her dizzy pain.

"So there's nothing to do about it," said Del, pinning her shawl. "We can't have anything to say to each other,—unless anybody should die, or anything; and of course I'm not wicked enough to think of that—Sene! Sene! what are you doing?"

Sene had risen slowly, stood upon the log, caught at an aspen-top, and swung out with it its whole length above the water. The slight tree writhed and quivered about the roots. Sene looked down and moved her marred lips without sound.

Del screamed and wrung her hands. It was an ugly sight!

"O don't, Sene, *don't!* You'll drown yourself! you will be drowned! you will be—O, what a start you gave me! What *were* you doing, Senath Martyn?"

Sene swung slowly back, and sat down.

"Amusing myself a little;—well, unless somebody died, you said? But I believe I won't talk any more to-night. My head aches. Go home, Del."

Del muttered a weak protest at leaving her there alone; but, with her bright face clouded and uncomfortable, went.

Asenath turned her head to listen for the last rustle of her dress, then folded her arms, and with her eyes upon the sluggish current, sat still.

An hour and a half later, an Andover farmer, driving home across the bridge, observed on the river's edge—a shadow cut within a shadow—the outline of a woman's figure, sitting perfectly still with folded arms. He reined up and looked down; but it sat quite still.

"Hallo there!" he called; "you'll fall in if you don't look out!" for the wind was strong, and it blew against the figure; but it did not move nor make reply. The Andover farmer looked over his shoulder with a sudden recollection of a ghost-story which he had charged his grandchildren not to believe last week, cracked his whip, and rumbled on.

Asenath began to understand by and by that she was cold, so climbed the bank, made her way over the windy flats, the railroad, and the western bridge confusedly with an idea of going home. She turned aside by the toll-gate. The keeper came out to see what she was doing, but she kept out of his sight behind the great willow and his little blue house,—the blue house with the green blinds and red moulding. The dam thundered that night, the wind and the water being high. She made her way up above it, and looked in. She had never seen it so black and smooth there. As she listened to the roar, she remembered something that she had read— was it in the Bible or the Ledger?—about seven thunders uttering their voices.

"He's sorry for her, and all that," they said.

A dead bough shot down the current while she stood there, went over and down, and out of sight, throwing up its little branches like helpless hands.

It fell in with a thought of Asenath's, perhaps; at any rate she did not like the looks of it, and went home.

Over the bridge, and the canal, and the lighted streets, the falls called after her: "He's sorry for her, and all that." The curtain was drawn aside when she came home, and she saw her father through the window, sitting alone, with his gray head bent.

It occurred to her that she had often left him alone,—poor old father! It occurred to her, also, that she understood now what it was to be alone. Had she forgotten him in those two comforted, companioned years?

She came in weakly, and looked about.

"Dick's in, and gone to bed," said the old man, answering her look. "You're tired, Senath."

"I am tired, father."

She sunk upon the floor,—the heat of the room made her a little faint,— and laid her head upon his knee; oddly enough, she noticed that the patch on it had given way,—wondered how many days it had been so,—whether he had felt ragged and neglected while she was busy about that blue neck-tie for Dick. She put her hand up and smoothed the corners of the rent.

"You shall be mended up to-morrow, poor father!"

He smiled, pleased like a child to be remembered. She looked up at him,—at his gray hair and shrivelled face, at his blackened hands and bent shoulders, and dusty, ill-kept coat. What would it be like, if the days brought her nothing but him?

"Something's the matter with my little gal? Tell father, can't ye?"

Her face flushed hot, as if she had done him wrong. She crept up into his arms, and put her hands behind his rough old neck.

"Would you kiss me, father? You don't think I'm too ugly to kiss, maybe,—you?"

She felt better after that. She had not gone to sleep now for many a night unkissed; it had seemed hard at first.

When she had gone half-way up stairs, Dick came to the door of his room on the first floor, and called her. He held the little kerosene lamp over his head; his face was grave and pale.

"I haven't said good night, Sene."

She made no reply.

"Asenath, good night."

She stayed her steps upon the stairs without turning her head. Her father had kissed her to-night. Was not that enough?

"Why, Sene, what's the matter with you?"

Dick mounted the stairs, and touched his lips to her forehead with a gently compassionate smile.

She fled from him with a cry like the cry of a suffocated creature, shut her door, and locked it with a ringing clang.

"She's walked too far, and got a little nervous," said Dick, screwing up his lamp; "poor thing!"

Then he went into his room to look at Del's photograph awhile before he burned it up; for he meant to burn it up.

Asenath, when she had locked her door, put her lamp before the looking-glass, and tore off her gray cape; tore it off so savagely that the button snapped and rolled away,—two little crystal semicircles like tears upon the floor.

There was no collar about the neck of her dress, and this heightened the plainness and the pallor of her face. She shrank instinctively at the first sight of herself, and opened the drawer where the crimson cape was folded, but shut it resolutely.

"I'll see the worst of it," she said with pinched lips. She turned herself about and about before the glass, letting the cruel light gloat over her shoulders, letting the sickly shadows grow purple on her face. Then she put her elbows on the table and her chin in her hands, and so, for a motionless half-hour, studied the unrounded, uncolored, unlighted face that stared back at her; her eyes darkening at its eyes, her hair touching its hair, her breath dimming the outline of its repulsive mouth.

By and by she dropped her head into her hands. The poor, mistaken face! She felt as if she would like to blot it out of the world, as her tears used to blot out the wrong sums upon her slate. It had been so happy! But he was sorry for it, and all that. Why did God make such faces?

She slipped upon her knees, bewildered.

"He *can't* mean any harm nohow," she said, speaking fast, and knelt there and said it over till she felt sure of it.

Then she thought of Del once more,—of her colors and sinuous springs, and little cries and chatter.

After a time she found that she was growing faint, and so stole down into the kitchen for some food. She stayed a minute to warm her feet. The fire was red and the clock was ticking. It seemed to her home-like and comfortable, and she seemed to herself very homeless and lonely; so she sat down on the floor, with her head in a chair, and cried as hard as she ought to have done four hours ago.

She climbed into bed about one o'clock, having decided, in a dull way, to give Dick up to-morrow.

But when to-morrow came he was up with a bright face, and built the kitchen fire for her, and brought in all the water, and helped her fry the potatoes, and whistled a little about the house, and worried at her paleness, and so she said nothing about it.

"I'll wait till night," she planned, making ready for the mill.

"O, I can't!" she cried at night. So other mornings came, and other nights.

I am quite aware that, according to all romantic precedents, this conduct was preposterous in Asenath. Floracita, in the novel, never so far forgets the whole duty of a heroine as to struggle, waver, doubt, delay. It is proud and proper to free the young fellow; proudly and properly she frees him; "suffers in silence"—till she marries another man; and (having had a convenient opportunity to refuse the original lover) overwhelms the reflective reader with a sense of poetic justice and the eternal fitness of things.

But I am not writing a novel, and, as the biographer of this simple factory girl, am offered few advantages.

Asenath was no heroine, you see. Such heroic elements as were in her—none could tell exactly what they were, or whether there were any: she was one of those people in whom it is easy to be quite mistaken;—her life had not been one to develop. She might have a certain pride of her own, under given circumstances; but plants grown in a cellar will turn to the sun at any cost; how could she go back into her dark?

As for the other man to marry, he was out of the question. Then, none love with the tenacity of the unhappy; no life is so lavish of itself as the denied life: to him that hath not shall be given,—and Asenath loved this Richard Cross.

It might be altogether the grand and suitable thing to say to him, "I will not be your wife." It might be that she would thus regain a strong shade of lost self-respect. It might be that she would make him happy, and give pleasure to Del. It might be that the two young people would be her "friends," and love her in a way.

But all this meant that Dick must go out of her life. Practically, she must make up her mind to build the fires, and pump the water, and mend the windows alone. In dreary fact, he would not listen when she sung; would not say, "You are tired, Sene"; would never kiss away an undried tear. There would be nobody to notice the crimson cape, nobody to make blue neck-ties for; none for whom to save the Bonnes de Jersey, or to take sweet, tired steps, or make dear, dreamy plans. To be sure, there was her father; but fathers do not count for much in a time like this on which Sene had fallen.

That Del Ivory was—Del Ivory added intricacies to the question. It was a very unpoetic but undoubted fact that Asenath could in no way so insure Dick's unhappiness as to pave the way to his marriage with the woman whom he loved. There would be six merry months, perhaps, or three; then slow worry and disappointment; pretty Del accepted at last, not as the crown of his young life, but as its silent burden and misery. Poor Dick! good Dick! Who deserved more wealth of wifely sacrifice? Asenath, thinking this, crimsoned with pain and shame. A streak of good common sense in the girl told her—though she half scorned herself for the conviction—that even a crippled woman who should bear all things and hope all things for his sake might blot out the memory of this rounded Del; that, no matter what the motive with which he married her, he would end by loving his wife like other people.

She watched him sometimes in the evenings, as he turned his kind eyes after her over the library book which he was reading.

"I know I could make him happy! I *know* I could!" she muttered fiercely to herself.

November blew into December, December congealed into January, while she kept her silence. Dick, in his honorable heart, seeing that she suffered, wearied himself with plans to make her eyes shine; brought her two pails of water instead of one, never forgot the fire, helped her home from the mill. She saw him meet Del Ivory once upon Essex Street with a grave and silent bow; he never spoke with her now. He meant to pay the debt he owed her down to the uttermost farthing; that grew plain. Did she try to speak her wretched secret, he suffocated her with kindness, struck her dumb with tender words.

She used to analyze her life in those days, considering what it would be without him. To be up by half past five o'clock in the chill of all the winter mornings, to build the fire and cook the breakfast and sweep the floor, to hurry away faint and weak over the raw, slippery streets, to climb at half past six the endless stairs and stand at the endless loom, and hear the endless wheels go buzzing around, to sicken in the oily smells, and deafen at the remorseless noise, and weary of the rough girl swearing at the other end of the pass; to eat her cold dinner from a little cold tin pail out on the stairs in the three-quarters-of-an-hour recess; to come exhausted home at half past six at night, and get the supper, and brush up about the shoemaker's bench, and be too weak to eat; to sit with aching shoulders and make the button-holes of her best dress, or darn her father's stockings till nine o'clock; to hear no bounding step or cheery whistle about the house; to creep into bed and lie there trying not to think, and wishing that so she might creep into her grave,—this not for one winter, but for all the winters,—how should *you* like it, you young girls, with whom time runs like a story?

The very fact that her employers dealt honorably by her; that she was fairly paid, and promptly, for her wearing toil; that the limit of endurance was consulted in the temperature of the room, and her need of rest in an occasional holiday,—perhaps, after all, in the mood she was in, did not make this factory life more easy. She would have found it rather a relief to have somebody to complain of,—wherein she was like the rest of us, I fancy.

But at last there came a day—it chanced to be the ninth of January— when Asenath went away alone at noon, and sat where Merrimack sung his songs to her. She hid her face upon her knees, and listened, and thought her own thoughts, till they and the slow torment of the winter seemed greater than she could bear. So, passing her hands confusedly over her forehead, she said at last aloud, "That's what God means, Asenath Martyn!" and went back to work with a purpose in her eyes.

She "asked out" a little earlier than usual, and went slowly home. Dick was there before her; he had been taking a half-holiday. He had made the tea and toasted the bread for a little surprise. He came up and said, "Why, Sene, your hands are cold!" and warmed them for her in his own.

After tea she asked him, would he walk out with her for a little while, and he in wonder went.

The streets were brightly lighted, and the moon was up. The ice cracked crisp under their feet. Sleighs, with two riders in each, shot merrily by. People were laughing in groups before the shop-windows. In the glare of a jeweler's counter somebody was buying a wedding-ring, and a girl with red cheeks was looking hard the other way.

"Let's get away," said Asenath,—"get away from here!"

They chose by tacit consent that favorite road of hers over the eastern bridge. Their steps had a hollow, lonely ring on the frosted wood; she was glad when the softness of the snow in the road received them. She looked back once at the water, wrinkled into thin ice on the edge for a foot or two, then open and black and still.

"What are you doing?" asked Dick. She said that she was wondering how cold it was, and Dick laughed at her.

They strolled on in silence for perhaps a mile of the desolate road.

"Well, this is social!" said Dick at length; "how much farther do you want to go? I believe you'd walk to Reading if nobody stopped you!"

She was taking slow, regular steps like an automaton, and looking straight before her.

"How much farther? Oh!" She stopped and looked about her.

A wide young forest spread away at their feet, to the right and to the left. There was ice on the tiny oaks and miniature pines; it glittered sharply under the moon; the light upon the snow was blue; cold roads wound away through it, deserted; little piles of dead leaves shivered; a fine keen spray ran along the tops of the drifts; inky shadows lurked and dodged about the undergrowth; in the broad spaces the snow glared; the lighted mills, a zone of fire, blazed from east to west; the skies were bare, and the wind was up, and Merrimack in the distance chanted solemnly.

They were alone there,—they two, and God.

"Dick," said Asenath, "this is a dreadful place! Take me home."

But when he would have turned, she held him back with a sudden cry, and stood still.

"I meant to tell you—I meant to say—Dick! I was going to say—"

But she did not say it. She opened her lips to speak once and again, but no sound came from them.

"Sene! why, Sene, what ails you?"

He turned, and took her in his arms; he hid the sky and snow from her sight; she felt his breath upon her hair.

"Poor Sene!"

He kissed her, feeling sorry for her unknown trouble. She struggled at his touch. He kissed her again. She broke from him, and away with a great bound upon the snow. She stood out against the sky, panting hard like a hunted thing.

"You make it so hard! You've no right to make it so hard! It ain't as if you loved me, Dick! I know I'm not like other girls! Go home, and let me be!"

But Dick drew her arm through his, and led her gravely away. "I like you well enough, Asenath," he said, with that motherly pity in his eyes; "I've always liked you. So don't let us have any more of this."

So Asenath said nothing more.

The sleek black river beckoned to her across the snow as they went home. A thought came to her as she passed the bridge—it is a curious study what wicked thoughts will come to good people!—she found herself considering the advisability of leaping the low brown parapet; and if it would not be like Dick to go over after her; if there would be a chance for them, even should he swim from the banks; how soon the icy current would paralyze him; how sweet it would be to chill to death there in his arms; how all this wavering and pain would be over; how Del would look when they dragged them out down below the machine-shop!

"Sene, are you cold?" asked puzzled Dick. She was warmly wrapped in her little squirrel furs; but he felt her quivering upon his arm, like one in an ague, all the way home.

About eleven o'clock that night her father waked from an exciting dream concerning the best method of blacking patent-leather; Sene stood beside his bed with her gray shawl thrown over her night-dress.

"Father, suppose some time there should be only you and me—"

"Well, well, Sene," said the old man sleepily,—"very well."

"I'd try to be a good girl! Could you love me enough to make up?"

He told her indistinctly that she always was a good girl; she never had a whipping from the day her mother died. She turned away impatiently; then cried out and fell upon her knees.

"Father, father! I'm in a great trouble. I haven't got any mother, any friend, anybody. Nobody helps me! Nobody knows. I've been thinking such things—O, such wicked things—up in my room! Then I got afraid of myself. You're good. You love me. I want you to put your hand on my head and say, 'God bless you, child, and show you how.'"

Bewildered, he put his hand upon her unbound hair, and said: "God bless you, child, and show you how!"

Asenath looked at the old withered hand a moment, as it lay beside her on the bed, kissed it, and went away.

There was a scarlet sunrise the next morning. A pale pink flush stole through a hole in the curtain, and fell across Asenath's sleeping face, and lay there like a crown. It woke her, and she threw on her dress; and sat down for a while on the window-sill, to watch the coming-on of the day.

The silent city steeped and bathed itself in rose-tints; the river ran red, and the snow crimsoned on the distant New Hampshire hills; Pemberton, mute and cold, frowned across the disk of the climbing sun, and dripped, as she had seen it drip before, with blood.

The day broke softly, the snow melted, the wind blew warm from the river. The factory-bell chimed cheerily, and a few sleepers, in safe luxurious beds, were wakened by hearing the girls sing on their way to work.

Asenath came down with a quiet face. In her communing with the sunrise helpful things had been spoken to her. Somehow, she knew not how, the peace of the day was creeping into her heart. For some reason, she knew not why, the torment and unrest of the night were gone. There was a future to be settled, but she would not trouble herself about that just now. There was breakfast to get; and the sun shone, and a snow-bird was chirping outside of the door. She noticed how the teakettle hummed, and how well the new curtain, with the castle and waterfall on it, fitted the window. She thought that she would scour the closet at night, and surprise her father by finishing those list slippers. She kissed him when she had tied on the red hood, and said good-by to Dick, and told them just where to find the squash-pie for dinner.

When she had closed the twisted gate, and taken a step or two upon the snow, she came thoughtfully back. Her father was on his bench, mending one of Meg Match's shoes. She pushed it gently out of his hands, sat down upon his lap, and stroked the shaggy hair away from his forehead.

"Father!"

"Well, what now, Sene?—what now?"

"Sometimes I believe I've forgotten you a bit, you know. I think we're going to be happier after this. That's all."

She went out singing, and he heard the gate shut again with a click.

Sene was a little dizzy that morning,—the constant palpitation of the floors always made her dizzy after a wakeful night,—and so her colored cotton threads danced out of place, and troubled her.

Del Ivory, working beside her, said, "How the mill shakes! What's going on?"

"It's the new machinery they're h'isting in," observed the overseer, carelessly. "Great improvement, but heavy, very heavy; they calc'late on getting it all into place to-day; you'd better be tending to your frame, Miss Ivory."

As the day wore on, the quiet of Asenath's morning deepened. Round and round with the pulleys over her head she wound her thoughts of Dick. In and out with her black and dun-colored threads she spun her future. Pretty Del, just behind her, was twisting a pattern like a rainbow. She noticed this, and smiled.

"Never mind!" she thought, "I guess God knows."

Was He ready "to bless her, and show her how"? She wondered. If, indeed, it were best that she should never be Dick's wife, it seemed to her that He would help her about it. She had been a coward last night; her blood leaped in her veins with shame at the memory of it. Did He understand? Did He not know how she loved Dick, and how hard it was to lose him?

However that might be, she began to feel at rest about herself. A curious apathy about means and ways and decisions took possession of her. A bounding sense that a way of escape was provided from all her troubles, such as she had when her mother died, came upon her.

Years before, an unknown workman in South Boston, casting an iron pillar upon its core, had suffered it to "float" a little, a very little more, till the thin, unequal side cooled to the measure of an eighth of an inch. That workman had provided Asenath's way of escape.

She went out at noon with her luncheon, and found a place upon the stairs, away from the rest, and sat there awhile, with her eyes upon the river, thinking. She could not help wondering a little, after all, why God need to have made her so unlike the rest of his fair handiwork. Del came bounding by, and nodded at her carelessly. Two young Irish girls, sisters, —the beauties of the mill,—magnificently colored creatures,—were singing a little love-song together, while they tied on their hats to go home.

"There *are* such pretty things in the world!" thought poor Sene.

Did anybody speak to her after the girls were gone? Into her heart these words fell suddenly, "*He* hath no form nor comeliness. *His* visage was so marred more than any man."

They clung to her fancy all the afternoon. She liked the sound of them. She wove them in with her black and dun colored threads.

The wind began at last to blow chilly up the staircases, and in at the cracks; the melted drifts out under the walls to harden; the sun dipped above the dam; the mill dimmed slowly; shadows crept down between the frames.

"It's time for lights," said Meg Match, and swore a little at her spools.

Sene, in the pauses of her thinking, heard snatches of the girls' talk.

"Going to ask out to-morrow, Meg?"

"Guess so, yes; me and Bob Smith we thought we'd go to Boston, and come up in the theatre train."

"Del Ivory, I want the pattern of your zouave."

"Did I go to church? No, you don't catch me! If I slave all the week, I'll do what I please on Sunday."

"Hush-sh! There's the boss looking over here!"

"Kathleen Donnavon, be still with your ghost-stories. There's one thing in the world I never will hear about, and that's dead people."

"Del," said Sene, "I think to-morrow—"

She stopped. Something strange had happened to her frame; it jarred, buzzed, snapped; the threads untwisted, and flew out of place.

"Curious!" she said, and looked up.

Looked up to see her overseer turn wildly, clap his hands to his head, and to hear a shriek from Del that froze her blood; to see the solid ceiling gape above her; to see the walls and windows stagger; to see iron pillars reel, and vast machinery throw up its helpless, giant arms, and a tangle of human faces blanch and writhe!

She sprang as the floor sunk. As pillar after pillar gave way, she bounded up an inclined plane, with the gulf yawning after her. It gained upon her, leaped at her, caught her; beyond were the stairs and an open door; she threw out her arms, and struggled on with hands and knees, tripped in the gearing, and saw, as she fell, a square, oaken beam above her yield and crash; it was of a fresh red color; she dimly wondered why,—as she felt her hands slip, her knees slide, support, time, place, and reason, go utterly out.

"At ten minutes before five, on Tuesday, the tenth of January, the Pemberton Mill, all hands being at the time on duty, fell to the ground."

So the record flashed over the telegraph wires, sprang into large type in the newspapers, passed from lip to lip, a nine days' wonder, gave place to the successful candidate, and the muttering South, and was forgotten.

Who shall say what it was to the seven hundred and fifty souls who were buried in the ruins? What to the eighty-eight who died that death of exquisite agony? What to the wrecks of men and women who endure unto this day a life that is worse than death? What to that architect and engineer who, when the fatal pillars were first delivered to them for inspection, had found one broken under their eyes, yet accepted the contract, and built with them a mill whose thin walls and wide, unsupported stretches could never keep their place unaided?

One that we love may go to the battle-ground, and we are ready for the worst: we have said our good-bys; our hearts wait and pray: it is his life, not his death, which is the surprise. But that he should go out to his safe, daily, commonplace occupations, unnoticed and uncaressed,—scolded a little, perhaps, because he leaves the door open, and tells us how cross we are this morning; and they bring him up the steps by and by, a mangled mass of death and horror,—that is hard.

Old Martyn, working Meg Match's shoes,—she was never to wear those shoes, poor Meg!—heard, at ten minutes before five, what he thought to be the rumble of an earthquake under his very feet, and stood with bated breath, waiting for the crash. As nothing further appeared to happen, he took his stick and limped out into the street.

A vast crowd surged through it from end to end. Women with white lips were counting the mills,—Pacific, Atlantic, Washington,—Pemberton? Where was Pemberton?

Where Pemberton had blazed with its lamps last night, and hummed with its iron lips this noon, a cloud of dust, black, silent, horrible, puffed a hundred feet into the air.

Asenath opened her eyes after a time. Beautiful green and purple lights had been dancing about her, but she had had no thoughts. It occurred to her now that she must have been struck upon the head. The church-clocks were striking eight. A bonfire which had been built at a distance, to light the citizens in the work of rescue, cast a little gleam in through the *débris* across her two hands, which lay clasped together at her side. One of her fingers, she saw, was gone; it was the finger which held Dick's little engagement ring. The red beam lay across her forehead, and drops dripped from it upon her eyes. Her feet, still tangled in the gearing which had tripped her, were buried beneath a pile of bricks.

A broad piece of flooring that had fallen slantwise roofed her in, and saved her from the mass of iron-work overhead, which would have crushed the breath out of Hercules. Fragments of looms, shafts, and pillars were in heaps about. Some one whom she could not see was dying just behind her. A little girl who worked in her room—a mere child—was crying between her groans for her mother. Del Ivory sat in a little open space, cushioned about with reels of cotton; she had a shallow gash upon her cheek; she was wringing her hands. They were at work from the outside, sawing entrances through the labyrinth of planks. A dead woman lay close by, and Sene saw them draw her out. It was Meg Match. One of the pretty Irish girls was crushed quite out of sight; only one hand was free; she moved it feebly. They could hear her calling for Jimmy Mahoney, Jimmy Mahoney! and would they be sure and give him back the handkerchief? Poor Jimmy Mahoney! By and by she called no more; and in a little while the hand was still. The other side of the slanted flooring some one prayed aloud. She had a little baby at home. She was asking God to take care of it for her. "For Christ's sake," she said. Sene listened long for the Amen, but it was never spoken. Beyond, they dug a man out from under a dead body, unhurt. He crawled to his feet, and broke into furious blasphemies.

As consciousness came fully, agony grew. Sene shut her lips and folded her bleeding hands together, and uttered no cry. Del did screaming enough for two, she thought. She pondered things calmly as the night deepened, and the words that the workers outside were saying came brokenly to her.

Her hurt, she knew, was not unto death; but it must be cared for before very long; how far could she support this slow bleeding away? And what were the chances that they could hew their way to her without crushing her?

She thought of her father, of Dick; of the bright little kitchen and supper-table set for three; of the song that she had sung in the flush of the morning. Life—even her life—grew sweet, now that it was slipping from her.

Del cried presently, that they were cutting them out. The glare of the bonfires struck through an opening; saws and axes flashed; voices grew distinct.

"They never can get at me," said Sene. "I must be able to crawl. If you could get some of those bricks off of my feet, Del!"

Del took off two or three in a frightened way; then, seeing the blood on them, sat down and cried.

A Scotch girl, with one arm shattered, crept up and removed the pile; then fainted.

The opening broadened, brightened; the sweet night-wind blew in; the safe night sky shone through. Sene's heart leaped within her. Out in the wind and under the sky she should stand again after all! Back in the little kitchen, where the sun shone, and she could sing a song, there would yet be a place for her. She worked her head from under the beam, and raised herself upon her elbow.

At that moment she heard a cry:

"Fire! *fire!* GOD ALMIGHTY HELP THEM,—THE RUINS ARE ON FIRE!"

A man working over the *débris* from the outside had taken the notion— it being rather dark just there—to carry a lantern with him.

"For God's sake," a voice cried from the crowd, "don't stay there with that light!"

But while this voice yet sounded, it was the dreadful fate of the man with the lantern to let it fall,—and it broke upon the ruined mass.

That was at nine o'clock. What there was to see from then till morning could never be told or forgotten.

A network twenty feet high, of rods and girders, of beams, pillars, stair-ways, gearing, roofing, ceiling, walling; wrecks of looms, shafts, twisters, pulleys, bobbins, mules, locked and interwoven; wrecks of human crea-tures wedged in; a face that you know turned up at you from some pit which twenty-four hours' hewing could not open; a voice that you know crying after you from God knows where; a mass of long, fair hair visible here; a foot there; three fingers of a hand over there; the snow bright-red under foot; charred limbs and headless trunks tossed about; strong men carrying covered things by you, at sight of which other strong men have fainted; the little yellow jet that flared up, and died in smoke, and flared again, leaped out, licked the cotton-bales, tasted the oiled machinery, crunched the netted wood, danced on the heaped-up stone, threw its cruel arms high into the night, roared for joy at helpless firemen, and swallowed wreck, death, and life together out of your sight,—the lurid thing stands alone in the gallery of tragedy.

"Del," said Sene, presently, "I smell the smoke." And in a little while, "How red it is growing away over there at the left!"

To lie here and watch the hideous redness crawling after her, springing at her!—it had seemed greater than reason could bear, at first.

Now it did not trouble her. She grew a little faint, and her thoughts wandered. She put her head down upon her arm, and shut her eyes. Dreamily she heard them saying a dreadful thing outside, about one of the overseers; at the alarm of fire he had cut his throat, and before the flames touched him he was taken out. Dreamily she heard Del cry that the shaft behind the heap of reels was growing hot. Dreamily she saw a tiny puff of smoke struggle through the cracks of a broken fly-frame.

They were working to save her, with rigid, stern faces. A plank snapped, a rod yielded; they drew out the Scotch girl; her hair was singed; then a man with blood upon his face and wrists, held down his arms.

"There's time for one more! God save the rest of ye,—I can't!"

Del sprang; then stopped,—even Del,—stopped ashamed, and looked back at the cripple.

Asenath at this sat up erect. The latent heroism in her awoke. All her thoughts grew clear and bright. The tangled skein of her perplexed and troubled winter unwound suddenly. This, then, was the way. It was better so. God had provided himself a lamb for the burnt-offering.

So she said, "Go, Del, and tell him I sent you with my dear love, and that it's all right."

And Del at the first word went. She sat and watched them draw her out; it was a slow process; the loose sleeve of her factory sack was scorched.

Somebody at work outside turned suddenly and caught her. It was Dick. The love which he had fought so long broke free of barrier in that hour. He kissed her pink arm where the burnt sleeve fell off. He uttered a cry at the blood upon her face. She turned faint with the sense of safety, and with a face as white as her own he bore her away in his arms to the hospital, over the crimson snow.

Asenath looked out through the glare and smoke with parched lips. For a scratch upon the girl's smooth cheek, he had quite forgotten her. They had left her, tombed alive here in this furnace, and gone their happy way. Yet it gave her a curious sense of relief and triumph. If this were all that she could be to him, the thing which she had done was right, quite right. God must have known. She turned away, and shut here eyes again.

When she opened them, neither Dick nor Del, nor crimsoned snow, nor sky, were there, only the smoke writhing up a pillar of blood-red flame.

The child who had called for her mother began to sob out that she was afraid to die alone.

"Come here, Molly," said Sene. "Can you crawl around?"

Molly crawled around.

"Put your head in my lap, and your arms about my waist, and I will put my hands in yours,—so. There! I guess that's better, isn't it?"

But they had not given them up yet. In the still unburnt rubbish at the right some one had wrenched an opening within a foot of Sene's face. They clawed at the solid iron pintles like savage things. A fireman fainted in the glow.

"Give it up!" cried the crowd from behind. "It can't be done! Fall back!" —then hushed, awe-struck.

An old man was crawling along upon his hands and knees over the heated bricks. He was a very old man. His gray hair blew about in the wind.

"I want my little gal!" he said. "Can't anybody tell me where to find my little gal?"

A rough-looking young fellow pointed in perfect silence through the smoke.

"I'll have her out yet. I'm an old man, but I can help. She's my little gal, ye see. Hand me that there dipper of water; it'll keep her from choking, maybe. Now! Keep cheery, Sene! Your old father'll get ye out. Keep up good heart, child! That's it!"

"It's no use, father. Don't feel bad, father. I don't mind it very much."

He hacked at the timber; he tried to laugh; he bewildered himself with cheerful words.

"No more ye needn't, Senath, for it'll be over in a minute. Don't be downcast yet! We'll have ye safe at home before ye know it. Drink a little more water,—do now! They'll get at ye now, sure!"

But out above the crackle and the roar a woman's voice rang like a bell:

"We're going home to die no more."

A child's notes quavered in the chorus. From sealed and unseen graves, white young lips swelled the glad refrain,—

"We're going, going home."

The crawling smoke turned yellow, turned red. Voice after voice broke and hushed utterly. One only sang on like silver. It flung defiance down at death. It chimed into the lurid sky without a tremor. For one stood beside her in the furnace, and his form was like unto the form of the Son of God. Their eyes met. Why should not Asenath sing?

"Senath!" cried the old man out upon the burning bricks; he was scorched now, from his gray hair to his patched boots.

The answer came triumphantly,—

"To die no more, no more, no more!"

"Sene! little Sene!"

But some one pulled him back.

17. Technology and Landscape

Illustrations

1. *The Great Palace Reclining-Chair Route.*

2. *American Autumn, Starucca Valley, Erie Railroad, 1865.*

3. *Night Scene at an American Railway Junction, 1876.*

4. *Accident on the Pennsylvania Central Railroad, February 6, 1864.*

5. *Sand Dunes, Carson Desert, Nevada, 1870.*

6. *Teams, Passing Through the Snow, On the Road, Sierra Nevada, 1866.*

7. The Musquito Trail, Rocky Mountains of Colorado, 1875.

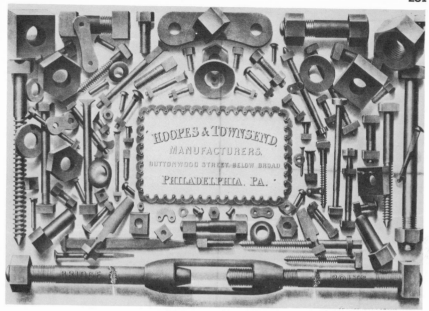

8. *Bridge Bolts, 1868.*

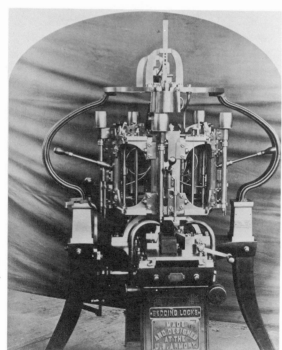

9. *Machine for cutting lock beds in musket stocks, 1876.*

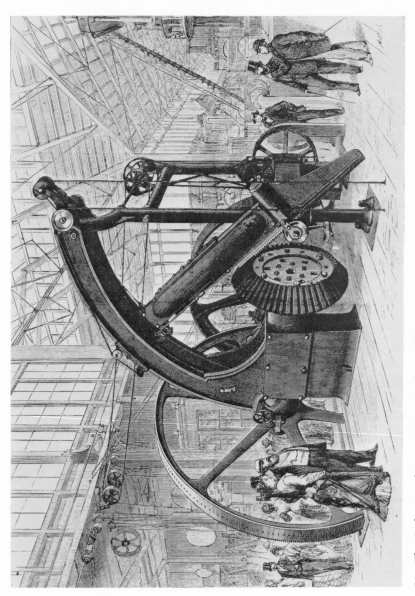

10. *The Corliss Bevel-Gear-Cutting Machine, 1876.*

11. *The New York and Brooklyn Suspension-Bridge, Cable Anchorage, Brooklyn, 1883.*

12. *Our Centennial—President Grant and Dom Pedro Starting the Corliss Engine, 1876.*

18. Pulp Fiction for Boys

Although their points of view and their values differed enormously, writers such as the radical libertarian Whitman, the arch-conservative William Graham Sumner, and the fundamentalist evangel T. De Witt Talmage all condemned the phenomenon known as "story-paper fiction." The immediate sources for this body of ephemeral "sensation" fiction were sentimental, Gothic, and historical romance, whipped up into an entirely escapist fantasy-world, a world of vicarious horrors and thrills. No one was able, either then or now, to claim any redeeming values, social or aesthetic, for pulp potboilers—although W. H. Bishop hints at the conclusion of his critique that they might at least encourage the habit of reading. What troubled all commentators, though, was the ready availability, especially for children, and the tenacity of the hold of cheap adventure stories on the minds of the young. Clearly here was a problem directly tied to industrialization, in which aesthetic, social, and moral values converged. Modern technology provided the means of production and circulation, in steam-powered rotary presses and extended railroad trunk lines, as well as the audience of poorly or uneducated workers and their children, who enjoyed few other sources of entertainment. Story-paper fiction in this period was one of the first symptoms of "mass" urban culture—a culture of sensation, escapism, and dangerously brutalized emotions.

The conservative and the fundamentalist assaults on pulp fiction had something in common: both were concerned with the threat to social stability. In *Night Sides of City Life* (1878), Talmage, a Brooklyn evangelical minister and prolific writer against the sins of the city, described "impure literature" as the first gate to hell. "No one—mark this—no one systematically reads the average novelette of this day and keeps either integrity or virtue . . . there are a million men and women in the United States reading themselves into hell!" Sumner's vocabulary is less hysterical and far more precise, but he too senses a kind of damnation. "It is impossible," he writes in "What Our Boys Are Reading" (*Scribner's Monthly*, 1878) "that so much corruption should be afloat and not exert some influence." His concern is with the "view of life"—"so base and false as to destroy all manliness and all chances of true success"

—in stories which celebrate feats of physical strength and barroom codes of drinking and swearing, which encourage boys to cheat their fathers and to run away in search of adventures. Even boys from respectable families are reading stories which, he writes as a flat summation, "are indescribably vulgar."

Bishop, a minor novelist, graduated from Yale in 1867, and was a frequent contributor to the established periodicals. Some of his novels and travel books appeared serially in *Atlantic* and *Harper's*.

Story-Paper Literature

W. H. BISHOP

The Yates boy, aged fifteen, desired to run away. He confided the intention to his sister, and she naturally conveyed it to his parents. His father summoned him before him, and said, "There is no need of your running away. If you will let me know any town or village in the country to which you desire to go, you shall be set down there with your trunk. I will give you a sum of money, furthermore, to find some kind of occupation, so that you may know by actual experience the value of the good home you have left." The offer was declined, with abashed thanks. It was not what his imagination pictured. He waited, and after a little time turned up missing, as the saying is, with two guns and a pointer dog. He returned from Chicago broken with ague, but departed again for the Cuban war, and has not since been heard of. His escapades were laid, with a show of reason, to the sensational romances, in which it appeared he was much absorbed.

Such stories are common. One day, it is three boys who are arrested at Patterson on their way to Texas, on the proceeds of a month's rent they have been sent to pay, but have appropriated instead. Another, three Boston boys do us the honor to believe that more adventures are to be found in New York than at home, and arrive with a slender capital of

W. H. Bishop, "Story-Paper Literature," *Atlantic Monthly*, XLIV (1879), 383–393.

four dollars and a half to seek them; are robbed of even this by more knowing gamins of the place, and spend several nights in the station-house before they can be reclaimed. Again, a group of runaways is found behind a New Jersey haystack playing poker, with a knife and a revolver before each one, as the custom is with all well-regulated desperadoes. A late boy-murderer confessed that he had wanted to hide in a cave and prowl and kill, and that he believed he got the idea from his reading.

This last extreme is rare, and the imaginations which go to the others are of an unwaveringly logical kind, which amounts to want of balance. A grain of common sense keeps down the imitative impulse in the majority of cases. They feel that, fine, and possibly veracious, as it all is, it is not, somehow, exactly adapted to their personally taking a part in it. We out-grow it,—for I make no doubt there are those who read this who have known something of the feeling from their own experience; and it would be a poor reader indeed who had had no amicable relations with pirates, avengers, dead-shots of the plains, and destroyers in his youth. We go to our counting-room, our machine-shop, our corner grocery, our law office, as the case may be. We shoot nobody at all, and do our plundering, if plunder we must, within the law, decorously, by light weights and short measures, by managing a company or borrowing of a friend. The remem-brance alone survives as a source of the very general enjoyment that is got out of mock heroics.

But let notice be given that it is not an especially humorous point of view that is sought for the story-paper literature. It is an enormous field of mental activity, the greatest literary movement, in bulk, of the age, and worthy of very serious consideration for itself. Disdained as it may be by the highly cultivated for its character, the phenomenon of its existence cannot be overlooked.

The taste for cheap fiction is by no means confined to this country. America leads in this form of publication in the kind of papers mentioned; but romances that do not appear to be of a greatly higher order are almost as profuse with the venders of reading matter at Paris, Turin, or Cologne as here, and not a daily paper on the continent of Europe, in any language, but has its scrap of a continued story, its *feuilleton*, in every issue.

Our story papers, damp from the press and printed very black, upholster all the news-stands, but we shall study them in a more leisurely way at a stationer's. Shall we choose this dingy one at the Five Points, where the grocery and wood and coal business is combined with the other; or this pretentious store under a lofty new tenement house in the German quarter, with the joints already warping apart, the paint blistered, and a plate-glass window cracked by uneven settling? Let it be rather one of the stuffy little, but more prosperous, ones of the up-town avenues. Some late numbers dangle from the edge of the low awning, under which it is necessary to stoop. A bell attached to the door jingles sharply. The interior is festooned with school satchels and jumping-ropes. Mother Carey's, Mother Shipton's, the Egyptian, the Hindoo, and the Golden Wheel of Fortune dream books, the Wild Oats, the Larry Tooley, the Eileen Alanna, the Love Among the Roses, song and dance books, in gaudy covers, ornament the window, among the tops and marbles.

The story papers, the most conspicuous stock in trade, are laid out on the front counter, neatly overlapped, so as to show all the titles and frontispieces. Ten are already in, and more to come,—the Saturday Night, the Saturday Journal, the Ledger, the Weekly, the Family Story Paper, the Fireside Companion. Near them on the glass case, in formidable piles, are the "libraries." These are, omitting the prominent examples which do the same sort of service for standard works, pamphlets reprinting at a dime and a half dime the stories which have appeared as serials in the papers. There are papers which, finding this practice a diversion of interest, distinctly announce that their stories will not reappear, and that their fascinations can be enjoyed only at original sources.

No far-reaching memory is needed to recall when the Ledger was the only journal of this kind. Its notorious prosperity gave rise to a swarm of imitators, eager to share the profits of so good a field. New York is still the great point of supply, but Chicago and some other Western cities have begun to find their account in similar publications for their tributary territories. As the new aspirants arise, it was necessary for each to set up its own peculiar claim to favor. One assumes to be the exclusive family story paper; another offers its readers microscopes, chromos, and supplements; others provide the fullest contents; others go upon the reputations of writers whose abilities to captivate are known: Colonel Tipton Slasher will write— Mrs. Jennie Smith Ringwood, whose power of passion development— Max Shorthorn, without a peer for pungent humor and drollery — A brilliant corps conceded to be, etc., etc. It would be a mistake to suppose there are not distinctions of reputation here, as among their betters.

But that was a splendid new department opened when it was observed where the most ardent class of patrons came from. They are boys. We may observe it ourselves, if we will give a little heed to the progress of the traffic on publication days. A middle-aged woman, with a shawl over her head and a half peck of potatoes in a basket, stops in for one; a shop-girl on her way home from work; a servant from one of the good houses in the side streets, come on her own account, or possibly for a school-girl mistress. But with them, before them, and after them come boys. They begin to read already as they walk away, and thread the streets without heeding their bustle. To-morrow the elevator boy will have the latest number of Cloven-Hoof the Demon, as he rides you up and down at the hotel or the business block. It will be hidden under many a jacket in school-hours. A shock-headed boy from the streets—his case has not heretofore been made public—set by a family to tidy up their cellar for the spring, was found perusing it, seated on a broken stool, and reaching vaguely for such things as might be in the neighborhood in the mean time.

The adventures in the adult papers were not beyond the capacity of the boys; but one, and then another, conceived the idea of conciliating their especial interest in making a paper for them, till this branch, with its Boys' Journal, Boys of New York, Boys of America, Boys of the World, Young Men of New York, Young Men of America, has become rather the larger of the two. The heroes are boys, and there are few departments of unusual existence in which they are not seen figuring to brilliant advantage. They are shown amply competent as the Boy Detective, the Boy Spy, the Boy Trapper, the Boy Buccaneer, the Boy Guide, the Boy Captain, the Boy Robinson Crusoe, the Boy Claude Duval, and the Boy Phœnix, or Jim Bludsoe, Jr., whose characteristic is to be impervious to harm in burning steamboats and hotels, exploding mines, and the like.

Occasionally, girls are similarly engaged, as the Girl Brigand and the Girl Dead-Shot, but are so few as to indicate clearly how very much less reliance is placed upon patronage from this quarter. The girls, in fact, are under closer supervision, and are apt to have duties for their leisure hours in the household. They have less pocket money, and few of the ready means of replenishing it at a pinch of their enterprising brothers. With their slight experience with fire-arms and rough riding, too, it can hardly be supposed that the Girl Brigand appeals to them with the fascination that might be exercised by something more nearly within the ordinary possibilities of imitation. They must even be puzzled somewhat at such ideals, and wonder at the boys' admiration of them.

Still, there are not wanting some efforts to attach their interest, also, to stories of a more likely character. Such a one is The Adventures of Fanny Larkhall at an Academy for Young Ladies. The air of liveliness in the paper from which this is taken is raised to the highest point by printing each sentence in a separate paragraph. This young girl of twelve is first introduced as leaving her arithmetic lesson to go skating clandestinely in

Central Park. "Ma knows," she remarks, "that I have no talent for arithmetic, and she might encourage what little ability I have in some other direction." She is sent to boarding-school on the Hudson River, not far from a school at which her brother is a pupil. The teachers at both schools are very ridiculous in their appearance, and "mean," tyrannical, and downright wicked in their characters, all of which is of course to be resisted. Miss Larkhall is in the habit of saying "*biz*" for business, "*sassy*" for saucy. She will "get square" with her teachers, and if they want her they must come to her. At the end of a column of slangy impudence and defiance, rankling under her keen sense of injustice, she asks, What has she done wrong? Why was she being punished?

It may be said at once that the juvenile branch of this literature is the worse. Very much of it is bad without mitigation. There is certain trouble in life for the girl who follows this model, and grows up and marries one of the boys similarly inspired. It falls upon teachers and parents first, then upon themselves. Instructors in some of the schools report that every third boys reads such literature, and that he is the hardest to deal with. It is in him to resist something, to dare something, in his modest way. Prevented from engaging in hand-to-hand conflicts with howling savages, he can yet, if circumstances be favorable, break his teacher's watch-chain. The Boy Scout or the Boy Phœnix would never have thought of doing less. They are not indisposed to philosophize themselves about their reading. They say, "It makes you brave."

The lesson of the necessity of a complete armament is so well impressed that it is not strange it is remembered by any setting out on their adventures. The whole vast action pivots, as it were, around the muzzle of an extended revolver. Every frontispiece shows a combat. Here a milder one, however, in which a pirate, with a curious taste in bricabrac even for his class, is quaffing a draught from a goblet made of a jeweled skull.

"With a well-directed blow Remington stretched the villain at full length upon the floor."

"With a grating curse, the dying wretch thrust a revolver against the Avenger's breast, and fired." . . .

The fierce rivalry between numerous competitors tends to two results. The first is an increase in the number of the serial stories. Two are found to be carring *eight serials* each at a time. Two others have seven each, another six. None have less than five. What an enormous voracity is here! Overlapping as they do, a new one commencing as an old one finishes, how does the subscriber ever escape from their toils? It seems as if, unless he would forego from one to seven eighths of the value of his money, which is not a pleasant thing to do in the most prosperous circumstances, he must be interlocked with his journal as fast as if in the arms of an octopus.

The second is the increase in sensationalism. The earlier stories were more honest and simpler. Here, now, is a unique combat,—marine divers fighting over a corpse, with knives, under water. But does anything else that is new remain? It would seem as if the last limit had been reached. After the enormous carnival of red brotherhoods, border phantoms, ghouls, demons, sleuths, ocean blood-hounds, brotherhoods of death, masked terrors, and reckless rangers, all done with the poor facilities that poverty-stricken human language affords, one could well expect to find these authors in a gasping state, reduced to the condition of the cannibals of the Orinoco, who could only go up to the hills, and say to their deities, "Oh!"

The same is true of the illustrations. From the point of view of art, so far as art can be considered in them, the earlier were the best. The older representations, sometimes lightly and sketchily printed, of life on the plains and spirited combat, the bold young scouts in their fringed leggings, the lithe heroine, captured or saved, twisted across the back of a galloping steed, were not always without a certain grace in the attitudes. The modern vie with one another in lurid horror and repulsiveness. The Boys of New York has a great cut occupying three fourths of its folio page. It is done in harsh ruled lines, like the most frigid kind of mechanical drawing, and printed black, black, to be visible from the longest possible distance. Coarse as it is, it breathes the essence of madness and murder. The artist should draw none henceforth but demons. Two frightful desperadoes, dark like negroes, with gleaming eyeballs and mustaches of the stubby, thick, jet-black, gambler pattern, are fighting with knives (having fallen out between themselves) in a moving hotel elevator, in which they have taken refuge to escape two detectives in chase. One detective, bounding up the stairs, appears, with a ghastly face and cocked revolver in hand, at one of the openings, as they go by. The other—the boy hero, who is not like a boy, but some strange, brawny ape—is seen clinging, with shrieks, to a ring in the bottom of the elevator, which he has clutched the better to follow them, in danger, now that he has mounted, of falling from exhaustion into the black abyss below. It haunts one. It is a nightmare.

The means taken to bring the papers to notice are often as enterprising as their contents. Copies of the opening chapters are thrown in at the area railings, and printed, regardless of expense, to pique curiosity, in the daily papers. The attention of the households of upper New York was widely awakened recently by an invitation telegram, sealed and addressed, the envelope and message-blank exact, saying, *"The child is still alive. You are personally interested in all the details of A Sinless Crime, to appear in to-morrow's——."*

The villain in the story papers, as often as it is indicated clearly who he is, has no redeeming traits. The idea of mixed motives, still less the Bret Harte idea of moral grandeur illuminating lives of continuous iniquity, through their sharing a blanket or a canteen at the end with emigrants delayed in a snow-storm, has not penetrated here. It is no ordinary crimes the villains meditate, either. Murder might almost be called the least of them. The only merciful drawback to their malignity is their excessive simplicity. They go about declaring their intentions with a guilelessness often worthy of positive sympathy . . .

The good, on the other hand, are known to be good by a constant insistence upon it. We cannot doubt what we are so often assured of. It is generally necessary for the proper complication of incidents that appearances should for some time be much against them; but how immaculate they shine out in the end! The authors are often put to severe straits to bring this about. It is the difficult point of plot-making. How can it be that they seem bad enough to lay themselves open to all this tribulation, when they are in fact so good? Credulity and gentlemanly indulgence are much needed to accept the explanations vouchsafed. A hero is occasionally even so thoroughly involved that he has no idea of his own innocence. The crimes imputed to Sandy Beverly are murder and forgery, particulars about which, it would seem, there should be a tolerable degree of certainty in one's own mind. But he swoons when he learns that he has not done them. "The news of his innocence was too much for him to bear." . . .

The heroines have for the most part, like full-private James, no characteristic trait of any distinctive kind. She is very beautiful; she often has hair "purple-black" in color, and always "great" eyes of some of the desirable shades; but generally she is simply a precious bundle of goods to be snatched out of deadly perils, and plotted and fought about. She has little actively to do but clasp her hands together, and little to say except "Oh, how can I repay you, my noble, my generous preserver!" She dispenses with chaperonage in a way the first society can never be brought to approve of.

Vast ingenuity is used in supplying motives to the "sleuth-like" personages so numerously engaged throughout the narratives in persistent schemes of vengeance. The original grievance is often found to be very slight. Nor can we believe that the following is always so seriously meant as it is said to be. The "human blood-hound" and "destroying angel"— there is the remarkable phenomenon in one case where "his heart was as white as his face with rage, as he grasped his bowie and followed on the stranger's track"—is continually letting his victim give him the slip without reason. "See here! if you do that again," he seems to be saying, or, "If ever I set eyes on you once more, it will be the worse for you." The plots in fact do not hasten to their conclusion, but are dragged back and detained from it. Time after time the occasion for the avenger to do whatever he is going to is flagrantly then and there, but he does not do it.

As to their constructions, vast as the ground the stories now cover, they are few and simple. This is constant: that the villain gets himself into trouble by loving the heroine, who cares nothing about him. The hero lays himself open by stepping in, in the nick of time, to protect her from consequent schemes of vengeance. Now it is in a Fourteenth Street tenement house, now in a palace in Russian Moscow, now in mediæval Venice, and again at ancient Palmyra; but the repulsing with scorn, the protection, the schemes of vengeance, and their coming to naught are everywhere the same. It sometimes seems hard upon the villain. Everything is against him from the first. She very often has no cause of complaint in the world, to begin with, but an "instinctive repulsion." But once rejected, he has cause enough, it may well be believed.

The "woman scorned" is his counterpart, and the second great source of trouble. She appears in the midst of marriages, in the stories in which she takes part, and forbids the bans, so sure as the marriages are set to take place. With the unscrupulous guardian, who has the keepers of insane asylums to aid him in his projects; the persons changed at birth, or returning thirty years after they were supposed to be lost at sea; the reprobate father or brother arousing acute jealousies by being taken on his clandestine visits after money for a lover, I have mentioned most of the essential elements. Generally, in the shorter stories, of which each paper contains a number besides its serials, there is a great deal of Cinderella business. Poor and plain nieces or wards marry the fine gentleman, in spite of the supercilious daughter, after all.

It is not exalted game to pick to pieces works from which not too much is expected at the best, and the plain road has by no means been abandoned in search of absurdities. But the surprising thing to learn is that there is really so much less in them than might be expected. The admiration grows for the craving which can swallow, without misgiving, so grand a tissue of extravagances, inaneness, contradictions, and want of probable cause. The stories are not ingenious, even, and ingenuity was perhaps supposed to be their strong point.

It is not that they do not give epigrams, bright conversations, penetrating reflections. We can recollect when we skipped all that in the best of books, and desired only to rush headlong on with the movement. Poe, Cooper, Féval, Collins, Charles Reade, have written stories in which what the people do is of very much more interest than what they are; but in these is a kind of fatality; events hold together; they could not have been otherwise.

Though written almost exclusively for the use of the lower classes of society, the story papers are not accurate pictures of their life. They are not a mass of evidence from which, though rude, a valuable insight into their thoughts, feelings, and doings can be obtained by others who do not know them. The figures are like to nature only as much as those drawn without models by an inferior artist are. The product is dried and hectic. The writers do not seem to be telling anything they have seen and known, but following, at third and fourth hand, traditions above them which they have read. The most enlightened field of the novel is social history,—to portray James K. Jackson and Elizabeth May Johnson in relation to their surroundings and times, as the formal historians do Napoleon Bonaparte and Katharine of Aragon. This is a field into which they very superficially enter. Perhaps they consult their popularity in not doing so. A considerable part of their audience is not reflective. It has rather simple wants and aspirations. Lack of culture is a continuous childhood. A statement is enough; a demonstration is not necessary. It is only a tyrannical employer or an unprincipled guardian who prevents the attainment of perfect happiness. Do readers wish for profound and intimate observations made about them which they never think of making about themselves? George Eliot says of a heroine that she is "ardent, theoretic, and intellectually consequent"; Mrs. Ringwood, that she had a blue silk dress and a perfect form.

The Spotter Detective, or the Girls of New York, seemed to promise a glimpse into social life. John Blaine, a strangely handsome man, escapes from Sing-Sing prison. He had been sentenced for assault with intent to kill, but this was only because "he had not a hundred thousand dollars at his back to buy corrupt judges and jurors." Three beautiful young ladies, in entirely disconnected situations, and a lunatic on Randall's Island are greatly affected by the news. The lunatic at once returns to his senses, goes to the St. Nicholas Hotel, and demands in what is a fairly amusing passage, "Young man, I'll trouble you for that package I left in your safe. Room 440."

"It was another man that had 440 last night, and I never saw you before," the clerk replies.

"Oh, I didn't say it was last night. It was before your time. Look back eighteen months; say, two years ago." He had been stopping there, it seems, when suddenly seized with lunacy.

He receives his package, which contains five thousand dollars, and then becomes the Spotter Detective. The convict is described as being "a gentleman born." "Not that some feudal despot in the olden time had laid a knightly sword upon the shoulder of an iron-handed soldier stained with gore, and bade him, 'Rise up, Sir John Blaine.' No! John Blaine's father was a seaman bold, whose boast in his cups was, 'A wife in every port'; his mother a poor, weak girl, a child of Erin's green isle, the daughter of a buxom dame, who kept a sailor boarding-house." He makes his mysterious escapes, and keeps up the chase by concealing himself in the apartments of the three beautiful girls by turns. What is the secret of his mysterious power over them? Aha! that is the point! Well, they are in one way and another his daughters. One resides in an elegant mansion on Madison Avenue; another boards—young, single, blazing with diamonds, and moving in the finest circles, though quite unattended—at the Hoffman House; the third is a sewing-girl. The book is peculiar in not making it clear whether the characters are to be considered depraved or not. Most of them have the look of it, as the convict Blaine; a card sharper, Captain O'Shane, and another who is at the beginning a tramp as well, Captain Blackie; and the guardian, Elbert van Tromp. The latter agrees to secure his lovely ward and cousin in marriage to Captain Blackie in consideration of a commission of fifty thousand dollars on her fortune. There is no reason in the world, as he is young, handsome, and a "lady-killer," why he should not take her himself with the whole million, but he prefers this method. The marriage is solemnized, Blackie having, however, reformed. John Blaine kills the honest Spotter Detective, and gets clear, and no poetic justice at all is done. Two interwoven young millionaires fall in love with two working-girls, whom they meet at a glass-blowers' ball, visit them at their apartment, where they keep house together, and marry them. The influence of this part must be in the direction of an easy making of acquaintance, which by no means always turns out so happily.

There are a great many poor persons in the narratives, and the capitalist is occasionally abused, showing that an eye is kept on the popular movements of the day; but poverty is not really glorified. The deserving characters are almost sure to be secretly of good families, and in reduced circumstances only for a short time. Ordinary origin and a humdrum course of life at honest, manual labor are not much wanted even here. The names are selected for their distinction with as much care as those of fashionable New York up-town hotels. The responsiveness of the faces of the characters, particularly the bad ones, who ought to be more hardened, to their emotions is one of the points to note. They turn "sickly yellow," "ghastly pale," and "white, rigid, and haggard" with extraordinary frequency. . . .

There is a popular impression among people who attach weight to the expression, "truth stranger than fiction" (as though it were not truer, of course), and appreciate too little the difficulty of making something out of nothing, that the material is chiefly matter of pure invention. Such is not the case. The writers keep scrap-books of all the horrible circumstances coming under their notice, and put them together to suit. It is all in the papers. The liveliest ingenuity cannot stimulate the novelist to the desperate inventions of beings whose whole existence is at stake.

The fault is simply with the taste of such materials, its exclusive and fatiguing bent towards the unusual and terrible. "This is positively too ridiculous," as the man is said to have said coming home to dinner, after an annoying day in his business, and finding his whole family lying murdered. It is a catalogue of wild "sensations," which writers of a better grade are chary in dealing with, but in themselves they are true enough. Who will invent the Bender family, the Cox-Alston duel, Charley Ross, or that Chicago suicide who died by poison, shooting, hanging, setting his clothes on fire, and drowning in a bath-tub all at once, at the Palmer House?

And now, having begun to say something in their favor, let us see if anything more can be said. There are story papers and story papers. It may be that those of the cheapest and flashiest order have been too exclusively dwelt upon. Those popular novelists, Mrs. E. D. E. N. Southworth, Mrs. Ann H. Stephens, and May Agnes Fleming contribute Hearst Histories, Deserted Wives, and Brides of an Evening to the story papers, and shall one disparage what is found on the table of so many boudoirs, far indeed removed from the lower classes? Some reprint as serials, with their own matters, standard productions, like the Count of Monte Cristo, the Memoirs of Houdin the Conjurer, and Tom Cringle's Log. Others give away Shakespeare's Sonnets and the Bab Ballads for supplements. In general, in the libraries good literature is beginning to mingle among the bad in a very curious way. Robinson Crusoe, very much mangled, it is true, at half a dime, may be found in the Wide-Awake Library, sandwiched between Bowie Knife Ben and Death Notch the Destroyer.

This is a phase of the subject which would bear working out by itself. Perhaps it offers a solution of the problem how the literature of the masses is to be improved. Would the adults take Charles Reade, Hardy, Wilkie Collins, Dickens, Victor Hugo, and the boys Scott, Bulwer, Manzoni, G. P. R. James, Irving's brigand tales and Conquest of Granada, Poe's Gold Bug and Adventures of Arthur Gordon Pym, if they were as cheap as the others? Is it simply and only a question of cheapness, and has the taste of the audience of story-paper buyers been maligned?

These papers have editorial pages in which a variety of good advice is printed, calculated to counteract, if attended to, though it may possibly be neglected by those whom it could most serve, the unsettling influence of the body of the contents. They aim at the good graces of the family. There is a department of "answers to correspondents," embodying information on manners, morals, dress, education, the affections. Edith F. is informed that too many rings on the fingers are vulgar; Emma D. that pie should be eaten with a fork; and L. M. that there is no such thing as love at first sight. Any young lady, it is tartly said, to whom a young man should propose marriage at first sight would endeavor to restrain his impetuosity for a day or two, so as to discover from what lunatic asylum he had escaped, and have him returned to his keepers. There are short essays and reflections on housekeeping; the care of children; the advisability of cheerfulness and economy; of going early to bed and of rising early; even, somewhat strangely, on moderation and taste in reading. They are trite and Tupperish, but one learns these things somewhere for the first time, and then they are strikingly novel. Who was the profound writer in whom they were new to us? How could we know he took them from predecessors who originated them not far from January 1st of the year One?

In considering the real influence of these papers it must be reckoned, not upon those who have outgrown them, and been led by the study of better things to see their absurdity, but on those who remain immersed in them for lack of better ideals, or leave them only to read nothing at all. They are by no means needed to account for an adventurous spirit in human nature. Robinson Crusoe ran away to sea in the year 1632, when this kind of literature could have been very little prevalent. But they certainly foment it to the utmost. The first condition of a happy existence is the ability to support *ennui*. But the personages here are never exhibited attending to the ordinary duties of existence. Embarked in the chase for some lost child, abducted heiress, or secreted will, they rush hither and thither, without ever stopping, around the world, and around again, if need be; and when it is done they fall into a state of inanition, or at least they would, only at that very moment the story is done, also. The labors and sacrifices demanded are of too extreme a type to be valuable as examples. The heroes and heroines would die for each other at any time, but which would curb his temper in a provoking moment; which would get up first and make the fire, in case there were no servants?—but there always are servants, in troops.

Still, the best of the story papers reward virtue and punish vice. Their dependence upon the family keeps them, as a rule, free of dangerous appeals to the lower passions. Ranging over all countries and periods, they convey considerable information about history and foreign parts into quarters where very little would otherwise penetrate. They encourage a chivalrous devotion to woman, though they do not do much towards making her more worthy of it. The story papers, then,—it is not here a question of those that have been said to be positively bad,—are not an unmixed evil. The legitimate charge against them is not that they are so bad, but only that they are not better.

The great question is, Are they better than nothing? There are persons who read neither story-papers nor anything else. They are no doubt exemplary and superior in many relations of life, prudent in matters of sentiment, cool in business, with the extra time for use that might otherwise have been expended in flights of the imagination; but let us believe that they have secretly their follies, too, as much as if they believed in pirates, hidden treasures, and destroyers.

The taste for reading, however perverted, is connected with something noble, with an interest in things outside of the small domain of self, with a praiseworthy curiosity about the great planet we inhabit. One is almost ready to say that, rather than not have it at all, it had better be nourished on no better food than story papers.

But it is a pity it is no better. This is the last, as it was the first and the continuous reflection from a view of the enormous extent of this imaginative craving, and the means by which it is ministered to. There ought to be in it information of worth; a separation of sense from nonsense; characters which, without preaching, should remain in the memory, as a stimulus to better things in trying times.

19. Nude Women Question

Like pulp fiction, popular theater was also attacked as dissolute and indecent, and frequently with good reason. Of course from the time of the Puritan condemnation of the theater in seventeenth-century England, popular performances and recreations have been charged as evil, the devil's work, and fundamentalist ministers in America kept the theme alive during the nineteenth century. But several accounts indicate that popular theater in New York after the Civil War reached new levels of grossness. Whitman wrote in *Democratic Vistas* that contemporary dramatic *presentations* were "on a par with . . . ornamental confectionary at public dinners." Sentimental melodrama, variety shows, burlesque, and as Olive Logan points out, the song and dance revue spiced with titillation of bare legs and exposed bosoms, contributed to the low repute of the stage.

Olive Logan was introduced to the theater by her father, an actor, dramatist and manager, and made her debut at the age of fifteen. She was born in Elmira, New York, in 1839, raised in Cincinnati, spent much of her life traveling, was married three times, and died in England in 1909. Her career in the theater lasted about fifteen years, and after her retirement from the stage in 1868 she devoted herself to popular journalism, playwriting and lecturing. Her topics ranged widely, from accounts of travel to woman's rights and other social topics. A forceful though erratic figure, she had some degree of popularity in the 1870's. In this selection she brings together a feminist outrage and a moralistic fervor against the uses of sexuality in popular culture. The theme was a relatively minor one in the feminist attack on the subservient place of woman, but her treatment of it does reveal a certain shrewdness in identifying the sexual stereotype as a barrier to freedom.

About Nudity in the Theaters

OLIVE LOGAN

"Nude. Bare."—*Webster.*

"Bare. Wanting clothes, or ill-supplied with garments."—*Johnson.*

There were always great evils attaching to the theatrical profession. I have always deplored them deeply. Some of them I have touched upon in the preceding chapters. No one who has read my articles, or listened to my lectures, will say that I have not earnestly defended the theatrical profession,—as such. I have also said, honestly, how I loathe the evils which attach to it. In this feeling of loathing, I have expressed the sentiments of a large class of people who were, like myself, bred to the stage, but who could shut their eyes to the evils referred to.

Within a few years, these evils had grown to appalling dimensions. Decency and virtue had been crowded from the ranks by indecency and licentiousness. A coarse rage for nudity had spread in our theatres, until it had come to be the ruling force in them.

Seeing this truth, I shuddered at it. Seeing its effects, I mourned over them. In every place where I spoke of the stage, I denounced this encroaching shame; but I always coupled with denunciation of it defence of THE DRAMA.

At the Woman's Suffrage Convention in New York, in May, 1869, I denounced this thing again; but, as I was not speaking at length upon this subject, but only touched upon it in passing, and by way of illustration, I did not, as usual, defend THE DRAMA.

At once, there rose so wild a yell, as all the fiends from heaven that fell were furious at my course.

Certain portions of the press attacked me, and accused me of slandering the profession to which I once belonged. Anonymous letters poured in upon me at the office of the Authors' Union in a sort of flood, villifying me, upbraiding me, covering me with coarse and gross revilings.

I was asked to explain such base conduct. It was demanded that I

Olive Logan, "About Nudity in the Theaters," *Women and Theatres* (New York, 1869), 123–153.

should take back my rash and reckless statements. I was requested to remember that I had once been very glad to think well of the theatrical profession. How *dared* I say I could advise no honorable woman to turn to the stage for support?

In a word, I was put upon my defence.

Turning the matter over in my mind carefully, I came to the conclusion that I had in my hands an opportunity for doing a great deal of good by the simple course of making my defence.

And I concluded, also, that my testimony in this matter had peculiar weight, as coming from one who is of a dramatic family, and may be presumed to speak from close and immediate observation, if not from experience.

I, therefore, wrote the words which follow; and, in reproducing them here, I shall only express the sincere hope that when this book is read, the evil here treated of will be so much a thing of the past, that this chapter shall possess no other value than as a record of a dark page in the history of the theatre.

Though for some years I have not played a part in a theatre, I have not been altogether separated from association with its people. The ties which bind me to these people are strong and close. I never expect to sever them wholly; but they shall never prevent me from giving my allegiance to the cause of morality, virtue, honor, and integrity, though, as a consequence of this, the theatrical heavens fall.

That curse of the dramatic profession, for which editors, critics, authors, and managers struggle to find a fitting name, is my general theme in this article; which is, at the same time, my defence against the charge of slandering the dramatic profession.

That the *Tribune* calls the Dirty Drama, the *World* the Nude Drama, the *Times* the Leg Drama, and other journals various other expressive adjective styles of *drama*, I call the Leg *Business*, simply.

Does any one call the caperings of a tight-rope performer the Ærial Drama?—the tricks of an educated hog the Porcine Drama?

There is a term in use among "professionals" which embraces all sorts of performances in its comprehensiveness, to wit: The Show Business.

In this term is included every possible thing which is of the nature of an entertainment, with these three requirements: 1. A place of gathering. 2. An admission fee. 3. An audience.

This remarkably comprehensive term covers with the same mantle the tragic Forrest, when he plays; the comic Jefferson, when *he* plays; the eloquent Beecher, when he lectures; and the sweet-voiced Parepa, when she sings. It also covers with the same mantle the wandering juggler, who balances feathers on his nose; the gymnast, who whirls on a trapeze; the danseuse, who interprets the poetry of motion; the clown, who cracks stale jokes in the ring; the performer on the tight-rope, the negro minstrel, the giant and the dwarf, the learned pig, and the educated monkey. Therefore, it includes the clog-dancing creature, with yellow hair and indecent costume.

All these things being included in the show business, you see it is almost as wide a world as the outer world. It must be a very wide world which should include Mr. Beecher with the learned pig.

It must be a very wide world which should include Rachel, Ristori, Janauschek, and Lander with the clog-dancing creature of indecent action and attire.

But, by as good a right as you would call Mr. Beecher and the learned pig performers in the intellectual sphere, you would call Janauschek and the clog-dancing creature interpreters of THE DRAMA.

How, then, does it happen that in attacking these yellow-haired nudities, I am compelled to say that they disgrace the dramatic profession?

In this wise: These creatures occupy the temples of the drama; they perform in conjunction with actors and actresses, on the same stage, before the same audience, in the same hour. They are made legitimate members of our theatrical companies, and take part in those nondescript performances which are called burlesques, spectacles, what you will. They carry off the chief honors of the hour; their names occupy the chief places on the bills; and, as I said in my speech at the Equal Rights Meeting at Steinway Hall, they win the chief prizes in the theatrical world.

A woman, who has not ability enough to rank as a passable "walking lady" in a good theatre, on a salary of twenty-five dollars a week, can strip herself almost naked, and be thus qualified to go upon the stage of two-thirds of our theatres at a salary of one hundred dollars and upwards.

Clothed in the dress of an honest woman, she is worth nothing to a manager. Stripped as naked as she dare—and it seems there is little left when so much is done—she becomes a prize to her manager, who knows that crowds will rush to see her, and who pays her a salary accordingly.

These are simple facts, which permit of no denial. I doubt if there is a manager in the land who would dream of denying them.

There are certain accomplishments which render the Nude Woman "more valuable to managers in the degree that she possesses them." I will tell you what these accomplishments are, and you shall judge how far they go toward making her, in any true sense, an actress.

They are: 1. The ability to sing. 2. The ability to jig. 3. The ability to play on certain musical instruments.

Now that I have put them down, I perceive that they need explanation, after all; so complete is the perversion of everything pertaining to this theme, that the very language is beggared of its power of succinct expression.

To sing. Yes, but not to sing as Parepa sings; nor such songs as she sings. The songs in demand in this sphere are vulgar, senseless—and, to be most triumphantly successful, should be capable of indecent constructions, and accompanied by the wink, the wriggle, the grimace, which are not peculiar to virtuous women, whatever else they are. The more senseless the song, the more utterly it is idiotic drivel, the better it will answer in the absence of the baser requisites. Here is a specimen:

> "Little Bo-peep, she lost her sheep,
> And don't know where to fi-*ind* her;
> Leave her alone and she'll come home,
> And fetch her tail behi-*ind* her."

A simple nursery song; and, if men were babies, innocent and harmless in itself; but men are not babies, and the song is not sung in a simple or harmless manner, but with the wink or the idiotic stare that means a world, and sets the audience into an extatic roaring.

To jig. Let no one confound jig-dancing with the poetry of motion which is illustrated by a thoroughly organized and thorough-bred body of ballet-dancers.

Ballet-dancing is a profession by itself, just as distinctly as is singing in opera. A danseuse, like Fanny Ellsler or Taglioni, or, to come to the present moment, like Morlacchi, is no more to be ranked with these nude jiggers than an actress like Mrs. Lander is.

The ability to jig is an accomplishment which any of these nude creatures can pick up in a few weeks. A danseuse, who has any claim whatever to the title of *artiste,* must be bred to her profession through years of toil and study.

In this country, the ballet proper has had little illustration. Yet it is a branch of art,—not the noblest art, it is true; but, by the side of the jigging woman, almost rising to dignity.

To play on certain musical instruments. These instruments should be such as to look queer in a woman's hands,—such instruments as the banjo and the bugle.

Now, I am not saying that the ability to sing silly songs, to jig, or to play the banjo, in itself disgraces a woman, however little it may entitle her to my esteem. I am only calling attention to them as valuable aids to the nude woman in her business, and letting you judge whether they give her any right to the name of *actress*.

You, no doubt, will at once remark that these accomplishments have hitherto been peculiar to that branch of the show business occupied by the negro minstrel. But in the hands of the negro minstrel, these accomplishments amuse us without disgusting us. They are not wedded to bare legs, indecent wriggles, nor suggestive feminine leers and winks; nor is there a respectable minstrel band in the United States to-day which would tolerate in its members the *double entendres* which fly about the stages of some of the largest temples of the drama in this city. The minstrels would not dare utter them. Their halls would be vacated, and their business ruined. It requires that a half-naked woman should utter these ribaldrous inuendoes, before our fastidious public will receive them unrebukingly.

To what branch of the show business, then, do these creatures belong?

I answer, to that branch which is known by the names of variety-show, concert-saloon, music-hall, and various other titles, which mean nothing unless you already know what they mean.

No one in the show business needs to be told what a variety-show is. It certainly is not a theatre.

Until the reign of the nude woman set in, variety-halls were the resort of only the lowest and vilest, and women were not seen in the audience.

The nude woman was sometimes seen upon the stage, but she was only permitted to exhibit herself economically, for fear of cloying the public appetite.

Delicate caution! but how useless, her later career in our theatres has shown.

There, she is exhibited ceaselessly for three hours, in every variety which an indecent imagination can devise.

When the *Black Crook* first presented its nude women to the gaze of a crowded auditory, she was met with a gasp of astonishment at the effrontery which dared so much. Men actually grew pale at the boldness of the thing; a death-like silence fell over the house, broken only by the clapping of a band of *claqueurs* around the outer aisles; but it passed; and, in view of the fact that these women were French ballet-dancers after all, they were tolerated.

By slow and almost imperceptible degrees, this shame has grown, until to-day the indecency of that exhibition is far surpassed. Those women were ballet-dancers from France and Italy, and they represented in their nudity imps and demons. In silence they whirled about the stage; in silence trooped off. Some faint odor of ideality and poetry rested over them.

The nude woman of to-day represents nothing but herself. She runs upon the stage giggling; trots down to the foot-lights, winks at the audience, rattles off from her tongue some stupid attempts at wit, some twaddling allusions to Sorosis, or General Grant, or other subject prominent in the public eye, and is always peculiarly and emphatically herself,—the woman, that is, whose name is on the bills in large letters, and who considers herself an object of admiration to the spectators.

The sort of ballet-dancer who figured in the *Black Crook* is paralleled on the stage of every theatre in this city, except one, at this time.

She no longer excites attention.

To create a proper and profitable sensation in the breast of man, she no longer suffices. Something bolder must be devised,—something that shall utterly eclipse and outstrip her.

Hence, the nude woman of to-day,—who outstrips her in the boldest sense. And, as if it were not enough that she should be allowed to go unhissed and unrotten-egged, she must be baptized with the honors of a profession for which Shakespeare wrote!

Managers recognize her as an actress, and pay her sums ranging from fifty to a thousand dollars a week, according to her value in their eyes. Actresses, who love virtue better than money, are driven into the streets by her; and it becomes a grave and solemn question with hundreds of honorable women what they shall do to earn a livelihood.

I say it is nothing less than an insult to the members of the dramatic profession, that these nude women should be classed among actresses and hold possession of the majority of our theatres. Their place is in the concert-saloons or the circus tent. Theatres are for artists.

A friend said to me the other day that it was inconsistent in me to find indecency in women exposing their persons, when men constantly do the same; that, as an honest exponent of Woman's Rights, I ought to see no more immodesty in a woman dancing a jig in flesh-colored leggings than in a man performing a circus feat in the same costume.

I reply, that I think such shows are indecent in both sexes. Yet, nevertheless, in woman a thousand times more indecent than in man; for the simple reason, that the costume of the sexes in every-day life is different. To ignore this fact is to just wilfully shut one's eyes to a reasonable argument.

Women in society conceal all the lower part of their bodies with drapery,—and for good and sufficient reasons, which no man, who has a wife or mother, should stop to question.

But set this aside. Circus men, who strip to the waist in this fashion, don't claim to be actors.

Now, I come back to the words I said at the Woman Suffrage Convention. They have been variously reported by the newspapers. They were exactly as follows,—

"I can advise no honorable, self-respecting woman to turn to the stage for support, with its demoralizing influences, which seem to be growing stronger and stronger day by day; where the greatest rewards are won by a set of brazen-faced, clog-dancing creatures, with dyed yellow hair and padded limbs, who have come here in droves from across the ocean."

I have been astonished and pained at the extent to which the meaning of these words has been distorted. The press and my anonymous letter critics seem to be agreed in taking the view, that I attack, in these words, the profession in which I was reared, and all my family.

Some of the letters sent me are from religious people, encouraging me to go on; others are from actors and actresses, seeking to dissuade me,— not always in gentle language.

The first letter on which I lay my hands, so gross in its language that I suspect it to be from one of the nude women themselves, says,—

"You were, no doubt, satisfied with the stage so long as it paid. Now, don't swear at the bridge that carried you over."

Perhaps this person, being new to the country, thinks it is true, as a newspaper once said, that I was formerly a ballet-girl.

Hitherto, I have only laughed at this story, as on a par with that of the person who thought me a daughter of the negro preacher, Loguen; or that of the "dress reform" scarecrow, who believed me "formerly a ballad songstress."

I laugh at it no longer. I answer, in all gravity, that I never was a ballet-girl, nor even a jig-dancer.

It is true that I was once a member of the theatrical profession; so were my father and my mother; so were my five sisters; but I say with pride that never was there a Logan who sought any connection with the stage save in the capacity of a legitimate player.

There were no nude women on the stage in my father's day. Such exhibitions as are now made on the stage of many leading theatres were, in his day, confined to that branch of the show business known as the *Model Artists*,—another perversion of words; but most people know their meaning in their present acceptation.

Across this infamous bridge no Logan ever walked.

And, one by one, every member of our family has left the stage behind, until, at this writing, no one remains upon it; though of their number, there are seven still living who have trod the boards.

Here it is proper that I should say why I left the stage. The *Commercial Advertiser* and the *Philadelphia Dispatch* are the only journals I have seen which have intimated that my hatred of indecency is born of jealousy; thus implying that I ceased to be an actress because these nude women had encroached upon my territory so far that I was forced to leave, or do what they do.

This is not true. As for the nude women, their reign had not yet set in at the time I left the stage. But I was not forced from the stage at all. My success as an actress was always fully equal to my deserts; and, up to the very day I retired from the stage, I was in receipt of large sums for my services as an actress. As a star (in which capacity I played in the leading theatres of this country, from Wallack's, in New York, to McVicker's, in Chicago) my earnings were very large,—sometimes reaching one thousand dollars per week. When I played for a salary, the lowest sum I ever received—save when I was a mere child—was one hundred dollars per week.

I left the stage respecting it and many of its people; but my resolve was to live, henceforth, by my pen. I preferred literature to acting, simply on the score of congeniality; and I have never regretted the day when I turned to it. I love it with all my soul, and have several times refused most tempting offers to leave it and return to the stage.

How then, can I be *jealous* of these women? I am no longer a rival for their place in the theatres. No, it is no such ignoble feeling as this which animates me; it is a feeling of shame that the stage should be so degraded, the drama so disgraced, by the place the nude woman has taken, united to a feeling of sympathy with the numerous modest and virtuous actresses who are crowded from a sphere which they could adorn and honor,— crowded from it *not* by superior talent, nor even by greater beauty, but by sheer brazen immodesty, and by unblushing vice.

I take up next an anonymous letter, dated at Boston, and signed, "A Sister Member of the Profession."

The writer says she is a respectable actress, and professes to be ignorant that gross evils prevail in the theatrical world.

She refers to my letter in *The New York Times,* and asks at what theatre such questions were ever put to an applicant for employment.

In my letter to the *Times,* I said,—

"I referred the other night to decent young women who are not celebrities,—merely honest, modest girls, whose parents have left them the not very desirable heritage of the stage, and who find it difficult to obtain any other employment, being uneducated for any other. When these girls go into a theatre to apply for a situation now, they find that the requirements of manager are expressed in the following questions,—

"1. Is your hair dyed yellow?

"2. Are your legs, arms, and bosom symmetrically formed, and are you willing to expose them?

"3. Can you sing brassy songs, and dance the can-can, and wink at men, and give utterance to disgusting half words, which mean whole actions?

"4. Are you acquainted with any rich men who will throw you flowers, and send you presents, and keep afloat dubious rumors concerning your chastity?

"5. Are you willing to appear to-night, and every night, amid the glare of gas-lights, and before the gaze of thousands of men, in this pair of satin breeches, ten inches long, without a vestige of drapery upon your person?

"If you can answer these questions affirmatively, we will give you a situation; if not, there's the door."

At nothing have I been more astonished than at the manner in which this letter has been received by certain "professionals."

When one of our daily newspapers says that the streets of this city are in a filthy condition, does a resident of Fifth Avenue rush down to the editor's sanctum to call him a liar, and point him to the cleanliness of Fifth Avenue?

It seems incredible that any one could be so stupid as to imagine me making reference to such managers, for instance, as Edwin Booth, Mr. Field, of the Boston Museum, or Mrs. John Drew, of Philadelphia!

These managers, and a few like them, form the exception to the rule. To such, all honor! But it is a sufficient indication of the enormity of this shame to say that the rage for nudity has intruded in some shape upon the stage of every theatre in this city, *except one.*

Here is a list of the places in this city where the English drama claims, or has claimed, a place, at one time or another, in its highest or its lowest manifestations,—

Academy of Music,	Booth's,
Fisk's Grand Theatre,	Wood's Museum,
Fifth Avenue Theatre,	Theatre Comique,
Wallack's,	The Tammany,
New York Theatre,	The Waverly,
Olympic,	Niblo's Garden,
Broadway Theatre,	Bowery Theatre,
Theatre Français,	Pastor's Opera House.

Two of the above-named places are now closed; but, at this writing, it is rumored that one of them is to be opened for the use of a newly organized troupe of nude women.

Of this whole list, there is but one (Booth's, which is only a few months old) which can claim that it has always been free from any symptom of this licentious fever.

"Four weeks from this time," says the *New York Review* of May 15, "there will be only two theatres in New York that will offer dramatic works. The rest will be show-shops, having as little to do with dramatic art as so many corner groceries."

As to the questions themselves, as printed above, they are, of course, suppositious. It is not said that managers put these exact questions to applicants. It is said that *"the requirements of managers are expressed in these questions."*

This is strictly true.

It is not necessary, I suppose, to give with the accuracy of a criminal trial report the exact questions which pass between managers and actresses who seek for employment. Their purport is unmistakable. Take this one which was asked a beautiful and modest young woman whom I have known for years, an actress by profession, who was quietly edged out of her last situation because she carried decency and womanly reserve too far in the presence of an audience which cheered to the echo the nude creatures who trod the same stage with her,—

"Are you up in this style of business?"

This question needed no interpreter,—for the manager pointed, as he spoke, to one of the members of his company, photographed in an immodest attitude, with her legs clad in flesh-colored silk and her body in a tight-fitting breech-cloth, richly embroidered.

She was not "up in" this sort of business; she sought employment as *an actress*; there was none for her, and she went away, to apply with like results at other theatres.

She sought employment, as a respectable actress, at fifteen or twenty dollars a week. She would have refused five hundred dollars a week salary to do what the nude woman does.

If the above instance does not indicate managerial requirements sufficiently, take these statements from managerial lips,—

"Devil take your legitimate drama! I tell you if I can't draw the crowd otherwise, I'll put a woman on my stage without a rag on her."

So said a manager of this city in the hearing of a dozen people; and the disgusting remark was bandied about from mouth to mouth as if it had been wit.

A proprietor of one of the theatres above-named, where a legitimate play was running without paying expenses, rubbed his dry old hands together, and said,—

"Aha! we must have some of those *fat young women* in this place to make it draw."

I go down to Boston for a moment, where lives this anonymous letter-writing actress who is so singularly ignorant of what is passing about her, to mention the rumor which was set afloat *by a manager* of a certain one of the blonde nudities, to the effect that she was once the mistress of the Prince of Wales.

This manager deemed it to his interest to keep this vile story afloat. It gave an added piquancy to the creature who nightly wriggled about his stage in a dress of silk that fitted her form *all over* as tightly as a glove.

I stay in Boston long enough to note that, in the late Working-woman's Convention there, a lady related the trials of a young friend of hers, who went upon the stage and endured insult and wickedness from managers. The same lady corroborated my own observations, with the statement, that managers look upon the girls they employ as women of the town.

My anonymous "sister member of the profession" has been fortunate beyond most actresses of this period, in coming in contact with nothing of this sort.

I return to New York, to direct attention to that manager of blonde nudities who has won, probably, the most money for his speculations in yellow hair and padded legs of any one in the business.

This person is an Englishman,—said to be, by birth, a gentleman (in the English or aristocratic sense of the word), and who, on entering the theatrical world, concealed his real name.

It is known that this man is a most licentious and shameless *roué*, who publicly boasts of the number of blonde women who have been his mistresses at different times; who actually perpetrated the monstrous indecency of making these infamous boasts in a speech at a dinner where women were present!

Among other things this disgraceful creature said was this: that a certain woman who had broken her professional engagement with him ought to have remembered the fact that she had once been his mistress, and had borne him children!

This infamous boast was coupled with the jeering remark that, in spite of the fact that he had no legal claim upon her services, he had a *moral one* in the fact just stated.

Shame! that such a monster as this should be permitted to remain in this country, the master of a drove of nude women, who are exhibiting themselves nightly to crowded houses, at the largest theatre on Broadway, and fill his already gorged pockets at the expense of disgrace to the dramatic profession, and distress to many of its members!

Were he to be hooted and stoned through the streets of this city, and packed off to England, covered with obloquy, it would be well. But packing him off would hardly rid the stage of this curse, since there are plenty of men besides him who are as vile as he, in all save the infamy of boasting.

With a sigh of relief, I turn to another anonymous letter, dated at New Haven, and signed "One who loves Jesus."

The writer of this letter is evidently a woman. It is tender and sweet in tone. "I assure you," says the good lady, "your noble stand will be esteemed by all good, moral people." I have abundant proof of that; and if I, in my turn, can lead all such people to think more gently of good and true actors and actresses, I shall thank heaven with a full heart.

"As a child of God," this letter says, "I must esteem the theatre as the devil's play-house."

There was a time, not very long ago, when I should have taken great offence at this. That time is past. I recognize the devil's play-house in the theatre where the nude woman jigs and wriggles.

If there be any such actual entity as that same old theological devil, I can easily imagine him kicking up his hoofs in Mephistophilean joy at the harvests that are falling into his lap from the temples of the nude.

But, dear lady,—you who write me from New Haven,—on the middle ground where I stand, I see what you can not see, and know what you can not know. All theatres do not deserve the stigma of this term. It is true that the theatres which still remain devoted to the drama proper are very, very few; but there are such; and they are no more the "devil's- play-house" than is the concert-room where Parepa sings. They are not consecrated to the service of God, it is true; but, at least, they are not given over to the devil's work.

I respect the theatre in its purity. I respect the actor who is an artist,— even the harmless clown of the pantomime, who makes us laugh without offending decency. That I love so many good and lovely women who are actresses, is my chief reason for deploring the reign of a class of women who are neither good nor lovely,—but coarse, indecent, painted, padded, and dyed.

If it were possible to treat the Nude Woman Question, and leave the nude woman herself out of it, I should be glad to do so. I am the last to wish to give pain to any person; but, in the path of clear duty, there is no choice. When it becomes a question between suffering, struggling virtue, and vice which rolls in luxury, and gathers unto itself wealth by the sheer practice of its wickedness, no woman who loves honor in her sex can hesitate as to the course to be taken.

The spirit of most of the anonymous letters I have received is one which might well cause me to hesitate in the path I have chosen, if fear were stronger in me than principle. But neither the sneers of low-class news-papers, nor the threats of anonymous correspondents, shall have weight with me. I see no other way to effect a cure of this nude woman evil but to make it odious. To that end, I shall do what in me lies. This article is but a beginning. I shall not cease to combat the encroachments of the nude woman upon the domain which should be occupied by true artists, and by virtuous men and women.

Firm in the belief that this indecent army *can* be routed, I call on all honorable souls, both in and out of the profession, to stand by my side and strike hard blows. We shall get hard blows in return, no doubt; but poor indeed must be the panoply of that warrior who can not hold his own against the cohorts of the nude woman. Whatever falls on my head in consequence of my words, I promise to give thrust for thrust. I do not fear the issue.

"Thrice is he armed that hath his quarrel JUST."

20. A Burlesque of Art Criticism

Humor was a basic ingredient of the popular culture which began to develop in America before the Civil War. Out of the comic tales and narratives of the old Southwest and of rural New England there emerged something like a nationally recognized American "type"—a character generous and affectionate, open to experience, free-booting, and sly and shrewd in his dealings with the world. The American comic type was also fundamentally irreverent toward high-sounding and pretentious language, usually identified with a European or Eastern antagonist. His point of view was generally that of "the common man." Frontier and Down East comedy remained highly popular after the war; new editions of works like Augustus Baldwin Longstreet's *Georgia Scenes* and Joseph G. Baldwin's *Flush Times in Alabama and Mississippi* continued to appear.

After the war a new and younger group of comedians emerged—more topical in their themes, more sophisticated in their literary style, and less defensive about their status as comedians. While in the earlier period the writer of humor usually set himself apart from his characters by means of an obviously educated and respectable diction, in the postwar period humorists frequently assumed the name of their characters and became identified with them, as Charles Farrar Browne (Artemus Ward), David Ross Locke (Petroleum V. Nasby), Henry Wheeler Shaw (Josh Billings)—and of course, Samuel L. Clemens (Mark Twain). The device of the comic name or mask permitted the artist, especially in platform performances, to present himself as a speaker of dialect, as slightly disreputable, as irreverent, as a wise fool, or as Mark Twain said, an "inspired idiot." The great popularity of these humorists suggests that they performed an important function for American culture—a function best described as a form of self-mockery.

When the outbreak of the Civil War closed the Mississippi River to steamboat traffic, Samuel Clemens, who had spent four years as apprentice and pilot on the river, looked for another occupation. After a brief episode with a band of volunteers in the war, he left for the far west in 1861, tried his hand at mining, became a reporter in Virginia City, and in 1864 arrived in California, where he met Bret Harte in the editorial offices of *The Californian* in San Francisco. He wrote "The Jumping Frog of Calaveras County" in this period, the story which launched his career and introduced the name Mark Twain to Eastern audiences. The following is one of several pieces he published in *The Californian* between 1864 and 1866. It shows his mastery of one of the characteristic devices of Western humor—the extended digression which, while seeming to avoid the "point" altogether (the art criticism), is really a deadpan commentary on it.

An Unbiased Criticism

MARK TWAIN

The Editor of *The Californian* ordered me to go to the rooms of the California Art Union and write an elaborate criticism upon the pictures upon exhibition there, and I beg leave to report that the result is hereunto appended together with bill for same.

I do not know anything about Art and very little about music or anatomy, but nevertheless I enjoy looking at pictures and listening to operas, and gazing at handsome young girls, about the same as people do who are better qualified by education to judge of merit in these matters.

After writing the above rather neat heading and preamble on my foolscap, I proceeded to the new Art Union rooms last week, to see the paintings, about which I read so much in the papers during my recent three months' stay in the Big Tree region of Calaveras county; [up there, you know, they read *everything*, because in most of those little camps they have no libraries, and no books to speak of, except now and then a patent-office report, or a prayer-book, or literature of that kind, in a general way, that will hang on and last a good while when people are careful with it, like miners; but as for novels, they pass them around and wear them out in a week or two. Now there was Coon, a nice bald-headed man at the

Mark Twain, "An Unbiased Criticism," *The Californian* (March 18, 1865); reprinted in *Sketches of the Sixties* (San Francisco, 1927), John Howell (ed.), 158–165.

hotel in Angels' Camp, I asked him to lend me a book, one rainy day: he was silent a moment, and a shade of melancholy flitted across his fine face, and then he said: "Well, I've got a mighty responsible old Webster-Unabridged, what there is left of it, but they started her sloshing around, and sloshing around, and sloshing around the camp before I ever got a chance to read her myself, and next she went to Murphy's, and from there she went to Jackass, and now, by G—d, she's gone to San Andreas, and I don't expect I'll ever see that book again; but what makes me mad, is that for all they're so handy about sashshaying around from shanty to shanty and from camp to camp, none of 'em's ever got a good word for her. Now Coddington had her a week, and she was too much for *him*—he couldn't spell the words; he tackled some of them regular busters, tow'rd the middle, you, know, and they throwed him; next, Dyer, *he* tried her a jolt, but he couldn't *pronounce* 'em—Dyer can hunt quail or play seven-up as well as any man, understand me, but he can't *pronounce* worth a d—n; he used to worry along well enough, though, till he'd flush one of them rattlers with a clatter of syllables as long as a string of sluice-boxes, and then he'd lose his grip and throw up his hand; and so, finally, Dick Stoker harnessed her, up there at his cabin, and sweated over her, and cussed over her, and rastled with her for as much as three weeks, night and day, till he got as far as R, and then passed her over to 'Lige Pickerell, and said she was the all-firedest dryest reading that ever *he* struck; well, well, if she's come back from San Andreas, you can get her and prospect her, but I don't reckon there's a good deal left of her by this time; though time was when she was as likely a book as any in the State, and as hefty, and had an amount of general information in her that was astonishing, if any of these cattle had known enough to get it out of her;" and ex-corporal Coon proceeded cheerlessly to scout with his brush after the straggling hairs on the rear of his head and drum them to the front for inspection and roll-call, as was his usual custom before turning in for his regular afternoon nap]; but as I was saying, they read everything, up there, and consequently all the Art criticisms, and the "Parlor Theatricals *vs.* Christian Commission" controversy, and even the quarrels in the advertising columns between rival fire-proof safe and sewing machine companies were devoured with avidity. Why, they eventually became divided on these questions, and discussed them with a spirit of obstinacy and acrimony that I have seldom seen equalled in the most important religious and political controversies. I have known a Grover & Baker fanatic to cut his own brother dead because he went for the Florence. As you have already guessed, perhaps, the county and township elections were carried on these issues alone, almost. I took sides, of course—every man had to—there was no shirking the responsibility; a man must be one thing or the other, either Florence or Grover & Baker, unless, of course, he chose to side with some outside machine faction, strong enough to be somewhat formidable. I was a bitter Florence man, and I think my great speech in the bar-room of the Union Hotel, at Angels', on the night of the 13th of February, will long be remembered as the deadliest blow the unprincipled Grover & Baker cabal ever got in that camp, and as having done more to thwart their hellish designs upon the liberties of our beloved country than any single effort of any one man that was ever made in that county. And in that same speech I administered a scathing rebuke to the *"Lillie Union and Constitution Fire and Burglar Proof Safe Party,"* (for I was a malignant Tilton & McFarland man and would break bread and eat salt with none other), that made even the most brazen among them blush for the infamous and damnable designs they had hatched and were still hatching against the Palladium of Freedom in Calaveras county. The concluding passage of my speech was considered to have been the finest display of eloquence and power ever heard in that part of the country, from Rawhide Ranch to Deadhorse Flat. I said:

"FELLOW-CITIZENS: A word more, and I am done. Men of Calaveras—men of Cuyote Flat—men of Jackass—BEWARE OF CODDINGTON! [Cheers.] Beware of this atrocious ditch-owner—this vile water-rat—this execrable dry-land shrimp—this bold and unprincipled mud-turtle, who sells water to Digger, Chinaman, Greaser and American alike, and at the self-same prices—who would sell you, who would sell me, who would sell us ALL, to carry out the destructive schemes of the *'Enlightened* [Bah!] *Freedom & Union Grover & Baker Loop-Stitch Sewing Machine Party* [groans] of which wretched conglomeration of the ruff-scruff and rag-tag-and-bob-tail of noble old Calaveras he is the appropriate leader—BEWAR-R-E of him! [Tremendous applause.] Again I charge you as men whom future generations will hold to a fearful responsibility, to BEWARE OF CODDINGTON! [Tempests of applause.] Beware of this unsavory remnant of a once pure and high-minded man!* [Renewed applause.] Beware of this faithless modern Esau, who would sell his birthright of freedom and ours, for a mess of pottage!—for a mess of tripe!—for a mess of sauerkraut and garlic! —for a mess of anything under the sun that a Christian Florence Patriot would scorn and a Digger Indian turn from with loathing and disgust!**

---

* He used to belong to the Florence at first.   M. T.

** I grant you that that last part was a sort of a strong figure, seeing that that tribe are not over-particular in the matter of diet, and don't usually go back on anything that they can chaw.   M. T.

[Thunders of applause.] Remember Coddington on election day! and remember him but to damn him! I appeal to you, sovereign and enlightened Calaverasses, and my heart tells me that I do not appeal in vain! I have done. [Earthquakes of applause that made the welkin tremble for many minutes, and finally died away in hoarse demands for the villain Coddington, and threats to lynch him.]

I felt exhausted, and in need of rest after my great effort, and so I tore myself from my enthusiastic friends and went home with Coddington to his hospitable mansion, where we partook of an excellent supper and then retired to bed, after playing several games of seven-up for beer and booking some heavy election bets.

The contest on election day was bitter, and to the last degree exciting, but principles triumphed over party jugglery and chicanery, and we carried everything but the Constable (Unconditional Button-Hole Stitch and Anti-Parlor Theatrical candidate), and Tax Collector (Moderate Lillie Fire-Proof and Fusion Grover & Button-Hole Stitch Machines), and County Assessor (Radical Christian Commission and Independent Sewing Machine candidate), and we could have carried these, also, but at the last moment fraudulent hand-bills were suddenly scattered abroad containing sworn affidavits that a Tilton & McFarland safe, on its way from New York, had melted in the tropical sunshine after fifteen minutes' exposure on the Isthmus; also, that the lock stitch, back stitch, fore-and-aft, forward-and-back, down-the-middle, double-and-twist, and the other admirable stitches and things upon which the splendid reputation of the Florence rests, had all been cabbaged from the traduced and reviled Button-Hole Stitch and Grover & Baker machines; also, that so far from the Parlor-Theatrical-Christian-Commission controversy being finished, it had sprung up again in San Francisco, and by latest advices the Opposition was ahead. What men could do, we did, but although we checked the demoralization that had broken out in our ranks, we failed to carry all our candidates. We sent express to San Andreas and Columbia, and had strong affidavits—sworn to by myself and our candidates—printed, denouncing the other publications as low and disreputable falsehoods and calumnies. whose shameless authors ought to be driven beyond the pale of civilized society, and winding up with the withering revelation that the rain had recently soaked through one of Lillie's Fire and Burglar-Proof safes in San Francisco, and badly damaged the books and papers in it; and that, in the process of drying, the safe warped so that the door would not swing on its hinges, and had to be "prized" open with a butter-knife. O, but that was a rough shot! It blocked the game and saved the day for us—and just at the critical moment our reserve (whom we had sent for and drummed up in Tuolumne and the adjoining counties, and had kept out of sight and full of chain-lightning, sudden death and scorpion-bile all day in Tom Deer's back-yard,) came filing down the street as drunk as loons, with a drum and fife and lighted transparencies, (day-light and dark were all the same to *them* in *their* condition), bearing such stirring devices as:

"*The Florence is bound to rip, therefore,* LET HER RIP!"
"*Grover & Baker, how are you* NOW?"
"*Nothing can keep the Opposition cool in the other world but Tilton & McFarland's Chilled Iron Safes!*" etc., etc.

A vast Florence machine on wheels led the van, and a sick Chinaman bearing a crippled Grover & Baker brought up the rear. The procession reeled up to the polls with deafening cheers for the Florence and curses for the "loop stitch scoun'rels," and deposited their votes like men for freedom of speech, freedom of the press and freedom of conscience in the matter of sewing machines, provided they are Florences.

I had a very comfortable time in Calaveras county, in spite of the rain, and if I had my way I would go back there, and argue the sewing machine question around Coon's bar-room stove again with the boys on rainy evenings. Calaveras possesses some of the grandest natural features that have ever fallen under the contemplation of the human mind—such as the Big Trees, the famous Morgan gold mine which is the richest in the world at the present time, perhaps, and "straight" whisky that will throw a man a double somerset and limber him up like boiled maccaroni before he can set his glass down. Marvelous and incomprehensible is the straight whisky of Angels' Camp!

But I digress to some extent, for maybe it was not really necessary to be quite so elaborate as I have been in order to enable the reader to understand that we were in the habit of reading everything thoroughly that fell in our way at Angels, and that consequently we were familiar with all that had appeared in print about the new Art Union rooms. They get all the papers regularly every evening there, 24 hours out from San Francisco.

However, now that I have got my little preliminary point established to my satisfaction, I will proceed with my Art criticism.

The rooms of the California Art Union are pleasantly situated over the picture store in Montgomery street near the Eureka Theatre, and the first thing that attracts your attention when you enter is a beautiful and animated picture representing the Trial Scene in the *Merchant of Venice*. They did not charge me anything for going in there, because the Superintendent was not noticing at the time, but it is likely he would charge you or another man twenty-five cents—I think he would, because when I tried to get a dollar and a half out of a fellow I took for a stranger, the new-comer said the usual price was only two bits, and besides he was a heavy life-member and not obliged to pay anything at all—so I had to let him in for a quarter, but I had the satisfaction of telling him we were not letting life-members in free, now, as much as we *were*. It touched him on the raw. I let another fellow in for nothing, because I had cabined with him a few nights in Esmeralda several years ago, and I thought it only fair to be hospitable with him now that I had a chance. He introduced me to a friend of his named Brown, (I was hospitable to Brown also,) and me and Brown sat down on a bench and had a long talk about Washoe and other things, and I found him very entertaining for a stranger. He said his mother was a hundred and thirteen years old, and he had an aunt who died in her infancy, who, if she had lived, would have been older than his mother, now. He judged so because, originally, his aunt was born before his mother was. That was the first thing he told me, and then we were friends in a moment. It could not but be flattering to me, a stranger, to be made the recipient of information of so private and sacred a nature as the age of his mother and the early decease of his aunt, and I naturally felt drawn towards him and bound to him by a stronger and a warmer tie than the cold, formal introduction that had previously passed between us. I shall cherish the memory of the ensuing two hours as being among the purest and happiest of my checkered life. I told him frankly who I was, and where I came from, and where I was going to, and when I calculated to start, and all about my uncle Ambrose, who was an Admiral, and was for a long time in command of a large fleet of canal boats, and about my gifted aunt Martha, who was a powerful poetess, and a dead shot, with a brick-bat at forty yards, and about myself and how I was employed at good pay by the publishers of THE CALIFORNIAN to come up there and write an able criticism upon the pictures in the Art Union—indeed I concealed nothing from Brown, and in return he concealed nothing from me, but told me everything he could recollect about his rum old mother, and his grand-mother, and all his relations, in fact, And so we talked and talked, and exchanged these tender heart-reminiscences until the sun dropped far in the West, and then Brown said, "Let's go down and take a drink."

21. A Popular Artist

Winslow Homer (1836–1910)

Homer's early work was almost entirely in lithography, illustration, and magazine drawings. His later stature as America's most celebrated artist owes much to his work through the 1860's and early 1870's, when his graphics could be seen in the pages of Harper's Weekly, which had begun publication as a profusely illustrated journal in the late 1850's. This was not the only outlet for his prints—he did a series of "Campaign Sketches" in lithography for the Boston publisher Louis Prang in 1863—but many of his best and most memorable pictures appeared in the influential Weekly.

Apart from the importance of this early work in black and white graphics upon the style and technique of his later oils and watercolors—an influence expressed chiefly in the dramatic directness of statement, the clarity and strength of outline and mass—the Harper's pictures show Homer as the master of a style appropriate both to media and to theme. The themes themselves are "popular" in the sense that they are drawn from vernacular life rather than conventional studio ideals of "art." Many of his prints are illustrations for stories—or contain stories themselves. Their meaning, the feeling with which they are invested, is immediately accessible—nothing is hidden or covert or "literary" in the manner of academic painters. Moreover, Homer's subjects are "topical" in two senses: they are drawn directly from public experiences like the war, and they correspond to feelings and moods widespread among Americans.

During the war he visited the front in Virginia as "special artist" for Harper's, and his prints are unsurpassed for their truthful evocation of camp life. Like many Americans, after the war, Homer turned his eye and mind to country life, especially life of the farm, the summer resort, the ocean beach. His images of young women and of uncouth rural boys were especially popular. "He can almost be said to have invented the American Girl," Lloyd Goodrich has written. Goodrich points out that Homer's depictions of rural life are free from nostalgic idealization, that they have "the conviction of utter authenticity." This is a remarkable achievement for so public an artist in a period when sentimentality and mawkishness were frequent notes. But Homer possessed what Goodrich calls a "primal freshness of vision," a quality of seeing and recording which links him with the best writing of the period—Whitman's poetry of the 1850's, and Mark Twain's prose of the 1870's and 1880's.

1. *A Bivouac Fire on the Potomac, 1861.*

2. *The War for the Union—A Cavalry Charge, 1862.*

3. *The Army of the Potomac—A Sharp-Shooter on Picket Duty, 1862.*

4. *The Straw Ride, 1869.*

HARPER'S WEEKLY
A JOURNAL OF CIVILIZATION

VOL. XIV.—No. 689.] NEW 'K, SATURDAY, MARCH 12, 1870. [SINGLE COPIES, TEN CENTS. $4.00 PER YEAR IN ADVANCE.

Entered according to Act of Congress, in the Year 1870, by H... ...r Brothers, in the Clerk's Office of the District Court of the United States, for the Southern District of New York.

"Thou shalt not covet thy neighbor's house, thou shalt not covet thy neighbor's wife, nor his servant, nor his maid, nor his ox, nor his ass, nor any thing that is his."

"Lord, have mercy upon us, and write all these thy laws in our hearts, we beseech thee."

5. *Tenth Commandment, 1870.*

6. *The Dinner Horn, 1870.*

7. *The Bathers, 1873.*

8. *The Nooning,* 1873.

9. *Snap the Whip, 1873.*

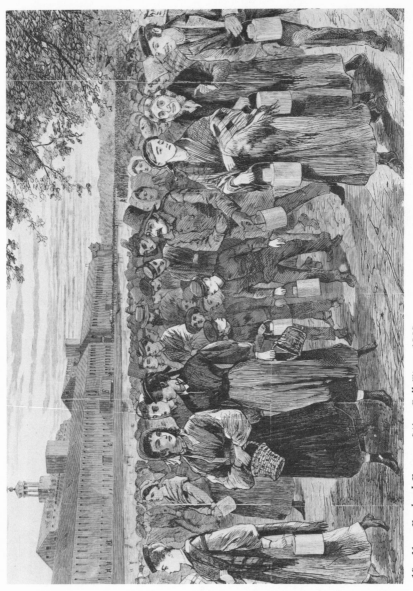

10. *New England Factory Life—Bell Time, 1868.*

11. *Station-House Lodgers, 1874.*

PART THREE

CULTURE AND DEMOCRACY

22. The Cultural Gap

In September, 1867, a letter signed "A Philistine" appeared in *The Nation* under the title "A Plea for the Uncultivated." The writer identified himself as one of "the great mass of workers, who are the mud, the common clay, upon whom conventional society may set its feet, but who cannot partake in the culture which is the chief good to be attained in life." His aim was to attack the invidious distinction by which some persons are admitted to the status of "cultivated" and others—men of science, men of affairs (merchants and manufacturers), and workers are excluded. This distinction, he argued, is unjust; it is based on a definition of culture as an essentially useless mental activity, the work of scholars who brood over dead languages. "We know that, except for our work, the culture of the scholar who despises our pursuits would be impracticable." The writer concludes that "merchants and traders and artisans" should stop accepting "their doom as Philistines, or weakly attempting to evade it by a smattering of literature or art," and claim for themselves "a position as high as that of others who now look down upon them by virtue of a clear perception of the fact that by their work the abundance of things is increased, the comfort of humanity promoted, the leisure of the scholar made possible, and true culture, or, as it has been well defined by Arnold, sweetness and light, diffused among all, and not monopolized by a few."

Charles Dudley Warner also addresses himself to the diffusion of "true culture," and it is significant that he and "A Philistine" would probably agree that "sweetness and light" is a universal, ennobling spirit. Warner was a graduate of Hamilton College (1851) and the University of Pennsylvania law school (1858); like other New Englanders in this period he turned from law to writing. He had spent some time in Missouri (1853–1854) as a railroad surveyor, an experience he exploits in *The Gilded Age*. He settled in Hartford in 1860, edited the Hartford *Courant*, and in addition to numerous books of essays and travel sketches, tried his hand at fiction. His major theme was the social responsibility of wealth, and his tone became sternly moralistic, which, as his friend Howells pointed out, tended to weaken his fiction. He was also a biographer of Washington Irving and Captain John Smith, a frequent lecturer at universities, and a contributor to periodicals.

What Is Your Culture to Me?

CHARLES DUDLEY WARNER

Twenty-one years ago in this house I heard a voice, calling me to ascend the platform, and there to stand and deliver. The voice was the voice of President North; the language was an excellent imitation of that used by Cicero and Julius Cæsar. I remember the flattering invitation—it is the classic tag that clings to the graduate long after he has forgotten the gender of the nouns that end in *um*—*orator proximus,* the grateful voice said, *ascendat, videlicet,* and so forth. To be proclaimed an orator, and an ascending orator, in such a sonorous tongue, in the face of a world waiting for orators, stirred one's blood like the herald's trumpet when the lists are thrown open. Alas! for most of us, who crowded so eagerly into the arena, it was the last appearance as orators on any stage.

The facility of the world for swallowing up orators, and company after company of educated young men, has been remarked. But it is almost incredible to me now that the class of 1851, with its classic sympathies and its many revolutionary ideas, disappeared in the flood of the world so soon and so silently, causing scarcely a ripple in the smoothly flowing stream. I suppose the phenomenon has been repeated for twenty years. Do the young gentlemen at Hamilton, I wonder, still carry on their ordinary conversation in the Latin tongue, and their familiar vacation correspondence in the language of Aristophanes? I hope so. I hope they are more proficient in such exercises than the young gentlemen of twenty years ago were, for I have still great faith in a culture that is so far from any sordid aspiration as to approach the ideal; although the young graduate is not long in learning that there is an indifference in the public mind with regard to the First Aorist that amounts nearly to apathy, and that millions of his fellow-creatures will probably live and die without the consolations of the Second Aorist. It is a melancholy fact that after a thousand years of missionary effort, the vast majority of civilized men do not know that *gerunds* are found only in the singular number.

I confess that this failure of the annual graduating class to make its

Charles Dudley Warner, "What Is Your Culture to Me?," *Scribner's Monthly* IV (1872), 470–478.

expected impression on the world has its pathetic side. Youth is credulous —as it always ought to be—and full of hope—else the world were dead already—and the graduate steps out into life with an ingenuous self-confidence in his resources. It is to him an event, this turning point in the career of what he feels to be an important and immortal being. His entrance is public and with some dignity of display. For a day the world stops to see it; the newspapers spread abroad a report of it, and the modest scholar feels that the eyes of mankind are fixed on him in expectation and desire. Though modest, he is not insensible to the responsibility of his position. He has only packed away in his mind the wisdom of the ages, and he does not intend to be stingy about communicating it to the world which is awaiting his graduation. Fresh from the communion with great thoughts in great literatures, he is in haste to give mankind the benefit of them, and lead it on into new enthusiasm and new conquests.

The world, however, is not very much excited. The birth of a child is in itself marvelous, but it is so common. Over and over again, for hundreds of years, these young gentlemen have been coming forward with their specimens of learning tied up in neat little parcels, all ready to administer, and warranted to be of the purest materials. The world is not unkind, it is not even indifferent, but it must be confessed that it does not act any longer as if it expected to be enlightened. It is generally so busy that it does not even ask the young gentlemen what they can do, but leaves them standing with their little parcels, wondering when the person will pass by who requires one of them, and when there will happen a little opening in the procession into which they can fall. They expected that way would be made for them with shouts of welcome, but they find themselves before long struggling to get even a standing-place in the crowd—it is only Kings, and the nobility, and those fortunates who dwell in the tropics, where bread grows on trees and clothing is unnecessary, who have reserved seats in this world.

To the majority of men, I fancy that literature is very much the same that history is; and history is presented as a museum of antiquities and curiosities, classified, arranged, and labelled. One may walk through it as he does through the Hotel de Cluny; he feels that he ought to be interested in it, but it is very tiresome. Learning is regarded in like manner as an accumulation of literature, gathered into great store-houses called libraries—the thought of which excites great respect in most minds, but is ineffably tedious. Year after year and age after age it accumulates—this evidence and monument of intellectual activity—piling itself up in vast collections, which it needs a lifetime even to catalogue, and through which the uncultured walk as the idle do through the British museum, with no very strong indignation against Omar who burnt the library at Alexandria. To the popular mind this vast accumulation of learning in libraries or in brains, that do not visibly apply it, is much the same thing. The business of the scholar appears to be this sort of accumulation; and the young student, who comes to the world with a little portion of this treasure, dug out of some classic tomb or mediæval museum, is received with little more enthusiasm than is the miraculous handkerchief of St. Veronica by the crowd of Protestants to whom it is exhibited on Holy Week in St. Peter's. The historian must make his museum live again; the scholar must vivify his learning with a present purpose.

It is unnecessary for me to say that all this is only from the unsympathetic and worldly side. I should think myself a criminal if I said anything to chill the enthusiasm of the young scholar, or to dash with any scepticism his longing and his hope. He has chosen the highest. His beautiful faith and his aspiration are the light of life. Without his fresh enthusiasm and his gallant devotion to learning, to art, to culture, the world would be dreary enough. Through him comes the ever-springing inspiration in affairs. Baffled at every turn and driven defeated from an hundred fields, he carries victory in himself. He belongs to a great and immortal army. Let him not be discouraged at his apparent little influence, even though every sally of every young life may seem like a forlorn hope. No man can see the whole of the battle. It must needs be that regiment after regiment, trained, accomplished, gay and high with hope, shall be sent into the field, marching on, into the smoke, into the fire, and be swept away. The battle swallows them, one after the other, and the foe is yet unyielding, and the ever-remorseless trumpet calls for more and more. But not in vain, for some day, and every day, along the line, there is a cry, "they fly, they fly," and the whole army advances, and the flag is planted on an ancient fortress where it never waved before. And, even if you never see this, better than inglorious camp-following is it to go in with the wasting regiment; to carry the colors up the slope of the enemy's works, though the next moment you fall and find a grave at the foot of the glacis.

What are the relations of culture to common life, of the scholar to the day-laborer? What is the value of this vast accumulation of higher learning, what is its point of contact with the mass of humanity, that toils and eats and sleeps and reproduces itself and dies, generation after generation, in an unvarying round, on an unvarying level? We have had discussed lately the relation of culture to religion. Mr. Froude, with a singular, reactionary ingenuity, has sought to prove that the progress of the century, so-called, with all its material alleviations, has done little in regard to a happy life, to the pleasure of existence, for the average individual Englishman. Into neither of these inquires do I purpose to enter; but we may not unprofitably turn our attention to a subject closely connected with both of them.

It has not escaped your attention that there are indications everywhere of what may be called a ground-swell. There is not simply an inquiry as to the value of classic culture, a certain jealousy of the schools where it is obtained, a rough popular contempt for the graces of learning, a failure to see any connection between the first aorist and the rolling of steel rails, but there is arising an angry protest against the conditions of a life which make one free of [on?] the serene heights of thought and give him range of all intellectual countries, and keep another at the spade and the loom, year after year, that he may earn food for the day and lodging for the night. In our day the demand here hinted at has taken more definite form and determinate aim, and goes on, visible to all men, to unsettle society and change social and political relations. The great movement of labor, extravagant and preposterous as are some of its demands, demagogic as are most of its leaders, fantastic as are many of its theories, is nevertheless real, and gigantic, and full of a certain primeval force, and with a certain justice in it that never sleeps in human affairs, but moves on, blindly often and destructively often, a movement cruel at once and credulous, deceived and betrayed, and revenging itself on friends and foes alike. Its strength is in the fact that it is natural and human; it might have been predicted from a mere knowledge of human nature, which is always restless in any relations it is possible to establish, which is always like the sea, seeking a level, and never so discontented as when anything like a level is approximated.

What is the relation of the scholar to the present phase of this movement? What is the relation of culture to it? By scholar I mean the man who has had the advantages of such an institution as this. By culture I mean that fine product of opportunity and scholarship which is to mere knowledge what manners are to the gentleman. The world has a growing belief in the profit of knowledge, of information, but it has a suspicion of culture. There is a lingering notion in matters religious that something is lost by refinement, at least that there is danger that the plain, blunt, essential truths will be lost in æsthetic graces. The laborer is getting to consent that his son shall go to school, and learn how to build an undershot wheel or to assay metals; but why plant in his mind those principles of taste which will make him as sensitive to beauty as to pain, why open to him those realms of imagination with the illimitable horizons, the contours and colors of which can but fill him with indefinite longing?

It is not necessary for me in this presence to dwell upon the value of culture. I wish rather to have you notice the gulf that exists between what the majority want to know and that fine fruit of knowledge concerning which there is so wide-spread an infidelity. Will culture aid a minister in a "protracted meeting?" Will the ability to read Chaucer assist a shop-keeper? Will the politician add to the "sweetness and light" of his lovely career if he can read the Battle of the Frogs and the Mice in the original? What has the farmer to do with the Rose Garden of Saadi?

I suppose it is not altogether the fault of the majority that the true rela-tion of culture to common life is so misunderstood. The scholar is largely responsible for it; he is largely responsible for the isolation of his position, and the want of sympathy it begets. No man can influence his fellows with any power who retires into his own selfishness, and gives himself to a self-culture which has no further object. What is he that he should absorb the sweets of the universe, that he should hold all the claims of humanity second to the perfecting of himself? This effort to save his own soul was common to Goethe and Francis of Asissi; under different mani-festations it was the same regard for self. And where it is an intellectual and not a spiritual greediness, I suppose it is what an old writer calls "laying up treasures in hell."

It is not an unreasonable demand of the majority that the few who have the advantages of the training of college and university, should exhibit the breadth and sweetness of a generous culture, and should shed every-where that light which ennobles common things, and without which life is like one of the old landscapes in which the artist forgot to put sunlight. One of the reasons why the college-bred man does not meet this reason-able expectation is that his training, too often, has not been thorough and conscientious, it has not been of himself; he has acquired, but he is not educated. Another is that, if he is educated, he is not impressed with the intimacy of his relation to that which is below him as well as that which is above him, and his culture is out of sympathy with the great mass that needs it, and must have it, or it will remain a blind force in the world, the lever of demagogues who preach social anarchy and misname it progress. There is no culture so high, no taste so fastidious, no grace of learning so delicate, no refinement of art so exquisite, that it cannot at this hour find full play for itself in the broadest fields of humanity; since it is all needed to soften the attritions of common life, and guide to nobler aspirations the strong materialistic influences of our restless society.

One reason, as I said, for the gulf between the majority and the select few to be educated is, that the college does not seldom disappoint the reasonable expectation concerning it. The graduate of the carpenter's shop knows how to use his tools—or used to in days before superficial training in trades became the rule. Does the college graduate know how to use his tools? Or has he to set about fitting himself for some employment, and gaining that culture, that training of himself, that utilization of his information which will make him necessary in the world? There has been a great deal of discussion whether a boy should be trained in the classics or mathematics or sciences or modern languages. I feel like saying "yes" to all the various propositions; for heaven's sake train him in something, so that he can handle himself, and have free and confident use of his powers. There isn't a more helpless creature in the universe than a scholar with a vast amount of information over which he has no control. He is like a man with a load of hay so badly put upon his cart that it all slides off before he can get to market. The influence of a man on the world is generally proportioned to his ability to do something. When Abraham Lincoln was running for the legislature the first time, on the platform of the improvement of the navigation of the Sangamon river, he went to secure the votes of thirty men who were cradling a wheat-field. They asked no questions about internal improvements, but only seemed curious whether Abraham had muscle enough to represent them in the legislature. The obliging man took up a cradle and led the gang round the field. The whole thirty voted for him.

What is scholarship? The learned Hindu can repeat I do not know how many thousands of lines from the Vedas, and perhaps backwards as well as forwards. I heard of an excellent old lady who had counted how many times the letter A occurs in the Holy Scriptures. The Chinese students who aspire to honors spend years in verbally memorizing the classics—Confucius and Mencius—and receive degrees and public advancement upon ability to transcribe from memory without the error of a point, or misplacement of a single tea-chest character, the whole of some book of morals. You do not wonder that China is to-day more like an herbarium than anything else. Learning is a kind of fetish, and it has no influence whatever upon the great inert mass of Chinese humanity.

I suppose it is possible for a young gentleman to be able to read—just think of it, after ten years of grammar and lexicon, not to know Greek literature and have flexible command of all its richness and beauty, but to read it—it is possible, I suppose, for the graduate of college to be able to read all the Greek authors, and yet to have gone, in regard to his own culture, very little deeper than a surface reading of them; to know very little of that perfect architecture and what it expressed; nor of that marvelous sculpture and the conditions of its immortal beauty; nor of that artistic development which made the Acropolis to bud and bloom under the blue sky like the final flower of a perfect nature; nor of that philosophy, that politics, that society, nor of the life of that polished, crafty, joyous race, the springs of it and the far-reaching still unexpended effects of it.

Yet as surely as that nothing perishes, that the Providence of God is not a patchwork of uncontinued efforts, but a plan and a progress, as surely as the pilgrim embarkation at Delf Haven has a relation to the battle of Gettysburg, and to the civil rights bill giving the colored man permission to ride in a public conveyance, and to be buried in a public cemetery, so surely has the Parthenon some connection with your new State capital at Albany, and the daily life of the vine-dresser of the Peloponnesus some lesson for the American day-laborer. The scholar is said to be the torchbearer, transmitting the increasing light from generation to generation, so that the feet of all, the humblest and the lowliest, may walk in the radiance and not stumble. But he very often carries a dark lantern.

Not what is the use of Greek, of any culture in art or literature, but what is the good to me of your knowing Greek, is the latest question of the ditchdigger to the scholar—what better off am I for your learning? And the question, in view of the inter-dependence of all members of society, is one that cannot be put away as idle. One reason why the scholar does not make the world of the past, the world of books, real to his fellows and serviceable to them, is that it is not real to himself, but a mere unsubstantial place of intellectual idleness, where he dallies some years before he begins his task in life. And another reason is, that while it may be real to him, while he is actually cultured and trained, he fails to see or to feel that his culture is not a thing apart, and that all the world has a right to share its blessed influence. Failing to see this, he is isolated, and, wanting his sympathy, the untutored world mocks at his superfineness and takes its own rough way to rougher ends. Greek art was for the people, Greek poetry was for the people; Raphael painted his immortal frescoes where throngs could be lifted in thought and feeling by them; Michael Angelo hung the dome over St. Peter's so that the far-off peasant on the Campagna could see it, and the maiden kneeling by the shrine in the Alban hills. Do we often stop to think what influence, direct or other, the scholar, the man of high culture, has to-day upon the great mass of our people? Why do they ask, what is the use of your learning and your art?

The artist, in the retirement of his studio, finishes a charming, suggestive, historical picture. The rich man buys it and hangs it in his library, where the privileged few can see it. I do not deny that the average rich man needs all the refining influence the picture can exert on him, and that the picture is doing missionary work in his house; but it is nevertheless an example of an educating influence withdrawn and appropriated to narrow uses. But the engraver comes, and, by his mediating art, transfers it to a thousand sheets, and scatters its sweet influence far abroad. All the world, in its toil, its hunger, its sordidness, pauses a moment to look on it— that gray sea-coast, the receding *Mayflower*, the two young Pilgrims in the foreground regarding it, with tender thoughts of the far home—all the world looks on it perhaps for a moment thoughtfully, perhaps tearfully, and is touched with the sentiment of it, is kindled into a glow of nobleness by the sight of that faith, and love, and resolute devotion, which have tinged our early history with the faint light of romance. So art is no longer the enjoyment of the few, but the help and solace of the many.

The scholar who is cultured by books, reflection, travel, by a refined society, consorts with his kind, and more and more removes himself from the sympathies of common life. I know how almost inevitable this is, how almost impossible it is to resist the segregation of classes according to the affinities of taste. But by what mediation shall the culture that is now the possession of the few, be made to leaven the world and to elevate and sweeten ordinary life? By books? Yes. By the newspaper? Yes. By the diffusion of works of art? Yes. But when all is done that can be done by such letters missive from one class to another, there remains the need of more personal contact, of a human sympathy, diffused and living. The world has had enough of charities. It wants respect and consideration. We desire no longer to be legislated for, it says, we want to be legislated with. Why do you never come to see me but you bring me something? asks the sensitive and poor seamstress. Do you always give some charity to your friends? I want companionship, and not cold pieces; I want to be treated like a human being who has nerves and feelings, and tears too, and as much interest in the sunset, and in the birth of Christ, perhaps, as you. And the mass of uncared-for ignorance and brutality, finding a voice at length, bitterly repels the condescensions of charity; you have your culture, your libraries, your fine houses, your church, your religion, and your God, too; let us alone, we want none of them. In the bear-pit at Berne, the occupants, who are the wards of the city, have had meat thrown to them daily for I know not how long, but they are not tamed by this charity, and would probably eat up any careless person who fell into their clutches, without apology.

Do not impute to me Quixotic notions with regard to the duties of men and women of culture, or think that I undervalue the difficulties in the way, the fastidiousness on the one side, or the jealousies on the other. It is by no means easy to an active participant to define the drift of his own age; but I seem to see plainly that unless the culture of the age finds means to diffuse itself, working downward and reconciling antagonisms by a commonness of thought and feeling and aim in life, society must more and more separate itself into jarring classes, with mutual misunderstandings and hatred and war. To suggest remedies is much more difficult than to see evils; but the comprehension of dangers is the first step towards mastering them. The problem of our own time—the reconciliation of the interests of classes—is as yet very illy defined. This great movement of labor, for instance, does not know definitely what it wants, and those who are spectators do not know what their relations are to it. The first thing to be done is for them to try to understand each other. One class sees that the other has lighter or at least different labor, opportunities of travel, a more liberal supply of the luxuries of life, a higher enjoyment and a keener relish of the beautiful, the immaterial. Looking only at external conditions, it concludes that all it needs to come into this better place is wealth, and so it organizes war upon the rich, and it makes demands of freedom from toil and of compensation which it is in no man's power to give it, and which would not, if granted over and over again, lift it into that condition it desires. It is a tale in the Gulistan, that a king placed his son with a preceptor, and said,—"This is your son; educate him in the same manner as your own." The preceptor took pains with him for a year, but without success, whilst his own sons were completed in learning and accomplishments. The king reproved the preceptor, and said,—"You have broken your promise, and not acted faithfully." He replied,—"O king, the education was the same, but the capacities are different. Although silver and gold are produced from a stone, yet these metals are not to be found in every stone. The star Canopus shines all over the world, but the scented leather comes only from Yemen." " 'Tis an absolute, and, as it were, a divine perfection," says Montaigne, "for a man to know how loyally to enjoy his being. We seek other conditions, by reason we do not understand the use of our own; and go out of ourselves, because we know not how there to reside."

But nevertheless it becomes a necessity for us to understand the wishes of those who demand a change of condition, and it is necessary that they should understand the compensations as well as the limitations of every condition. The dervish congratulated himself that although the only monument of his grave would be a brick, he should at the last day arrive at and enter the gate of Paradise, before the king had got from under the heavy stones of his costly tomb. Nothing will bring us into this desirable mutual understanding except sympathy and personal contact. Laws will not do it; institutions of charity and relief will not do it.

We must believe, for one thing, that the graces of culture will not be thrown away if exercised among the humblest and the least cultured; it is found out that flowers are often more welcome in the squalid tenement-houses of Boston than loaves of bread. It is difficult to say exactly how culture can extend its influence into places uncongenial and to people indifferent to it, but I will try and illustrate what I mean, by an example or two.

Criminals in this country, when the law took hold of them, used to be turned over to the care of men who often had more sympathy with the crime than with the criminal, or at least to those who were almost as coarse in feeling and as brutal in speech as their charges. There have been some changes of late years in the care of criminals, but does public opinion yet everywhere demand that jailers and prison-keepers and executioners of the penal law should be men of refinement, of high character, of any degree of culture? I do not know any class more needing the best direct personal influence of the best civilization than the criminal. The problem of its proper treatment and reformation is one of the most pressing, and it needs practically the aid of our best men and women. I should have great hope of any prison establishment at the head of which was a gentle-man of fine education, the purest tastes, the most elevated morality and lively sympathy with men as such, provided he had also will and the power of command. I do not know what might not be done for the viciously inclined and the transgressors, if they could come under the influence of refined men and women. And yet you know that a boy or a girl may be arrested for crime, and pass from officer to keeper, and jailer to warden, and spend years in a career of vice and imprisonment, and never once see any man or woman officially, who has tastes, or sympathies, or aspirations much above that vulgar level whence the criminals came. Anybody who is honest and vigilant is considered good enough to take charge of prison birds.

The age is merciful and abounds in charities; houses of refuge for poor women, societies for the conservation of the exposed and the reclamation of the lost. It is willing to pay liberally for their support, and to hire ministers and distributors of its benefactions. But it is beginning to see that it cannot hire the distribution of love, nor buy brotherly feeling. The most encouraging thing I have seen lately is an experiment in one of our cities. In the thick of the town the ladies of the city have furnished and opened a reading-room, sewing-room, conversation-room, or what not, where young girls, who work for a living and have no opportunity for any culture, at home or elsewhere, may spend their evenings. They meet there always some of the ladies I have spoken of, whose unostentatious duty and pleasure it is to pass the evening with them, in reading or music or the use of the needle, and the exchange of the courtesies of life in conversation. Whatever grace and kindness and refinement of manner they carry there, I do not suppose is wasted. These are some of the ways in which culture can serve men. And I take it that one of the chief evidences of our progress in this century is the recognition of the truth that there is no selfishness so supreme—not even that in the possession of wealth—as that which retires into itself with all the accomplishments of liberal learning and rare opportunities, and looks upon the intellectual poverty of the world without a wish to relieve it. "As often as I have been among men," says Seneca, "I have returned less a man." And Thomas à Kempis declared that "the greatest saints avoided the company of men as much as they could, and chose to live to God in secret." The Christian philosophy was no improvement upon the pagan in this respect, and was exactly at variance with the teaching and practice of Jesus of Nazareth.

The American scholar cannot afford to live for himself, nor merely for scholarship and the delights of learning. He must make himself more felt in the material life of this country. I am aware that it is said that the culture of the age is itself materialistic, and that its refinements are sensual; that there is little to choose between the coarse excesses of poverty and the polished and more decorous animality of the more fortunate. Without entering directly upon the consideration of this much-talked-of tendency, I should like to notice the influence upon our present and probable future of the bounty, fertility, and extraordinary opportunities of this still new land.

The American grows and develops himself with few restraints. Foreigners used to describe him as a lean, hungry, nervous animal, gaunt, inquisitive, inventive, restless, and certain to shrivel into physical inferiority in his dry and highly oxygenated atmosphere. The apprehension is not well founded. It is quieted by his achievements the continent over, his virile enterprises, his endurance in war and in the most difficult explorations, his resistance of the influence of great cities towards effeminacy and loss of physical vigor. If ever man took large and eager hold of earthly things and appropriated them to his own use, it is the American. We are gross eaters, we are great drinkers. We shall excel the English when we have as long practice as they. I am filled with a kind of dismay when I see the great stock-yards of Chicago and Cincinnati, through which flow the vast herds and droves of the prairies, marching straight down the throats of Eastern people. Thousands are always sowing and reaping and brewing and distilling, to slake the immortal thirst of the country. We take, indeed, strong hold of the earth; we absorb its fatness. When Leicester entertained Elizabeth at Kenilworth, the clock in the great tower was set perpetually at twelve, the hour of feasting. It is always dinner-time in America. I do not know how much land it takes to raise an average citizen, but I should say a quarter section. He spreads himself abroad, he riots in abundance; above all things he must have profusion, and he wants things that are solid and strong.

On the Sorrentine promontory, and on the island of Capri, the hardy husbandman and fisherman draws his subsistence from the sea and from a scant patch of ground. One may feast on a fish and a handful of olives. The dinner of the laborer is a dish of polenta, a few figs, some cheese, a glass of thin wine. His wants are few and easily supplied. He is not over-fed, his diet is not stimulating; I should say that he would pay little to the physician, that familiar of other countries whose family office is to counteract the effects of over-eating. He is temperate, frugal, content, and apparently draws not more of his life from the earth or the sea than from the genial sky. He would never build a Pacific railway, nor write an hundred volumes of commentary on the Scriptures; but he is an example of how little a man actually needs of the gross products of the earth.

I suppose that life was never fuller in certain ways than it is here in America. If a civilization is judged by its wants, we are certainly highly civilized. We cannot get land enough, nor clothes enough, nor houses enough, nor food enough. A Bedouin tribe would fare sumptuously on what one American family consumes and wastes. The revenue required for the wardrobe of one woman of fashion would suffice to convert the inhabitants of I know not how many square miles in Africa. It absorbs the income of a province to bring up a baby. We riot in prodigality, we vie with each other in material accumulation and expense. Our thoughts are mainly on how to increase the products of the world, and get them into our own possession.

I think this gross material tendency is strong in America, and more likely to get the mastery over the spiritual and the intellectual here than elsewhere, because of our exhaustless resources. Let us not mistake the nature of a real civilization, nor suppose we have it because we can convert crude iron into the most delicate mechanism, or transport ourselves sixty miles an hour, or even if we shall refine our carnal tastes so as to be satisfied at dinner with the tongues of ortolans and the breasts of singing-birds.

Plato banished the musicians from his feasts because he would not have the charms of conversation interfered with. By comparison, music was to him a sensuous enjoyment. In any society the ideal must be the banishment of the more sensuous; the refinement of it will only repeat the continued experiment of history—the end of a civilization in a polished materialism, and its speedy fall from that into grossness.

I am sure that the scholar, trained to "plain living and high thinking," knows that the prosperous life consists in the culture of the man, and not in the refinement and accumulation of the material. The word culture is often used to signify that dainty intellectualism which is merely a sensuous pampering of the mind, as distinguishable from the healthy training of the mind as is the education of the body in athletic exercises from the petting of it by luxurious baths and unguents. Culture is the blossom of knowledge, but it is a fruit blossom, the ornament of the age but the seed of the future. The so-called culture, a mere fastidiousness of taste, is a barren flower.

You would expect spurious culture to stand aloof from common life, as it does, to extend its charities at the end of a pole, to make of religion a mere *cultus*, to construct for its heaven a sort of Paris, where all the inhabitants dress becomingly, and where there are no Communists. Culture, like fine manners, is not always the result of wealth or position. When monsigneur the archbishop makes his rare tour through the Swiss mountains, the simple peasants do not crowd upon him with boorish impudence, but strew his stony path with flowers, and receive him with joyous but modest sincerity. When the Russian Prince made his landing in America the determined staring of a bevy of accomplished American women nearly swept the young man off the deck of the vessel. One cannot but respect that tremulous sensitiveness which caused the maiden lady to shrink from staring at the moon when she heard there was a man in it.

The materialistic drift of this age, that is, its devotion to material development, is frequently deplored. I suppose it is like all other ages in that respect, but there appears to be a more determined demand for change of condition than ever before, and a deeper movement for equalization. Here in America this is, in great part, a movement for merely physical or material equalization. The idea seems to be well-nigh universal that the millennium is to come by a great deal less work and a great deal more pay. It seems to me that the millennium is to come by an infusion into all society of a truer culture, which is neither of poverty nor of wealth, but is the beautiful fruit of the development of the higher part of man's nature.

And the thought I wish to leave with you, as scholars and men who can command the best culture, is that it is all needed to shape and control the strong growth of material development here, to guide the blind instincts of the mass of men who are struggling for a freer place and a breath of fresh air; that you cannot stand aloof in a class isolation; that your power is in a personal sympathy with the humanity which is ignorant but discontented; and that the question which the man with the spade asks about the use of your culture to him, is a menace.

23. Toward a Democratic Culture

The 1871 Text of *Democratic Vistas* was based on two essays Walt Whitman had published in *The Galaxy* several years earlier, "Democracy" (December, 1867) and "Personalism" (May, 1868). Whitman was living in Washington at the time, where he remained until his stroke in 1873, when he moved to his brother's house in Camden, New Jersey. He had come to Washington in 1862, and devoted himself to comforting wounded soldiers in hospitals there and in nearby Virginia by reading to them, bringing gifts of food, providing paper and envelopes for letters, occasionally writing letters for the disabled, and even dressing wounds. The sufferings he witnessed and tried to mitigate affected him profoundly, and strengthened his compassion and his confidence in the people to make extreme sacrifices for democracy. At the war's end he secured a clerkship in an office in the Department of the Interior, but was fired about a year later, in 1865, when the Secretary discovered he was the author of *Leaves of Grass*, still considered a "scandalous" book. This episode was widely publicized by his indignant friends, and helped win him a wider audience, especially abroad.

As the selection reprinted here makes clear, *Democratic Vistas* was first conceived more or less as a reply to Carlyle's "Shooting Niagara: and After?" which appeared in August, 1867. Carlyle is the "venerable and eminent persons" referred to here; the three paragraphs addressed directly to him ("my venerable friend") were removed from the 1871 edition and replaced by a much condensed note. Carlyle had attacked democracy as a "swarmery," or the "Gathering of Men in Swarms," and equality as "delirious absurdity": "any man equal to any other; Quashee Nigger to Socrates or Shakespeare . . . shall we say?" "By far the notablest case of Swarmery, in these times," he wrote, "is that of the late American War, with Settlement of the Nigger Question for results"—a question he saw as basically that of the relation between servant and master. Writing mainly against the Reform Bill of 1867 which extended the suffrage to large sections of the English working class, Carlyle ridiculed the millennial hopes of the supporters of universal suffrage: "Bring in more voting; that will clear away universal rottenness, and quagmire of mendacities." Instead he argued that "commanding and obeying" is the basis of all human culture, and that rather than equality, society needed a "hero," a natural and practical "aristocrat," to "deliver the world from its swarmeries."

In his reply Whitman shifts the emphasis from political to cultural equality and stresses the ideal of the independence of the individual. But in disagreement his conception of the unrealized "People" may have something in common with Carlyle's version of the traditional yeomanry which respected work and had dignity, just as his Bard resembles Carlyle's "Practical Aristos" who coerces chaos ("dirt, disorder, nomadism, disobedience, folly and confusion") into cosmos.

Democracy

WALT WHITMAN

After the rest is said—after many time-honored and really true things for subordination, experience, rights of property, etc., have been listened to, and acquiesced in—after the valuable and well-settled statement of our duties and relations in society is thoroughly conned over and exhausted— it remains to bring forward and modify everything else with the idea of that Something a man is, standing apart from all else, divine in his own right, and a woman in hers, sole and untouchable by any canons of religon, politics, or what is called modesty or art.

The radiation of this truth, practically a modern one, is the history and key of the most significant doings of our immediately preceding three centuries, and has been the political genesis and life of America. Advancing visibly, it still more advances invisibly. Underneath the fluctuations of the expressions of society, as well as the movements of the politics of the leading nations, we see steadily pressing ahead, and strengthening itself,

Walt Whitman, "Democracy," *The Galaxy* IV (1867), 919–933.

even in the midst of immense tendencies toward aggregation, this image of completeness in separatism, of individual personal dignity, of a single person, either male or female, characterized in the main, not from extrinsic acquirements or position, but in the pride of himself or herself alone; and, as an eventual conclusion and summing-up, the simple, but tremendous and revolutionary, idea that the last, best dependence is to be upon Humanity itself, and its own inherent, normal, full-grown qualities, without any superstitious support whatever.

The purpose of Democracy—supplanting old belief in the necessary absoluteness of established dynastic rulership, temporal, ecclesiastical, and scholastic, as furnishing the only security against chaos, crime, and ignorance—is, through many transmigrations, and amid endless ridicules, arguments, and ostensible failures, to illustrate, at all hazards, this doctrine of the sovereignty and sacredness of the individual, coëqual with the balance-doctrine that man, properly trained, may and must become a law, and series of laws, unto himself, surrounding and providing for, not only his own personal control, but all his relations to other individuals, and to the State; and that, while other theories, as in the past histories of nations, have proved wise enough, and indispensable perhaps for their conditions, *this,* as matters now stand in our civilized world, is the only Scheme worth working from, as warranting results like those of Nature's laws, reliable, when once established, to carry on themselves.

With such for outset, and a silent, momentary prayer that we may be enabled to tell what is worthy the faith within us, we follow on.

Leaving unsaid much that should properly prepare the way for the treatment of this many-sided matter of Democracy—leaving the whole history and consideration of the Feudal Plan and its products, embodying Humanity, its politics and civilization, through the retrospect of past time (which Plan and products, indeed, make up all of the past, and a major part of the present)—leaving unanswered, at least by any specific and local answer, many a well-wrought argument and instance, and many a conscientious declamatory cry and warning—as, very lately, from an eminent and venerable person abroad—things, problems, full of doubt, dread, suspense, (not new to me, but old occupiers of many an anxious hour in city's din, or night's silence), we still may give a paragraph or so, whose drift is opportune. Time alone can finally answer these things. But as a substitute in passing let us, even if fragmentarily, throw forth a thought or two—a short direct or indirect suggestion of the premises of the theory, that other Plan, in the new spirit, under the new forms, started here in our America.

As to the political section of Democracy, which introduces and breaks ground for further and vaster sections, few probably are the minds, even in these republican States, that fully comprehend the aptness of that phrase, "THE GOVERNMENT OF THE PEOPLE, BY THE PEOPLE, FOR THE PEOPLE," which we inherit from the lips of Abraham Lincoln; a formula whose verbal shape is homely wit, but whose scope includes both the totality and all minutiæ of the lesson.

The People! Like our huge earth itself, which, to ordinary scansion, is full of vulgar contradictions and offence, Man, viewed in the lump, displeases, and is a constant puzzle and affront to the merely educated classes. The rare, cosmical, artist-mind, lit with the Infinite, alone confronts his manifold and oceanic qualities; but taste, intelligence and culture (so-called), have been against the masses, and remain so. There is plenty of glamour about the most damnable crimes and hoggish meannesses, special and general, of the Feudal and dynastic world, with its *personnel* of lords and queens and courts, so well-dressed and so handsome. But the People are ungrammatical, untidy, and their sins are gaunt and ill-bred.

Literature has never recognized the People, and, whatever may be said, does not to-day. Speaking generally, the tendencies of literature, as pursued, are to make mostly critical and querulous men. It seems as if, so far, there were some natural repugnance between a literary and professional life, and the rude spirit of the Democracies. There is, in later literature, a treatment of benevolence, a charity business, rife enough; but I know nothing more rare, even in this country, than a fit scientific estimate and reverent appreciation of the People—of their measureless wealth of latent power and capacity, their vast, artistic contrasts of lights and shades— and in America, their entire reliability in emergencies, and a certain breadth of historic grandeur, of peace or war, surpassing all the vaunted samples of the personality of book-heroes, in all the records of the world.

The movements of the late war, and their results, to any sense that studies well and comprehends them, show that Popular Democracy practically justifies itself beyond the proudest claims and wildest hopes of its enthusiasts. Probably no future age can know, as we well know, how the gist of this fiercest and most resolute of the world's warlike contentions resided exclusively in the unnamed, unknown rank and file; and how the brunt of its labor of death was, to all essential purposes, Volunteered. The People, of their own choice, fighting, dying for their own idea, insolently attacked by the Secession-Slave-Power, and its very existence imperilled. Descending to detail, entering any of the armies, and mixing with the private soldiers, we see and have seen august spectacles. We have seen the alacrity with which the American-born populace, the peaceablest and most good-natured race in the world, and the most personally independent and intelligent, and the least fitted to submit to the irksomeness and exasperation of regimental discipline, sprang, at the first tap of the drum, to arms—not for gain, nor even glory, nor to repel invasion—but for an emblem, a mere abstraction—for the life, *the safety of the Flag*. We have seen the unequalled docility and obedience of these soldiers. We have seen them tried long and long by hopelessness, mismanagement, and by defeat; have seen the incredible slaughter toward or through which the armies (as at first Fredericksburg, and afterward at the Wilderness), still unhesitatingly obeyed orders to advance. We have seen them in trench, or crouching behind breastwork, or tramping in deep mud, or amid pouring rain or snow, or under forced marches in hottest Summer (as on the road to get to Gettysburg), vast suffocating swarms, divisions, corps, with every single man so grimed and black with sweat and dust, his own mother would not have known him; his clothes all dirty, stained and torn, with sour, accumulated sweat for perfume, many a comrade, perhaps a brother, sun-struck, staggering out, dying, by the roadside, of exhaustion—yet the great bulk bearing steadily on, cheery enough, hollow-bellied from hunger, but sinewy with unconquerable resolution.

We have seen this race proved by wholesale by drearier, yet more fearful tests—the wound, the amputation, the shattered face or limb, the slow, hot fever, long, impatient anchorage in bed, and all the forms of maiming, operation and disease. Alas! America have we seen, though only in her early youth, already to hospital brought. There have we watched these soldiers, many of them only boys in years—marked their decorum, their religious nature and fortitude, and their sweet affection. Wholesale, truly! For at the front, and through the camps, in countless tents, stood the regimental, brigade and division hospitals; while everywhere amid the land, in or near cities, rose clusters of huge, whitewashed, crowded, wooden barracks, (Washington City alone, at one period, containing in her Army hospitals of this kind, 50,000 wounded and sick men)—and there ruled Agony with bitter scourge, yet seldom brought a cry; and there stalked Death by day and night along the narrow aisles between the rows of cots, or by the blankets on the ground, and touched lightly many a poor sufferer, often with blessed, welcome touch.

I know not whether I shall be understood, but I realize that it is finally from what I learned in such scenes that I am now penning this article. One night in the gloomiest period of the war, in the Patent Office Hospital, as I stood by the bedside of a Pennsylvania soldier, who lay, conscious of quick approaching death, yet perfectly calm, and with noble, spiritual manner, the veteran surgeon, Dr. Stone (Horatio Stone, the sculptor), turning aside, said to me that though he had witnessed many, many deaths of soldiers, and had been a worker at Bull Run, Antietam, Fredericksburg, etc., he had not seen yet the first case of man or boy that met the approach of dissolution with cowardly qualms or terror. My own observation fully bears out the remark.

What have we here, if not, towering above all talk and argument, the plentifully-supplied, last-needed proof of Democracy, in its personalities?

Grand, common stock! to me the accomplished and convincing growth, prophetic of the future; proof undeniable to sharpest sense, of perfect beauty, tenderness and pluck, that never Feudal lord, nor Greek nor Roman breed, yet rivalled. Let no tongue ever speak in disparagement of the American races, North or South, to one who has been through the war in the great Army hospitals.

—Meantime, Humanity (for we will not shirk anything) has always, in every department, been full of perverse maleficence, and is so yet. In downcast hours the Soul thinks it always will be—but soon recovers from such sickly moods. I, as Democrat, see clearly enough (none more clearly), the crude, defective streaks in all the strata of the common people; the specimens and vast collections of the ignorant, the credulous, the unfit and uncouth, the incapable and the very low and poor. The eminent person, in his conscientious cry just mentioned, sneeringly asks whether we expect to elevate and improve politics by absorbing such morbid collections and qualities therein. The point is a formidable one, and there will doubtless always be numbers of solid citizens who will never get over it. Our answer is general, and is involved in the scope and letter of this article. We believe the object of political and all other government (having, of course, provided for the police, the safety of life, property, and the basic common and civil law, always first in order) to be, among the rest, not merely to rule, to repress disorder, etc., but to develop, to open up to cultivation, to encourage the possibilities of all beneficent and manly outcroppage, and of that aspiration for independence, and the pride and self-respect latent in all characters. (Or, if there be exceptions, we cannot, fixing our eyes on them alone, make theirs the rule for all.)

The mission of government, henceforth, in civilized lands, is not authority alone, not even of law, nor by that favorite standard of the eminent writer, the rule of the best men, the born heroes and captains of the race (as if such ever, or one time out of a hundred, got into the big places, elective or dynastic!)—but, higher than the highest arbitrary rule, to train communities through all their grades, beginning with individuals and ending there again, to rule themselves.

What Christ appeared for in the moral-spiritual field for Human-kind, namely, that in respect to the absolute Soul, there is in the possession of such by each single individual, something so transcendent, so incapable of gradations (like life), that, to that extent, it places all beings on a common level, utterly regardless of the distinctions of intellect, station, or any height or lowliness whatever—is tallied in like manner, in this other field, by Democracy's rule that men, the Nation, as a common aggregate of living identities, affording in each a separate and complete subject for freedom, worldly thrift and happiness, and for a fair chance for growth, and for protection, in citizenship, etc., must, to the political extent of the suffrage or vote, if no further, be placed, in each and in the whole, on one broad, primary, universal, common platform.

The purpose is not altogether direct; perhaps it is more indirect. To be a voter with the rest is not so much; and this, like every institute, will have its imperfections. But to become an enfranchised man, and now to stand and start without humiliation, and equal with the rest; to commence, or have the road cleared to commence, the grand experiment of development, whose end, perhaps requiring several generations, may be the forming of a full-grown manly or womanly Personality—that *is* something. To ballast the state is also secured, and in our times is to be secured, in no other way.

We do not (at any rate I do not) put it either so much on the ground that the People, the masses, even the best of them are, in their latent or exhibited qualities, essentially sensible and good—nor on the ground of their rights; but that, good or bad, rights or no rights, the Democratic formula is the only safe and preservative one for coming times. We endow the masses with the suffrage for their own sake, no doubt; then, still more, from another point of view, for community's sake. Leaving the rest to the sentimentalists, we present Freedom as sufficient in its scientific aspects, cold as ice, reasoning, clear and passionless as crystal.

Democracy too is law, and of the strictest, amplest kind. Many suppose (and often in its own ranks the error) that it means a throwing aside of law, and running riot. But, briefly, it is the superior law, not alone that of physical force, the body, which, adding to, it supersedes with that of the spirit. Law is the unshakable order of the universe forever; and the law over all, and law of laws, is the law of successions; that of the superior law, in time, gradually supplanting and overwhelming the inferior one.

(While, for myself, I would cheerfully agree—first covenanting that the formative tendencies shall be administered in favor, or, at least not against it, and that this reservation be closely construed—that until the individual or community show due signs, or be so minor and fractional as not to endanger the State, the condition of tutelage may continue, and self-government must abide its time.)

—Nor is the esthetic point, always an important one, without fascination for highest aiming souls. The common ambition strains for common elevations, to become some privileged exclusive. The master sees greatness and health in being part of the mass. Nothing will do as well as common ground. Would you have in yourself the divine, vast, general law? Then merge yourself in it.

And, topping Democracy, this most alluring record, that it alone can bind, and ever seeks to bind, all nations, all men, of however various and distant lands, into a brotherhood, a family. It is the old, yet ever-modern dream of Earth, out of her eldest and her youngest, her fond philosophers and poets. Not this half only, this Individualism, which isolates. There is another half, which is Adhesiveness or Love, that fuses, ties and aggregates, making the races comrades, and fraternizing all. Both are to be vitalized by Religion (sole worthiest elevator of man or State) breathing into the proud, material tissues, the breath of life. For at the core of Democracy, finally, is the Religious element. All the Religions, old and new, are there. Nor may the Scheme step forth, clothed in resplendent beauty and command, till these, bearing the best, the latest fruit, the Spiritual, the aspirational, shall fully appear.

—Portions of our pages we feel to indite with reference toward Europe more than our own land, and thus, perhaps not absolutely needed for the home reader. But the whole question hangs together, and fastens and links all peoples. The Liberalist of to-day has this advantage over antique or medieval times, that his doctrine seeks both to universalize as well as individualize. The great word Solidarity has arisen.

How, then (for in that shape forebodes the current deluge)—how shall we, good-class folk, meet the rolling, mountainous surges of "swarmery" that already beat upon and threaten to overwhelm us? What disposal, short of wholesale throat-cutting and extermination (which seems not without its advantages), offers, for the countless herds of "hoofs and hobnails," that will somehow, and so perversely get themselves born, and grow up to annoy and vex us? What under heaven is to become of "nigger Cushee," that imbruted and lazy being—now, worst of all, preposterously free? etc. Never before such a yawning gulf; never such danger as now from incarnated Democracy advancing, with the laboring classes at its back. Woe the day; woe the doings, the prospects thereof! England, or any respectable land, giving the least audience to these "servants of the mud gods," or, utterly infatuate, extending to them the suffrage, takes swift passage therewith, bound for the infernal pit. Ring the alarum bell! Put the flags at half mast! Or, rather, let each man spring for the nearest loose spar or plank. The ship is going down!

Be not so moved, not to say distraught, my venerable friend. Spare those spasms of dread and disgust. England, after her much-widened suffrage, as she did before, will still undergo troubles and tribulations, without doubt; but they will be as nothing to what (in the judgment of all heads not quite careened and addled), would certainly follow the spirit, carried out in any modern nation, these days, of your appeal or diatribe. Neither by berating them, nor twitting them with their low condition of ignorance and misery, nor by leaving them as they are, nor by turning the screws still tighter, nor by taking even the most favorable chances for "the noble Few" to come round with relief, will the demon of that "unanimous vulgar" (paying very heavy taxes) be pacified and made harmless any more. Strangely enough, about the only way to really lay the fiend appears to be this very way—the theme of these your ravings. A sort of fate and antique Nemesis, of the highest old Greek tragedy sort, is in it (as in our own Play, or affair, rapidly played of late here in the South, through all the acts—indeed a regular, very wondrous Eschuylean piece—to that old part First, that bound and chained unkillable Prometheus, now, after twenty-three hundred years, very grandly and epico-dramatically supplementing and fully supplying the lost, or never before composed, Second and Third parts). Your noble, hereditary, Anglo-Saxon-Norman institutions (still here so loudly championed and battled for in your argument) having been, through some seven or eight centuries, thriftily engaged in cooking up this mess, have now got to eat it. The only course eligible, it is plain, is to plumply confront, embrace, absorb, swallow (O, big and bitter pill!) the entire British "swarmery," demon, "loud roughs" and all. These ungrateful men, not satisfied with the poor-house for their old age, and the charity-school for their infants, evidently mean business—may-be of bloody kind. By all odds, my friend, the thing to do is to make a flank movement, surround them, disarm them, give them their first degree, incorporate them in the State as voters, and then—wait for the next emergency.

Nor may I permit myself to dismiss this utterance of the eminent person without pronouncing its laboriously-earned and fully-deserved credit for about the highest eminence attained yet, in a certain direction, of any linguistic product, written or spoken, to me known. I have had occasion in my past life (being born, as it were, with propensities, from my earliest years, to attend popular American speech-gatherings, conventions, nominations, camp-meetings, and the like, and also as a reader of newspapers, foreign and domestic)—I therefore know that trial to one's ears and brains from divers creatures, alluded to by sample, and well-hetchelled in this diatribe, crow-cawing the words Liberty, loyalty, human rights, constitutions, etc. I, too, have heard the ceaseless braying, screaming blatancy (on behalf of my own side), making noisiest threats and clatter stand for sense. But I must now affirm that such a comic-painful hullabaloo and vituperative cat-squalling as this about "the Niagara leap," "swarmery," "Orsonism," etc. (meaning, in point, as I make out, simply extending to full-grown British working-folk, farmers, mechanics, clerks, and so on—the "industrial aristocracy," indeed, there named—the privilege of the ballot, or vote, deciding, by popular majorities, who shall be designated to sit in one of the two Houses of Parliament, if it mean anything), I never yet encountered; no, not even in extremest hour of midnight, in whooping Tennessee revival, or Bedlam let loose in crowded, colored Carolina bush-meeting.

But to proceed, and closer to our text.

The curse and canker of Nations politically has been—or, at any rate, will be, as things have come to exist in our day—the having of certain portions of the people set off from the rest by a line drawn—they not privileged as others, but degraded, humiliated, made of no account. We repeat it, the question is, finally, one of Science—the science of the present and the future. Much quackery teems, of course, yet does not really affect the orbic quality of the matter. To work in, if we may so term it, and justify God, his divine aggregate, the People (or, the veritable horned and fluke-tailed Devil, *his* aggregate, then, since you so convulsively insist upon it, O, eminence!)—this, without doubt, is what Democracy is for; and this is what our America means, and is doing—may I not say, has done? If not, she means nothing more, and does nothing more than any other land. And as, by virtue of its cosmical, antiseptic power, Nature's stomach is fully strong enough not only to digest the morbific matter always presented, not to be turned aside, and perhaps, indeed, intuitively gravitating thither—but even to change such contributions into nutriment for highest use and life—so American Democracy's. That is the lesson we, these days, send over to European lands by every western breeze.

And, truly, whatever may be said in the way of abstract argument, for or against the theory of a wider democratizing of institutions in any civilized country, much trouble might well be saved to those European lands by recognizing this palpable fact (for a palpable fact it is), that some form of such democratizing is about the only resource now left. *That,* or chronic dissatisfaction continued, mutterings which grow annually louder and louder, till, in due course, and pretty swiftly in most cases, the inevitable crisis, crash, dynastic ruin. Anything worthy to be called statesmanship in the Old World, I should say, among the advanced students, adepts, or men of any brains, does not debate to-day whether to hold on, attempting to lean back and monarchize, or to look forward and democratize—but *how,* and in what degree and part, most prudently to democratize. The difficulties of the transfer may be fearful; perhaps none here in our America can truly know them. I, for one, fully acknowledge them, and sympathize deeply. But there is Time, and must be Faith; and Opportunities, though gradual and slow, will everywhere be born. And beaming like a star, to any and to all, whatever else may for a while be quenched, shines not the eternal signal in the West?

—There is (turning home again) a thought, or fact, I must not forget— subtle and vast, dear to America, twin-sister of its Democracy—so ligatured indeed to it, that either's death, if not the other's also, would make that other live out life, dragging a corpse, a loathsome, horrid tag and burden forever at its feet. What the idea of Messiah was to the ancient race of Israel, through storm and calm, through public glory and their name's humiliation, tenacious, refusing to be argued with, shedding all shafts of ridicule and disbelief, undestroyed by captivities, battles, deaths —for neither the scalding blood of war, nor the rotted ichor of peace could ever wash it out, nor has yet—a great Idea, bedded in Judah's heart— source of the loftiest Poetry the world yet knows—continuing on the same, though all else varies—the spinal thread of the incredible romance of that people's career along five thousand years—so runs this thought, this fact, amid our own land's race and history. It is the thought of Oneness, averaging, including all; of Identity—the indissoluble Union of These States.

—The eager and often inconsiderate appeals of reformers and revolutionists are indispensable to counterbalance the inertness and fossilism making so large a part of human institutions. The latter will always take care of themselves. The former is to be treated with indulgence, and even respect. As circulation to air, so is agitation and a plentiful degree of speculative license to political and moral sanity. Indirectly, but surely, goodness, virtue, law (of the very best) follow Freedom. These, to Democracy, are what the keel is to the ship, or saltness to the ocean.

The gravitation-hold of Liberalism will be a more universal ownership of property, general homesteads, general comfort—a vast, intertwining reticulation of wealth. No community furnished throughout with homes, and substantial, however moderate, incomes, commits suicide, or "shoots Niagara." As the human frame, or, indeed, any object in this manifold Universe, is best kept together by the simple miracle of its own cohesion, and the necessity and profit thereof, so a great and varied Nationality, occupying millions of square miles, were firmest held and knit by the principle of the safety and endurance of the aggregate of its middling property owners.

So that, from another point of view, ungracious as it may sound, and a paradox after what we have been saying, Democracy looks with suspicious, ill-satisfied eye upon the very poor, and on the ignorant. She asks for men and women well-off, owners of houses and acres, and with cash in the bank—and with some cravings for literature, too; and must have them, and hastens to make them. Luckily, the seed is already well-sown, and has taken ineradicable root.

—Huge and mighty are our Days, our republican lands—and most in their rapid shiftings, their changes, all in the interest of the Cause. As I write, the din of disputation rages around me. Acrid the temper of the parties, vital the pending questions. Congress convenes; the President sends his Message; Reconstruction is still in abeyance; the nominations and the contest for the twenty-first Presidentiad draw close, with loudest threat and bustle. Of these, and all the like of these, the eventuations I know not; but well I know that behind them, and whatever their eventuations, the really vital things remain safe and certain, and all the needed work goes on. Time, with soon or later superciliousness, disposes of Presidents, Congressmen, party platforms, and such. Anon, it clears the stage of each and any mortal shred that thinks itself so potent to its day; and at and after which (with precious, golden exceptions once or twice in a century), all that relates to sir potency is flung to moulder in a burial-vault, and no one bothers himself the least bit about it afterward. But the People ever remains, tendencies continue, and all the idiocratic transfers in unbroken chain go on. In a few years the dominion-heart of America will be far inland, toward the West. Our future National Capitol will not be where the present one is. I should say that certainly, in less than fifty years, it will migrate a thousand or two miles, will be re-founded, and every thing belonging to it made on a different plan, original, far more superb. The main social, political spine-character of The States will probably run along the Ohio, Missouri and Mississippi Rivers, and west and

north of them, including Canada. Those regions, with the group of powerful brothers toward the Pacific (destined to the mastership of that sea and
its countless Paradises of islands), will compact and settle the traits of
America, with all the old retained, but more expanded, grafted on newer,
hardier, purely native stock. A giant growth, composite from the rest,
getting their contribution, absorbing it to make it more illustrious. From
the North, Intellect, the sun of things—also the idea of unswayable Justice,
anchor amid the last, the wildest tempests. From the South, the living
Soul, the animus of good and bad, haughtily admitting no demonstration
but its own. While from the West itself comes solid Personality, with blood
and brawn, and the deep quality of all-accepting fusion.

Political Democracy, as it exists and practically works in America,
supplies a training-school for making grand young men. It is life's gym-
nasium, not of good only, but of all. We try often, though we fall back
often. A brave delight, fit for freedom's athletes, fills these arenas, and
fully satisfies, out of the action in them, irrespective of success. Whatever
we do not attain, we at any rate attain the experiences of the fight, the
hardening of the strong campaign, and throb with currents of attempt at
least. Time is ample. Let the victors come after us. Not for nothing does
evil play its part among men. *Vive*, the attack—the perennial assault! *Vive*,
the unpopular cause—the spirit that audaciously aims—the courage that
dies not—the never-abandoned efforts, pursued the same amid opposing
proofs and precedents.

—Once, before the war, I, too, was filled with doubt and gloom. A
traveller, an acute and good man, had impressively said to me, that day—
putting in form, indeed, my own observations: I have traveled much in the
United States, and watched their politicians, and listened to the speeches
of the candidates, and read the journals, and gone into the public houses,
and heard the unguarded talk of men. And I have found your vaunted
America honey-combed from top to toe with infidelism, even to itself and
its own programme. I have marked the brazen hell-faces of succession and
slavery gazing defiantly from all the windows and doorways. I have everywhere found, primarily, thieves and scalliwags arranging the nominations
to offices, and sometimes filling the offices themselves. I have found the
North just as full of bad stuff as the South. Of the holders of public offices
in the Nation, or in the States, or their municipalities, I have found that
not one in a hundred has been chosen by any spontaneous selection of the
outsiders, the people, but all have been nominated and put through by
little or large caucuses of the politicians, and have got in by electioneering,
not desert. I have noticed how the millions of sturdy farmers and me-

chanics are thus the helpless supple-jacks of comparatively few politicians. And I have noticed more and more, the alarming spectacle of parties usurping the Government, and openly and shamelessly wielding it for party purposes.

Sad, serious, deep truths. Yet are there other, still deeper, amply confronting, dominating truths. Over those politicians, and over all their insolence and wiles, and over the powerfulest parties, looms a Power, too sluggish may-be, but ever holding decisions and decrees in hand, ready, with stern process to execute them as soon as plainly needed, and at times, indeed, summarily crushing to atoms the mightiest parties, even in the hour of their pride.

Far different are the amounts of these things from what, at first sight, they appear. Though it is no doubt important who is elected President or Governor, Mayor or Legislator, there are other, quieter contingencies, infinitely more important. Shams, etc., will always be the show, like ocean's scum; enough if waters deep and clear make up the rest. Enough, that while the piled embroidered shoddy gaud and fraud spreads to the superficial eye, the hidden warp and weft are genuine, and will wear forever. Enough, in short, that the race, the land which could raise such as the late rebellion, could also put it down.

The average man of a land at last only is important. He, in These States, remains immortal owner and boss, deriving good uses, somehow, out of any sort of servant in office, even the basest; because (certain universal requisites, and their settled regularity and protection, being first secured), a Nation like ours, in the formation state, trying continually new experiments, choosing new delegations, is not served by the best men only, but sometimes more by those that provoke it—by the combats they arouse. Thus national rage, fury, discussion, etc., sublimer than content. Thus, also, the warning signals, invaluable for after times.

What is more dramatic than the spectacle we have seen repeated, and doubtless long shall see—the popular judgment taking the successful candidates on trial in the offices—standing off, as it were and observing them and their doing for a while, and always giving, finally, the fit, exactly due reward.

—When I pass to and fro, different latitudes, different seasons, beholding the crowds of the great cities, New York, Boston, Philadelphia, Cincinnati, Chicago, St. Louis, San Francisco, New Orleans, Baltimore—when I mix with these interminable swarms of alert, turbulent, good-natured, independent citizens, mechanics, clerks, young persons—at the idea of this mass of men, so fresh and free, so loving and so proud, a singular awe falls upon me. I feel, with dejection and amazement, that among our geniuses and talented writers or speakers, few or none have yet really spoken to this people, or absorbed the central spirit and the idiosyncrasies which are theirs, and which, thus, in highest ranges, so far remain entirely uncelebrated, unexpressed.

Dominion strong is the body's; dominion stronger is the mind's. What has filled, and fills to-day our intellect, our fancy, furnishing the standards therein, is yet foreign. The great poems, Shakespeare included, are poisonous to the idea of the pride and dignity of the common people, the life-blood of Democracy. The models of our literature, as we get it from other lands, ultramarine, have had their birth originally in courts, and basked and grown in castle sunshine; all smells of princes' favors. For esthetic Europe is yet exclusively feudal.

The literature of These States, a new projection, when it comes, must be the born outcrop, through all rich and luxuriant forms, but stern and exclusive, of the sole Idea of The States, belonging here alone. Of course, of workers of a certain sort, we have already plenty, contributing after their kind; many elegant, many learned, all complacent. But, touched by the National test, they wither to ashes. I say I have not seen one single writer, artist, lecturer, or what not, that has confronted the voiceless but ever erect and active, pervading, underlying will and typic Aspiration of the land, in a spirit kindred to itself. Do you call those genteel little creatures American poets? Do you term that perpetual, pistareen, pasteboard work, American art, American opera, drama, taste, verse? I think I hear, echoed as from some mountain-top afar in the West, the scornful laugh of the Genius of These States.

—Democracy, in silence, biding its time, ponders its own ideals, not of men only, but of women. The idea of the women of America (extricated from this daze, this fossil and unhealthy air which hangs about the word, Lady), developed, raised to become the robust equals, workers, and even practical and political deciders with the men—greater than man, we may admit, through their divine maternity, always their towering, emblematical attribute—but great, at any rate, as man, in all departments; or, rather, capable of being so, soon as they realize it, and can bring themselves to give up toys and fictions, and launch forth, as men do, amid real, independent, stormy life.

—Then, as toward finale (and, in that, overarching the true scholar's lesson), we have to say there can be no complete or epical presentation of Democracy, or any thing like it, at this day, because its doctrines will only be effectually incarnated in any one branch, when, in all, their spirit is at the root and centre. How much is still to be disentangled, freed! How long it takes to make this world see that it is, in itself, the final authority and reliance!

Did you, too, suppose Democracy was only for elections, for politics, and for a party name? I say Democracy is only of use there that it may pass on and come to its flower and fruits in manners, in the highest forms of interaction between men, and their beliefs—Democracy in all public and private life, and in the Army and Navy. I have intimated that, as a paramount scheme, it has yet few or no full realizers and believers. I do not see, either, that it owes any serious thanks to noted propagandists or champions, or has been essentially helped, though often harmed, by them. It has been and is carried on by all the moral forces, and by trade, finance, machinery, intercommunications, etc., and can no more be stopped than the tides, or the earth in its orbit. Doubtless, also, it resides, crude and latent, well down in the hearts of the fair average of the American-born people, mainly in the agricultural regions. But it is not yet, there or anywhere, the fully-received, the fervid, the absolute faith.

I submit, therefore, that the fruition of Democracy, on aught like a grand scale, resides altogether in the future. As, under any profound and comprehensive view of the gorgeous-composite Feudal world, we see in it, through the long ages and cycles of ages, the results of a deep, integral, human and divine principle, or fountain, from which issued laws, ecclesia, manners, institutes, costumes, personalities, poems (hitherto unequalled), faithfully partaking of their source, and indeed only arising either to betoken it, or to furnish parts of that varied-flowing display, whose centre was one and absolute—so, long ages hence, shall the due historian or critic make at least an equal retrospect, an equal History for the Democratic principle. It, too, must be adorned, credited with its results; then, when it, with imperial power, through amplest time, has dominated mankind—has been the source and test of all the moral, esthetic, social, political, and religious expressions and institutes of the civilized world—has begotten them in spirit and in form, and carried them to its own unprecedented heights—has had monastics and ascetics, more numerous, more devout than the monks and priests of all previous creeds—has swayed the ages with a breadth and rectitude tallying Nature's own—has fashioned, systematized, and triumphantly finished and carried out, in its own interest, and with unparalleled success, a New Earth and a New Man.

—Thus we presume to write, as it were, upon things that exist not, and travel by maps yet unmade, and a blank. But the throes of birth are upon us; and we have something of this advantage in seasons of strong formations, doubts, suspense—for then the afflatus of such themes haply may fall upon us, more or less; and then, hot from surrounding revolution, our speech, though without polished coherence, and a failure by the standard called criticism, comes forth, real at least, as the lightnings.

And may-be, we, these days, have, too, our own reward (for there are yet some, in all lands, worthy to be so encouraged). Though not for us the joy of entering at the last the conquered city—nor ours the chance ever to see with our own eyes the peerless power and splendid *eclat* of the Democratic principle, arrived at meridian, filling the world with effulgence and majesty far beyond those of past history's kings, or all dynastic sway; there is yet, to whoever is eligible among us, the prophetic vision; the joy of being tossed in the brave turmoil of these times—the promulgation and the path, obedient, lowly reverent to the voice; the gesture of the god, or holy ghost, which others see not, hear not—with the proud consciousness that amid whatever clouds, seductions, or heart-wearying postponements, we have never deserted, never despaired, never abandoned the Faith.

Selected
Bibliography

Blair, Walter · *Native American Humor, 1800–1900*. New York, 1937.

Bremner, Robert H. · *From the Depths: The Discovery of Poverty in the United States*. New York, 1956.

Bruce, Robert V. · *1877: Year of Violence*. New York, 1959.

Burchard, John and Albert Bush-Brown · *The Architecture of America*. Boston, 1961.

Cochran, Thomas C. and William Miller · *The Age of Enterprise: A Social History of Industrial America*, rev. ed. New York, 1961.

Cochran, Thomas C. · "Did the Civil War Retard Industrialization?" in *The Economic Impact of the Civil War*, ed., Ralph Andreano. Cambridge, 1967.

Curti, Merle · *The Growth of American Thought*. New York, 1951. *Probing Our Past*. New York, 1955.

Hart, James D. · *The Popular Book: A History of America's Literary Taste*. Berkeley, 1950.

Hofstadter, Richard · *Anti-Intellectualism in American Life*. New York, 1963.

Kirkland, Edward Chase · *Dream and Thought in the Business Community, 1860–1900*. Ithaca, N. Y., 1956.

Larkin, Oliver W. · *Art and Life in America*. New York, 1957.

Luckhurst, Kenneth · *The Story of Exhibitions*. London, 1951.

Marx, Leo · *The Machine in the Garden*. New York, 1964.

May, Henry · *Protestant Churches and Industrial America*. New York, 1963.

Miller, Perry, ed. · *American Thought, Civil War to World War I*. New York, 1954.

Mott, Frank Luther • *Golden Multitudes*. New York, 1947.

A *History of American Magazines, 1865–1885*. Cambridge, 1938.

Mumford, Lewis • *The Brown Decades, A Study of the Arts of America, 1865–1895*. New York, 1931.

Nevins, Allan • *The Emergence of Modern America, 1865–1878*. New York, 1927.

Potter, David • *People of Plenty: Economic Abundance and the American Character*. Chicago, 1954.

The South and the Sectional Conflict. Baton Rouge, 1968.

Pressly, Thomas J. • *Americans Interpret Their Civil War*. Princeton, 1954.

Raleigh, John Henry • *Matthew Arnold and American Culture*. Berkeley, 1957.

Rose, Willie Lee • *Rehearsal for Reconstruction*. Indianapolis, 1964.

Ross, Earle D. • *Democracy's College: The Land-Grant Movement in the Formative Stage*. Iowa State College, 1942.

Rourke, Constance • *Trumpets of Jubilee*. New York, 1927.

Santayana, George • "The Genteel Tradition in American Philosophy," in *Winds of Doctrine*. New York, 1913.

Schlesinger, Arthur Meier • *The Rise of the City, 1878–1898*. New York, 1933.

Smith, Henry Nash • *Popular Culture and Industrialism, 1865–1890*. New York, 1967.

Trachtenberg, Alan • *Brooklyn Bridge, Fact and Symbol*. New York, 1965.

Walker, Robert H. • *The Poet and the Gilded Age*. Philadelphia, 1963.

Williams, Raymond • *Culture and Society, 1780–1950*. London, 1959.

Wilson, Edmund • *Patriotic Gore: Studies in the Literature of the American Civil War*. New York, 1962.

Woodward, C. Van, ed. • *The Comparative Approach to American History*. New York, 1968.